Cultural Identity
and Ethnicity
in the Pacific

D1198705

Cultural Identity and Ethnicity in the Pacific

Edited by
Jocelyn Linnekin
and
Lin Poyer

University of Hawai'i Press

HONOLULU

Paperback edition 1996

96 97 98 99 00 01   5 4 3 2 1

Library of Congress Cataloging-in-Publication Data

Cultural identity and ethnicity in the Pacific /

Jocelyn Linnekin and Lin Poyer.

p.   cm.

Includes bibliographical references.

ISBN 0–8248–1208–5

1. Ethnicity–Oceania.   2. Oceania–Social life and customs.

I. Linnekin, Jocelyn, 1950–   II. Poyer, Lin, 1953–

GN662.C77   1990

306'.098—dc20   89–5228   CIP

ISBN 0–8248–1891–1 (pbk)

University of Hawai'i Press books are printed

on acid-free paper and meet the guidelines

for permanence and durability of the Council

on Library Resources

CONTENTS

Cultural Identity
and Ethnicity
in the Pacific

1

Introduction

JOCELYN LINNEKIN

AND LIN POYER

This book discusses ways in which Pacific Islanders make distinctions between themselves and others. The organization and conceptual bases of group identities in the Pacific have received relatively little comparative treatment, perhaps because the disparate social forms found in Oceania have defied attempts at generalization. In Barth's pioneering work on ethnicity, he set aside "pelagic islands" as a special case (1969, 11).[1] Until recently many Western observers have assumed that Pacific Island societies were geographically isolated and culturally homogeneous, with self-evident and unproblematic group boundaries. Such assumptions restrict the existence of self-conscious cultural identity to the period following extensive contact with Europeans and other foreigners.

The historical and ethnographic material presented here contradicts such easy generalizations. Except, arguably, for the outlying island groups of Polynesia, precontact Oceanic societies were far from isolated. Micronesians and Melanesians, especially, participated in complex exchange networks and interisland political arrangements long before the arrival of Europeans. Even Polynesians on far-flung outliers knew of mythic-historical others. Larger island groups such as Hawaii, New Zealand, and Pohnpei were characterized by internal variations in language and social practice. Yet a close look at formulations of cultural identity in several Pacific Island societies does reveal some striking contrasts with the Western paradigm of ethnicity. Cross-cultural comparison thus highlights—and calls into question—certain commonly held presuppositions of Western social science.

Theories of Ethnicity

The starting premise of this volume is that there are alternative schemes of conceptualizing cultural differences, based on different theories of the origins and meaning of human variability, and that these cultural propositions structure social behavior. To make these alternative models explicit, we use the terms *cultural identity* and *ethnicity* in distinctive ways. We use *ethnicity* to refer to a set of theories based on the proposition that people can be classified into mutually exclusive bounded groups according to physical and behavioral differences; moreover, these ascriptions are "presumptively determined by . . . origin and background" (Barth 1969, 13). In this view, people are as they are because they were born to be so. Changes in external circumstances can affect but not completely alter identity. Groups of people sharing biological ancestry are readily seen as units, and social units are readily identified as sharing putative ancestry. When physical and cultural differences are believed to correlate, this notion glides easily into a racial theory of identity. In ethnic ideologies blood, seed, and transmitted substance figure prominently, if not exclusively, in determining an individual's group membership. *Ethnicity* therefore describes both the Western popular theory of group identity and a theoretical construct developed by Western social scientists.[2]

This Western ethnotheory of ethnicity shares with the American concept of kinship (see Schneider 1968, 1984) the premise that cultural affiliations reflect blood ties and have a predetermined, inevitable quality (Handler and Linnekin 1984). Ethnicity is seen as a natural, unambiguous bond "in the blood"—a conceptualization that emerges as social action in different scenarios, from "us versus them" to the melting pot (Fishman 1983). So pervasive are these assumptions that social scientists have not consistently distinguished ethnicity as a Western ethnotheory from ethnicity as an analytic tool. In his review of the concept, Ronald Cohen (1978, 385) points out that few authors even bother to define ethnicity, despite cogent criticism of its uncritical use (e.g., Aronson 1976; Blu 1980; Galaty 1982; Handler 1985a; LeVine and Campbell 1972; MacCannell 1984; Moerman 1965, 1968). Since Boas, it has been an anthropological truism that culture does not reside in the genes, but the assumption that an ethnic group is a "biologically self-perpetuating" unit was and to some extent still is entrenched in the social-scientific view of ethnicity (see, e.g., Barth 1969, 10–11; De Vos 1975; Enloe 1973, 17; Keyes 1981, 5–6; Smith 1981, 65–66; Stack 1986).

Over the past three decades cross-cultural studies have greatly increased the subtlety and sophistication of the questions we ask about the nature of ethnicity. Reviews of ethnicity theory indicate the range and complexity of the intellectual tasks now facing the field (Cohen 1978; Muga 1984; Reminick 1983; Yinger 1985). We cannot provide our own such review here but wish to acknowledge recent contributions that bear directly on the goals of this volume. Three theoretical developments in particular have promoted the conceptual separation of Western premises about the nature of group identity from the social-scientific study of cultural differences.

First, the divergence between "primordialist" and "circumstantialist" analyses (Glazer and Moynihan 1975) directed attention to the relationship between understandings of personal identity and group identity. Much of the ongoing debate has focused on the relative weight of "cultural givens" (Smith 1981, 66) versus situational factors in the definition of ethnicity (discussions include Drummond 1980, 1981; Hechter 1986; Jayawardena 1980; Nagata 1981; Norton 1983; Stack 1986). The primordialist position in anthropology was explicated in a seminal essay by Clifford Geertz (1973, 255–310), who drew on concepts initially formulated by the sociologist Edward Shils (1957). In the primordialist paradigm certain fundamental affiliations—place, kin, language, religion, custom—have an "overpowering coerciveness" (Geertz 1973, 259) and are viewed "as 'natural' attachments in the same sense as kinship" (Smith 1981, 66). Although writers since Barth have acknowledged that ethnic boundaries do not necessarily rely on any measurable cultural content, most continue to hold that ethnic identity is a fundamental and universal reality of social life: "ethnicity, as one type of primordial assumption about the nature of human identity, can be found in all types of societies, industrial as well as nonindustrial" (Keyes 1981, 27; cf. Isaacs 1975; Schwartz 1982).

In contrast, the "circumstantialist" or "instrumentalist" position sees ethnic attachments as "epiphenomenal and malleable" (Hechter 1986, 13), a function of historically variable social and political conditions. Most writers in this vein have taken a political economy approach, exploring the relationship between ethnicity and "power relations within a context of conflict" (Bourgois 1988, 328; for a seminal essay see Vincent 1974). Circumstantialists see ethnic identity becoming salient as a result of interaction with cultural others (Salamone 1985), categorization by the dominant society (Green 1981), peripheral development (Bourgois 1988; O'Brien 1986), or political mobilization (Rothschild 1981; Wallerstein 1973).

What we might call the "modern synthesis" in ethnicity theory attempts to incorporate insights from both primordialist and circumstantialist positions (see Castile and Kushner 1981; De Vos and Romanucci-Ross 1982). Keyes (1981), for example, argues for the strength of primordial ties but acknowledges situational factors as well as the cultural construction of ethnic categories (see also Nagata 1981). Yet, although Keyes states that ethnicity "derives from a *cultural* interpretation of descent" (emphasis added), the premise is still that objectively given cultural and ancestral differences are at the root of identity

ascriptions: certain "givens" at birth are "subject to cultural elabora-
tion . . . sex, locality and time of birth, physiological features that are
recognized as marks of biological inheritance, and social descent or links
with forebears" (1981, 5). Within the synthesis, ethnicity is still perceived to be grounded in differences of descent and origin. Yet the interest generated by the lengthy primordialist-circumstantialist debate has
been essential to gaining perspective on Western preconceptions about
personal and group identity.

A second significant development has been the recognition of the role
of colonialism and economic transformation in shaping the social structural and behavioral dimensions of cultural identity. Insightful studies
have demonstrated the recent historical origins and contingent quality
of "tribal" and similar groupings (e.g., O'Brien 1986) and have emphasized the role of world-system expansion in the formation of
group boundaries (MacCannell 1984; Stack 1981; Wolf 1982). As
we shall explain below, regional and global historical processes have
been and continue to be significant in shaping Pacific Island identities.

Advances in symbolic anthropology have produced a third line of
argument important to our approach in this volume. This is the application of semiotic theory to ethnographic cases in which emblems of differentiation appear to be at least as important as competition for scarce
economic resources in the creation and reproduction of cultural units.
These anthropologists have explored the active symbolic construction
and "invention" of cultural identity in the present (Bentley 1987; Blu
1980; Clifford 1988; Galaty 1982; Handler 1984; Handler and Linnekin
1984; Landsman 1985, 1987; Linnekin 1983; Poyer 1988a). Although
this approach has been criticized for ignoring material factors, it has
forced students of ethnicity to see cultural representations as more than
epiphenomena of pragmatic political pursuits. Recognition of identity
as symbolically constituted was a necessary precursor to the analyses of
Pacific cases presented here.[3]

This volume, then, is part of a growing effort to integrate cultural
and structural approaches into a dialectical understanding of group
identity. But, while the chapters that follow address issues that are the
conventional stuff of ethnicity studies—how stereotypes operate in face-
to-face interactions, how identities may shift according to situation,
how colonization has affected group boundaries—they do so without
presupposing the source of these differences. Instead, we are initially
concerned with the cultural dimensions of identity; that is, with symbols, meanings, and indigenous categories. Indeed, this perspective represents the unique contribution that anthropologists can make to the
analysis of cultural identity. Pacific Islanders may or may not share

Western assumptions about what makes others the same or different. In other words, Oceanic ethnotheories are not necessarily ethnic theories.

Oceanic Cultural Identities

Oceania comprises three geographic areas, roughly representing three distinct cultural regions: Melanesia, Micronesia, and Polynesia. Language, social organization, levels of political integration, and cultural practice vary among these regions (and among populations within them), but social scientists have formulated Pacific-wide generalizations on the basis of historical relationships and certain broad similarities (introductions to the peoples of the Pacific include Alkire 1978 and Oliver 1975, 1989).[4] Geographical constraints in conjunction with historical contingencies have produced considerable variation in local definitions of group identity and in intergroup relations. Trade, political contact, and religious movements take strikingly different forms among the physically close but culturally distinctive populations of Papua New Guinea and among the geographically dispersed atolls of eastern Micronesia. Precontact voyages of exploration, political competition among European colonial powers, and World War II are only a few of the historical events that have dramatically altered relationships among Pacific Island societies.

Other writers before us have pointed out problems of fit between the Western model of ethnicity and the perception and organization of cultural differences in the Pacific. The issue of ethnic identity in Oceania has surfaced particularly in studies of relocated communities and migrant enclaves (Chapman 1985; Lieber 1977b). Howard and Howard (1977), for example, describe a resettled Rotuman community's transformation into an ethnic group on Fiji. Similarly, Lieber found that interactions between migrant Kapingamarangi and cultural others on Pohnpei crystallized a concept of Kapingamarangi identity (1977b, 60–61; see also chapter 4), and Larson links intense Tikopia concern with maintaining custom to the existence of a Tikopia outpost in the Russell Islands (1977, 260).

Martin Silverman (1977a, 6) writes that the ways in which such relocated groups define themselves—and are defined by others—"seem similar to what in other parts of the world is described under the rubric of 'ethnicity.' " His cautious wording and reference to "other parts of the world" are telling. Do Pacific Islanders have salient group identities only in migrant or colonial contexts? The evidence presented herein does not support such a conclusion. In Melanesia one finds examples of numerous self-defined, distinct groups within a small area, as well as socially salient bush/grassland and bush/sea contrasts (Schwartz 1982). Kainantu (Watson, chapter 2) and Mandok (Pomponio, chapter 3) identities are certainly politicized, though at a "level of scale" (Cohen 1978, 396) quite different from that of ethnic groups within nation-states. Micronesians, too, develop distinctive stereotypes based on perceived differences in tradition, dialect, and custom among groups (Flinn, chapter 5; Poyer, chapter 6).

The predominant theme in the literature, then, expressed by Barth as well as by Pacific ethnographers, is that there is something unique about cultural boundaries in Oceania, but anthropologists have found it difficult to specify the crucial "difference that makes a difference" between Pacific and Western constructions of identity. Our goal is not to silence the debate; on the contrary, we hope to raise provocative questions about the conceptualization and organization of cultural differences, both in the Pacific and elsewhere. We suggest that Oceanic and Western views are characterized by fundamentally different theories about the determination of identity. In brief, we venture to propose an Oceanic theory of cultural identity that privileges environment, behavior, and situational flexibility over descent, innate characteristics, and unchanging boundaries. We hasten to qualify this lofty generalization by noting that the contrast is to some extent a matter of emphasis rather than an either/or distinction. Though ethnic models are particularly salient in Europe and North America, social categories invoking descent and shared biological substance are certainly found in other areas of the world—including the Pacific. Nonetheless, we believe the general contrast is valid.

Because of its relatively recent colonial history, the Pacific is a fruitful area for studying the interaction between indigenous notions of identity and the economic and political contingencies posed by the intrusion of nation-states. Colonization abruptly brought Pacific societies under the sway of metropolitan centers and imposed a uniform political and economic system over vast areas. Colonial control intensified interaction between island peoples, and perhaps most significantly, created market centers, classic arenas for the negotiation of social boundaries. Contact with the West also introduced a competing theory of group identity as based wholly or primarily on common descent.

This volume therefore addresses two general questions. First, what are the indigenous assumptions that underlie prevailing categorical distinctions among Pacific peoples? Second, how have local modes of group ascription changed as a consequence of the colonial encounter? The chapters that follow attempt to answer these questions for a set of Oceanic societies that differ in indigenous epistemologies and in the shape of their encounters with the non-Pacific world.

Lamarckian and Mendelian Models

Since cultural identity in the present is the outcome of interaction between indigenous theory and historical process, every ethnographic case can properly be called unique. The specific premises underlying Oceanic social ascriptions are therefore variable, as is the relative flexibility or rigidity of boundaries. Yet, in general, Pacific theories of cultural identity differ strikingly and systematically from theories based on the ethnicity paradigm. At the root of this contrast are epistemological differences about what constitutes a person, and a distinctive theory of ontogeny. Western paradigms of group identity rely both on a biological theory of inheritance and on a psychological model of a discrete, bounded individual. Social-psychological investigations of the relationship between personal and ethnic identity are founded on these assumptions (see Austin and Worchel 1979; Group for the Advancement of Psychiatry 1987; Jacobson-Widding 1983; Strauss 1977; Tajfel 1982). Personal identity in Pacific Island societies is constructed of different cultural materials (White and Kirkpatrick 1983).[5] An understanding of community identity must take into account cultural philosophies of personhood.

Lieber (chapter 4) develops the notion of consocial personhood—which sees persons defined through "their social placement" (Geertz 1973, 390) as nodes of relationships—as distinct from the Western concept of a physically bounded, genetically determined, self-actuating individual (see Geertz 1973, 364–367, 389–391; Schutz 1962). Using Kapingamarangi theories of personhood as an example, Lieber suggests that a Pacific concept of the consociate underlies local understandings of how children become adults and of what motivates human behavior. For Pacific Islanders, much of what determines a person's behavior, feelings, and self-perception is environmental, consisting in the physical and social relationships that nurture a growing child and form the context in which the adult acts. This concept of a person as a node of social relationships profoundly informs such critical Oceanic institutions as kinship, adoption, land rights, and title systems.

James Watson's (chapter 2) presentation of "Lamarckian" identity suggests that consocial personhood may be the essential underpinning of Oceanic notions of group affiliation through a causative process of environmental imprinting on the person. The theory popularly identified as Lamarckian states that acquired characteristics are heritable (*pace* Lamarck).[6] A Lamarckian/Mendelian distinction is a useful way of contrasting a theory that emphasizes the role of social relationships in determining an individual's essential characteristics from one that emphasizes biological inheritance of substance as the determinant of identity. Oceanic explanations for why members of a group share certain traits are based on the premise that people are as they are primarily because of external situation and experience. Shared identity comes from sharing food, water, land, spirits, knowledge, work, and social activities. As Watson's Kainantu informant succinctly phrased it, "other people do other things" because they live in different physical and social worlds.

As Watson makes clear, the Lamarckian notion posits a relationship between environment and biological substance very different from Western theories of individual development. In the Lamarckian model, parental experience, actions, and performed relations with people, plants, soil, and other parts of the environment affect the constitution of the individual at the level of ontogeny. In contrast, the Mendelian model, which we are associating with the Western concept of ethnicity, sees individual identity as determined more or less irrevocably by descent and predictable from facts of parentage—hence Keyes' statement that "ethnicity is a form of kinship reckoning" (1981, 6). The Mendelian model dichotomizes shaping influences before and after birth as two qualitatively different sets of factors; the Lamarckian model sees no such discontinuity. In essence the two models refer to the social ramifications of different cultural constructions of biology.[7] Pierre van den Berghe has recently taken the Mendelian concept of ethnicity to its logical conclusion by espousing sociobiology. Van den Berghe now argues that ethnicity and race

> are extensions of kinship, and, therefore the feelings of ethnocentrism and racism associated with group membership are extensions of nepotism between kinsmen . . . ethnocentrism and racism, too, are deeply rooted in our biology and can be expected to persist even in industrial societies . . . nepotism and ethnocentrism are biologically evolved mechanisms serving the pursuit of individual self-interest. (1981, xi–xii)

In contrast, the Lamarckian premise holds that where you live and how you behave are at least as important as biological parentage in determining who you are socially. A corollary to the Lamarckian proposition running directly counter to the concept of ethnicity is that people are not simply born into social groups but may—in fact, must—become members through their actions. In Oceanic societies identity is continually demonstrated, a matter of behavior and performance.[8] An analogy can be drawn here to Sahlins' (1985, 25–31) concept of "performative structures," which he proposed in the Hawaiian context. "By relative contrast," to paraphrase Sahlins, Pacific Islanders can be said to construct their identities out of practice. Substance is not merely acquired from one's parents but may derive equally from living in a place. We are suggesting here that Oceanic cultural identities "are made as well as born" (Sahlins 1985, 28).

The chapters that follow explore these general propositions about cultural identity in Oceania—consocial definitions of personhood and Lamarckian ideas of the acquisition of essential characteristics—in cases from Melanesia, Micronesia, Polynesia, and Australia. Indigenous theories of identity in the Pacific are of course variable, locally and regionally. The Melanesian Mandok (Pomponio, chapter 3), maritime middlemen traders of the Siassi Islands, define themselves by what they do and where they do it. And certainly Hawaiians (Linnekin, chapter 7) and Maori (Sinclair, chapter 10; Dominy, chapter 11) emphasize ties to the land and have indigenous metaphors of shared substance, such as blood and bone. Recognizing the variability of such specific cultural constructions, if it is possible to generalize about regional differences, Melanesian constructs tend to emphasize place as the basis of shared substance (see Bonnemaison 1985). Polynesian notions seem to place more stress on performed relations and behavioral criteria. The Micronesian societies represented here perceive their social worlds as constellations of exchanging groups and differentiate themselves from one another on the basis of a variety of criteria.

Yet in ascriptions of personal and local group identity, certain higher-level presuppositions are shared throughout Oceania: that people can voluntarily shift their social identities, that a person can maintain more than one identity simultaneously, and that behavioral attributes—such as residence, language, dress, participation in exchanges—are not only significant markers but are also effective determinants of identity. Moreover, fundamental Oceanic premises about the acquisition of cultural identity may persist in social relations even in the face of major political and economic changes, and in spite of the introduction of Western-influenced ethnic categories.

Formulations of Cultural Identity: A Continuum

The arrangement of chapters in this volume roughly charts an increasing organization into social units that approach Western-style ethnic groups: mutually dichotomizing, politically instrumental populations with relatively stable boundaries, defined by ancestry according to Mendelian premises and corresponding to "sociocultural differences at a particular level of scale" (Cohen 1978, 396). Socially, the continuum thus outlined traces a process of closure, a gradual limiting of the range of affiliations that are activated in social relationships.

A major problem with employing the rubric of ethnicity is precisely that it is Western ethnotheory and therefore may ignore significant distinctions—both internal and external—recognized by local people themselves. For this reason the goal of this volume is to investigate, rather than to assume, the formulation of distinctions within and among Pacific societies. The apparent cultural homogeneity of many Micronesian and Polynesian island societies has tempted scholars to assume geographic determinism: that cultural boundaries coincide naturally with the physical boundaries of island groups. The ethnographic examples presented herein do not support the notion that cultural and ecological boundaries in the Pacific are isomorphic. They certainly do not coincide, for instance, among the Kainantu (Watson, chapter 2; see Schwartz 1982 for an analogous situation among the Manus peoples of the Admiralties). Here small, self-identified groups easily incorporate people of diverse origins (cf. Marshall 1975, 165; Poyer, chapter 6). Despite what to an observer appear as miniscule behavioral and emblematic differences, these groups actively maintain separate, coherent identities.

Oceanic groups elsewhere were internally differentiated along kin, status, and territorial lines long before the intrusion of colonialism. Indeed, such nonethnic distinctions were the primary modes of structuring relationships in precontact times. Polynesian societies were characterized by more or less acute differentiation between chiefs and commoners. In highly stratified chiefdoms such as Hawaii, this categorical and social distinction entailed mutual stereotyping of behavioral characteristics and even the attribution of different origins—the Polynesian identification of chiefs as sea people and foreign, and the symbolic identification of commoners with the land. Like other scholars, Barth (1969, 27) notes that rank distinctions such as these are not "ethnic" because of stipulated common kinship and permeable boundaries. In another example, for most of its known history Pohnpei (Eastern Caroline Islands) did not recognize an identity as a single society and was not united under a single ruler (Petersen 1977). Boundaries between Pohnpei's chiefdoms were socially salient and politicized to the extent that they were grounds for warfare. Sapwuahfik's sectional identities (Poyer, chapter 6) and Maori tribes (Sinclair, chapter 10; see also Linnekin, chapter 7) offer analogous examples of internal structural differentiation in the face of apparent cultural homogeneity.

Such internal differentiation, however, is different in structure and significance from ethnicity in the sense in which we use it here. The formation of ethnic groups in the island Pacific characteristically reflects the influence of Western (and in the Micronesian case, Japanese) categories and institutions. We believe that ethnic group organization was absent in the precolonial Pacific. By now it should be clear that we do not mean to suggest that precontact Pacific Islanders did not postulate cultural differences, or that these identities were unreflective. Regardless of their degree of contact with Western institutions, Oceanic groups are often quite self-conscious and insistent about their identities. Yet as suggested above, these groups maintain separate cultural identities within pluralistic social environments, and their theories of affiliation consistently emphasize context, situation, performance, and place over biological descent.

The Lamarckian paradigm can partially explain the apparent fluidity of social boundaries in many Pacific societies, where individuals are likely to possess multiple, nested affiliations in a conceptual hierarchy (see Cohen 1978; Linnekin, chapter 7). In contrast, ethnicity is categorical. In precontact Oceania, the Yap "empire" (see Flinn, chapter 5) perhaps most closely approximated a system of dichotomizing, complementary groups along the lines of Barth's (1956, 1969) organizational model. Here island communities were tied into a wider tributary and exchange network and their separate identities were salient in that context. But even in this case, no evidence exists that group identity was seen as categorical, innate, and superordinate.

Our point is that ethnicity as it is perceived today was not an imperative categorical affiliation in precontact Oceania. More broadly, this conclusion implies that ethnic identity is not primordial, but must be seen as emerging under certain historical circumstances. Howard and Howard (1977, 165) propose that the "crucial question" for understanding the development of ethnic groups is "under what conditions does ethnicity become the superordinate symbol within a social system?" The arrangement of chapters in this volume provides a series of ethnographic cases with which we can address this question.

Development of Ethnic Groups

The political scientist Joseph Rothschild (1981, 20) notes that anthropologists were relatively late in discovering politicized ethnicity. In part this is because most anthropologists have worked in small-scale non-Western societies, but the lag also reflects our disciplinary tendency to view indigenous societies as naive isolates. The colonial expansion of states in the Pacific imposed new administrative definitions on native peoples and in turn provoked shifts in self-perception. Self-categorization continues to evolve in the postcolonial era. Today, state-level politics is the most potent factor in the ongoing transformation of Pacific cultural identities. Throughout the island Pacific, cultural identity has become or is in the process of becoming politicized. As Rothschild points out, even in Western Europe "ethnic political consciousness" has not always been historically salient; it emerged as a force only in the past two centuries (Rothschild 1981, 13). This "modern surge of politicized ethnicity" has created an international model for political action (Rothschild 1981; Smith 1981) in which Pacific Islanders are now participating.

The early chapters of this volume examine cultural identity in societies that do not formulate their social categories by opposition to an alien metropolitan center, and where the Lamarckian theory of identity prevails. Pulap (Flinn, chapter 5) and Sapwuahfik (Poyer, chapter 6) seem to represent the incipient development of ethnic groups as these islanders become increasingly involved in the political arena of their pluralistic new nation, the Federated States of Micronesia. The final four chapters describe Oceanic societies where indigenous peoples have become minorities in their own lands. In Hawaii, New Zealand, and Australia, Pacific peoples have been subordinated and disenfranchised. Accordingly, they tend to adopt the political tools of other groups struggling against dominant colonial powers. At this end of the continuum of emerging ethnicity, incorporation within nation-states has led to the institutionalization of a biological model of identity in which cultural differences are perceived to be unambiguous, exclusive, and enduring.

In this context, Hawaiians (Linnekin, chapter 7), Maori (Sinclair, chapter 10; Dominy, chapter 11), and Australian Aborigines (Tonkinson, chapter 9) begin to see themselves as part of the "Fourth World" and start to turn Western notions of cultural boundaries to their own political advantage, often formulating an explicitly countermetropolitan identity. Although at the national level these groups are classified and may define themselves as races or ethnic groups, we suggest that concepts of consocial personhood and Lamarckian social identity often prevail in the casual ascriptions made in everyday interpersonal relations. In these cases it may be appropriate to differentiate ethnicity as an ethnotheory from the social organization of ethnic groups; we suggest that one may occur without the other—at least temporarily. It remains to be seen whether Western ideological influence and the political division of the Pacific world along ethnic lines will succeed in reproducing the Western theory of ethnicity in local communities. The final chapters of this volume offer some evidence to the contrary, that at least in Hawaii and New Zealand, Oceanic formulations of cultural identity have begun to penetrate into the institutions and administrative categories of the dominant society. Our continuum does not, therefore, chart an ineluctable transition from Lamarckian to Mendelian premises about identity.

The impacts of colonialism in the Pacific are both conceptual—the introduction of foreign models—and practical—the introduction of invasive political and economic structures. During the colonial era the Pacific Islands were incorporated into a world system of material and social relations; each island group became tied to a metropolitan center dominated by foreigners. Economic viability came to hinge on external and seemingly arbitrary factors. Vital decisions were no longer the province of the local community, the extended kin network, or customary authorities. Moreover, the concept of ethnicity became entrenched in a host of laws and administrative policies that still operate throughout the colonial and postcolonial Pacific. The nature and uses of cultural differentiation were substantially altered in this context. Confronted with political systems organized along Western lines, modern Pacific Islanders are pressured to formulate their group identity in Western terms.

The imposition of foreign social models makes cultural identity problematic both in thought and in action. "Who I am" now determines what I can and cannot do, can and cannot have, can and cannot be. Ethnicity (as defined by the metropolitan power) may conflict with the contingent and situational character of indigenous cultural identity, but it becomes nonetheless a limitation on personal action and a challenge to local theories of consocial personhood. Social relationships and biography no longer determine personal identity; an arbitrary and externally imposed categorization comes increasingly to shape a person's life.

Modes of political action are easier to gauge than evanescent shifts in self-perception. In Oceania today we see the metamorphosis of cultural identities into interest groups, organized for action at various political levels. The goals of aboriginal peoples in the Pacific match those of the victims of colonial domination elsewhere in the world: economic security, political sovereignty, civil rights, human dignity, social equality. A form of international structural relativity is at work in the pursuit of these goals: an interest group formed on the basis of cultural identity provides an organizational match for the political structures of domination and a base for alliances with similar movements elsewhere in the Pacific and in the world.

Ethnic political movements in the Pacific, like similar movements elsewhere in the postcolonial world, often explicitly define themselves by opposition to what they see as the undesirable attributes of Euro-American culture (see Dominy, chapter 11). The formation of an ethnic group is often accompanied by the emergence of an objectified concept of indigenous lifeways and more rigid notions of identity. By unifying under the banner of a shared tradition people can act more effectively in a pluralistic political arena. The self-conscious and directed redefini-

tion of certain acts, artifacts, and values as traditional—a familiar phenomenon in European ethnic revivals (Hobsbawm and Ranger 1983)—
is equally characteristic of contemporary Pacific nationalism (see Linnekin, chapter 7). A difficult question, for scholars and ethnic
nationalists alike, is the extent to which this objectification indexes culture change—the adoption of foreign modes of self-perception.

Scholars disagree about whether consciousness of tradition in the
Pacific is indigenous or whether this awareness reflects introduced cate-
gories such as "culture." Howard and Howard note the influence of
Western education on the way Rotumans conceptualize cultural units.
They perceptively point out that the ethnic group concept is founded on
Western premises about the boundedness of culture and society—premises that are formally institutionalized by colonial administrations. The
Western assumption that cultural units coincide with geographically
defined political units clearly created a basis for conceptualizing a
bounded Rotuman community, "despite the fact that the traditional system was characterized by groupings with highly permeable social
boundaries" (1977, 191).

The relatively recent preoccupation with *kastom* 'custom' in Melanesia, particularly in new nations such as Vanuatu (Larcom, chapter 8;
see also Keesing and Tonkinson 1982; Tonkinson 1982a, b), similarly
suggests the influence of Western notions of culture and society (cf.
Handler 1984). In 1973, Larcom (1982, 331–332) found Malakulans
uninterested and uncomprehending when asked about their past customs. But in 1981 they were "acutely aware of *kastom* as a body of past
traditions to be revitalized . . . something representing past authenticity in counterpoint to Western values" (see also Lindstrom 1982; Linnekin 1983; Tonkinson 1982a). Linnekin (chapter 7) elaborates on the processes involved in such objectification (see also Larcom, chapter 8;
Sinclair, chapter 10).

Keesing (1982a, 297–298) acknowledges the influence of international political ideologies, primarily nationalism, on Melanesian
appeals to kastom but he points out that "other, older sources" are also
behind modern traditional consciousness in Melanesia. He finds indigenous cultural precedent for "the idea of codifying 'custom.' " One may
of course recognize cultural precedent as well as introduced ideological
models for concepts such as kastom. What seems distinctively Western
about the notions of culture that surface in modern Pacific politics,
however, is their rigidity when compared with indigenous premises
about identity.

As political consciousness develops, culture becomes a subject of public discourse and, as for the Mewun of Vanuatu (Larcom, chapter 8), of
disagreement and negotiation. Ideology in the Marxian sense thereby

expands its realm as a distorter of immediate relations among persons. A world in which identity is formed by face-to-face social relations is transformed into one where it is defined by a status and role influenced if not determined by ethnicity. To some extent, participation in a global economic and political order requires this; in a nation of a million people we cannot know each other biographically as in an atoll community. But even as Oceanic concepts of identity come to resemble Western ones in their general form, the ethnographic content of those cultural identities remains encouragingly diverse. In espousing kastom, the Pacific Way, the Micronesian Way, Maoritanga, and so on, Pacific Islanders are asserting their right, their capability, and their willingness to reject aspects of Western culture and to retain crucial features of indigenous lifeways and world view. From an anthropologist's point of view this commitment to cultural diversity, a phoenix rising from the ashes of the threat of Western uniformity, is a hopeful sign for the future. The maintenance of cultural distinctiveness is of course a two-edged sword, for such differences offer ready excuses for oppression. But cultural differences are also recognized—and not just by anthropologists—as a source of richness in human life and a pool of alternative ways of being, a vital resource of workable options for the world's future.

NOTES

Our thanks go to Richard Handler, Alan Howard, Michael D. Lieber, and James B. Watson for valuable critiques of earlier versions of this chapter, and to the other members of the Association for Social Anthropology in Oceania symposium, Cultural Identity in Oceania, for inspiration and comments. For the failings of the chapter, we alone are responsible.

1. A key argument in Barth's (1969) seminal essay is that ethnic boundaries are created and maintained through mutual interaction—an important challenge to "primordialist" assumptions. But he does not completely forsake the culture-historical notion that an isolated population such as an island group would develop an ethnic identity *in situ*. In his later discussion of cultural variability in Melanesia, Barth (1971) speaks of local cultural units as "local syndromes" and "systems," however, not as ethnic groups.

2. This model is of course not limited to the West; in Asia, for example, one may find more or less similar Mendelian theories of identity. We refer to the ethnicity model as Western in this volume, however, because it has been elaborated primarily by American and European social scientists and because most colonial powers in the Pacific have been Western nations.

3. Cultural identities are symbolically constituted in the sense that the criteria determining ascription to such groups are cultural constructs rather than naturally given attributes. The arbitrariness of ethnic categories refers to their semiotic nature, not to any lack of real-world effect.

4. Although the aboriginal peoples of Australia are not properly speaking "Pacific Islanders," we have included a chapter on Aboriginal identity because of historical and structural analogues to "Fourth World" Pacific Island peoples. The situation of Aborigines in Australia—outnumbered and landless in their own homeland—is in many ways similar to that of Hawaiians and Maori.

5. The concept of personhood, with its developmental and emotional implications, is explored for a number of Pacific Island societies in White and Kirkpatrick (1985). Their volume expands our understandings of the significance of cultural constructions of the person by exploring identity in terms of the community as well as the individual social actor.

6. We admit to a degree of distortion as we remove Lamarck's idea from its disciplinary context. We use the term only as an analogy to characterize a general theory that stresses the malleability and the contemporary acquisition of identity.

7. We are indebted to Michael D. Lieber and James B. Watson for clarification of the Lamarckian notion and its implications.

8. The theme of cultural identity as contingent on situation and context is prevalent in recent ethnographic studies of Pacific Island societies (see, e.g., Carroll 1975; Marshall 1975).

2

Other People Do Other Things: Lamarckian Identities in Kainantu Subdistrict, Papua New Guinea

JAMES B. WATSON

What is cultural identity among many-neighbored small groups, living in close proximity and nearly identical to one another in the main features of their daily activity, organization, and exchange relationships? What sort of stereotypes prevail where tiny outgroups are known by the score, and yet each nevertheless assumes its own distinct identity and that of every other? What sense of a common local heritage develops in each such little group? And which of these self-ascribed features are viewed as their own, either not shared with every outgroup, or not shared with any? Finally and centrally, how are these ethnic differences or diacritics thought to arise and characterize each group? Even if primordially given, these differences are somehow perpetuated or reproduced through time. In comparing themselves to peers, in short, who do members of these groups think they are, and what do they think makes them so?

The aboriginal peoples of Papua New Guinea's Eastern Highlands are organized in autonomous polities, some with as few as one or two hundred members. Many if not most of these local peoples experience episodes of radical revision in their membership. Most groups are formed in a highly fluid sociopolitical field, intermittently marked by relocations, realignments, and the patriation of alien immigrants who have been expelled by hostile neighbors from their own lands elsewhere. Restless or disgruntled insiders split off to form new groups; refugee outsiders are recruited from time to time to reinforce the ranks of those remaining. To the literal-minded genealogist, the long-term kinship and continuity of each such group seem confused, even compromised.

A truncated local sense of history nevertheless contains the frequent events of fission and fusion. In spite of ongoing exchanges of personnel, a common and ostensibly continuous local identity immerses not only long-established elements of the community but, in time, the descendants of recent immigrants. Even though the broad outlines of this

17

recurring confluence of people may be known, at least for recent generations, the unity and distinctiveness of each small group is proclaimed
by insiders and tacitly assumed outgroups. Moreover, local identity is
asserted and assumed without the need of much specification. The unity
of each people is sufficiently proven in their residence and in their performance, ample proof apparently that they not only have their fate in
their own hands but also have unique talent and temperament. Members of each group are also presumed to possess a unique magical competence, imparted to their young through habituation and tutelage and
not readily shared with outsiders.

This chapter examines the basis of local distinctiveness in the face of
apparent cultural uniformity. How are numerous tiny, fluid local
groups differentiated in practice and in ideology? What are the conceptual principles that guarantee and define a distinctive identity for each
group? As an ethnographer working in Kainantu Subdistrict, I came to
a paradoxical conclusion: no matter how numerous, small, near, and
nearly identical the polities of the Eastern Highlands may be, no matter
how permeable their boundaries or how checkered the history of their
membership, they will consider themselves and will be thought to be
distinct ethnic units. The very political reality that qualifies, if not contradicts, the claim of continuous, consistent, genealogical identity also
helps to impose a pragmatic separateness and unity on these small polities. That political reality is greatly aided by the awareness of magic
and indigenous principles of growth and inculcation. In the broadest
sense the implication of these principles can be characterized as
Lamarckian, as distinct from Mendelian.

The name of Lamarck has long been used loosely to label the inheritance of acquired traits as distinct from a genetically regulated inheritance. Some fifty years ago Ginzburg (1933, 22) observed that "in its
bearing on sociology the Lamarckian theory has sometimes been interpreted inaccurately as implying the inheritance of mental training." In
this sense, he noted, the Lamarckian model is cited in contrasting mental or cultural evolution to biological evolution. This loose, revisionist
usage has nonetheless persisted. In a recent acknowledgment, Gould
(1979, 28) concedes that there is good reason to approve so serviceable a
distinction, despite its departure from Lamarck's original intention.
Not only by now firmly established, he points out, the model in which
acquired characters are inherited is well suited to the modern theory of
culture, whereas it fails to accord with the findings of contemporary
biology: "Human cultural evolution, in strong opposition to our biological history, is Lamarckian in character. What we learn in one generation, we transmit directly by teaching and writing."

Except for the evolutionary implication, to which I will later return,

the Kainantu theory of cultural identities is arguably Lamarckian in
this derivative modern sense. Such an argument emphasizes the importance of characters acquired directly from the environment. The origin,
continuity, or replacement of these characters over time is clearly linked
in Kainantu thought to the place in which, and to the people among
whom and by whose efforts, persons are formed. The relevance to the
comparative study of cultural identity is that in Kainantu theory an
inheritance involving parental seed or substance is much less clearly
projected. These points will be elaborated below.

The Ethnographic Context

For eighteen months in 1953–1954 and twelve months in 1963–1964 I
lived successively in each of five different local groups in the Kainantu
Subdistrict of the Eastern Highlands Province (then District) of Papua
New Guinea (then the Territory of New Guinea). The main purpose of
the initial fieldwork was to compare the responses to colonial contact of
two different peoples, thereby ascertaining how they might resemble or
differ from each other in various measures of acculturation. Indigenous,
de facto cultural differences were thus a prime concern of this research,
including whatever recognition and meaning such differences might
have for the people themselves—their own self-awareness, cultural
identity, views of others, and instrumental ethnicity. During this project
my wife, infant daughter, and I were successively the guests of a relatively large Agarabi group and two smaller Tairora-speaking groups.
The latter two sites were chosen because of the probability that they differed from each other in the duration or intensity of their colonial contact.

A central concern for the second research, conducted as part of the
Micro-evolution Project (Watson 1963),[1] was, as the term *micro-evolution* suggests, the differentiation of the numerous small local societies of
this region of the Central Highlands. Thus, again, the research emphasis was favorable to the recognition of physical, linguistic, and cultural
differences, small or large, among local peoples. At least incidental to
this focus was what use the people involved might make of the differences they recognized.

As a supplement to the main research, my wife and I (as well as some
other members of the team) took part in the LeVine-Campbell Cross-
Cultural Study of Ethnocentrism (LeVine and Campbell 1972). In connection with that project we used the elaborate *Ethnocentrism Field
Manual*, including a schedule devised for data gathering in some twenty
situations comprising several continents (LeVine and Campbell 1972,

245–296). In 1964 we interviewed numerous residents of Batainabura, one of the two Tairora-speaking communities in which we lived during that study.[2] Although the comparative findings of the ethnocentrism project have yet to be published, at least one observation can be made, and it has bearing on the discussion to follow. The *Ethnocentrism Field Manual* anticipated interviewing informants of a given community about the neighboring peoples whom they distinguished as "outgroups." The format of the schedule allowed for no more than four or five outgroups, yet in using the definitions provided, informants could list between forty and sixty outgroups. A composite inventory—collating the responses of four informants—yielded well in excess of that number of outgroups.

Clearly the outgroups anticipated in the field manual—ethnic or linguistic if not "tribal" congeries—differed from the outgroups recognized by Kainantu informants. They recognized each local group as a separate people and, if close enough to be known sufficiently, spoke of them as such. Phratries were also peoples, to be sure, and with increasing distance a local group would increasingly tend to be blurred or merged with its larger phratry. Kainantu informants also recognized and could describe ethnolinguistic congeries comprising a number of phratries and an even larger number of local groups. In short, while larger collectivities were recognized in one set of terms or another, local groups of as few as a hundred souls also could be regarded as outgroups in their own right and in that sense as separate and distinguishable peoples.

The Sociopolitical Background of Cultural Identity in Kainantu

In the 1960s the peoples of Kainantu Subdistrict were living as they always had, in numerous small local groups, each linked to various outgroup partners by marital or well-remembered military exchanges. In the majority of cases each group's neighbors and alliance partners were within a day's walking distance. Many could be reached in half a day or less, so intergroup visiting was frequent. The nearest neighbors could usually be reached within an hour or two, and the hamlets of a single local community were typically within calling distance—usually a walk of minutes, seldom as much as an hour. In some cases one could reach hamlets of other communities by voice since long-distance calling, with its own linguistic conventions, is well developed. In a few cases one could call out to people of a different phratry, but in an area of well-remembered warfare this proximity was exceptional and uneasy.

Phratries, their constituent communities, and even the tiny hamlets into which many of the latter were subdivided, were all separately named and distinguished. The sense of locality and coresidence was well particularized in the immediate vicinity of each group. What I refer to here as the local or territorial community—what Pataki-Schweizer (1980) has called the "bounded complex"—was the most autonomous and probably also the most continuous political entity. Except when very small, phratries were normally looser collectivities, and at the other end of the scale hamlets were more or less submerged in the communities they composed.

Political life had been dynamic and fluid in this area for at least several generations before the coming of Europeans. At any level of organization, the length of time a particular membership stayed together varied by chance. Phratries could grow not only through natural increase but more precipitously from the sudden influx of outsiders—dispossessed refugees fleeing their own territory—who might be recruited to join a local community. By no means uncommon, the same event could also lead to weakening or splitting of a phratry by diluting the common interest and identity of its member communities. The loyalties of refugees naturally favored their immediate sponsors and coresidents, whose interests sometimes diverged from those of other factions of the phratry. Through the recruitment of outsiders hamlets could also become increasingly independent of the community within which they arose.

Thus in the 1960s some 25,000 to 40,000 Kainantu people lived in numerous small, proximate, lately warring and highly fluid polities, loosely joined (a) in genealogically premised phratries and (b) in politically premised exchange partnerships, but relatively independent of one another at the level of local, territorial communities. For a discussion of the meaning of cultural identity or ethnicity, several further facts stand out against this background:

1. At every level throughout most of the vicinity there is a profound similarity of production and social organization.

2. Consequent upon this similarity is the redundant—in the sense of duplicative, not excessive—capability of neighboring groups for cooperation, since they are all largely alike in what they can offer in exchange.

3. A number of languages, and within some languages distinct dialects, subdivide the area into speech communities, the largest (Tairora) having some eleven thousand speakers, the smallest (Binumarien) a few hundred.

4. Roughly coincident with the speech communities or their constituent dialects are recognized ethnic differences, some of which are apparent to neighbors.

5. Crosscutting at least the larger of these ethnolinguistic congeries is a further variegation of practice or belief, remarkable if minute, some of it known to both the people so distinguished and their neighbors, some ostensibly known only to the people themselves, and some evidently recognized by neither the group itself nor by others of the vicinity. In this instance my inquisitiveness, as well as my successive residence in a series of different communities, apparently brought to light previously unrecognized differences between groups, in one or two cases to the surprise of the people concerned.

In this last point I have characterized a cultural variegation that, though often minute, seemed remarkable to me—a purely personal reaction, of course, dependent on what my previous acquaintance with ethnology had led me to expect. In a discussion of ethnicity and its indigenous uses, however, a note of clarification is needed. We are describing, after all, a relatively small number of human beings in one particular corner of the earth, people who, like their country, appear to most of the outside world as not only uniform but perhaps even monotone. It was in this light that I found it astonishing—as did some of the people themselves—that two villages, sharing virtually the same dialect and linked by marriage and a tradition of common descent, differed on a point that left both of them incredulous. In one community ghosts are known by fairly frequent—and most unwelcome—contact with the living, while in the other no one has ever seen a ghost. In the former village ghosts are recognized by an unforgettable visage graphically reported to those happily spared the experience, while in the latter people consider the idea of such an encounter equally unappealing but most unlikely.

As used here, "diacritics" are the claimed points of difference between groups, insofar as these are recognized and emphasized by members of the groups concerned. Recognition and emphasis vary from group to group as well as from one diacritic to another. Recognition varies most overtly in how closely ingroup and outgroup perceptions are matched on specific points of ethnic difference. A perfect match is arguably impossible, even when insiders and outsiders both recognize what is ostensibly the same point of ethnic difference and give it much the same relative emphasis. Wholly unilateral diacritics doubtless occur, on the other hand, at least in Kainantu, as in the case of purported differences that one party flatly disclaims or simply ignores. Any demonstrable intergroup difference might of course be diacritical for an observer, but such differences may not serve as diacritics for given actors. Some differences are simply unknown, and some known differences may be thought too trivial for emphasis. In other words, diacritics are selectively recognized and emphasized in practice.

Wholly unrecognized as a point of local difference, for instance—its discovery in fact astonishing to the principals themselves—are the divergent ideas of ghostly apparitions described above. This rather sharp difference of local belief does (or did) not constitute a diacritic for the actors. The same may well be true, again, of a guardian of the afterworld, a lusty hermaphrodite who is vivid only to the members of one of two groups while scarcely known to the other. Despite the groups' historical and spatial closeness, only the first group views its territory as lying on the route to the land of ghosts. While sharing the general respect for local expertise, members of the second group are less clear about the precise path of the lately dead in reaching the afterworld.

As for what I have called unilateral diacritics, Kainantu peoples widely say of each other that certain local beliefs and practices are private, some deliberately so. To the extent that such guardedness prevails, the unilateral diacritics of Kainantu may well be fairly numerous as, based solely on their own privacy and the belief that others follow them in this, group members take for granted significant differences between themselves and others, differences that cannot always be specified. To give an idea of the diversity of Kainantu diacritics, at least the tiny sample that came to light in the field, the following list is more or less randomly drawn from notes or memory. I have roughly grouped them, moreover, as an outsider's common sense might suggest. To complement the picture, I include a single diacritic, one almost certainly recognized throughout the vicinity, that uniformly distinguishes any Kainantu people from the distant salt makers to the south.

1. Among *skills or powers* ascribed to certain peoples or localities one finds renown for making arrows of extraordinary efficacy (although now more widely made, particular types of arrows still bear the local name of the originators); pottery making; lime making; salt making, as mentioned above, a universally known import from the south; rain-making magic (e.g., Kainantu peoples such as the Arogara, occupying the forested Kratke foothills); ownership of the annual *orana* ritual; and *ampu* (Tairora *hampu*), an elaborate rite for ensorcelling wanted brides and thus attracting them without paying brideprice, especially from neighboring enemies. (This last practice is limited as far as I know to certain northern Tairora and Agarabi-speaking peoples.)

2. *Resources* believed to be more or less locally distinctive include
magically potent water for promoting the growth of pigs; superior
seed for winged beans; distinctive bananas required for the *orana*
ritual, found only in the territories of the ritual sponsors and said to
be capable of growing nowhere else; potting clay—this despite the
admission that seemingly identical deposits occur among certain
nonpotters whose art, it was nevertheless maintained, would surely
fail them if they tried to use this material; and local soils unusually
favorable to the growing of yams, kudzu, and other specific crops.

3. *Local landscape features* associated with the ethnic identity of those
who hold the given territory include forest versus *kunai* 'grassland'
habitats; the large limestone cliffs or outcroppings of a certain people; a limestone rock shelter whose back wall is smoke stained by the
fires of the spectral inhabitants; the pair of giant monoliths found in
the forest of Batainabura and representing the rivalrous Two Brothers, whose myth is famous in the region (Vincent 1973); isolated
small monoliths found standing in certain territories, their erection
ascribed to ancestors and the stones themselves endowed with special power as rubbing stones for pigs, beneficial to their growth and
health (cf. Watson and Cole 1977, fig. 10); and the pandanus tree in
whose trunk is embedded a stone axe that no outsider may hope to
pull free. Held as private local knowledge, this last landscape feature is thus a frankly unilateral diacritic.

4. *Distinctive local artifacts* include the bustle skirts (made from a reed
of limited distribution) of certain Gadsup women and their neighbors, worn for dancing because with movement they bounce and
rustle audibly; the bark cooking drums used with earth ovens; and
the carven tree-fern figurines of Batainabura and perhaps other forest peoples.

To an outsider the foregoing diacritics may seem a decidedly mixed
bag, the sense of miscellany no doubt accentuated by the very act of list-
ing them. An exhaustive list of Kainantu diacritics would surely be
many times longer, its effect perhaps still more miscellaneous. From a
Kainantu point of view, in any case, the categories suggested here may
be somewhat extraneous. Although not arranged by conscious intent,
the order of the listed categories may nevertheless loosely suggest which
items are considered more weighty or definitive of local identity. As I
endeavor to show below, the operating premise of Kainantu diacritics
seems to imply the convergence of what I shall call a "proprietary landscape" with local history or ancestral tradition, and of these in turn

with competence, power, belief, and practice, all together making for distinctive ethnic character and *pari passu* thus for interethnic difference. In that light, the wearing of reed skirts (as opposed to bark), or the use of bark drums to increase the content of an earth oven, could hardly rank in weight with the immediacy and influence of limestone cliffs, with arrow-making or pottery-making power, with the sponsorship of rituals, with the magic for controlling rain, or with similar diacritics.

Whether or not "minute" is the correct descriptor, such cultural variegation is all the more remarkable if one stops to think how soon much of it may vanish from sight, and how many detailed local differences must have already disappeared. If no standardized ethnography were written for several decades and one was then based wholly on contemporary observations, Kainantu cultures might then appear thoroughly homogeneous. The task of regional synthesis, its broad outlines already quite plain at the time of my fieldwork, would be trouble free indeed. Given the evident similarities of local ecology, organization, and ideology, Kainantu practice and belief would blend convincingly into a single culture, perhaps with remnant ethnolinguistic differences marking its only subvariants. Peeling off the layers of acculturation might seem all the more straightforward since all of the innovation would have occurred in so short a time. Most of the lost differences might well be untraceable once the fragile diversity they represented in the 1960s was irretrievably blurred.

This minute diversity, which I take to be transient, underscores two points with respect to cultural identity and its local manifestations. The first point is that, transient or not, minute or not, ample diacritics are available for differentiating the small groups that interact in the Kainantu area. That, to the external observer, these peoples differ in relatively small matters and are alike in many of the larger features of their lives could well be thought a central fact of local ethnicity. In this light the frequent mixing, splitting, and merging of erstwhile separate groups might seem to make a viable ethnicity of micropolities even more surprising. But I doubt that *multum in parvo* is a sufficient key to the local identification process.

The second point is that local identifications do not correspond precisely or predictably to a repertoire of contrastive traits. The tacit acceptance of difference is the salient characteristic of Kainantu intergroup relations, quite apart from any list of potential ethnic differentiators. The little that is known about another group represents much more that is assumed or implied, and seemingly need not be known. The claim of ethnic distinctiveness lies deeper than the surface manifestations that illustrate it and is therefore invulnerable to the minuteness or transience that an ethnographer might perceive. The prevailing assumption is that in a principled way peoples *are* different—whether or not the details can be specified. Initially I was impressed that local ethnic theorists could indeed, when pressed, substantiate their many identities. To be candid, it gave me some satisfaction as an ethnographer to discover a richness in little differences. I gradually came to be more impressed, however, with how little the claims relied on the palpable contrasts. Although I am concerned with the content of local differences, this chapter focuses on the principles underlying cultural identity in Kainantu and hence the use of that content. My primary interest here is the process of differentiation, not the catalog of diacritics used locally as cultural markers. Indeed, to Kainantu peoples the latter are secondary to the a priori assertion of difference.

Before turning to principles, however, I will first touch briefly on one important aspect of group differentiation: the linguistic diversity and the mixing of peoples of different speech in this region. Over half a dozen languages are spoken in the immediate vicinity of Kainantu, and all of the communities I resided in have close social ties to at least one community of alien speech. Often two or three other languages are represented in these linkages. Many communities of the vicinity have incorporated refugees who arrived speaking a language other than that of their hosts. With time, if the refugees remain, their original language may be lost, but probably not without a distinct residue of the sounds, words, attitudes, and cultural practices they brought with them. In some communities in the 1960s there were refugees or their descendants still speaking their original language—albeit some as bilinguals, resulting in their designation by the community (from Pidgin) as "hapkas." At least one community has three languages said to be in active use.

The Use of Diacritics

Neither a catalog of traits nor a cultural taxonomy forms the basis of cultural identity in Kainantu. Behavioral and cultural diacritics are certainly recognized, and considering the region's size and overall uniformity, a surprising wealth of diacritics is available for discriminating among local peoples. This fact raises the question, what if diacritics were indeed the hinge of local ascriptions of ethnicity? Would there be sufficient cultural uniqueness to provide distinctive "emblems" (Schwartz 1963) for every group in the Kainantu area whose neighbors treat them distinctly?

Pataki-Schweizer (1980, 137) has carefully tabulated the number and size of territorially autonomous communities among roughly 24,000

Kainantu as of the early 1960s. The survey includes all but two of the
largest ethnolinguistic series represented in the area. The tabulated peoples, comprising the major part of the local population, are presumably
representative of the vicinity as a whole at that time. Within their number are an even 100 local communities, each with an average population of 240 (standard deviation 113), each occupying an average of 4.9
square miles (standard deviation 3.3). The total area represented is
485.9 square miles, so that population density averages 49 per square
mile. If the two remaining large ethnolinguistic populations were
included, the figures would be augmented by perhaps 15,000 to 20,000
individuals and another 50 or so local communities, making a total of
approximately 150 such communities or "bounded complexes."

To be sure, none of these 150 communities must deal with all the rest
—or even with a majority of them—at any given moment, if ever.
Indeed, many were known by little more than name and perhaps by
some incident or ascribed trait, some feature of their country, some salient personage, or a legendary or mythical event. The number of outgroups named by each of four Batainabura informants, as previously
noted, ranged from 40 to 60, including certain ethnolinguistic series and
phratries as well as local communities. Of this number their active
neighbors—those who engage them in frequent first-hand exchanges,
hostile or friendly—may be perhaps a third or so. The people of each
community could conceivably stereotype their immediate neighbors
and active partners, finding a memorable attribute to associate with
each. In my experience, however, while no one would doubt the reality
of differentiation by locality, the various neighbors might not agree on
the same stereotype. Diacritics one neighbor considered unique to a
particular group might also include some other group in the eyes of a
different neighbor, and so forth; the permutations are nearly endless.

In a seminar on ethnicity some years ago I described the Kainantu situation under a title something like "The Ethnicity of Numerous, Small,
Neighboring Groups." Accustomed to the grosser differentiation of large
ethnic minorities in modern nations, or to the cultural identities of
whole nations or regions, some members of the seminar could not agree
that I was even addressing ethnicity. Of course I was not speaking of an
ethnic situation of the sort they were used to considering, for the very
point of my paper was to present a markedly different scenario—yet
one in which cultural identification was basic, even profound, though
at the surface minutely defined. More than one member of the group
remained unpersuaded; one insisted that no more was at issue in
Kainantu than petty local prejudices similar to those of small villages in
Europe. Believing that political autonomy and the need to deal with
their neighbors in matters of war and peace set the villages of Kainantu

apart from those of the modern world, or even those of medieval Europe, I seek now to demonstrate how, despite the fluidity and number of independent groups in Kainantu, each group views a plethora of others as ethnically distinct.

As diacritics are locally known and used, they are most assuredly not the summation of presumed differences. Indeed, they could not be since local peoples do not profess to know all that is different about their neighbors. As acknowledged above, they naturally have more complete knowledge of some neighbors than of others. Diacritics are used to provide confirmation, to exemplify, to illustrate, to mark the telling instance. Description, enumeration, classification might seem to emerge with sufficient probing, especially if the probing itself provides an order that may be lacking in the indigenous scheme. Unless I am wrong, however, any semblance of systematics would be illusory. Diacritics prove what is already presumed—that different peoples do indeed differ, as indigenous assumptions about the formation and identification of peoples would predict. Diacritics are thus merely the overt manifestation of the historical process by which local peoples are believed to have differentiated. Particular attributes are not the sum of ethnic differences but the tips of ethnic icebergs—large segments of which one does not know and may never expect to discover.

The premise in Kainantu is that the process of group formation produces uniformity among the membership in shared knowledge, experience, speech, and behavior. Correlatively, if belonging to one group makes members alike in their uniqueness, members of other groups must be unique in their own way. But to know everything that is different about one's neighbors, it would be necessary to know in detail all that is shared by the members of every single personnel. As I have argued, there is much to know in the Kainantu area. Some of this knowledge is hard for outsiders to acquire, and the members of any one community have no practical need to know all the differences between themselves and the members of other communities, least of all those beyond a radius of, say, fifteen to twenty miles. With many of these communities the relations are tenuous, transient, distant, or virtually nonexistent. During my fieldwork I discovered that an inquisitive outsider can turn up differences heretofore unrecognized by lifelong residents. Often, though not always, my informants accepted such revelations with a notable lack of surprise or even interest. Some such knowledge is clearly useful, but exhaustiveness or avid information seeking is irrelevant, except perhaps to ethnographers.

That association makes for similarity and distantiation for difference is probably one of those primal ideas that can be found in one expression or another in much of the world. The question then becomes what "association" means in different cultural contexts, as well as what are the meaningful similarities and differences. Whenever I asked members of one community why those of another group differed in some particular trait, the commonest response was "because their fathers/ancestors taught them so." I now wonder what other answer I expected, but at the time I occasionally longed for some ecological, historical, sociological, or psychological insight. I have come to believe that my informants' answer was not only adequate but accurate, a correct expression of the indigenous view and not simply a stopgap response to an unfamiliar question.

People become what they are made to become by their forebears, whose power and influence over them, in Kainantu, exceed precept and example. In the next few paragraphs I will detail certain incidents that illuminate the cultural identity of Kainantu peoples and the means by which identity is produced. Margaret Mead once remarked that the small local groups of New Guinea represent a characteristically open society. I take this to mean that there are few characters that would indelibly qualify or disqualify individuals for admission to a particular group. In any case, that view appears to hold for Kainantu local groups, presuming that the prospective recruits are persons from the known region and hence initially share a great deal with the group they join. Among the beliefs, values, and sentiments shared by a local community are not only such profound, regionwide convictions as the prevalence of magical influences, but also beliefs about the distinctiveness of local peoples and how the differences originate.

The Taro on the Rock

With respect to local identity and its recognition I can recall no more telling incident than the one I have come to call "the taro on the rock." One afternoon in 1964 I found myself high on a steep grassy ridge in the territory of another group, immediate neighbors of the people among whom I was living but strongly hostile to them. Atop this ridge, stark against the sky when seen from my village across the valley, were three huge limestone boulders, each approximately the size of a large two-story house. Being so prominent, as well as having the special significance of stone outcrops, these three boulders were landmarks and quite likely were named. We had already been joined on our climb by several men from the nearby village, concerned to know our purpose in their territory. In the course of conversation with them, we learned several curious things about the ridge and the boulders. As we turned the corner of one of the boulders, a local man pointed out a path up its far side.

By clinging to small bushes growing from the rock and using seams in the rock for toeholds one could ascend to the top. And thus was discovered a taro garden on the more or less flat top of the boulder, planted there by a man from the village. The path was evidently his.

Perhaps it would be inaccurate to call this the last place on earth one would seek to plant taro when there is no shortage of suitable ground in the valley below, much closer to the village. Within the surrounding region taro is planted in various odd little pockets such as former latrine pits, sunken graves, and soggy spots sometimes deliberately created for the purpose. Taro is locally known to love damp soil and is usually planted in low ground and damp places. So I naturally asked why taro was planted up here, high on a windswept ridge. As I suggested possible reasons, the local men told me that it was not the droppings of high-roosting birds, nor the limestone itself, nor a deposit of rich soil that was somehow trapped on top of the rock. Indeed, the top of the rock had no natural soil of its own and the owner of the garden consequently had to carry the soil by hand, in small packets of banana leaves, following the vertical path up the side of the boulder, to plant his taro on top. Moreover, he had to keep adding soil from time to time because the rain kept washing it away.

Then why did he do it? Here I was stumped. The father of the garden was not himself among us and, typical in my experience, his fellow villagers professed an inability to answer. My question, they pointed out, should be asked of the man whose work it was. I think they may have known, or at least they could have offered a good guess, but all the same their reluctance to do so did not come wholly as a surprise. Nor did I press them beyond indicating how remarkable the fact seemed. I was content to comply with what appeared to be the etiquette of the country and felt sure I could learn about the improbable taro garden once back in my village. So unlikely a practice would surely be noted by the people next door, even though enemies, and its reason would be known.

I was wrong. I could find no one in my village who admitted ever having heard about the taro, nor would anyone venture to suggest why taro would be planted in such a place. I was not only wrong, however, in thinking they would know. Even more surprising, I was wrong in supposing they would be interested. No one seemed particularly impressed at learning of the practice nor did anyone find it remarkable not to have heard of it before. Furthermore, no one was in the least inclined to speculate about the possible reasons for the taro on top of the rock. Unable to understand this indifference, I endeavored to justify my own curiosity—the obvious difficulty of carrying up the dirt, the availability of ample taro ground much closer to the village, and so forth.

Failing to engage anyone else's curiosity, I eventually tried their

patience. If I had to have an explanation for what I had learned, someone finally suggested by way of changing the subject, I could ask X,
whom everyone knew, the next time he visited our village. Though
from the enemy group whose country lay at the foot of the mountain, X
regularly came to see his friends in our village. He was the only man
from that entire community whom they trusted, they often said, and
thus the only one who could safely enter their territory. More to the
point, X and his fellow villagers were part of the same enemy phratry as
the owner of the problematical taro.

Meanwhile I was reminded, with some hint of resignation, that for as
long as I had known them, the villagers had patiently answered my
numerous questions concerning the different local peoples and practices
of the surrounding country. After all, as everyone well knew, their enemies across the valley also kept the bodies of their dead in caves. "Isn't
that the very reason you went over there today: because that is something we do not do here and you wanted to see it? Why do they do it?
Because their ancestors taught them to do it—and of course because
they have caves. Our ancestors did not teach us to do that, nor do we
have caves. If they had taught us to do it, we would surely do it." This
remonstration closed with a remark I found memorable, though I doubt
the speaker was trying to be terse or dramatic. "Those are other people," he said. "Other people do other things."

When X later visited the village, incidentally, I asked him about the
taro. He echoed the point about other people. Even though admittedly
of the same phratry as his own village, these particular people were
known to have practices his village did not have—cave burial, for
instance. While denying any knowledge of the taro, he suggested it
probably wasn't the only thing different about them. The core members
of that group were originally refugees from elsewhere. They had doubtless brought some of their old ways with them. "Elsewhere" in this case
was the territory of the original phratry from which this group had been
forced to flee, about ten miles or so distant from where we were standing, but nevertheless peoples of the same speech as X and those of the
village where I lived.

Coupled with other experience of the area, this incident suggests a
number of leads. First, although areas of ignorance are readily professed, even in the case of immediate neighbors, there is a sufficient general knowledge of ethnic differentiation to permit nearby peoples, even
ones of the same language, to believe they differ from one another. Second, so firmly rooted is the assumption of differences that the report of
previously unknown differences may be superfluous, hence of little
interest. Such differences are already in principle anticipated, and even
additional information has no certainty of exhausting what still remains

unknown. Third, different practices are directly ascribed to the efforts and inculcation of forebears. Fourth, even at short distances from a given community and even among a few hundred people comprising the same small phratry and sharing a single language, the presence of exotic or unfamiliar practices is perfectly conceivable if not anticipated. Fifth, there is no inevitable sense of impropriety, perverseness, or opprobrium in unfamiliar practices. On the contrary, informants some-times suggest they might themselves practice such behavior but for the fact that their forebears did not teach it to them, or that they lack the opportunity. In short, the people of any one locality naturally differ from the people of any other locality.

At least one more point must be made here, though this anecdote alone is insufficient to support it. Many ethnic differences are covert and conventionally unknown, and there may be a positive reluctance to admit knowing of them. The ridgetop taro gardener's fellow villagers denied knowing his motives. They referred the question to the gardener himself although, in his absence, this obviously meant leaving the ques-tion hanging. To be sure, not only was I living in the village of their ene-mies, I was a stranger with no right to their knowledge. But I have been obliquely answered on other, less sensitive issues. This particular defer-ence concerned the behavior of an individual, not a community. Informants told me on other occasions that not just collectivities else-where have practices known only to themselves and unmentioned by others, but that individuals too have private practices. This sense of pri-vacy is ultimately sanctioned by magical belief, containing for the insider a sense of power and propriety, and for the outsider a sense of danger. The point is not to claim yet one more revelation about the magic pervading the indigenous cultures of Papua New Guinea or those of Kainantu. It is rather to suggest that understanding the meaning of identity—both the indigenous meaning and the meaning of indigenous —also requires recognizing the pervasiveness of magic. This theme will become clearer in considering indigenous ideas about the process of eth-nic (and individual) differentiation.

The Forest and the Grassland

In Kainantu as doubtless elsewhere in New Guinea a distinction is made between forest or bush peoples and grassland or kunai peoples. It is one of those categorical contrasts defining no single people uniquely but serving rather to differentiate opposite sets. The distinction is fairly overt and was frequently made in reference both to other peoples and to the speaker's own people. Essentially the same distinction has been widely noted by regional ethnographers. Both in being dyadic and in turning on an opposition of landscape and niche, bush/grassland is reminiscent of the more familiar Melanesian dichotomy of bush/beach. In both cases, moreover, the bush side of the line is projected as coinciding with a lesser degree of sophistication and politico-cultural dominance. Again, exemplifying Tylor's observation of a century ago ([1871] 1920, I:113), a greater mastery of magic is associated with the less dominant and less sophisticated bush.

In Kainantu, kunai connotes greater bellicosity, initiative, and aggressiveness, more pigs, more brokerage and political manipulation, as well as more proficient gardening, along with fewer or a less frequent use of wild forest foods. Bush peoples, on the other hand, are proud of understanding the forest, having greater control over and consequently being at much less risk from its powerful substances, wild creatures, and supernatural denizens. Bush people naturally have more opportunity to hunt and appear to do so more often. (If close enough to forest neighbors, grassland folk may sometimes be given hunting rights in their neighbors' territory.) Pride in salubrious local waters seems to be quite general but is if anything more pronounced in the case of "water from the bush." Certain secondary crops, such as introduced white potatoes and the once more important kudzu *(Pueraria lobata)*, are said —at least by grassland folk—to grow better in the bush. Bush people take pride in their abundance of timber for fencing and houses and in the ease of finding firewood. Unless themselves totally bereft of trees, moreover, even grassland peoples look down upon neighbors who, unable to claim a piece of forest, are compelled to build dwellings entirely with bamboo and thatch and to seek poor substitutes for good firewood and fencing. The list of contrasts could doubtless be lengthened by itemizing obvious resource differences as well as matters of character, culture, and temperament.

In transcending the mere possession and use of different resources, the bush/grassland contrast seems consistent with other ideas about cultural identity in this area. A local folktale will illustrate. A man from the kunai went to visit his kinsman in a bush village. Arriving at the village, however, the visitor found that his kinsman had gone to inspect his garden in the bush. Along the path to the kinsman's garden the visitor was startled by an unfamiliar creature crossing in front of him. When he pursued it, it tried to escape down a hole, but the man managed to seize hold of its tail before it disappeared completely. Trying to pull the creature out, the visitor found it much too strong but the sounds of the struggle reached his kinsman in the garden nearby, and the latter came running to see what had happened. His straining kinsman urged him to help pull the creature out of the hole so that they could have meat. Dismayed at seeing what had happened, the local man shouted to him to let go. Doing as he was told, the puzzled visitor looked to his kinsman for an explanation. "Oh my poor kinsman," lamented the local man, "you are in great danger of your life. You are not from here and you do not know our country. It is perilous for you to meddle with our creatures. You should not have laid a hand on that python for now you may die from it. I could do it if I wanted to, since I am from here and know the things of this land. But you do not know them, and now you must return at once to your own village. Perhaps you will thereby be able to overcome the sickness that threatens you. If you stay here, you will not get well." Returning home to the grassland without delay, the unfortunate man found it was too late for him. He sickened and died.

Unlike their unfortunate forebear, grassland folk seemed fully cognizant of pythons and other forest perils by the time I heard this story. The dichotomy it projects seems real enough. I once watched a group of children from a bush village terrify H, a full-grown kunai friend of mine, by chasing him with a dead python they had been swinging like a jump rope. His obvious horror and protest at their play disclosed his kunai vulnerability to these mischievous children of the bush, and the temptation to tease him with the snake was more than they could resist. The python was destined to be eaten, but H refused any part of it, insisting that neither he nor anyone else from his village would eat such a thing, as it would certainly cause them great harm. At the same time H was aware that pythons are food in the bush and did not expect eating this one to be fatal to our hosts, since they were accustomed to touching and eating pythons.

The Legacy of Land and Forebears

While not inborn, the indigenous competence of bush people in dealing with things of the bush is nonetheless profoundly stamped in them. It is not simply a matter of technical knowledge—such as how to handle or cook a python—but is rather an essential part of his being that the bush person can freely do such things while someone from the grassland can do so only at his peril. Familiarity with the magical powers of the bush and knowledge and certainty in dealing with them, including an immunity to the inherent danger, have simply not been imparted to the latter. The indigenous inheritance is partly a question of parentage but is not fundamentally genetic. It is partly a question of tutelage but is not limited to verbal instruction. The ancestors' legacy is transmitted through growing up in a particular community where, thanks to the peculiar powers of its members, a unique competence is instilled in the young, infusing them and forming them after the community's own local character. Indigenous identity is partly a question of belonging to the country itself, imbibing the local waters and ingesting the foods that spring from the local soil.

These substances are themselves efficacious and naturalizing, which is to say they are magical. And their efficacy or magic is unique, different from the efficacy of the water, food, and soils of other places—not in being able to slake thirst or satisfy hunger but in making indigenous those who constantly partake of them and whose very growth is made by means of them. Local waters, tasting different, therefore *are* different, made so presumably by the land in which they rise or flow. Home waters are the very best for neutralizing alien magic. That does not mean that alien waters or foods are always dangerous to outsiders, though some waters may be dangerous, and some foods—pythons, for instance—clearly are inappropriate for those unaccustomed to them. But local waters and foods will not do for the transient consumer what they do for the person who consistently uses them.

If the people come to have the land in them, the land likewise comes to have the people in it. This means for the newborn that the collective heritage of their predecessors is present in the land into which they have been born—their gardens, their animals, their food and their water, their knowledge, skill, immunities, competence, power. These forebears lived from the same land, grew up with its strength, defended it, were often named for it (and it for them), imprinted their story upon it, tilled it, dwelt upon it, hunted it, are buried in it or on it, were familiar with its nonhuman denizens, including those we call supernatural. The local person knows the abode of at least the more singular local demons and in approaching any known abode addresses its resident, reminding it that he too belongs to the place, is no trespasser, and deserves to enter or pass unmolested within the demon's range. The sense of a proprietary landscape is shared by both human and demon.

In a previous analysis (Watson 1983) I concluded that environment is by far a larger factor in local identification than any direct, somatic inheritance or genetic substance received from parents. Magic is the principal or most potent nexus between environment and the person. If we limit the discussion to the shared, collective identity of persons, we may specify the magical ways in which environment is decisive. Some prenatal effects differentiate individuals of the same group, as when an expectant parent carefully observes the principal precautions or, through imprudence or inadvertence, bring unfavorable influences to bear upon the unborn. These possibilities too are environmental rather than congenital in character, and thus they strengthen the basic proposition. But unless they occur quite generally in the community, they are not of direct interest for understanding cultural identity. The collective influence upon any and every unborn child of a given group is in the community's effort to provide a safe haven for its expectant parents and for itself, its wisdom in assuring that safety, and its guardian role in maintaining intact the collective-ancestral-terrigenous mold.

The newborn infant does not seem to be thought of as a predetermined being awaiting inevitable fulfillment, carrying within itself a programmed nature destined to unfold step by step, thus progressively being completed and revealed. In short, the newborn may be much closer to the tabula rasa of classical theory than to the preencoded creatures of modern genetics. The fairly frequent references in Melanesia to "growing" a child and to the "hard work" entailed in this activity would seem to bear out this idea, as does the large amount of ritual that is essential to the purpose. It may be significant, incidentally, that ears and hearing are closely connected with understanding, reason, choice, and decision—broadly speaking, with thinking. This seems consistent with the idea of a recipient being, one malleable and unformed but ready for formation, as distinct from a being whose innate potential for development entails (or precludes) a substantial gift, talent, or propensity that the external environment can promote or hinder only to a limited extent.

One could counter my characterization of Kainantu and Western notions of identity formation by pointing to other peoples who, perhaps no more or less than Kainantu, recognize the unformed character of young children and the importance of training yet are able to accept that significant aspects of their maturation or destiny are immanent. To sharpen the contrast, Kainantu peoples do not deny the palpable physical evidence of maturation. But they believe that individual development entails the acquisition of important, intangible qualities, which must be nurtured through individual and collective effort. In the Kainantu conception, the individual's physical growth, strength, industry, and prowess clearly also benefit from such effort. Without belaboring the latent or explicit racism of many Western peoples, I point to their prevalent Mendelian ideas. By comparison, the notion of an immutable personal and physical inheritance does not figure prominently in the Kainantu view of human development. One of the best arguments for this environmentally based theory of cultural identification or ethnicity is found in local concept and practice with respect to the developmental cycle.

A Lamarckian Identity

There is little in Kainantu ethnic theory to suggest a Mendelian model of inheritance, that is, a process whereby somatically fixed traits are transmitted in genetic succession from past to present generations and are impervious to the short-term change of surroundings. Physical attributes such as blood, bone, heart, brain, and physique, even when seen to differentiate individuals, do not loom large among the ethnic distinctions that are conventionally of greatest interest. Ethnically distinctive characters are not for the most part, if at all, transmitted in a direct physical sense from progenitors to progeny. In the intergenerational continuity or discontinuity of ethnic character in Kainantu, ethnicity appears as a communal and environmental imprint. Identity is thus a matter of social and cultural succession in a particular locality.

How does the physical role of paternity and maternity enter into the differentiation of members of one community from those of another? Kainantu informants readily distinguish the male and female contributions to progeny, but the essential question is not sexual identity or its source in one parent or the other. Rather the question is whether individuals of either sex or both impart, directly and somatically, an inheritance of cultural, ethnic, temperamental, or other local and collectively distinctive qualities. Semen is essential and, to be sure, is essentially male in Kainantu; but how does the semen of males from one group differ from that of males in another? And does it differentiate the male children of one group from those of another? The notion of a seminal difference from male to male would be worth remarking, in any case, but the immediate issue concerns its significance in communal terms. Do the males of different groups—bush groups as opposed to grassland groups, let us say—have different seed by means of which their children inherit distinctive bush or grassland proclivities? And should this be the case, what originally differentiated this seed and how indelible is its stamp if, say, posterity abandon the bush or the grassland?

Indelible though the stamp of the bush may be in those it marks, I find in local ideas of intergroup difference no indication that bush characters are transmitted from progenitors to progeny along a procreational pathway. Most of what is believed to make peoples distinctive, I conclude, results from what the community itself, in the widest sense, does to or for its children, in forming them and especially in promoting their growth and maturation. What makes the members of one group alike in this respect, and what therefore makes them different from the members of other groups, is not only acquired in large measure postnatally and as a part of maturation but is in essence a collective stamp, a communal donation. I have therefore used the name of the great eighteenth-century French biologist to suggest the profoundly environmental sense of Kainantu ethnic inheritance (Watson 1983). The idea of a fixed and collectively distinct somatic endowment seems less elaborated or more ambiguous in the Kainantu context.

The bush/kunai distinction is an appropriate test and illustration of the relevance of the Lamarckian model to Kainantu ideas of cultural identity. As a dichotomy bush and kunai are not alone enough to characterize peoples individually, except to others of the opposite kind. Each category, that is, represents numerous politically independent localities. Yet the principles of identification underlying the bush/grassland contrast, while generally more salient, are essentially the same as the principles tacitly assumed to govern the more particular identification of local polities. Bush/kunai stereotyping is typically done in broad strokes, however, involving some of the most overt and explicit criteria of identity. Local polities are differentiated with less overt and less universally acknowledged diacritics. Granting the Lamarckian character of the bush/grassland distinction, how well does the model fit the distinctions Kainantu people make between one local polity and another?

In Kainantu terms the vulnerability or immunity of individuals to the powers of the forest is an ethnic attribute that distinguishes whole social groups, both in their own eyes and in those of outsiders. These diacritics are not genetically inherited or imparted, but reflect familiarity, custom, habituation, and an acquired accommodation to the creatures, things, spirits, and terrigenous powers of a particular locale, aided by the instruction and the ritual and magical proclivities of parents and other elders of a community. Immunization through exposure is a central part of the identification process, including the idea of innoculation, a notion pervading Kainantu magical practice. The same principles surface in discussions of the difference between one local group and the next.

In this light the views of Kainantu peoples virtually preclude a racist or biologistic approach to ethnic differentiation. It is true that, even given a Mendelian premise, one is by no means compelled to take a racist view of cultural or ethnic differences. But with an initial and dominant premise of biological history, the Mendelian must go on to recognize the separate boundaries of ethnic or cultural history. He is otherwise likely to formulate arguably racist conclusions. From a Kainantu standpoint, in contrast, the initial or dominant premise posits a kind of cultural history. It would be difficult thus for Kainantu ethnic differences to be conflated with somatic differences in a biologistic approach to the differentiation of socially separate peoples. Traditional Kainantu ethnicity, in other words, is quite unlikely to take root in race. What the future portends for Kainantu ideology in the national setting is another question.

In its evolutionary premise, as earlier noted, the Lamarckian model does not nicely fit Kainantu ethnicity. Kainantu ideas of ethnic differentiation and inheritance, as far as I can see, are not even tacitly evolutionary. However, identities are not believed to be everlasting. Indeed, the premise seems rather than ethnic differences only endure as long as the conjunction of a people and a land. In the case of bush/grassland distinctiveness, this continuity might well be thought as timeless as the forest and the grassland. With individual communities, however, some qualification is evident. In political and military terms, at least, Kainantu communities have recognized histories. Their rise and fall are well known to local chroniclers, as are their episodes of fusion and fission. It is understandable, I think, that these checkered communal careers are nevertheless not viewed as part of some global process akin to progress or evolution.

Local cultural identities can change. Such a perception is hardly surprising in light of so much historical movement (*turbulence* would not be an excessive term), including the recurrent relocation of people in small or large numbers and their consequently shifting allegiances. With the influx of a sizable bloc of refugees, especially if they speak a different language, a community may for a time be recognized as an ethnic composite (thus the "hapkas" communities noted earlier). It will be so viewed by its neighbors, moreover, who will tend to attribute not only language but other local singularities to this circumstance. In one example, the differential suicides of one sex were said to be unprecedented in the older, preimmigrant community. A suicide, whether or not involving the immigrants or their children, may thus be ascribed to the influence of the refugee element.

On such grounds members of a community in which I was living insisted that their enemies nearby, who were actually of the same speech, differed in practice and in knowledge. These particular enemies were closely allied to a third group—likewise enemies of the first—that did in fact speak a foreign language. Being fairly constant allies as well as neighbors, both enemy groups had a number of obvious bilinguals, though none whose first language could not be determined. Implying a kind of contamination through association, it could be said (despite practical experience) that neither enemy group spoke the same language as their common enemy, among whom I was living. The same principle that explains how individuals acquire their ethnic characteristics—from those with whom they share their lives—thus appears to describe how a community's ethnic identity is formed, how it can change, and how it is distanced from the identity of outsiders. Here again the revisionist Lamarckian model seems to fit.

People Who Have the Same Story

Despite demographic movements and the rise and fall of communities, local rhetoric asserts the cohesiveness of the home community. Continu-

ity and fidelity to a common present are derived from a common past
that flows uninterrupted from the mythical beginning of time. Side by
side with this mythic charter is a substantial body of oral history detailing multiple and complex movements of people, departures and arrivals
in a landscape of recurrent consanguineal rupture and alien merger. In
light of these local histories, how do Kainantu conceptualize the continuity mythically implied in pedigrees, identities, loyalties, ethnicity?

In ethnic terms individuals assume the identity of the communities in
and through which they are formed. The distinctive foods and waters,
magical power, and the whole community's ritual efforts affect their
being, moving them toward manhood or womanhood. These and the
works of founders and forebears in gardening, swine keeping, marriage,
and warfare have created and maintained the bond between land and
people. The observer can only conclude that all of these preconditions
and past actions signify more than lineage in any genealogical or procreational sense. Are we then saying that an environmentally and
socially acquired cultural identity counts for more than descent? Or is
this merely the form of descent that Kainantu peoples recognize?

In one light Kainantu ethnicity is the conjunction of individual and
societal histories. Concluding a long conversation about groups and
communal identities, one man observed that in each local instance we
were speaking of "people who have the same story." *Story* in his and
doubtless other Kainantu languages is a word also referring to accounts
of legendary or mythical antecedents. Those antecedents may themselves, indeed, be spoken of as story folk, beings, or personages. Not sur-
prisingly, accounts of story people typically describe how various customs, landmarks, names, beliefs, groups, or fraternal kindreds first
came to be. "People with the same story" is thus a notion clearly applicable to the unbroken communal inheritance conventionally ascribed,
despite a checkered history, to each local society.

More than that, however, the same story can actively contain in a single unbroken continuum the episodes of fusion and alien confluence
that make up many Kainantu histories. Not only sharing but themselves
contributing to the same story with the older elements of a community,
the children of immigrants will in time come to be distinguished by that
common story as fully as the children of older residents. No Kainantu
chronicler can relate the story of every people known to him. But he has
no doubt that each land and people has its particular story, one that
matches his own in its basic lineaments if not its unique details.
Whether or not stronger in some absolute sense, the proprietary landscape, linked by story to its human inhabitants, affords effective local
identities under conditions in which genealogical descent might well be
unavailing.

NOTES

The initial period of fieldwork in 1953–1954 was supported by the Ford Foundation. The 1963–1964 research, as part of the Micro-evolution Project, was supported by the National Science Foundation.

1. The research team for the Micro-evolution Project included four other ethnographers, each concerned with a different but adjacent language group, as well as linguists, a geographer, a physical anthropologist, and archaeologists. The monographs so far published on the basis of this work have appeared in a series, Anthropological Studies in the Eastern Highlands of New Guinea (Littlewood 1972; McKaughan 1973; Robbins 1982; Watson 1983; Watson and Cole 1977). The Tairora monograph (Watson 1983) is immediately relevant to this chapter.

2. A verbatim translation of all of the responses of the interviewees has been published by the Human Relations Area Files (Watson and Watson 1972).

3

Seagulls Don't Fly into the Bush: Cultural Identity and the Negotiation of Development on Mandok Island, Papua New Guinea

ALICE POMPONIO

Seagulls don't fly into the bush.
When their wings are tired, they
float on driftwood.
—Mandok proverb

In this chapter I explore what might be considered a Lamarckian case with a Mendelian twist. The Siassi Islands of Papua New Guinea have long been noted in the anthropological literature as the hub of the Vitiaz trade system (Harding 1967). Though their identity as "middlemen traders" has been recognized and studied from an economic point of view (Allace 1976; Brookfield and Hart 1971; Freedman 1967; Harding 1967), the influence of this system on individual and community identity had not been pursued until it emerged as an important issue for Mandok Islanders deciding whether or not to send children on to secondary education (Pomponio 1983; Pomponio and Lancy 1986). To refer to the Mandok solely as middlemen, however, misses an important component of their cultural identity.[1] What is important to them, as I shall demonstrate, is that they are *maritime* middlemen. Their conception of who they are, and why, utilizes notions of descent and blood familiar to Westerners, but only as a description of parameters for an individual's being. The proof of one's identity lies in the absorption of "substance" and daily behavior appropriate to a particular place—in this case, the sea.

Mandok is a ten-acre raised coral islet lying just south of the high island of Umboi in the Siassi Islands,[2] which separate New Britain from the mainland (Map 1). The resident population of Mandok in 1980 was 537—270 males, 267 females. The Mandok are a composite of immi-

43

grants from other parts of Siassi, West New Britain, and the Tami Island area, which includes Malasiga on the New Guinea mainland. Most Mandok who claim to be descendants of the original settlers of the island trace their ancestry back first to Aromot (about eight miles to the northeast) and ultimately to Kilenge, in the Cape Gloucester area of West New Britain. According to the genealogical data available to me, the original migrants to Mandok came from Aromot Island well before 1700 and were an established community before the eruption of Long Island (cf. Blong 1982). Most Mandok and Aromot Islanders consider themselves to derive from the same stock. Over the years many customs, linguistic expressions, and family lines were imported through trade from throughout the Vitiaz and Dampier straits. Through time, however, the Mandok and residents of other small islands have transformed themselves from sedentary horticulturalists from Kilenge, Tolokiwa, or Umboi Island to mobile maritime middlemen who connect these diverse areas through trade.

Although the documentation is scant, most genealogies reveal at least one male forebear who migrated to Mandok following a feud in his home place. These events parallel very closely different episodes in the Siassi creation myth, the Legend of Namor (see Pomponio 1983, 72–121). Speculation about the relationship between empirical events and these mythical episodes is beyond the scope of this discussion. It is important to note, however, that the Mandok behave as if they have always lived on Mandok, even though the migration to the Siassi area is relatively recent. Though consistently acknowledging their varied origins in different points along the trade circuit, Mandok are quick to point out the differences between themselves today and the stock from which they came, with a slightly superior air. These points will be developed further below.

To illustrate the conjuncture of values, goals, and motivations implied by the Mandok identity as mobile, maritime middlemen, I examine an apparent paradox. Mandok Island was originally chosen for a study of the cultural basis of achievement motivation because in 1978 Mandok children had scored among the highest in a battery of cognitive tests and because since the late 1960s, Mandok graduates of the educational system had distinguished themselves by high achievement and rapid upward social mobility. When I arrived on Mandok in 1979, however, I confronted the following facts:

1. No Mandok children had been sent to high school from 1976 to 1979, and of the nine chosen to attend high school in 1980, only four were actually sent. In a survey of sixty-two provincial schools conducted by the provincial superintendent of education, Mandok's

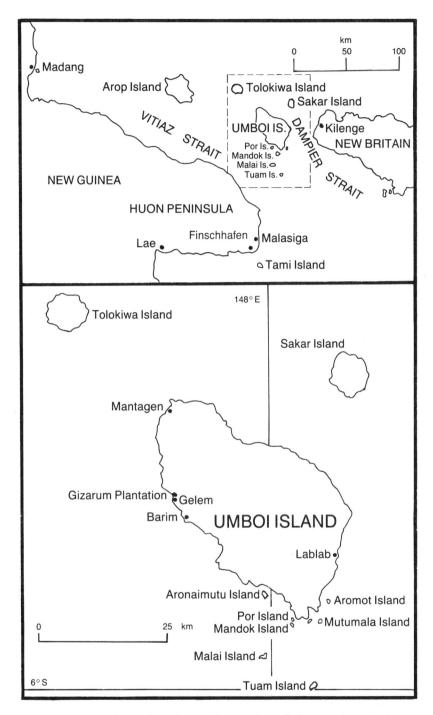

Map 1. *Top,* **Siassi District, Papua New Guinea;** *bottom,* **enlarged view of Umboi Island and nearby islands. Drawn by Diana Breneiser-Renfro.**

sixth grade class of 1979 was rated poor, on the basis of national exam scores (Isoaimo 1980).

2.   Although the Mandok are historically renowned middlemen and traders, and are regarded by their neighbors as entrepreneurs, their experiences with cash cropping and a market economy repeatedly proved disastrous.

3.   When the Catholic mission decided to sell their boat to the village communal business society to encourage local enterprise in Mandok, the result was a disabled boat, a defaulted loan, a bankrupt business society, and a divided village.

The explanation for these events and their outcomes lies in Mandok notions of investment and achievement and in their cultural identity as maritime middlemen and traders, in conjunction with political and economic developments in Papua New Guinea since the 1930s. Of the latter, particularly relevant are post-1960 policies aimed at promoting economic development throughout the country in preparation for national independence (achieved in 1975).

Development in Siassi has always been synonymous with cash cropping. From the administration's point of view, cash cropping for the small islanders had always implied resettlement to Umboi Island. I have argued elsewhere (Pomponio 1983; Pomponio and Lancy 1986) that for many Papua New Guineans, educating their children may constitute their major role in national development. Given Mandok's lack of land and their historical role as maritime middlemen and traders, the islanders participate in Western education as a "development project." The benefits of this particular project were consistent with traditional patterns of leadership and achievement, which stress physical mobility out and back from a central location, mental shrewdness, knowledge concerning investment/return ratios, multilingualism, creative abilities (e.g., carving for men, incising trochus-shell armlets for women), manipulation of social relationships, travel, and profitable trade. In this chapter I suggest that Mandok behavior vis-à-vis the school and other development projects does not represent a paradox, but rather indicates that Mandok people are making rational choices based on their cultural values.

My approach is based on Foster's reformulations of Barth's (1969) theory that ethnic identity is the result of a community's shared categories, which form the basis of their interactions with each other and with outsiders to the community. In Foster's work on Mon traders in Thailand (1974, 1977), he departs from the widely held view of trade as a peace-maintaining mechanism (see Harding 1970 for a discussion of this in Siassi) and maintains instead that trade generates tension between the trader and his customers. He further contends that the Mon are successful traders largely because they consistently maintain a certain cultural distance from the people with whom they trade. He asserts, moreover, that it is good business to do so.

The Mandok differ from the Mon in several important respects. First, Mandok trade operates primarily as a subsistence barter system and is not rooted in commerce. Second, the Mandok notion of trade as an occupation is specifically bracketed within a maritime subsistence economy. A three-sided aspect to Mandok cultural identity therefore emerges: they are "sea people" as opposed to "bush people"; they are episodically mobile, not solely sedentary; and they are primarily subsistence middlemen who distribute other peoples' produce, not horticultural producers. Nevertheless, Foster's general point, that traders consciously cultivate and maintain a separate ethnic identity and that it is good business to do so, is quite applicable and appropriate to the Mandok case.

The maintenance of diverse ethnic identities under conditions of intensive interaction has long been recognized as characteristic of Melanesian societies (Mead 1967). This feature has not, however, been pursued in detail with respect to the relationship between subsistence economy—specifically recognizing trade as a subsistence economy—and cultural identity. The Mandok data suggest a direct relationship between the primary mode of subsistence in a given society and the cultural identity that patterns its members' goals and motivations for achievement (cf. LeVine 1966). Thus, rather than describing fishermen who trade, my approach views the Mandok as maritime middlemen who fish.

In this chapter I will outline the important categories that define Mandok cultural identity and their definitions of economic achievement. I will then review Mandok development history in three separate but interrelated contexts—the school, cash cropping, and *bisnis* 'business'—to demonstrate that from the beginning the Mandok interpreted their interactions with government, mission, and school officials from the perspective of trading relationships, and that at every critical juncture the Mandok have made conscious decisions reflecting a view of themselves as mobile, maritime middlemen. Contingencies of an impinging cash economy notwithstanding, they intend to retain this view.

Mandok assumptions about who they are and the way in which their identity patterns their relationships with others provide the cultural backdrop for understanding their attitudes and behavior toward schooling, cash cropping, and the purchase of the mission boat. Given Man-

dok cultural identity, sending children to school in town centers became
in 1963 a major adaptive strategy in a rapidly changing economic environment, born out of a perceived trade relationship between village,
mission, and government. The initial benefits that accrued from sending children to secondary schools subsidized the declining overseas trading system and, for a short time, allowed the Mandok to repel repeated
attempts to relocate them to Umboi Island to become sedentary horticulturalists and cash croppers. Education became not only a subsidy to
the declining overseas trading system and a boon to the local status
mobility system, but perhaps more important, it also offered an alternative to relocation. With the approach of national independence, however, administrative policy changes combined to make education a losing investment from the Mandok point of view. Finally, I argue that the
purchase of the mission boat was in keeping with Mandok perceptions
of who they are and why—an attempt at participating in government-
or mission-sponsored development programs in a manner they perceived to be appropriate to their identity.

Cultural and Geographic Variability in Siassi

Mandok is situated in the Siassi District of Morobe Province. Siassi District has always been treated politically as if it contained a homogeneous population. However, there are significant differences among island
populations. Within the boundaries of Siassi, local people draw clear
distinctions among themselves based on geography, language, economy,
and place of origin. Harding (1967) and Freedman (1967) have noted
that the small islanders of Siassi are a relatively homogeneous population in terms of language, economy, rituals, and cultural identity, especially in contrast to the different populations on Umboi Island. Linguistic and economic differences contribute to local perceptions that the
two constitute different worlds. The small islanders refer to the Umboi
peoples in general as "the Umboi," or "those Umboi people"; in turn,
Umboi peoples refer to small islanders in general as "the islanders."
    Finer distinctions based on language are also made. Siassi District
contains four major language groups. One can divide Umboi diagonally
from northeast to southwest, separating two of these groups. Speakers
of the third language group live in Barim, Mantagen, Aronaimutu
(bilingual), Tolokiwa, and Arop islands. The last language is that of the
Siassi Islanders proper, who speak two different but mutually intelligi-
ble dialects of Mutu, an Austronesian language.[3]
    The subsistence economies of the different populations correspond to
geographical and linguistic groupings. Umboi and its satellite islands

to the west, Tolokiwa and Arop, depend primarily on swidden horticulture and arboriculture. These are inland bush people for the most part, depending on the land for their subsistence. Gardeners on northwest Umboi depend on taro as their staple crop, whereas those on southeast Umboi are sweet potato and yam growers. In contrast, small islanders historically were fishermen and traders. When Harding (1967) described Siassi as the central hub of the Vitiaz trade system, he referred mostly to Aromot, Mandok, Malai, and Tuam. Voyaging in huge two-masted sailing canoes (produced only on Aromot and Mandok), Siassi traders connected mainland New Guinea with West New Britain through the distribution of material culture, rituals, magical spells, and raw materials. The only indigenous crafts in this area were canoe building, fishnet weaving, carving, weaving of pandanus sleeping mats, and the production of incised trochus-shell armlets.

The Mandok also trade with Umboi Island communities for vegetable staples and raw materials. In this barter system, the cultural value of comparable toil balances out to the satisfaction of the traders. The Umboi people do not really manufacture anything—the mountain people of the northwest dig red ochre out of the soil; the lowlanders of the southeast obtain the raw materials traded with the small islanders from the bush. Their labor goes into their gardens. On the other hand, by Western standards the Mandok (and other small islanders) do not work hard. They spend comparatively more time on their crafts than they do on fishing. If the fishing is good, one day's catch will convert into one to two weeks' worth of vegetables. The nutritional balance of trade is obvious—the Umboi gardeners rely on the small islanders for protein supplements, and the islanders rely on the Umboi for their vegetable staples and for variety in their fruit and vegetable diet.

Despite this interdependence, an opposition between sea people and bush people pervades relations between Siassi small islanders and the people of Umboi. In describing other communities the Mandok use the expression *diran to* '(group of) people from,' meaning a group that is rooted in and derives its identity and vitality from a place. Thus they describe themselves as being *diran to te* 'people of the sea.' This is in direct contrast to *diran to su* 'people of the bush.' Having traveled to distant shores and returned with a wealth of material goods and stories, the Siassi small islanders, as traders, enjoyed in precontact times a more cosmopolitan status than the Umboi bush peoples.

In precontact times the underlying status rivalry between the small islanders and Umboi bush communities found expression in competitive feasting. A general atmosphere of cooperation and peaceful coexistence prevails today, but not without occasional setbacks (some of which will be discussed below). This asymmetrical relationship is shifting as cash cropping and participation in a market economy increase. The ethnic distinctions inherent in the classification of sea or bush, however, retain their significance as cultural categories in defining populations and in patterning behavior between groups.

Although frequent intermarriage, trade, and generally congenial relations prevail among the islands of Siassi, there remains an underlying current of competition and parochialism. If a Malai woman, A, marries a Mandok man, she is always referred to as "Malai A," or "that Malai woman," particularly in times of disagreement. Each small island population has a vested interest in maintaining its identity vis-à-vis the others. This seems to be a common feature of trading societies (see, for example, Foster 1974). Interisland differentiation and competition consistently surface both in informants' accounts and in patrol reports for the area, and have stood in the way of attempts to unify Siassi into one political body or organization. The competition is especially marked between the small islanders and Umboi bush communities but is tempered by networks of interlacing trade and kin relations and the perception that all depend on one another for survival.

Maritime Trade as a Cultural System

Maritime trade is the major subsistence activity and the major category through which the Mandok pattern their relationships with others. Though the overseas trade system has declined drastically since the early part of this century, especially since the early 1950s, trade as a "cultural system" (Geertz 1966) persists in Mandok outlook and social relationships. Trade was the operant cultural category by means of which the Mandok interpreted and patterned their relationships with the mission, the government, and the school. In this section I shall briefly describe the importance of the sea and the centrality of waterborne trade in Mandok culture.

The sea is a major source of food, the highway to other communities, and the foundation of ceremonial life for the Mandok. Most Mandok subsistence activities focus on the reefs and on the nearby mangroves that skirt the southern tip of Umboi. The general sexual division of sea labor is that men fish off the reefs with large nets in which they catch several varieties of large schooled fish and dugong, while women collect shellfish on the reefs and in the mangroves. Women also go diving for several species of sea clam (*Tridachna* spp.) in the deeper channels off the larger reefs and farm immature sea clams close to Mandok. These provide emergency resources for the lean times. Women also engage in hook-and-line fishing. Teenagers and younger children collect shellfish, go hook-and-line fishing, and more recently engage in underwater spearfishing. Exploitation of the sea is not only a major source of protein but also provides a basis for overseas and local trade. The Mandok traditionally traded for all of their plant staples, and even though they do garden today, they still rely on local trade for the greater part of their vegetable foods.

For the Siassi Islanders, trade implies sailing. Knowledge of the sea, winds, and stars is crucial to overseas sailing in the precarious Vitiaz and Dampier straits. In pre-European times men who were renowned sailors and good navigators were therefore highly regarded. Along with maritime knowledge, such a man would also possess the magical incantations to control the weather, wind, and seas, and in some cases, the sorcery by which to control or destroy his rivals. A traditional leader would combine as many elements as possible to expand his wisdom and enhance his renown. However, merely having the talent or the personality to lead is not enough: one must demonstrate that power continually. Before pacification and missionization, demonstrating prowess entailed aggressive overseas trade, navigation and sailing skills, competitive feasting, sorcery, multilingualism, and social networking to establish and maintain trade alliances. Definitions of manhood stressed creative abilities, mental shrewdness, knowledge concerning economic investment/return ratios, and manipulation of social relationships. Finally, all of these displays and trading exploits must be carried out with the aplomb of a "man of wisdom."

Out of this constant travel and trade emerged a big-man status system oriented not toward the accumulation of land and wealth in a sedentary environment, but toward manipulation and management of others' products through mobility and trade—that is, the control and redistribution of wealth (Sahlins 1963).[4] I call this kind of system "middleman culture." Though recognizably Melanesian (see for example Harding 1967; Freedman 1967), it is distinct from the more familiar patterns of entrepreneurship studied to date in Melanesia in three crucial respects: (1) the relative lack of land or utilization of land resources (horticulture and pig husbandry) as a basis for the local economy; (2) the emphasis on trade as a primary, rather than secondary, feature of the subsistence economy, and as a standard for evaluating entrepreneurial talents and achievements; and (3) a social and distributive system that militates against the accumulation of significant amounts of wealth and favors instead the control and manipulation of goods, food, and people.

Siassi big-men are not "men of anger" (Valentine 1963) or warriors. They are craftsmen, clever investors, and men of knowledge. They succeed not by overpowering their adversaries physically, but by outsmarting them—not by production, but by clever manipulation. Through

generations of trading they have transformed a landless society of mav-
erick immigrants into a patterned system of seagoing salesmen, trading
their own and others' products for profit. This profit is then recycled
into their own system of exchanges, politics, and prestige. By connect-
ing the geographical endpoints of this far-flung trade system to their
own central location they not only control the rates of exchange, but
also maintain to a great extent a monopoly of access to valued goods
(Harding 1967).

Maritime Metaphors for Humanness

If, as Michael Lieber suggests (chapter 4), local theories of knowing lie
beneath ethnic stereotypes and categories, and if these theories are
expressed through notions of Lamarckian inheritance of behavioral
characteristics—"doing other things" (Watson, chapter 2)—then Mandok behavior with respect to the school and other development projects
can be understood in terms of a fundamental epistemology: they do
what they do because they are who they are, and vice versa. There are
several points to make in this context. First, Mandok perceptions of
themselves as sea people (as opposed to Umboi bush people) are analogous to Tairora bush/grassland distinctions in Kainantu (Watson, chapter 2). Moreover, the differences between what "we" do and what
"they" do are not just a matter of differential access to environmental
resources and concomitant differences in technical knowledge, but are
founded on the realization that such knowledge constitutes an essential
part of a person's being.

The second and related point concerns Watson's notion of a collective
heritage of one's predecessors present in the land on which Tairora are
born. There is a similar notion of the collective heritage of Mandok
forebears being present in the sea and in all the technical forms of
knowledge that surround its exploitation, such as constructing fishnets,
carving canoes and bowls, and trading across its boundaries (Pomponio 1983). The Mandok cognate to the "guardian role" of the individual Tairora in "maintaining intact the collective-ancestral-terrigenous
mold" (Watson, chapter 2) might be the "marigenic mold." An interesting facet of Mandok perceptions of their essential identity is that,
despite the fact that they originally migrated from primarily bush locations, through subsequent generations the Mandok seem to have absorbed the autochthonous essence of a maritime habitat. A sedentary
and horticultural status quo pervades Mandok mythical and ritual symbolism, yet the defining feature that separates the founders from
present-day Mandok cultural identity is the breaking away from the

previous pattern and the creation of a new cultural tradition. This is what I meant by my earlier statement that the Mandok "behave as if they have always lived on Mandok."

These events and symbols suggest that notions of Lamarckian inheritance need not be static but can through time be selected and cultivated consciously (cf. Larcom, chapter 8). In this case there is a definite selection of traits and customs related to a seafaring lifestyle, and moving away from life in the bush. The Mandok data also suggest that expressions that may upon first hearing be construed as "Mendelian" (e.g., use of terms such as *blood, line or lineage,* and other expressions that imply inherited biological traits) are in fact situationally or contextually reformulated appropriations of ontogeny.[5]

The product of the combination of land and sea symbolism is illustrated in Mandok notions of personhood. Similar to members of other Melanesian societies, the Mandok often identify themselves by reference to particular environmental features that are most significant to their subsistence economy. For instance, most Melanesian horticulturalists express concepts of the self and humanness in terms of botanical metaphors. Thus, in those areas where yams are the primary staple and highest prestige crop, yams frequently symbolize the physical body and concepts of growth (Fortune [1932] 1963; Tuzin 1972). Where taro is the primary staple crop, human beings are described in terms of taro parts, growth, and reproduction (Panoff 1968; Kahn 1986). Other Melanesian societies use pandanus (Herdt 1981), pigs (Goodale 1985), or cassowaries (Gell 1975) as metaphors for humanity.

One distinctive feature of Mandok exegetical style in describing the form of the human body is the use of both plant and oceanographic metaphors for the self. For example, the firstborn child is referred to as the "head of the tree." When describing where in the body the *anunu* 'self, likeness, reflection, life substance' resides, one informant explained that "the *anunu* resides inside of the container" (i.e., the skin of the body). However, instead of continuing these metaphors to describe the body as a tree (body) with bark (skin) and sap (blood) (cf. Panoff 1968), Mandok describe the human body as like a clamshell with or without meat inside it. One informant explained it to me as follows:

> Just like we say the women go diving for mollusks and I say that Atai Tuku put Manbog Sirig[6] inside the *diwar* 'empty clamshell', it is like this. When there is meat inside, it is a *gol* 'clam', and the clam lives inside of the *gol patu* 'clamshell'. But after you take the meat out, then the clamshell is a *diwar*, an empty shell you see lying about the beach. All right, it is the same with humans—the *anunu* 'life substance' resides inside the skin. Once the *anunu* goes out of the body you die—the *anunu* becomes a ghost, and a man is then a corpse.

Not the least of these types of metaphorical analogies, the sea also provides the Mandok with the foundations for their ceremonial life. Mandok social organization emphasizes patrilineality, primogeniture, and relative age. Inherent in this system is a definite notion of limited good (Foster 1965). That is, children share the "substance" of their parents and other kin, which is conceived of in terms of the combination of blood, food, and work (cf. Lieber, chapter 4). Firstborns, because they constitute the first issue of a marriage, are believed to have more of the important life (marigenic and biogenetic) substance than the other children.

The transubstantial nature of Mandok personhood is evidenced by their belief that firstborns can be "created" through adoption, and adoption is not limited to married couples. In fact many children (thirteen of eighty-one, or 16 percent of my sample) are adopted specifically for this purpose. Beliefs and customs surrounding adoption offer a clear contrast with Western Mendelian concepts of personhood—the important substance here is not contained in blood or semen, but food and work (i.e., caretaking). By feeding and caring for a child, the substance of the adult is transferred to that child. The referent in this case is not shared biogenetic substance but a substance conceived in terms of the fruits of human effort, close association, and enduring solidarity. For the Mandok, most of these sources of substance are found in, on, or near the sea.

Each new major accomplishment of a firstborn child is publicly recognized and celebrated with feasting cycles and food distributions. Most of Mandok ceremonial life celebrates these first accomplishments of the firstborn. An extended discussion of these feasts is not possible here, but some comment regarding their symbolic emphasis on the sea and its products is pertinent. Those ceremonies that illustrate most clearly the value of the sea to the Mandok are those that introduce the child to subsistence activities and those that initiate the child into the ceremonial life of the village.

The child's introduction into socioeconomic activities is formalized in two major celebrations, each of which concerns maritime activity. These are the first canoe paddle, called "net fishing," and the first sea crossing. In a boy's first canoe paddle, the men of the village take him out and show him for the first time how men catch fish or dugong in the great nets. For girls, the analogous ceremony is called "mouth of the clam." The girl is taken on the reef by all the women of the village and shown how to dive for sea clams or to cull the two important types of mangrove clams. When either boys or girls return, the entire village turns out to greet them on the beach and barrage them with dried coconut husks, splash them with seawater, and generally celebrate by drenching everyone in the sea.

The first sea crossing celebrates the child's first voyage across the Vitiaz or Dampier Strait. Traditionally this implied that the child was introduced to his or her father's overseas trade partnerships. These partnerships are expressed in kinship terms and passed down through generations, and are therefore an important feature of the continuation of the overseas trade network. The crossing also symbolizes for the Mandok both their mobility and their ability to overcome obstacles. Thus physical mobility is symbolically linked with social and political mobility. The firstborn child, male or female, "cuts the path" for future siblings and is shown how to overcome the major geographical barriers that separate the Mandok from significant sources of their livelihood. The ceremony itself is performed by the women who live on the opposite side of the village from the child. They dress up in ridiculous attire, dance and clown their way across the village, again to douse the child and his/her entire patrilineal extended family with buckets of seawater. The child's father, in turn, provides a pig and a food distribution for the entire village.

For any of these ceremonies, the child may actually be too young to participate. The important factor for the Mandok, however, is the public acknowledgment of the child's right to engage in those subsistence activities crucial to Mandok survival: fishing and trade. The precise timing of particular feasts may vary according to the resources available to the sponsor, the child's father and/or paternal grandfather. The motivating ideology can be shown, however, to demonstrate a fairly clear-cut pattern that reflects how Mandok notions of the physical, social, and moral development of an individual are related to the sea and maritime activities. They also illustrate that social/political mobility and physical mobility imply each other.

Having validated and marked officially the child's physical and socio-economic development with rituals, the next formal stage in the growth of a child pertains to moral or spiritual development. This stage requires a brief description and explanation of the *nakamutmut*, the masked figures that play a prominent role in the ceremonies and the dancing feasts associated with them. A detailed discussion of the role of the masked figures is beyond the scope of my discussion here. However, their role in symbolizing the Mandok premise that life comes from the sea cannot be ignored. The nakamutmut is a central character in the firstborn child's first dancing feast and provides the symbolic coagulant for various formal aspects of Mandok law, moral order, and knowledge. The masked figure supervises the superincision of boys, and later ritually beats all children in the final stages of this category of initiation. Rather than analyzing the ceremonial details, I shall limit my presentation to the cultural/symbolic significance of the figure's presence.

Nakamutmut are named most often after significant environmental features of their places of origin, such as reefs, mangroves, sand cays, prominent boulders, and other distinctively maritime landmarks. These places represent the apical ancestral roots of the family or the patrilineal lines to which they belong. The figures consist of a mask with various plumes and significant decorations attached to long strands of sago fronds. As the figure dances, the fronds swish and sway in rhythm to the beat of the drums, much as reef grass undulates with the alternating currents of the sea. The nakamutmut may also be named after significant events in Mandok maritime history. For example, one figure is said to commemorate the Great Gitua Shipwreck, in which many Mandok were lost at sea.

A particular feasting cycle begins when a masked figure is "pulled up," as the Mandok say. At dawn on the day on which it is to arrive in the village to start the cycle, it appears on the reef off that part of the village in the direction from which its roots are traced. Later in the day the firstborn child is painted, dressed in all of his/her dancing feast regalia, presented to the figure, and introduced to the dance. The Mandok say that the nakamutmut bring food to the village. Many feasts are given in their presence. When they are pulled up and escorted out, the usual feasting foods of taro (or manioc) pudding, sweet potato, and pork must be supplemented by a clam chowder made of large sea clams or mangrove clams. When the cycle ends years later, the masked figure is escorted out in the same direction from which it came. These events dramatize further that life itself arises from the sea.[7]

Against this backdrop of Mandok cultural identity and prestige categories, I now turn to a discussion of recent political and economic events in Papua New Guinea that have affected Mandok's involvement with national development. This discussion in turn will lead to an understanding of my second assertion, that the Mandok from the very beginning interpreted their relationships with governments, mission, and school from the standpoint of investments in trade.

Education and Development on Mandok

Mandok's waxing and waning support of secondary education reflects reversals of administrative policy from the mission period through the 1970s. In the early years of the mission phase of education, the Mandok sent four youths to Kilenge for basic literacy and catechistic training. Education was suspended during World War II and resumed around 1948, again with the purpose of basic literacy, numeracy, and religious instruction. Those who had been educated in Kilenge or Rabaul for one to three years were employed by the mission to teach basic literacy, arithmetic, and catechism to village children on Mandok.

In 1960 a permanent mission house and school were constructed on Por Island, six hundred meters from Mandok. Students attending this school were later sent to larger mission schools near plantations in Kilenge and Rabaul and to high school in Rabaul. Although they feared sending the children to distant shores to attend high school, parents were required to put almost no money into this venture. Moreover, the children were in town centers and within reach either of family trade relations or relatives employed at the mission-owned plantations. The students saw visible evidence of progress in the towns and via their school experience became a part of the process of national development. Through their children's experiences and successes, Mandok parents also felt that they played an active role in national development.

As the seat of local government and mission headquarters changed, so did the location of the high schools to which Mandok students were sent. Depending on the year of entry into form I (grade 7), Mandok students were sent to high schools in Rabaul, Dreggarhafen (near Finschhafen), Madang, or Lae. All of these locations, again, were town centers along or extending established trade routes (except Lae, which was easily accessible by this time by commercial boat). With the exception of the school in Dreggarhafen, the Catholic mission ran all of the schools. The children, then, while far from home, were never far from a support group. Moreover, this was during the 1960s, when education was identified with national development, so the children were encouraged not only by their parents but also by the personnel and circumstances of the time to aspire to well-paying town jobs and rapid upward mobility.

By this time the overseas trade system had declined markedly, a result of an influx of more desirable European goods and easier access to distant places due to the services of commercial boats. Trade partners who had previously depended on Mandok traders for valued goods could now get them for themselves. Moreover, the introduction of cash meant that the Mandok, along with the rest of the country, needed and sought wage employment from Europeans. For the Mandok, this was achieved primarily through the education and later employment of children. The children, by securing town jobs, subsidized the declining trade system by sending cash and goods back to the village. Mandok traders were thus able to increase their trade networks in two ways. First, by visiting children at schools they visited the towns and established new connections. Second, by entering into the cash economy the children themselves opened up a new trade route of sorts. In this way, Mandok parents strengthened their economic base and staved off the demise of the trade system. In addition, they evaded several government attempts to relocate the village to Umboi Island, as discussed below.

Cash Cropping, Relocation, and *Bisnis* in Siassi, 1960–1980

The post–World War II administration in Siassi was concerned with increasing a depleted population as a result of overrecruitment for labor. Islanders were encouraged to "[improve] subsistence gardens and [to encourage] the development of local industries and cash-crops as an inducement to the people to seek cash on their own island" (Patrol Report 1, 1952, 4). By 1960, however, administrative officials were concerned with overpopulation and resettlement of the small islands, especially Aromot and Mandok (Patrol Reports 9, 11, 1961–1962). Although different possible sites on Umboi were considered, old feuds, new religions, and traditional rivalries between the small islanders and several Umboi communities interfered with the program. The breakdown of local trade was also offered as an explanation for the islanders' reluctance to relocate to Umboi. In the end, no one moved (for a more complete discussion of these events see Pomponio 1983, 271–278).

The above factors notwithstanding, I suggest that the real obstacle to resettlement was embedded in Mandok (and other small islanders') perceptions of themselves as mobile sea people rather than sedentary horticulturalists. The patrol officer at the time noted that, though small islanders did acquire land for gardens, they made only halfhearted attempts at horticulture (Patrol Report 1, 1952, part II:7). The problem as he interpreted it was that "Islanders claim they are fishermen and as such cannot be expected to toil in gardens in the same way as 'bush natives' " (Patrol Report 1, 1952, 7).

This interpretation goes a long way toward explaining why the same problems regarding relocation persist today, despite a current policy of peaceful coexistence between the Lutheran and Catholic missions and the resumption of local trade. Both missions have initiated several gardening projects on Umboi over the years, with varying results that reflect a cultural identity based on indigenous subsistence economy more than religious affiliation. For example, the Umboi Islanders have widened their horticultural base and are now engaged in the production of copra and cocoa.[8] The major obstacles to Umboi gardeners seem to be the attention required to grow cash crops and the perennial problem of transporting their products to market in Lae or Madang (Ploeg 1984). The Mandok, like most other small islanders, have cultivated a few more coconut trees for copra production but do not have the land resources or the transportation facilities to support large-scale cash cropping. Despite several opportunities to gain more land since 1960 (Pomponio 1983, 269–298), the Mandok have declined to exploit them in any significant way. They did increase their land parcel on Umboi somewhat in 1980, but they staunchly refused to move.

Despite mission and government attempts to encourage the Mandok to grow cash crops, they preferred other opportunities for cash accumulation—the Melanesian maritime traders' analogue to Kapingamarangi fishermen's interactions with outsiders (Lieber, chapter 4). Shell diving remained a popular, if sporadic, means of local employment for the small islanders throughout the early 1970s.[9] This was a profitable activity from the islanders' point of view because they stayed at home and "repopulated," which initially pleased the government, and earned cash, which pleased themselves. Patrol officers reported the villagers' willingness to participate in "development," and noted a need for closely supervised projects to help with the transition to a market economy (cf. Patrol Report 11, 1961–1962, 9–13; and 2, 1970–1971, app. A). In addition, throughout the 1960s there was talk of initiating a fishing industry in Siassi (Patrol Report 2, 1970–1971, 7). None of these suggestions ever came to fruition. The important point from the Mandok perspective, however, is that during this same period children were being sent to school and obtaining jobs, and shell diving was available as an alternative means of obtaining cash for villagers living on Mandok. Under these circumstances, why should the small islanders garden?

The government's move to reduce the resources committed to education, beginning in 1970, hit the Mandok very hard for several reasons. First, education that had been free or had required only a token fee now cost a great deal in tuition, clothing, and transportation. The School Localization Program, intended to encourage children to stay in school, had the opposite effect on the Mandok. Instead of going to high school in mission or town centers, Mandok students were assigned first to Gelem High School on the west side of Umboi, and then (as now) to Siassi High School in Lablab, on the east side of Umboi.[10] The students were no longer surrounded by kin, no longer in urban centers, and no longer supported by the Catholic mission. Both Gelem and Lablab high schools, while government subsidized, were originally Lutheran mission high schools.

Worse still from the students' point of view was that they now had to work in the school gardens, labor that they perceived to be far more demanding and demeaning than the fishing and reef-gathering activities in which they would be participating at home. The first-generation Mandok students who were sent to Kilenge and Rabaul during the mid-1960s were seventeen to nineteen years old when they entered form I— according to Mandok concepts of physical and moral development, on the verge of adulthood. In contrast, students who were attending school on Umboi from 1970 on were aged from twelve to fourteen—too young, by Mandok standards, to be expected to do heavy garden work. Thus, when the students complained that they were being overworked and underfed in their bush high schools, the parents felt sorry for them and were angry at the schoolteachers for what they felt to be unreasonable and cruel exploitation of "mere children."

Although several alternatives to high school were made available, from the Mandok parents' perspective, the closer the country came to independence, the fewer incentives they had to participate in development. In contrast to rising school fees and general inflation, the average Mandok man's access to money has either remained constant (in the case of sales of carvings in Lae or to occasional tourist boat passengers) or declined (in the case of young men leaving for temporary employment as plantation laborers). The deficit between available income and expenditures was made up by remittances from educated and employed Mandok youths in towns. This additional income, however, provided only a temporary reprieve for the villagers. Until the late 1960s anyone who was literate and numerate could count on finding a job, but by 1970 a college-level degree or diploma was necessary for all but the most menial jobs. Even these were in short supply. From the villagers' perspective, then, they were (and still are) paying more and getting much less in return.

These disincentives have accumulated to the point that parents today view school as a losing investment. Interest in school, at both the community and high school levels, has plummeted since the early 1970s. Attendance at the Por-Mandok Community School has shown a pattern of dropouts, and parental participation is very lax. Achievement scores of Mandok children in the national grade 6 exam declined sharply between 1975 and 1980, reaching an all-time low in 1979 (Isoaimo 1980). The Mandok have quite consciously and rationally adjusted their participation in schooling to reflect the likely return on their investment. As one parent of school-age children phrased it, "Why should I spend my [hard-earned] money and send him to school, if I know he'll only be back again in a few years empty-handed [i.e., jobless]? Then I'll have to start all over again to teach him village things so he can eat and have a good life here."

These attitudes have apparently been transmitted to the children, who are moderating their classroom performance accordingly. However, though parents initiated their own retrenchment policy regarding education, their eagerness to participate in development did not wane; it was replaced with another project, which promised bigger and better (i.e., more culturally suitable) returns than either cash cropping or education. This was the attempt to initiate a village communal *bisnis* enterprise by buying the mission boat.

The Boat That Sank the Village

To comprehend the havoc that this particular project wrought on the village, a brief description of significant features of Mandok social organization and a summary of the economic and political climate of the time are necessary. Mandok Village is divided sociogeographically into two sections: Mata to the east, and Sangup, the west side of the village. Though always differentiated, in the past few years these geographic designations have become synonymous with the eventual split of the island into two competing business societies, the Sunrise Society and the Mandok Society. Each half of the village accommodates specific groups of *runai* 'patrilineal groups'. Though the Mandok insist that the patrilineages are all equal, in times of stress or when pushed by circumstances, some are more equal than others. Specifically, those patrilineages whose Mandok founders were the first lot of settlers on each island are said to "boss" the village. It is from these groups that Mandok leaders emerge. These runai all trace their ancestry to sites on or near the sea.[11]

Thus, the important feature of patrilineage membership or village residence is not west side/east side of Mandok, but the sea/bush origins of the first settler of any given *lain* 'group, lineage' and the founders' rights of the very first immigrants to Mandok. Even though these migrations occurred several generations ago, Mandok notions of transmission of blood and heritability of personality, intelligence, and leadership qualities through bloodlines retain these distinctions (cf. Watson, chapter 2). Such a conceptualization, to continue the terminology offered in chapter 1, is clearly Mendelian. However, the Lamarckian emphasis is seen by the fact that those lineages that derive from bush locations are less powerful politically than those from sea locations.

The west side of the village enjoys higher status than the east side because members of these patrilineal groups are perceived to be more closely and fundamentally rooted in Mandok marigenic substance and therefore have the right to lead. Men from the east side are considered to be, as one young man whispered to me during a village debate, "just so much driftwood." That is, their ancestry is less valued and therefore they are not considered rightfully eligible to assume positions of leadership within the village. We might also speculate a certain analogical association between the first immigrants to Mandok and firstborn children. That is, not only are the first residents served first, for example, in marigenic substance, they are also charged with "cutting the path" for subsequent arrivals—hence the fact that most, if not all, Mandok leaders were from the west side of the village.

By the mid-1970s the cumulative effects of education, labor migration, rural development projects, and approaching national independence had produced a leadership crisis on Mandok. The generation that had held power was growing old. Men in the thirty to forty-five age group had received only minimal literacy training; some had experience as plantation laborers. Younger men who would have been considered capable of assuming leadership were instead in towns advancing their education or working in semi- to highly skilled jobs. There were thus no true leaders to succeed those presently in power. The combined perception of a village brain drain and the swiftness of the changes brought about by the Europeans necessitated some serious reevaluation of the future of the village.

The Catholic mission had trained several Mandok to crew mission boats, and a few to captain them. Their extensive knowledge of the reef system and winds, and their general orientation to the sea, were invaluable in the treacherous Vitiaz and Dampier straits, which separated the different parishes in Siassi from the mission's mainland headquarters in Rabaul (later Lae). Some of these men served on the mission boat, the M. V. *Jawani*, which was used to supply the mission with its staples, and also to shuttle cargo and personnel between islands in Siassi and other mission posts.

When trade stores came to Siassi in the mid-1960s, the mission helped to establish a store and trained its clerks to prepare the Mandok for independence and self-sufficiency. The villagers pooled their capital to form the Mandok Society, a villagewide business cooperative that controlled a copra drier and the village trade store. Coconut trees were planted on the limited land on Umboi for copra production. Proceeds from copra sales were used to stock the trade store with goods previously obtainable only in the towns, such as tinned meats and fish, rice, razor blades, cookies, pens, paper, envelopes, fishhooks, and fishing tackle. Trade-store profits were put in a village communal fund, from which people could borrow money for such expenses as school fees.

Around 1976–1977, the Mandok Society wanted to buy the *Jawani*. They envisioned that instead of paying for boat services, they could run their own business, hauling copra and cargo produced by other communities in Siassi to markets in Lae and Rabaul. They would also gain thereby a reasonable alternative to relocating the village to the Umboi bush—an alternative consistent with their perceived historical prominence as Siassi middlemen. After much deliberation and public debate about the merits of such an undertaking, the Mandok Society bought the boat. They used about 4000 *kina* (approximately $5640 U.S.) of the society's funds and borrowed the balance from the PNG Banking Corporation and the Development Bank.

At that time two captains on Mandok were capable of running the boat for the village. Each was literate and numerate, had worked on plantations, and had some experience with running boats. However, the two men happened to be from different bloodlines and from the two opposing factions of the village. The first, whom I will call A, was from a long line of respected leaders of Mandok. Although not a firstborn child, he was the first son of a very prominent leader and patrilineal group elder. Since his patrilineage is considered by village standards to produce the rightful heirs to Mandok leadership positions, he was tacitly expected to follow in his father's footsteps. The second man, B, was from the Mata (east) side of the village. Though also from a respectable lineage, he was not a firstborn son and therefore not considered to be as strong a contender in Mandok terms. He did, however, have more experience in handling motorized boats and in working on plantations than did A. B, who spearheaded the campaign to buy the boat, also had many young kinsmen who could assist as his crew.

The purchase of the *Jawani* began to reveal internal political strains. The Sunrise Society emerged as a direct competitor to the Mandok Society, with their own copra drier and trade store. The competition between the two societies for control over the boat escalated into a true village schism: extended families were split, customary exchanges of food and betel nut between relatives from different factions were suspended, violent threats went back and forth. When the boat broke down, the Mandok Society defaulted on loan payments, and the boat was repossessed and resold by the bank. The communal fund disappeared as a source of cash for school fees and other projects.

The debate over the boat resurfaces today every time either side of the village initiates any sort of new project. Two popular interpretations of what happened represent different levels of analysis of a complex event. The first view states simply that the village was trying to go from fishing and gardening to a business economy overnight. Never having had any experience in market economics, the villagers could not handle this sudden switch and things fell apart. The second view points to long-standing political and status differences in the village. According to this theory, the boat offered a focal point for a revolt of underlings. Now that the east side of the village had access of European knowledge, cash, and goods, they felt they could gain access to local power by manipulating control over the *Jawani*. By utilizing B's experience and knowledge of boatmanship they tried to rewrite the laws of Mandok leadership and overthrow the existing power structure.

Both of these analyses are accurate and true, to a certain extent. The significance of this case, however, does not lie in historical accuracy— determining "what really happened"—but in the pattern of interactions and the choices made at important junctures. Once again individual Mandok discovered an alternative business enterprise to the one being promoted by outsiders, and this alternative kept some of the population mobile and most of it on Mandok instead of moving to Umboi. Unfortunately internal social and political tensions, and ignorance of the nuances of credit financing and market economics, combined to produce a disaster instead of a success.

When I arrived on Mandok in October 1979, the village was trying to get back together socially and economically, but the wounds were still fresh. In fact, in many ways the situation had worsened. Just before Christmas 1979, a third copra drier was erected by one lineage for their personal use and profit. This caused a stir that climaxed at a public meeting in the village plaza. Many Mandok feared another split in the village. One man accused the owners of the new copra drier of poaching his coconuts. Finally the church elders decided not to have the copra drier blessed until the matter was cleared up—a solution that all accepted for the time being. When I left Mandok in February 1981, the unblessed copra drier remained, as one church councillor described it, "a building with sin." This decision seemed to make an acceptable statement to the village at the time; it did not, however, solve the issue of what to develop next.

Moving the School to Umboi

As if there were not enough turmoil, yet another relocation scheme was being launched. The education system's emphasis on rural development and "better community life" required teachers to sponsor community projects in their schools. In the latter part of 1980, the two schoolteachers initiated a project that would move the school to the garden area of Umboi. The Por-Mandok Community School is so named because it is located on Por Island, detached physically from the Mandok community. Neither island has garden land, making community land development impossible.

The teachers were both from bush areas and felt more comfortable in the bush and with land-development projects. A major concern of all teachers who have worked on Mandok is food, because their sole source is the trade store on Mandok. Especially during my field stay, after two years of ravaged gardens, this was a big problem. By moving the school to Umboi, the teachers felt that the children could learn to garden and grow their own food; they would also have land on which to develop other community projects. Encouraged by educated and employed Mandok who had returned for the Christmas holidays, the elders decided to start building the new school on Umboi in late November. Once the Christmas feasting cycles began, however, the buildings were left unfinished; the 1981 school year opened on Por.

The Mandok had apparently decided informally against the project to move the school. The village did decide, however, to buy an icebox to start a fishing business and pooled their money for that. This enterprise lasted approximately five months. Transport and money-management problems, and the fact that a freezer with a generator was placed on a different island, made the Mandok fishing venture less profitable. Yet the establishment of the fishing business and the commitment of the villagers to really do it this time inspired the opening of several new trade stores on Mandok. These two were short-lived for the most part, "rising and falling like the tide," leaving "always a debt" (Fr. Frans Lenssen, pers. comm., 1982).

In 1984 the two sides of the village joined again to form one business society, "Matasangup," which unites verbally and symbolically the two formerly opposing halves of the village (Fr. Frans Lenssen, pers. comm., 1984). This time the village was united around several freezers and a generator for a fishing business. The catch was to be kept in the village freezers until it could be air freighted to Lae (Lewis Kusso-Alless, pers. comm., 1985). That project failed, partially due to transportation costs, partially because of interisland rivalries. In 1986 the Finschhafen Siassi Kabwuum Development Authority (FISIKA) established a subsidiary called the Siassi Development Corporation. FISIKA officials hope to overcome both transport and sociopolitical problems by the operation of a bulk store and a fishing business for all of Siassi. Only time will tell if the tide has reversed, to reiterate Father Frans' metaphor.

Conclusion: A Middleman Culture's Interpretations of Development

Mandok involvement with Western schooling, cash cropping, and their ill-fated purchase of the mission boat represent separate but related episodes of the same saga. Taken together, these incidents reveal a consistent pattern of behavior in the face of cultural, economic, and political changes that are outside their control and that threaten their cultural identity as seafaring middlemen. Mandok reactions to cash cropping, education, and business are patterned by their orientation to the sea and their perception of themselves as middlemen and traders. Their choices at each point were based on the Mandok view that appropriate investments are those that befit their mobile middleman culture. Each government, mission, or school initiative to have the Mandok relocate was countered with an alternative that kept the Mandok villagers on their island, and also kept at least part of the population mobile. As the trade system started deteriorating with increased migrant labor, and migrant labor opportunities then declined with the suspension of labor recruitment, trochus collecting and education were seized upon to fill the economic gap. Trochus collecting kept the men at home and employed, and education provided a long-range investment with surplus human resources (i.e., children).

Education not only provided cash input to the village, but more important perhaps for the Mandok, it subsidized the declining trade system. In the early years of secondary education, the high schools to which Mandok children were sent were in mission or government centers and were located at points along traditional trade routes. Just as Harding predicted for migrant laborers, educated youths became a new trade system of sorts by supplying access to goods and cash to relatives at home.

When secondary education no longer fulfilled parents' expectations for adequate returns on their school fees, local carving and vocational schools presented other opportunities—but these promises too were unfulfilled. Combining the funds of the entire village to purchase the mission boat seemed to be a logical and appropriate next step. The Mandok saw themselves as having the rights to this kind of knowledge and therefore concluded that they—as opposed to other islanders, and certainly as opposed to the Umboi bush people—should organize the distribution of Siassi produce. The fact that they also had men who were trained and experienced both in European ways and in European boats reinforced this idea. In many ways, the promises of a village business centered around the mission boat also offered Mandok the opportunity to outdo the Umboi gardeners in development. Again, this competition is a reformulation of traditional relationships between the small islanders and Umboi communities. After all, why should the Mandok garden like bush people, when they could regain their prominence as kings of the sea and traders and, instead of producing, could distribute the bush peoples' products and thereby acquire cash directly?

The series of frustrated attempts at relocation, land purchase, and disputes over rights to land resources documented in patrol reports since the 1960s provides further evidence of the status rivalry between the sea people and the bush people. However, competition between Mandok village factions turned the game against themselves in the face of ignorance of the nuances of market economics and credit finance. The lines of cleavage were inherent in the social structure of the village—the issue of the boat brought these antagonisms and rivalries to the surface. In short, even though the items traded and the means of achieving renown had changed somewhat with the coming of Europeans, the fundamental motivations, goals, and culturally acceptable routes to achievement remained constant.

A Mendelian model as described by Lieber (chapter 4) makes two major assumptions: (1) there is a difference between being (inner composition) and behavior, and (2) behavior is a surface manifestation of what is within. Although I would not describe the Mandok sense of personhood as totally consocial or Lamarckian in this sense, there is a systematic association between levels at which substances are associated with identity and the nature of the larger social system within which what one does makes a difference. Whether this is a byproduct or a necessary condition of a middleman trading society is beyond the scope of the present discussion. However, the relationship between these elements cannot be ignored as important factors in Mandok cultural identity.

Most often for the small islanders, development solutions formulated by outsiders have entailed plans to relocate to Umboi Island and new projects for cash cropping. But Mandok aspirations and standards of excellence are tied to their cultural identity as mobile maritime traders rather than sedentary horticulturalists. Time and again the Mandok have responded to development pressures by staying on their island. Their feelings were perhaps best expressed by a Mandok father during a heated debate over the 1980 attempt to move the school to Umboi Island: "Go ahead and move the school to Muru, and see what you get. You think once you move the children you can call yourselves Mandok anymore? Ha! You'll be bush people, just like the Umbois! Our skin is strong because we wash in the sea. You watch—the children will grow up to be all skin and bones if they live in Muru." Another informant, perhaps more eloquently, cited the proverb that appears at the beginning of this chapter.

For generations the Mandok have enjoyed an existence analogous to that of seagulls, scavenging bits and pieces of culture and material resources from throughout the Vitiaz and Dampier straits, lighting only briefly at key islands and villages in their journey. Their proverbial nest is on Mandok; their home is on the sea. Implicit in this proverb is the Mandok judgment that life traveling on the sea is more advanced than life in the bush. From the Mandok perspective, to invest in a school system or any other project that promises to transform cosmopolitan mobile sea people into isolated sedentary bush people is tantamount to

expecting seagulls to become land birds. This metamorphosis would
entail more than a loss of status in the local sociopolitical system—it
would change their autochthonous essence, alter their cultural identity,
and sacrifice their continuity in marigenic substance. For the Mandok,
this seems to be a price too high.

NOTES

I gratefully acknowledge the following for providing funding for the project:
from 1979 to 1980: the Papua New Guinea Department of Education, Research
Branch; Bryn Mawr College, Frederica de Laguna Fund for Anthropological
Research; and the Morobe Province Research Center. From 1986 to 1987: the
Wenner-Gren Foundation for Anthropological Research and St. Lawrence University. Many thanks are also due to Jocelyn Linnekin, Michael Lieber, and the
other members of the Cultural Identity in Oceania panel for their insightful
comments, criticisms, and suggestions. Ultimate responsibility for the interpretation and final product of those efforts is of course entirely mine.

1. Note that the Mandok, while different, are not unique among Melanesian
societies in depending on trade for subsistence. Other notable examples are the
Murik Lakes (K. Barlow and D. Lipset, pers. comm., 1982), Chambri Lakes
(Gewertz 1983), and Ponam Island, Manus Province (Carrier 1979, 1981a,
1981b).

2. There is some confusion in the usage of different names for the parts of
Siassi District. Politically the entire area is known as Siassi. Locally, the small
coral islets that ring the southern tip of Umboi are considered Siassi Islands
proper, and Umboi is referred to as the mainland. I use the terms as follows:
Siassi to refer to the entire area; *islands, small islanders,* to refer to the small
coral islets of Aromot, Mutumala, Mandok, Aronaimutu, and the two somewhat larger islands of Malai and Tuam. The three major islands, Umboi, Arop,
and Tolokiwa, are referred to by name.

3. Harding (1967, 123) and Freedman (1967, 4) refer to this as "Siassi language." Speakers of the language have no name for it, referring merely to "our
language," but Umboi Islanders in the Kaimanga group call it "island," or "the
islanders' language" after the local term for island. More recently Hooley and
McElhanon (1970; see also Hooley 1971, 1976) refer to both the languages of
southeast Umboi and the islanders' language as members of the "Siassi Family."
They distinguish the language of the small islanders as Mutu, and this is the
name that I use. Note also that Hooley and McElhanon call the language
spoken on southeast Umboi "Mangab," which is the Mutu term for this area.

4. Carving, fishnet weaving, and trochus-armlet production constitute the
major exceptions to the Mandok pattern of being distributors rather than producers. Note however that the Mandok, while producing, are not producing
food. A major distinguishing feature of the Siassi trade system, from the Mandok perspective, is that in both overseas and local trade the overwhelming balance of trade is aimed at trading nonedible (ceremonial) items for food—pigs
and staple vegetables.

5. I am indebted to Michael Lieber for this line of thinking. Responsibility for any misappropriation or distortion of his ideas is, however, mine.

6. Atai Tuku and Manbog Sirig are protagonists in the Myth of the Sea Eagle.

7. Although the masked figures are sources of ceremonial life, they are also sources of danger. Their construction and their mysteries are the exclusive knowledge of men. Women and children are forbidden to see their construction or touch the figure. During the dance, women avert their eyes from directly looking into the mouth of the figure, for fear of death. The nakamutmut are also the symbolic repositories of Mandok traditional law and custom, as are masked figures elsewhere in Melanesia (see Sack 1972; Zelenietz and Grant 1981).

8. Rice and Robusta coffee cultivation were also attempted but by the early 1960s were acknowledged to be failures due to neglect (Patrol Report 9, 1961–1962, 7).

9. Despite the market slumps of the 1950s and 1960s, and the depletion of the reefs with regard to these species, trochus and green snail shells were still listed in 1970 as one of the items of Siassi produce being sold to Gizarum plantation (Patrol Report 1, 1970–1971, 2).

10. Although 1971–1972 marks the beginning of the decline of Mandok high school enrollments, Gelem High School was better situated, from the Mandok point of view, than Lablab. The Mandok maintain fairly intensive trade and intermarriage with Barim (west coast of Umboi) and Aronaimutu Island. The children were therefore still within reach of kin and/or trading relations.

11. I have listed these elsewhere (Pomponio 1983, 285) as Aromot, Barim, Kilenge, or Malasega. My thanks to Lewis Kusso-Alless (pers. comm., 1984), for clarifying for me the fact that connections to Barim and Malasega are matrilineal and are therefore less important in determining patrilineage membership.

4

Lamarckian Definitions of Identity on Kapingamarangi and Pohnpei

MICHAEL D. LIEBER

The major concern of this chapter is how identities of communities in Oceania and the stereotypes built on these identities are generated. I locate the generating principles at the level of cultural premises rather than that of political-historical contexts (the latter approach is that taken in several other chapters in this volume). By describing Kapinga-marangi and Pohnpei notions of personhood and their stereotypes of several local populations, I show that, while Kapingamarangi (hereafter Kapinga) and Pohnpeians share ideas of consocial personhood and environmental determinism, their perceptions of local groups differ significantly. The difference is, in large measure, the outcome of very different assumptions about the meaning and location of political power in the two societies. These different cultural assumptions are critical in shaping the colonial experiences of these societies and, thus, the modern identities of these communities.

Consocial Personhood and Lamarckian Stereotypes

Whether or not we accept Linnekin and Poyer's cultural identity/ethnic identity distinction, community identity delineates a category of persons to which definitive attributes are ascribed. Community identity is thus a logical implication of a community's conception of the meaning of personhood. This assertion of a causal connection between communities' stereotypes and ideas of personhood implies a hierarchical ordering of categories of persons. Ethnic stereotypes are not different in structure from descriptions of other categories of persons in a community's repertoire; it is the level of inclusiveness that distinguishes a description of, say, members of a particular family from that of members of another community.

What it means to be a person is structured by people's ideas of how one becomes a person (i.e., by local theories of ontogeny). For this

71

reason we find consocial personhood linked with ontogenetic theories of environmental determinism to be common, if not universal, in Oceania.

Geertz (1973, 365), following the philosopher Alfred Schutz, describes consociates as "persons who encounter one another somewhere along the course of daily life." They are "involved with one another's biography." The person is not an individual in our Western sense of the term. The person is instead a locus of shared *biographies:* personal histories of people's relationships with other people and with things. The relationship defines the person, not vice versa (Errington 1974; Larcom, chapter 8; Lieber 1977a; Shore 1982). Persons are unique in the particular emphases they place on particular relationships and the styles by which they conduct them.

Consocial personhood can be and is enacted in very different sorts of social organizations, ranging from the ranked hierarchies of Samoa (Shore 1982) and Pohnpei (Riesenberg 1968) to the egalitarian Kaluli (Schieffelin 1976) and Tairora (Watson 1983). These differences in how consocial personhood is institutionalized shape differences in how biographies are structured and interpreted from one society to another. I will show, for example, that while Kapinga and Pohnpei share an identical concept of consocial personhood, the structures and contents of personal biographies of each are quite different. These differences at least partly determine what attributes of interaction each community takes into account in constructing stereotypes of the other.

James Watson, in chapter 2, contrasts a Lamarckian structure of community stereotypes characteristic of Kainantu peoples with the Western-style Mendelian structure of ethnic imagery. The thoroughgoing environmental determinism of Kainantu peoples shapes stereotypes that are thumbnail descriptions of how people from other communities typically act and interact—"other people do other things." These sociological sketches appear to be typical of Oceanic stereotypes. They contrast sharply with Western stereotypes, which are characterological; that is, stereotypes that designate character traits such as greediness, sloth, stupidity, and hypersexuality, which are popularly assumed to be inherited as biogenetic units.

It is clear from Watson's (chapter 2) and Pomponio's (chapter 3) accounts that Lamarckian structuring of identity is a folk theory (or theories) of ontogeny, which asserts precisely that biology and behavior covary. But Mendelian identity is also based on a folk theory of ontogeny that also often asserts that biology and behavior covary. Why is it, then, that Mendelian ontogeny generates an equation between race and ethnicity (i.e., racial theories of behavior), while Lamarckian ontogeny, in its Oceanic form, does not? Because these two very different theories of ontogeny, both culturally constituted, presuppose very different conceptions of the human soma.

Mendelian ontogeny holds that traits of physiognomy and character are inherited as units from one's parents through a single act of conception. Traits are inherited as properties of, as *parts* of persons. These properties are said to be generated by atomic units or corpuscles within the seed and egg, which interact to produce somatic capacities and propensities of character before birth. The child's social and physical environment affects him or her only after birth. Lamarckian ontogeny, in its Oceanic form, asserts that the developing fetus incorporates material from its parents throughout conception and gestation. It inherits somatic traits that include preformed relationships between people and plants, soil, animals, other objects, and other people that together constitute the parents' environment. These relationships are conveyed to the fetus as bodily substances that are transforms of the parents' constitutions and experiences before and during gestation. The same relationships continue to contextualize the child's experiences after birth unless, of course, the child is raised in a totally different place from that in which he or she was nurtured *in utero*. Lamarckian ontogeny assumes a plasticity of inherited substance not found in popular Mendelian ontogeny, whose units of substance are fixed once and for all at conception. It is this plasticity that confounds the sort of neat drawing of racial boundaries one sees attempted in the West. Racial theories require units of inherited substance that do not change with environment—Jews are supposed to continue to be greedy in New York or Jerusalem, or Poles to be stupid in Chicago as well as Warsaw.

What Kainantu, Mandok, and (as I will show) Kapinga inherit are transforms of relationships between people and between people and things. What people inherit in Mendelian ontogeny are properties, that is, parts of a whole person, through the fusion of parts of parts of persons—corpuscular units in seed and egg. Mendelian ontogeny yields individuals, describable in terms of their particular properties (just like any other object). Lamarckian ontogeny yields consociates, describable in terms of the manner in which they conduct their relationships. Consocial personhood follows logically from environmentally determined ontogeny just as the person as individual follows logically from Mendelian ontogeny.

Because Lamarckian identity incorporates social and environmental relationships in a theory of transformation into biological substance, I find the proposed distinction between cultural and ethnic identities in the introduction to be useful as a starting point for thinking about the

Oceanic data, but not very useful in organizing my ethnographic presentation. Lamarckian identity as described for Kainantu peoples, the
Mandok, and the Kapinga partake of both. It is not simply a matter of
emphasis. Descent, as construed by these communities, does in fact
delineate a boundary that includes some people and excludes others as
members. Biological substance, as construed by these communities,
does covary with behavior and is used to distinguish people from one
another. From this point of view, these communities are examples of
ethnic identity. That it is social relationships and relations between people and things that are inherited by people exemplifies cultural identity.
But the two are inextricably and logically fused. I will, therefore, use
the term *ethnic identity* to refer to identities of people as members of a
community vis-à-vis other, different communities throughout this ethnographic presentation. I now turn to the description of Kapinga personhood and ethnicity.

Kapingamarangi Personhood and Categories of Persons

Kapingamarangi is a tiny atoll located 485 miles south and west of
Pohnpei in the Eastern Caroline Islands (see Map 2). Its Polynesian
inhabitants number about 450 persons who subsist on locally available
coconut, taro, breadfruit, pandanus, and lagoon and deep-sea fish. The
thirty-one islets that comprise its 0.42 square miles of land area constitute the major resource for food, for copra, and for building materials
for houses, canoes, and gear.

Effective colonial control of the atoll began in 1914, when the Japanese colonial administration took control of Micronesia. During this
period the Kapinga founded a resettled community, called Porakied, on
Pohnpei 485 miles to the north. Since 1919, field-trip ships have ensured
continual movement of people between the atoll and Pohnpei. The population of the atoll has remained steady at about 450 people since the
1930s. The population of Porakied has grown from 120 people in 1943
to 600 people in 1982. Kapinga people's most intensive contacts with
other islanders have been on Pohnpei.

Kapinga define the person as a locus of social relationships, of shared
biographies. For example, people are differentiated from animals in
terms of the human ability to maintain different categories of relationship. People cite the facts that dogs and cats from the same litter often
mate with one another, or that a dog will readily mate with its mother,
saying "You see, animals don't know who their relatives are; people do."
Persons are describable in terms of their unique styles of conducting

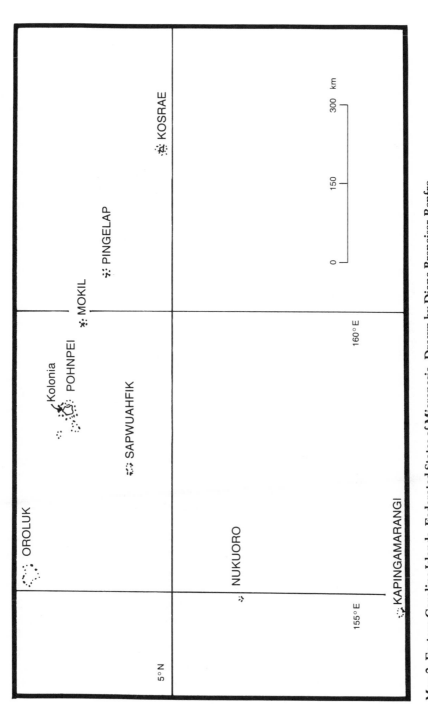

Map 2. Eastern Caroline Islands, Federated States of Micronesia. Drawn by Diana Breneiser-Renfro.

their relationships. Styles are cultivated as part of the process of maturation.

Special abilities, skills, interests, work habits, conversational topics, joking strategies, and the like come to define persons as unique. These definitive patterns, along with persons' known responses to particular kinds of situations, form the biography that others know. People abstract these patterns in talking about one another, and these abstractions are persons' reputations. Obviously, in situations where these patterns of conduct are the data on which people base their predictions of one another's responses, consistency of style is a minimal requirement of everyone. Kapinga can and do tolerate a wide range of violations of etiquette and moral interdictions, such as foul language, theft, bad temper, or stinginess, as long as one is consistent about it. Even insanity is tolerated with gentle good humor as long as one is consistently mad. While Kapinga do have labeled roles, such as kinship roles, leader of a work party, leader of the men's house, priest, and the like, only those involving avoidance relationships are useful for predicting a person's most likely response to a given situation. Consistency can be built in, as well as being built up.

The Inheritance of Acquired Characteristics

The process of repetitive experience that creates personal consistency begins before a person is born. Kapinga are explicit about the effect of repeated prenatal experiences on a fetus. What a woman sees and what both parents do during gestation can effect permanent bodily and behavioral predispositions in the developing baby. For example, pregnant women are told not to look at misshapen fruit or at monstrous things or images of any kind, lest the baby be similarly misshapen. They must look at only perfectly formed objects. If either parent engages in habitual lying or thievery during pregnancy, the child will be a habitual thief or liar.[1]

The inheritance of personal attributes owing to membership in larger categories of persons, such as families, is decidedly Lamarckian. Various families on Kapingamarangi, each of which is associated with a named ancestral residence compound, are known to possess and transmit behavioral dispositions such as industriousness, thievery, promiscuity, craftsmanship, intellectual virtuosity, witchcraft, fishing skill, and querulousness. Kapinga agree that these predispositions are part of a person's "flesh" and that they are inherited during conception. Informants were not very articulate about the processes by which such predispositions become part of the flesh. They rejected the suggestion that predispositions were inherited as units of substance, as corpuscles analogous to genes. Rather, they emphasized that the relationships to members of particular families is inherited, and that the patterns of acting are outcomes of those relationships, which are a part of a person's inherited biological substance.

When discussing the behavioral propensities of particular families, Kapinga recognize that not all persons in the category exhibit the purported characterisitics. Not all the men in the family associated with the compound, *ngeia holeu* 'north of the cult house', for example, are expert craftsmen, though the family is associated with that trait. Informants answer that the men who are not good craftsmen are more closely affiliated with other families of which they are a part. Some speculated that perhaps the substance from the father's side was stronger than that from the mother's side or vice versa. Two informants stated that the men who were raised at that compound were more likely to become good craftsmen. Most others stated that simply being part of that family made the difference. They talked as if it was more a matter of aptitude and osmosis than of learning as they understand it. Boys of the craftsman family seem to acquire craft skills with little or no effort while others must work hard to learn the skills without ever becoming as good at them. That the development of the particular behavioral trait is associated with particular compounds seems to owe to the fact that family relationships originate and are enacted in particular places.

It is at a different level of social category, male and female, that Kapinga appear to be most comparable to Kainantu and Mandok peoples regarding the association of people with locale, with substances, and with the inheritance of immunities. Females are centrally located on Kapingamarangi, working at house compounds and taro pits. Men are peripherally located, working at lagoon beaches, outer islets, the outer reef, and the deep sea. Women are associated with mud, which they create by mulching the sandy soil to grow taro—the Kapinga symbol of domestication. Men are associated with seawater and fish. These are natural associations in the sense that women and men are thought to do what they do not as a matter of convention, but as an inevitable expression of their constitutions.

Outer islets north of the central populated islets are women's domain, where they are immune to the depredations of a female spirit of those islets. Men are vulnerable to the spirit unless accompanied by a woman. Conversely, the islets south of the central islets are a male domain, and a malevolent male lagoon spirit there, to whom men are immune, will attack a woman unaccompanied by a man.

We see in the Kapinga data the same themes that Watson describes for Kainantu peoples—relation of people to locales, substances, and immunities to local dangers. But the relations are very differently dis-

tributed through the two social orders. Relations with natural substances define entire communities and sets of communities in Kainantu,
while they characterize only men on Kapingamarangi. Women are associated with processed substances that they themselves transform by
work, not by ingestion. Kapinga appear to be typical of Polynesian and
Micronesian societies in this respect, that is, the inheritance of a natural
inclination for a relationship with (usually processed) substances rather
than the inheritance of the transformed substances themselves. These
inherited relations, moreover, typically define categories of persons at a
level of social hierarchy lower than that of the entire community (e.g.,
Labby 1976; Lieber 1984; Petersen 1982a; Riesenberg 1968; Sahlins
1981).

Immunities show the same pattern. While immunities to local hazards delineate communities and regions in Kainantu, they distinguish
males and females at a lower order of social category on Kapingamarangi. Nonmembers of a community or region can acquire such
immunities through repeated contact with Kainantu people, while this
is not the case with Kapinga, who are, thus, non-Lamarckian in this
regard. The female-taro and male-fish relations are much more malleable, as Kapinga women participate in some kinds of fishing and
Kapinga men plant and care for taro on Pohnpei as the need arises.

The highest level of social category is that of Kapinga person, which
was defined in precontact times by a relation between people, the central islet of Touhou, and the gods. That relationship is set forth in the
Kapinga origin myth, which describes two canoes of castaways, one
containing a woman, Roua, and another her husband, Utamatua, his
followers, and local spirits from his home island, who pursued Roua to
Kapingamarangi, where she died. After several attempts to establish a
cult house for his spirits on various islets, Utamatua, his followers, and
his spirits take Touhou, a sandbar, and built it into a habitable islet.
Here, Utamatua buries his wife, builds the cult house over her grave,
and resides. Among older people today, Touhou continues to be a metaphor for the atoll, which is otherwise referred to as Kirinis (from the
British name, Greenwich). The physical transformation of the islet into
a residential and ritual center defines the population as an established
community. The relationship between Kapinga/non-Kapinga identity
and spirits inherited by persons was ritually expressed (until Western
contact) by the treatment of a castaway, who was not accorded a social
identity until a cult-house ritual was performed severing his or her relationship with the spirits of the home island. Thereafter the person was
given a Kapinga name and allowed to marry.

With the advent of the Japanese colonial administration in 1914,
Kapinga experienced within a five-year period the resident authority of
a Japanese administrator, a two-year drought and famine that resulted

in ninety deaths, the collapse of the traditional ritual system, conversion
to Christianity, resettlement on Pohnpei, regular contact by ship with
Pohnpei and other islands, and their first intensive contacts with people
of other islands. The way that Kapinga now define Kapinga identity
reflects the changes contingent on these events. Local gods lost their status as deities to a universal Jehovah, whom Kapinga worshiped equally
with other islanders in the same church and, on Pohnpei, in the same
congregation. Lesser spirits like the lagoon spirit continue to be associated with particular places, but they do not define a people as distinctive. The triadic link between local gods, places, and persons was severed, leaving the relation between place and person to delineate
differences between ethnic categories. Yet the assumption that relations
distinctive to people in particular places are inherited as part of one's
"flesh" remains unchallenged. It is hardly surprising, then, that genealogy categorically distinguishes Kapinga from non-Kapinga people.

Defining Kapinga Identity

A person without a Kapinga ancestor is not considered a Kapinga person, although such a person could be treated in the ways that Kapinga
treat one another if, for example, he or she had resided with Kapinga
people long enough to learn the language and customary expectations.
People with Kapinga ancestry, however, may or may not be thought of
as Kapinga, depending on the nature of their interactions with Kapinga
people.

In general, genealogical relations, social relationships, and the places
where these relations are (or are not) enacted combine to shape people's
biographies. Kapinga attend to the particular biographies when making
judgments about people's identities within the community (cf. Poyer,
chapter 6). Kapinga ancestry entitles one to the benefits and obligations
that inhere in kinship relations, yet one may choose not to commit oneself to them. On the other hand, a person without Kapinga ancestry
may spend his or her life in the Kapinga community and act in every
way like a Kapinga and still not be considered a Kapinga. A Kapinga
can spend his or her entire lifetime elsewhere and act in every way like a
non-Kapinga and still be considered a Kapinga. Or one who is part
Kapinga can be considered a Kapinga in some contexts and a non-
Kapinga in others. One's willingness to be involved in the most minimal
way in kinship relations—occasional visits—appears to be sufficient to
warrant the designation, "Kapinga person." The Lamarckian idea
underlies all of these combinations of descent, social interaction, and
place in attributing Kapinga or some other identity to particular
people.[2]

While one's ancestry delineates a boundary at least to the extent of clearly defining who is not a Kapinga, ancestry has its denotative limits. For example, people living in the Marshall Islands who are descendants of five Kapinga who migrated there in 1866 are considered to be Marshallese people, but should any of them come to Pohnpei or the atoll seeking their relatives (as one woman did in 1978), they would be considered Kapinga people. In such cases, Kapinga use the term *baahi* 'part, half, side' to emphasize the contribution of descent to one's identity (e.g., mother's side, father's side, Nukuoro side or part Nukuoro). That a person is part Kapinga (has a Kapinga side) entitles him or her to certain inalienable claims and obligations, principally those of kinship (see Lieber 1970, 1974). The Marshallese people mentioned above are Marshallese until they exercise their options contingent on their ancestry. The identification of one as Kapinga, then, is no different than the identification of one as a kinsman. While traceable descent confers rights on persons (such as rights over land or rights to adopt or foster a child), the exercise of those rights makes one a kinsman. This may require little more than showing up to help with work on a house or requesting to adopt a child (whether or not the request is pressed or repeated over time or followed through to the actual taking of the child). It is primarily through maintaining social relationships with kin that a part-Kapinga's Kapinga identity is affirmed.

Part-Kapinga, like adoptees in their adopters' households, are at a particular rhetorical disadvantage in the sometimes good-natured, sometimes malicious taunting and ribbing that constitutes much of casual social interaction. People can always attribute some undesirable act or statement to one's non-Kapinga heritage, particularly with younger people, whose awareness of their reputations among their peers leaves them very vulnerable to gossip and insult. A riposte such as "You're a haughty person, just like Kosraeans," both insults and excludes a part-Kosraean from his or her usual place in social interaction. Natural children sometimes taunt an adoptive sibling in much the same fashion (e.g., "Who are you to say anything? Is this your house?"). This sort of taunt can be used as humor as well. For example, a boy with a Mortlockese grandfather had grown up in Porakied and on the atoll, having only occasionally visited his Mortlockese relatives on Pohnpei. He was playing my guitar one day when a woman said to him, "Play us a song from your island." He smiled weakly while others chuckled at the joke. What made the remark a joke was that the young man had never been to the Mortlocks, spoke no Mortlockese, and could barely remember the names of the Mortlockese relatives he had met. The request was couched in a way that presupposed the experience of relationships in a particular place, conjured up by his grandfather, who was not specifically mentioned. Such a request made to a person who had actually spent time with non-Kapinga relatives on another island would not be considered humorous. Joke that it was, the implication of exclusion from present company was still there, and the boy's downward gaze indicated some discomfort.

Other imputations made to or about part-Kapinga are neither rhetorical nor humorous. One man with a part-Kapinga father and a Pingelapese mother was raised on Pingelap and Kosrae, coming to the atoll in his late teens after World War II. He married a Kapinga woman and had three children with her, also adopting a Pingelapese nephew. He spent all of his adult life in Porakied, with a few brief stays on the atoll. He is not well liked by Kapinga, who point to his social aggressiveness, his clannishness with regard to his family, and his relative lack of open-handedness as evidence of his Pingelapese heritage. More serious is the widespread belief that he is a sorcerer. This attribution carries a specific connotation of Pingelapese identity, since sorcery is not a Kapinga practice, and Pingelapese and Pohnpeians are thought to be powerful sorcerers. The accusation not only connotes Pingelapese identity, but also implies the experience of Pingelapese social relationships from which the skills could have been mastered.

Several Kapinga children have been adopted by Pohnpeians and Sapwuahfik people and have spent most of their lives with their adopters, neither speaking nor understanding the Kapinga language. In 1982 these people, four males and two females, were all described categorically as Kapinga persons by other Kapinga. Informants pointed out that all but one of them would visit their relatives in Porakied whenever they were in Kolonia. One girl, however, shunned any contact with Kapinga for much of her life. People said that they resented her attitude, her intention to *hai tangada Pohnpei* 'make (or establish) herself as a Pohnpeian' (cf. Poyer's description of the same process on Sapwuahfik in chapter 6). Rather than referring to the girl as a Pohnpeian, people simply wrote her off as someone to interact with. She eventually returned to Porakied in her late teens, which several Kapinga pointed out as being typical in one respect. Adoptees and part-Kapinga children raised elsewhere often have no contact with Kapinga people throughout their childhood, but they almost always attempt to establish relationships with their Kapinga kin during their teens. Rather than make categorical attributions, particularly about part-Kapinga, people have a wait-and-see attitude.

Consistent with Kapinga thinking about children adopted by non-Kapinga is the case of a Pingelapese boy who was adopted as an infant by his part-Kapinga, part-Pingelapese uncle. He grew up in Porakied on Pohnpei speaking Kapinga and has remained there; he is married to a Kapinga woman. This man is considered to be Pingelapese, although

Kapinga interact with him as they would with a Kapinga person. He
does, after all, know how to interact properly, since he has learned
through experience how Kapinga interact. Kapinga say of him, as they
say of Kapinga adopted by other islanders, that should he decide to go
and live permanently with his congeners, he would have an easier
adjustment than would a non-Pingelapese (or in the Kapinga case, non-
Kapinga) to the new social situation. When asked why this should be
the case, people were less than articulate, saying only that since he is
Pingelapese (or since Kapinga adoptees are Kapinga), he (or they)
would learn to speak and act properly much more quickly than those
not so endowed. This is perfectly consistent with statements that
Kapinga make about why people of a particular family seem to develop
a particular skill or predisposition more easily than others. It is a
Lamarckian statement.

Equally Lamarckian is the way Kapinga talk about two men adopted
as infants by Sapwuahfik people and who were raised on Sapwuahfik,
later marrying Sapwuahfik women and raising their families there. Neither of them speaks or understands Kapinga, although they occasionally
visit relatives in Porakied when they come to Pohnpei. One man holds
several positions of responsibility and is becoming prominent on Sapwuahfik. Kapinga point to him, saying that his growing importance in
the Sapwuahfik community is only to be expected, since he is part of the
family of smart or bright people. Another man, mentioned by Poyer in
chapter 6, has earned the reputation of a first-rate fisherman on Sapwuahfik. Kapinga explain this by pointing out that his father was a
member of the family of superior fishermen. His preeminence on Sapwuahfik is only to be expected. As Poyer points out in chapter 6, Sapwuahfik people expect this man to be a good fisherman because he is
Kapinga. Kapinga people have no such categorical expectation of themselves. Although all men are expected to fish, not all of them do, and of
those who do, only a few are thought to be expert fishermen. Kapinga,
unlike Mandok, do not define themselves in terms of how they make
their living. Fishing is important to Kapinga identity, but not identical
with it.

Contacts with Non-Kapinga

While Kapingamarangi had been more or less isolated from contacts
with outsiders on any regular basis before European contact in 1877,
Kapinga knew of other islands and other peoples through their own traditional history and through sporadic landings of castaways.

The isolation of Kapingamarangi ended in 1877 when the first British ship entered the lagoon (Emory 1965, 13). Other ships subsequently visited the island for trading and provisioning, bringing Europeans and Americans, some of whom remained on the island, and three of whom married there. Kapinga also came into contact with Melanesian and Polynesian crewmen and had their first contacts with Nukuoro, 164 miles to the north.

During the period of Japanese control over Micronesia Kapinga were resettled on Pohnpei in the district center, where the colonial administrative headquarters was located. The Kapinga were granted twenty-one acres of lease land in Kolonia Town, the district urban center, in late 1919. This area forms what is now Porakied Village (Lieber 1968, 1977a). The atoll and Porakied Village have maintained regular contact and a flow of persons since 1919. The most intensive contacts with other islanders and with colonial personnel have taken place on Pohnpei.

Kapinga on Pohnpei: 1919 to the Present

Kapinga living in Porakied in the 1920s found themselves at the periphery of Kolonia Town, a periurban administrative, commercial, and residential center populated and controlled mainly by the Japanese. Surrounding this central, densely packed town with its shops, hospital, administrative offices, docks, and Catholic and Protestant missions, were Pohnpeians, Sapwuahfik, Trukese, Palauans, Filipinos, and Nukuoro. Across the inlet that separates Porakied from Sokehs lived enclaves of Mokilese, Pingelapese, and Mortlockese people.

At the boundaries of Kolonia Town was the larger Pohnpei polity with its five chiefdoms—Net, U, Madolenihmw, Kiti, and Sokehs, each subdivided into named sections. Each had and still has its own ritual-political leaders, divided into two lines of chiefs: the *Nahnmwarki* 'paramount chief' line and the *Nahnken* 'talking chief' line, each consisting of ranked titles. The paramount chief outranked the talking chief, who outranked the second in the paramount line, and so on. Each section was similarly organized by chiefly lines of titles. The highest titles in chiefdoms and sections tended to be controlled by particular subclans of particular matrilineal clans.

Kapinga on Pohnpei were easily distinguishable from other islanders by their physiognomy and language, and their initial contacts tended to be tentative or hostile. But Kapinga quickly established a secure niche for themselves by having a virtual monopoly over the supply of deep-sea fish. Their identity as fishermen facilitated their integration with other islanders in all the various contexts of activity that regularly brought them together. These included employment by the government and private businesses, a Japanese school, church, and recreational activities.

Kapinga work crews were regularly transported to Pohnpei as road gangs, and some of these workers remained on Pohnpei to fish. Kapinga fishermen developed reciprocity relationships with Pohnpeian and other Micronesian landowners throughout the island. Some of these relationships, which Sahlins (1965) calls "trade friendships," evolved into kinship relations and resulted in Kapinga men receiving section titles in U during World War II. Very few of their contacts resulted in intermarriage, however—three with Pohnpeians and two with Mort-lockese before the war.

The postwar establishment of the U.S. Trust Territory of the Pacific Islands, with its interest in economic and political development of the area, greatly expanded the contexts of contact among islanders without initially changing the patterns of contact. The Japanese administration had already established a school and a hospital in Kolonia that trained and employed islanders. They had established elective offices and employed islanders in businesses and government services. The American administration expanded many of these programs. Each atoll and chiefdom on Pohnpei had its schools, dispensary, and municipal charters with chief magistrate and elective council. Pohnpei District, which included Mokil, Pingelap, Kosrae, Sapwuahfik (then Ngatik), Nukuoro, and Kapingamarangi, had a district legislature by the mid-1950s. Municipalities had cooperative retail stores and licensed private businesses, such as retail stores, restaurants, and pool halls. The administration used its schools to recruit islanders to bureaucratic positions in administrative departments, the hospital, and the schools. Government salaries accounted for both the bulk of the district's cash flow and for the capital to start new retail businesses. There has always been a good deal of competition for these jobs, not only among members of the various island enclaves, such as Mokilese and Pingelapese, but also among Pohnpei people of various chiefdoms and sections, and family, section, and ethnic group nepotism are expected from officeholders.

The Protestant church, in attempting to cope with an almost overnight expansion of the Kolonia population, responded by sponsoring the formation of local, mainly island enclave congregations. The first of these was inaugurated in the Kapinga village, Porakied, in 1951, with the construction of the first of several *sinagogee* 'synagogues', as they are called, where morning and evening vespers could be held, along with Sunday school, holiday celebrations, and weddings. Other enclaves rapidly established their own synagogues. Sunday morning services, meetings of the church governing board and other organizations, and larger holiday services continued to be held in the Protestant church in Kolonia. In addition to the usual interethnic contact at the mission church, the decentralization of some church activities promoted contact between ethnic enclaves through exchange programs, joint choir concerts, and joint services. Several marriages between Kapinga and Mortlockese resulted from these programs.

The American administration's policy with regard to island group minorities on Pohnpei differed sharply from that of its German and Japanese predecessors. The German administration used resettlement of out-island people on Pohnpei as a political strategy (Bascom 1950). The Japanese administration used resettlement for economic purposes, especially to ensure itself an adequate labor supply. Both administrations ensured these resettled communities independence from their Pohnpeian neighbors. The Japanese governor, for example, ordered the paramount chief of Net to stay out of Porakied and to cease interfering in its affairs in 1930 (Lieber 1968, 77).

By 1953, the American administration had articulated a melting pot policy for out-island groups on Pohnpei that is still the administrative dogma. The policy holds that out-islanders on Pohnpei, regardless of their island of origin, would eventually become Pohnpei citizens, voting in local elections, paying taxes, speaking Pohnpeian, and participating in the feasting and title system. Administrative practice was sometimes guided by this policy (e.g., in denying the Kapinga quit claim or any other title to Porakied land) and sometimes not. American economic policy since 1960 has probably had a far greater effect on enclave boundaries than the melting pot policy ever had. The Kapinga homestead community on Pohnpei illustrates this process (Lieber 1984).

The American district administrator on Pohnpei attempted to implement the melting pot policy by means of a homesteading program in 1954. Seeing potential overpopulation on the atolls, he initiated a pilot project using administration-controlled land in Madolenihmw to resettle people from Pis-Losap, Pingelap, and Kapingamarangi (Emerick 1960). Each homesteader, with a lease on three hectares of land, was expected to improve the land with subsistence and cash crops for an eventual fee simple deed, to pay head taxes and vote in island and local elections in Madolenihmw, to speak Pohnpeian, and to participate in the feasting and title system in Madolenihmw. The Pis-Losapese and the Pingelapese had little difficulty fulfilling these expectations. Kapinga were less successful as homesteaders, and by 1966, there were but fifty-four permanent Kapinga residents on the homesteads. They had become well integrated into local affairs and received section status and section titles in late 1965. Yet they were still considered Kapinga, both by Pohnpeians and by themselves. Because they took their titles at least partly as a strategy to establish their political independence from Porakied, they became a different kind of Kapinga people rather than a different kind of Pohnpei people. Moreover, a chiefly grant of a section or

chiefdom title on Pohnpei labels a particular position that has inherent
rights and obligations vis-à-vis other labeled positions in a particular
named place. A title implies nothing about one's place of origin. The
only implication a title has about place is the presupposed commitment
of the man holding the title to people in the place—section or chiefdom
—where he accepts the title and its obligations. Island of origin (ethnicity), therefore, is completely irrelevant to the traditional feasting and
title system on Pohnpei. Nor is a title relevant to Pohnpei identity, since
there were no Pohnpei titles as such (until 1975), only chiefdom and section titles.

From 1972 to 1975, Kapinga homesteaders gradually abandoned
their homestead village and returned to live in Porakied. During this
same period several Kapinga adopted by Pohnpeians and Kapinga who
had been living in Kolonia all returned to live in Porakied. These movements were part of a larger process of disengagement from Pohnpeians
and other Micronesians with whom regular contact had formerly been
maintained. Trade friendships had almost entirely lapsed by 1977.
Porakied had become a self-made ghetto. Kapinga went into Kolonia
Town for work, medical care, or business, but for little else.

The disengagement process appears to have been the Kapinga response to the rapid economic expansion during the 1960s and the early
1970s. During this time, administrative and government-sponsored services, programs, and paid positions expanded at an almost geometric
rate. The U.S. Trust Territory of the Pacific Islands budget in 1960 was
$6 million. By 1979 it was $96 million (not including agency grants and
private agencies). The consequent growth of the Kolonia Town population and work force helped raise the wholesale price of tuna from thirteen cents per pound in 1966 to ninety cents per pound in 1980. The
growth of tourism helped create a handicraft market worth $1 million a
year by 1980. Almost anyone could get cash through handicraft production, with males and females from ages twelve through eighty producing carvings, trivets, model canoes, baskets, pocketbooks, and shell jew-
elry. This ready source of cash allowed Kapinga to convert from a mixed
cash-subsistence production-reciprocity economy to a strictly cash economy by the mid-1970s. Kapinga perceived the American-sponsored
option of commercial entrepreneurship as providing for their wants
faster, more abundantly, and at less trouble and risk than reciprocal
trade relations in the Pohnpei domain. Trade friendships could, after
all, turn out to be exploitative, and Pohnpeians were feared as sorcerers
and blamed for several deaths in the 1960s and 1970s.

The disengagement process appeared to be affecting other enclaves as
well, who, with the growth of retail stores and bingo parlors in their
own communities, were doing their buying, socializing, and drinking at

home. The streets of Kolonia Town, which had teemed with people both day and night in the 1960s, were deserted at night save for two bars of unsavory reputation by 1977.

This process of disengagement affected even the Protestant church, long the safe house for interethnic contact. In 1979, the ruling council of ministers and deacons agreed that the Kolonia church, which had been the site of Sunday services for the entire Kolonia Town population, would henceforth be used only for islandwide activities, such as choral competition among local congregations throughout the island. This decision was attributed to the desire of Pohnpeian parishioners to rid themselves of out-islanders' control of the church. While this seemed to be the opinion of many of the men who were involved in the discussions, none of them with whom I spoke (including Kapinga, Pohnpeians, Nukuoro, and Mokilese) seemed to be unhappy with the outcome. Within eight months, Sunday services were being held almost exclusively in the local synagogues.

That the relationship between Pohnpeians and other cultural minorities on their island is more sensitive to colonial economic policy than to its melting pot ideology is underscored by the fact that the administration's decision to survey the Madolenihmw homestead lands for final quit claim (or disenfranchisement) in 1979 and 1980 resulted in one-sixth of the Porakied population returning to Madolenihmw. Most of those who left Porakied were still in Madolenihmw in 1982. They had reestablished their relationships with their Pingelapese and Pohnpeian neighbors, all of whom seemed pleased and not too surprised to see them back. While they could have considered the Kapinga abandonment of their homesteads as an implicit rejection of commitment to relationships with them, they did not. While the paramount chief could have taken away the homesteaders' section status and lifted their titles, he did not. They were doing what people do—maximizing their options (Lieber 1984; Silverman 1969).

Kapinga perceptions of their relations with other island communities, then, are very much a product of their colonial experience, particularly as an ethnic community on Pohnpei. They, like other out-island enclaves, came there under the aegis of colonial powers pursuing imperial interests. Three colonial administrations have established the conditions under which out-islanders remain and maintain themselves as ethnic minorities on Pohnpei. These conditions—political, economic, and religious—have varied from time to time, and the state of interethnic relations is highly sensitive to such variation. Analysis of the nature of interethnic relations is, thus, inseparable from the analysis of the relationship between each community and the colonial government, as the consideration of ethnic stereotypes demonstrates.

Kapinga and Pohnpeian Stereotypes

A comparison of Kapinga and Pohnpeian stereotypes of other islanders
shows both striking similarities and striking differences.[3] Both Kapinga
and Pohnpeian descriptions focus on observable aspects of people's
predilection for particular styles of action and interaction—they are
sociological sketches. Both are Lamarckian in their attributions of
inheritance of patterns of interaction peculiar to a particular place. But
when we compare the sorts of observations that Kapinga and Pohnpeians focus on, important differences in stereotypes emerge. I contend
that the differences are attributable to cultural differences between the
two communities, particularly in their differing conceptions of their
relationships with colonial powers.

Pohnpeians describing other ethnic groups focus on observable patterns of activity or predilections for particular arenas of activity. They
describe Kapinga, for example, as good fishermen and craftsmen and as
strong, hard workers. But they also think of Kapinga as lacking in ambition and foresight, as unable to plan ahead. From a Pohnpeian perspective, this is a reasonably accurate description. Other than a few men
who are active in feasting, even titled Kapinga avoid participation in
feasts on Pohnpei, a participation that presupposes careful planning
and allocation of one's time and resources over a period of years. Pohnpeians also point out that very few Kapinga have prepared themselves
for administrative or teaching jobs.

Pohnpeians see Pingelapese as messy, clannish, devout and active in
church affairs, and both shrewd and very aggressive. Examples of their
clannishness are their preference for en bloc voting whenever a Pingelapese runs for public office against a non-Pingelapese and their purported tendency to route administrative jobs to other Pingelapese whenever they are in a position to do so. What Pohnpeians appear to mean by
aggressiveness is the often-mentioned Pingelapese preference for achieving middle-echelon administrative jobs, the vigor with which they pursue those positions, and their consequent prominence in those positions
on Pohnpei.

Mokilese are described by most Pohnpeian informants as ambitious,
skilled, and crafty. What is so intriguing about this description is the use
of aggressive for Pingelapese and ambitious for Mokilese. When I asked
for examples, informants pointed to the prominence of Mokilese in
upper echelons of colonial administration—particularly in the former
Congress of Micronesia and the present Congress of the Federated States
of Micronesia—and in highly skilled technical jobs over which they
have a virtual monopoly, such as machinists and mechanics. They are
considered very subtle and charming while being very manipulative,
particularly in political contexts.

If one takes all of these stereotypes together, they do in fact describe something about the larger Pohnpei social order. Kapinga, to the extent that they are visible at all, are people of the marketplace. They are the suppliers of fish and the purveyors of handicrafts and are otherwise not very visible. Pingelapese have been prominent in church affairs on Pohnpei and in middle-level administration in various agencies, including the hospital and the education department. Mokilese are in fact prominent in upper-echelon administration, especially in Congress. For example, during elections for the Congress of the Federated States of Micronesia in 1979, Mokilese men were candidates for 60 percent of the seats allotted to Pohnpei State. Pohnpeians are prominent at all these levels. From their point of view, that is to be expected, for Pohnpeians consider Pohnpei to be very much their island. Their ethnic descriptions identify whom they believe to be their competitors for control over affairs on the island, and they allude to the contexts of competition. In each case, descriptions focus on the issue of control in the colonial arena. Pingelapese and Mokilese people have been and still are active in the feasting and title system, some having very high titles. Yet no Pohnpeian ever mentioned this in discussions about them. When asked why Kapinga, Pingelapese, and Mokilese are the way they are, Pohnpeian informants responded with answers such as, "They do what their parents did," or "They grow up with the *tiahk* 'customs' of their island."

Kapinga descriptions of other island groups put no emphasis on political position and greater emphasis on skills and interpersonal proclivities than do Pohnpeian descriptions. Pingelapese are considered dirty and "careless" in their personal habits, easily angered, clannish, vengeful, very enterprising, and very religious. They are considered powerful curers and sorcerers, good organizers of businesses, and hard workers for their families and friends. Kapinga never pointed to Pingelapese administrative positions in their descriptions.

Mokilese, according to Kapinga, are good at fishing, working, learning mechanical skills (such as boat building), and organizing. Several Kapinga referred to Mokilese as being very personable, but said that one never knows if a Mokilese is really one's friend. In discussing Mokilese organizing abilities, Kapinga informants pointed to their work in reorganizing the Kolonia Protestant church in 1980. While Kapinga recognize the prominence of Mokilese in Congress, they appear not to think of that fact as particularly definitive of Mokilese.

What strikes Kapinga as being distinctive about Pohnpeians is their haughtiness (putting themselves before others), their capacity for being extremely generous, and their unpredictable displays of almost gratuitous hostility. The charge of haughtiness has to do with the condescension with which Pohnpeians often treat Kapinga and with the ways that Kapinga see higher and lower ranking people interact. Kapinga cite numerous examples of Pohnpeian generosity, both on the part of chiefs and of ordinary people, particularly during World War II, when Kapinga had to leave Porakied and seek shelter in U and Kiti. At the same time, Kapinga fear Pohnpeians as sorcerers. They cite several deaths over the past few years that they attribute to sorcery by Pohnpeians who were supposedly friends of the deceased.

I asked about one other group, the Nukuoro, with whom the Kapinga have long had close relations of reciprocity and intermarriage. While Kapinga gave detailed descriptions, Pohnpeians ventured no opinions whatever, saying only that they did not know anything about them. One can predict that Nukuoro do not form a politically or socially visible group on Pohnpei, and this is in fact the case (Carroll 1977).

We see that three Pohnpeian ethnic stereotypes (and one category empty of content) concentrate attention on the place that each ethnic group holds in the larger colonial arena of commercial and administrative control over persons, resources, and policies. Each stereotype is referable to the particular sorts of contexts in which members of each out-island enclave exercise political and economic control in the colonial administrative domain. Kapinga concentrate their attention on those observable patterns of interaction that are relevant to face-to-face dyadic interaction, such as visiting, friendship, hospitality, and reciprocity. Generosity, fairness, and trustworthiness are attended to, while political position in the larger order is not.

The obvious question is, what accounts for this difference between the Pohnpeian focus on the distribution of control and the Kapinga focus on symmetrical, reciprocal relations? It can be partly explained by differences in how Kapinga and Pohnpeians institutionalize personhood and partly by different cultural premises that have shaped the ways in which the two peoples have experienced colonial domination.

The Pohnpeian Concept of the Person and Its Institutional Context

Pohnpeians appear to define personhood consocially, as do the Kapinga. Also like the Kapinga, Pohnpeians perceive the person's inner self as concealed and controlled, while the public demeanor presented to others is cultivated and subject to constant scrutiny. The greater the disparity between the inner content and the outer persona, the greater the respect accorded, especially to men, who are most subject to the constraints of shame and embarrassment (Falgout 1984, 116). Unlike the Kapinga, Pohnpeians do not cultivate personal uniquenesses as public styles. Elaborate rules of etiquette in fact standardize public demeanor. One's potentials and capabilities are expected to be demonstrated (and not talked about) when the occasion demands, for example, by showing courage when threatened, displaying one's agricultural skill in presentations to the paramount chief at feasts, or demonstrating one's songwriting skill when called upon at a feast to entertain. What a person's actual skills and capabilities are is the subject of much of everyday conversation (Falgout 1984, 121). These assessments, like those by Kapinga of one another, are partly based on what people are known to inherit from the experience of residence in particular places and from being members of particular families.

Matrilineal clans and subclans, whose histories of incorporation into the social order form a large portion of Pohnpeian accounts of the origin of their island, are associated with particular personal attributes, such as forcefulness, immunity to embarrassment, special virtuosity in certain kinds of cultivation, and luck (Falgout 1984, 124). Particular places on Pohnpei, from whole sections to subsections to individual farmsteads, are also associated with personal attributes said to be inherited cognatically. Petersen (1982a) tells us that the Awak section in U is associated with a spirit of political independence based on a long history of resistance to the domination of the paramount chief. Falgout gives examples of subsections and farmsteads whose histories are embedded in persons who grow up there as inherited personal attributes (1984, 122–123). These features of personal distinctiveness owing to place of birth and family are clearly Lamarckian.

The Lamarckian character of Pohnpeian social categories is further underscored by the fact that, according to Glenn Petersen (pers. comm.), one can change an infant's lineage by feeding it premasticated breadfruit from the land of its new lineage. The importance of substance here is striking in comparison with the Kainantu and Mandok. As in these two societies, the ingestion of substance from a place is constitutive of personal identity as part of a specific set of social relationships. But for Pohnpeians as for Kapinga, the substance is cultivated, a product of human labor. The level of social category, moreover, is not that of an entire community, but the lower-order category of lineage.

On Pohnpei, as on Kapinga, people's assessments of a person's potentials also depend on what Falgout (1984, 121) calls "running biographies," (i.e., personal histories of social interaction and distinctive achievement). But similarities to Kapinga personhood end here. The shape of Pohnpei personal biographies is determined by sets of relationships whose structure, while formally similar to the traditional Kapinga priesthood, permeates the Pohnpei social order in a way that the Kapinga priesthood never did. While Kapinga develop personal styles and specialties that publicly distinguish people as unique, the social order of Pohnpei accomplished the matter of public uniqueness through the distribution of chiefdom and section titles. These titles could be seen as roles, since they labeled specific tasks in the chiefdom or section organization before colonial domination. But the titles were far more than task labels. They were, and continue to be, all-encompassing personal identities, much as village titles are for the Balinese (Geertz 1973). Personal names on precolonial Pohnpei were never used in public, for they were known only to one's parents and oneself. Children were given appellative nicknames for use in reference and address until a man, or a woman's husband, received a title. Thereafter, one was referred to and addressed by the title. One's public career could be assessed by the succession of titles one acquired through activity in a section or state.

Chiefdoms and sections on Pohnpei have been and continue to be sociopolitical entities. The precolonial paramount chief was not only a sacred personage, but also the titular owner of all the land of his polity (Riesenberg 1968, 63). Working through the talking chief, he used both land and titles to control people, sections, and the relationships between sections. It was in the sections that cooperative activity was performed, including the production of crops and military hardware. The section was a military unit in warfare. The section chief was and continues to be responsible for the level of agricultural production and the performance of his section in local and state feasts. Like paramount chiefs, the section chief uses titles to reward and encourage participation in feasts and to punish lack of participation (Petersen 1982a).

A title on Pohnpei clearly constitutes a personal identity in a sociopolitical context. Personal identities are part and parcel of the identity and destiny of the section and chiefdom. But what of the island as a whole? That precolonial Pohnpeians had a sense of themselves as a single category is implied by their distinction between *tiahk en Pohnpei* 'customs of the island' and *tiahk en sapw* 'customs of the land' (referring to more local entities). What the content of the larger category might have been is not at all clear, however. Examination of the structure of Pohnpei oral history allows us to make some plausible inferences about that larger category.

Pohnpei oral history describes an ancient era during which the island was peopled by successive arrivals of canoes with people and spirits from elsewhere (Bernart 1977; Hambruch and Eilers 1936). Each new arrival marked a contribution of new people, new skills, and new elements of social practice to a developing social order. Accounts of later arrivals of groups of outsiders chronicle conquests by the immigrants, who assume political leadership in one or more states, sometimes changing the details of the local title structure, sometimes not. Some conquerors attempted to extend their domination to encompass the entire island, never with complete success. All became incorporated into the preexisting title system, most often as clans. Thus, later oral history of contact between Pohnpei and people of other islands is, like the earlier history, about the process of incorporation, but it is here a political history of warfare and subsequent negotiation. The point is that whatever the content of the category—Pohnpei person—before colonial domination, that identity had to do with the incorporation of social and cultural differences as a political process.

Precolonial Pohnpei identity, then, was political identity, as postcolonial identity has been, though clearly in a different way. This is equally true of Kainantu and Mandok, and of the Pulapese, whose identity as part of the Yapese empire was certainly politicized. One can cite Samoa (Shore 1982) and the precolonial Marshall Islands (Mason 1947), divided into groups of warring atolls under four paramount chiefs, as examples of precolonial politicized identities. The question is not whether politicized identity shapes boundaries between communities that we can call ethnic boundaries. This clearly has been the case since long before colonial contact. Instead, the question is, in what specific ways does the experience of colonial domination bring about change in the way communities identify themselves and one another? And at what levels of a social or cultural system are changes embedded and manifest? I will attempt to answer these questions by comparing Pohnpei and Kapinga responses to colonial domination.

Colonial Domination on Pohnpei and Kapingamarangi

Colonial contact began on Pohnpei in about 1830, and during the succeeding fifty years, Pohnpeians were exposed to European traders, ships' personnel, beachcombers, and missionaries. Pohnpei chiefs employed many of these people as liaisons in trade and by 1880 were quite familiar with them and their technology. Spain was the first power to try to establish colonial control, meeting with local resistance that culminated in its garrison being destroyed and sacked. The Germans, who assumed control from Spain in 1898, also met armed resistance but used military force to establish colonial domination on Pohnpei.

German policy was aimed at stripping the chiefs of political and economic power. A good deal of land was expropriated as "public domain" by the administration, and what remained was converted to plots held in fee simple by individuals. Land titles explicitly carried a clause limiting the number of feasts a landowner was obligated to give to the Nahnmwarki. The prohibition of warfare undermined the chiefs' military power, while conversion to Christianity removed the substance of their ritual power.

Although these changes had the socially differentiating effects for which they were designed, most of their demographic and political results were the opposite of what the Germans intended. Instead of settling people on their own lands, the new land laws resulted in increased personal mobility, since one could leave his land to go elsewhere for long periods without fear of violence or of the Nahnmwarki taking one's land and giving it to another. It also meant that one could pursue status aspirations in any number of other sections or chiefdoms, since one no longer had to worry about warfare in exercising one's options. Pohnpeians never considered abandoning their most important avenues for personal advancement, and chiefs still had the power to confer and remove titles. The avenues for competition had narrowed with the prohibition of warfare, but that simply put more emphasis on feasting as the principal means of attaining higher titles.

German policy aimed at obliterating the feasting and title system only succeeded in galvanizing a common response to the threat posed by the colonial regime to the very foundations of personal and group identities. That policy and the Pohnpei response to it resulted in permanently demarcating the colonial system and the traditional social order as separate, competing domains, encoded in the common phrase, "things of the office, things of the people." The Spanish and German colonial administrations provided the Pohnpeians' first experience with outside powers that would try to control the local social order without becoming part of it, violating the assumption of incorporation of outside conquerors.

Two other colonial policies made the emergence of separate domains and resulting ethnic identities on Pohnpei inevitable. One was that the colonialists thought of and treated Pohnpeians as a single category. Instead of distinguishing among polities on Pohnpei, colonialists lumped them together as on a par with Trukese, Mokilese, Kapinga, Palauans, etc. The categorical implications of the German threat to the feasting and title system reinforced this distinction as germane to Pohnpei people. Furthermore, German and Japanese use of resettlement of out-island groups served to contextualize the presence of the latter on Pohnpei. The colonial regime, after all, had brought them there, sponsored them, given them land expropriated from Pohnpei chiefs, and ensured their safety from encroachment by Pohnpeians. The very presence of particular out-island communities on Pohnpei, either as temporary laborers or as permanent settlers, was a political act in a colonial political context. Kapinga identity was politicized vis-à-vis Pohnpeians (whether or not the Kapinga ever realized it) as part of the same process that had politicized Pohnpeian identity. As Japanese and American administrations have incorporated Micronesians into the bureaucracy that controls Pohnpei, the issues of control in the colonial domain further elaborate the arenas in which politicized identities—ethnic identities—are competitively visible to Pohnpeians.

Ethnic identities are socially relevant today in the world of administrative contacts, bureaucratic positions, education, commerce, medical care, church, and recreational settings of bars, movies, sports competition, and pool halls. Even in the solidary context of trade friendships, the term for *friend* is neither the Pohnpei nor the Kapinga word, but the Japanese *kompani*. In this colonial context, Pohnpeians see their interests threatened by the colonialists' sponsorship of out-islanders for positions of authority in the distribution of jobs, land, and goods on what they still insist is their island. The Pohnpei tradition of resistance to colonial authority makes it clear that they may have resigned themselves to the reality of colonial control, but never to its legitimacy, as is demonstrated by the Pohnpeian vote against the Compact of Free Association with the United States in 1983 (Petersen 1984). Thus, ethnic identity and political, economic, and ritual control are seen as major, interrelated problems by Pohnpeians. It should not be surprising that this problem is reflected in the structure of modern Pohnpeian ethnic imagery.

We have already seen that the domain of traditional feasting and titles is one in which place of origin is irrelevant to the identities of the people involved. Ethnicity is irrelevant in that domain for that reason. If, for example, a man has a title in the Awak section of U, the fact that he may have been born and raised in another section or chiefdom or island is irrelevant to his relations with others at an Awak feast. Thus, Kapinga can accept section titles as a community and still remain Kapinga. Their titles are relevant in the feasting domain, and their identities as Kapinga are relevant in the colonial domain.

In the precontact period, authority on Kapingamarangi was vested in the owners or managers of land, in the headmen of men's houses, and, most important, in the ritual order of the priesthood, particularly in the high priest. The structure of the priesthood, as described by Emory (1965, 319 and the following pages), is a dual organization that is strikingly similar to both the Pohnpei and the Samoan title systems. Its two lines of priests, one under the ritual priest and the other under the "calling" priest, were asymmetrically ranked such that each position in the ritual priest's line outranked its counterpart in the other line. Like Pohnpei titles, eligibility for the priesthood was transmitted matrilineally. The ritual order was designed specifically to deal with the gods and with upkeep of the cult house. The relationship between people and gods in Kapinga ritual had one central focus—food and its abundance. The high priest maintained his position for only as long as he proved effective in using his relationship with the gods to ensure the provision of fish and plant food and safety of people from disaster, such as droughts.

The evolution of secular authority on Kapingamarangi is a postcontact phenomenon. A minor functionary of the men's house associated with the cult house became responsible for dealing with ship captains and other European visitors after 1877. His close association with these people yielded both personal wealth and economic power over the copra trade. He was known as the "king" by Europeans. By the time of the collapse of the priesthood in 1917, when it became clear that nothing that the succession of high priests could do was going to alleviate the drought, the Kapinga were more than willing to entertain the notion that their conception of the gods was mistaken. Relief from starvation and thirst in 1917 came not from the sky but from the hold of a government ship in the form of drinking coconuts and taro sent from Nukuoro along with a Nukuoro missionary and church elders. The conversion of the Kapinga population was accomplished in a matter of weeks, and by 1918 the old cult house had been burned to the ground. This left the "king" in the sole position of authority. It is critical to note that in both the precontact sacred and postcontact secular realms, the basis of authority was the responsibility for dealing with powerful outsiders—gods and foreigners.

Though the gods were no longer a social category to be reckoned with, the Kapinga never doubted the underlying premise that control originates ultimately from outside the island. There was a being named Jehovah that would take some time to comprehend, but there was a much more immediate colonial presence whose structure was not much different (or differently perceived) from the old gods. That the same techniques that seemed to work with the gods also worked to procure tangible benefits from the colonialists (sweet words, accommodation to expressed wishes, offerings of food and labor) lent to the colonial powers a legitimacy that Kapinga have never seemed to question. Secular and ritual authority were combined when the king became the leader of the new (Protestant) church. But this connection was severed in 1955 with the death of the last king. His son, nominated to succeed him, refused the position, opting instead to become the island's first chief magistrate. Church and secular authority have competed for preeminence in policy making since then, but Kapinga (even church members) often say, "If the church is supposed to lead us, then how is it that the 'office' (i.e., the government) is the one that provides the bags of rice?"

Control and its legitimacy are not an issue for Kapinga. The problem for them is how to get access to the valued resources that the colonialists control and avoid the hazards of dealing with powerful people. Kapinga see other islanders controlled by the same colonial power and struggling to get the same benefits. They see themselves, therefore, as related symmetrically to other islanders as more or less in the same boat. In contrast to Pohnpeian voters, Kapinga voted overwhelmingly for the Compact of Free Association with the United States, but only because it was the only alternative to total independence. The Kapinga would prefer the continued administrative authority of the United States to an independent nation that would involve transfer of control to local islanders like themselves. Yet it has been extremely confusing and frustrating for Kapinga to deal with an American administration that simultaneously expands its services to provide for islanders' welfare while demanding self-help proposals and ordinances (which they often veto) from the islanders. In other words, the Pohnpeian relationship to the colonial administration has been one of ambivalent resignation, mistrust, and competitive manipulation. The Kapinga relationship to the same administration has been one of unrequited dependency.

The difference between the Pohnpeian and the Kapinga ethnic stereotypes, then, is attributable to cultural differences in the organization of the two societies' perceptions of the larger social universe and, consequently, to differences in their responses to the same colonial administrations. In particular, the location of power and control in the two cultural universes structures Pohnpeian and Kapinga responses. For the Kapinga, the legitimacy of power depends on the agents of power remaining outside and apart from the local social order. For Pohnpeians, it is the opposite; legitimacy depends on the agents of power becoming incorporated into the social order.[4]

Conclusion: Culture and Identity

Linnekin and Poyer (chapter 1) posit a distinction between cultural and ethnic identities. These terms label what are ethnographically real differences among the societies described in this volume. There are those societies, such as Kapinga, Kainantu, Mandok, and Pulap, in which (what I call) ethnic identities are local affairs, concentrating on differences between categories of persons with whom people are in regular, face-to-face contact in various, specifiable contexts. There are also societies, such as Maori, Pohnpei, and Hawaii, in which ethnic identities have developed in contradistinction to colonial masters (and their agents). These identities become emblems of political constituencies that are engaged in struggles for enfranchisement. The objectification of the constituency's culture, body of custom, or community serves as a strategy for mobilizing adherents and legitimating both the constituency's identity and its claims on the dominant power. As labels for these obviously significant differences, the cultural/ethnic identity distinction forces us to direct attention to accounting for these differences. But these are undoubtedly gross differences painted in bold strokes. Closer examination of the ethnographic details of each case reveals more fine-grained differences in the processes that shape the identities of communities, lower-level groups and categories, and persons.

Just as politicized identities are not peculiar to Pohnpeians, Maori, and Hawaiians (who in some ways resemble what we think of as ethnic groups in our Western sense), neither is objectification of culture, custom, or community limited to these groups. There is ample evidence that objectification of culture, custom, and/or community is common in Oceania, particularly among migrant and relocated communities faced with reconciling traditional ideology with current realities in order to make a decision about some particular community problem (Kiste 1974; Larson 1977; Lieber 1977a; Schwimmer 1977; Silverman 1971, 1977b; Tonkinson 1977). Objectification in these cases is an internal affair of the community, emerging in discussion and debate as a necessary strategy for contextualizing the particular issue under consideration. For example, the struggle of the Kapinga homestead community (described above) to maintain their political autonomy from the Porakied community forced members of both groups to objectify the concept of "Kapinga community" and to delineate its components (Lieber 1977a, 56–58; Lieber 1984, 152). Tikopia resettled in the Russell Islands found themselves under constant pressure to reconcile custom (by which they define themselves as unique) with noncustomary expedients that enabled them to establish and maintain their new community. Eventually, the nature of custom became an explicit issue with the suggestion that the intent of a custom can be legitimately realized without replicating its exact form (Larson 1977, 260, 266). Banabans resettling on Rambi Island were forced to replicate a culture whose details were no longer clear to them. Banaban culture was and remains an explicit issue in this community (Silverman 1971, 1977b).

It is not the fact of politicized identities or the fact of the objectification of culture that distinguishes Oceanic communities as different in the processes of delineating identities, but the particular *forms* politicization and objectification take. These different forms are realized as parts of different cultural (symbolic) and sociopolitical *contexts*. More specifically, what we are analyzing are the relationships between particular communities and the precolonial, colonial, and postcolonial macrosystems that have structured relationships between local communities. These relationships constitute the context of which particular communities and their processes of identification are part (Bateson

1972, 275–276). To the extent that these relationships are different, then the contexts differ. Pohnpeians and Kapinga have had very different relationships with the same colonial administrations. The structure of the contexts within which they identify themselves and other communities and, therefore, the contexts themselves, are different. I have demonstrated that the culture of these two groups is the critical variable determining the difference between their larger sociopolitical contexts. These cultural differences have shaped both their responses to their contexts—colonial domination as interpreted by each—and to the other island groups that are parts of their different colonial contexts.

By way of contrast, Pohnpeians and Maori, with different colonial masters and history, have developed an almost identical response to colonialists. Both have invented new cultural domains to encompass the colonialists (Pohnpeian *mehn waii* and Maori *pakeha*) who could not and would not be incorporated into the native political system. The Pohnpei feasting and title system and the Maori *tangi* (chapter 10) have been identically recontextualized in the modern colonial context. Each serves not only its older ceremonial and political ends, but also emblematizes the distinction between the continuous, traditional domain and the discontinuous, intrusive colonial domain. Both have become diacritics of ethnic boundaries in Barth's (1969) sense.

My argument, then, is a cultural one. Understanding ethnicity in Oceania, as anywhere else, is possible only by understanding the cultural premises that constrain people's perceptions of the human world of which they are part. We must understand Oceanic cultures at several levels when confronting the problem of ethnicity. One is at the very abstract, implicit level of premises that define the person and human ontogeny—environmental determinism and its logical corollary of the consocial person. This level of premise surely distinguishes Oceanic thinking about categories of persons from their Euro-American counterparts but does not distinguish between different Oceanic societies. Distinctions between different Oceanic societies are found at a less abstract but still implicit level of premise about the relationship between the community and the structure of its environment, and at the yet less abstract level of premises about the structure of the relationships within which personhood is enacted. The highest order of premise appears to be commonly shared in Oceania, while the lower orders of premise show much more variability. I contend that this hierarchy of premises structures people's perceptions of others and of their contexts of interaction, and that they show a continuity between precolonial and colonial and postcolonial changes. The structure of particular regional and colonial systems, of economic and political conditions, surely matters in the

analysis of each ethnographic case, but only as these conditions are construed by the people we study. Human communities are not billiard
balls and cannot be analyzed as such.

NOTES

The data on which this chapter is based were collected during two periods of
field research, the first during 1965–1966 while working on the Pacific Displaced Communities Project (directed by Homer G. Barnett), and the second
during 1978–1980 and 1982 doing research partially supported by the Office of
Social Science Research and the Graduate School Research Fund at University
of Illinois at Chicago. I am indebted to James Watson, Emily Schultz, Mary
Catherine Bateson, Fred Errington, Deborah Gewertz, Ali Pomponio, and Lin
Poyer for their contributions to the thinking and writing that went into this
chapter.

1. While all of these interdictions presuppose a notion of environmental
determinism, we see that only those on how parents act are Lamarckian in the
strict sense of the term. Those interdictions on what the mother sees or how she
sits presuppose the child's being or looking different from the parents. That is
certainly determinism by the environment but just as certainly non-Lamarckian. I am grateful to Mary Catherine Bateson for pointing this out to me in a
personal communication.

2. Implied in both Lamarck's and the Kapinga versions of the Lamarckian
idea is fundamental duality between that which is more or less stable structure
(e.g., mammalian physiology) and that which is contingent on how the environment impinges on the population. In Kapinga terms the duality is manifest
as that which is categorical and that which is contingent (see Lieber 1984, 165–
167 for Kapinga and Pohnpei examples). While some sorts of identity are malleable, ambiguous, or contingent on the situation, such as one's family, other
identities such as male and female are categorical and do not vary with the situation. As Vern Carroll (1970a) has demonstrated for the Nukuoro, practices
such as adoption bring the categorical nature of the parent-child relationship
and biological assumptions underlying it into direct conflict with the premise
that social parenthood is contingent on the present needs, desires, and schemes
of one's kinsmen. Watson (1983) has demonstrated the pervasive implications of
the premise of a contingent universe for Tairora culture, Lamarckian identity
structure being one manifestation. Genealogy, as Watson has shown, is put at
the service of political contingencies to charter coresident personnel as a group.
One has or does not have a Tairora or Kapinga ancestor—and that is a difference that makes a difference. Given a Kapinga ancestor (and gender), however,
the attribution of identity is contingent on which ancestor and which family, on
the biographies of the ancestor's descendants, and on one's own biography.

3. I worked with 42 informants, mainly Pohnpeians, for two periods of six
weeks during 1978 and 1979 and again briefly during the summer of 1982. My
data on Kapinga stereotypes were collected first in 1966 from 280 adults of both

sexes and rechecked with 33 informants in 1982. I have not included group stereotypes from any groups other than Pohnpeians and Kapinga, however, because I do not think my data from the other groups are detailed or reliable enough to warrant their inclusion.

4. This is a perfect example of what Bateson (1972; Reusch and Bateson 1951) and Mead (1977) have called "end linkage."

5

We Still Have Our Customs: Being Pulapese in Truk

JULIANA FLINN

Although the concept of ethnicity developed in a Western context and connotes common biological inheritance (Linnekin and Poyer, chapter 1), recent writers on the subject have highlighted some important aspects of the formulation of group identities. Of particular importance to this chapter is the insight that cultural identity emerges through interaction with others, and may shift or crystallize under the impact of new external circumstances such as political changes or industrialization (De Vos and Romanucci-Ross 1975; Hicks 1977b). Group identity can be a manipulative tool in the pursuit of political power or economic advantage (Cohen 1969; Keyes 1981; Stone 1977; Vincent 1974). Other writers note that ethnic identity is often situationally variable (Berreman 1975; Hicks 1977a; Moerman 1965; Nagata 1974; Schiller 1977; Uchendu 1975). Individual group affiliation can be fluid and flexible; although boundaries between groups remain salient, personnel and cultural content can fluctuate (Barth 1969).

These observations are useful for understanding formulations of cultural identity among the people of Pulap, an atoll in the outer islands of Truk State in the Federated States of Micronesia. Pulapese cultural identity, like that of Sapwuahfik (Poyer, chapter 6), is not highly politicized as is aboriginal identity in Hawaii and New Zealand, where white, Western society is defined as the "other" (Dominy, chapter 11; Linnekin, chapter 7; Sinclair, chapter 10). Interaction with other islanders in Truk State is the principal arena in which Pulapese cultural identity is formulated. Pulapese use certain myths about their past, stories of historical events, and a number of indigenous customs to assert their unique cultural identity in this context.[1]

Pulap Atoll is the northernmost of the Western Islands in the Central Carolines and has two inhabited islets, Pulap and Tamatam. Pulap lies at the northern end of the reef and is much larger in area and population. Two other atolls in the Western Islands lie farther south: Puluwat, acknowledged as chief of the group, and Pulusuk. Pulap has about four

103

hundred people, the Western Islands as a whole about thirteen hundred (United States Department of State 1980).

The Western Islands are all low, coral atolls, as are the other outer islands of Truk: Namonuito Atoll to the north, the Hall Islands to the northeast, and the Mortlocks to the southeast (see Map 3). The centrally located islands of Truk Lagoon, including the administrative center of Moen, are volcanic high islands about 130 miles east of Pulap. The outer islands are serviced from Moen by government ships that ferry cargo, passengers, and services in and out of Truk Lagoon.

Pulap and the other Westerns have been the least touched by the outside world but have nonetheless been affected by the changes in administration of Truk. Although the Spanish discovered both Truk Lagoon and Pulap Atoll in the sixteenth century, Europeans largely ignored the area until the late 1800s, when German commercial interests led to a dispute with Spain over control of the islands. Germany eventually purchased the islands after the Spanish-American War. The major impact of German rule on the Western Islands was ending interisland warfare. Germans also forcibly took a few Pulap men to work elsewhere in Micronesia and tried unsuccessfully to purchase Pulap land for coconut plantations. Japan seized the islands in 1914 after declaring war on Germany. The Japanese then continued the practice of forced labor but also sent a few Pulap boys to school in Truk Lagoon. The United States took over in 1945 after World War II and implemented medical and educational programs. In July 1978 Truk joined Yap, Pohnpei, and Kosrae in ratifying the Constitution of the Federated States of Micronesia, and in 1986 a compact of free association negotiated with the United States was finally implemented.

These changing political, social, and economic realities have created changing contexts for negotiation of identities. Furthermore, Lieber (chapter 4) describes how cultural perceptions of other social groups interact with the political and economic context in shaping group identities. In the Pulap case, many attitudes and stereotypes reflect cultural beliefs about historical relations with other islands and with foreign administrations, and others have arisen more recently with increased contact with other islanders and new patterns of social interaction precipitated by the American administration. Pulapese traditionally traveled to, traded with, and fought against other Central Caroline Islanders, and Pulap beliefs about these relations continue today to structure relationships. Pulapese tend to interpret interaction with people of several other island groups as reflecting or resurrecting previous patterns. An election, for example, replays an old battle.

The contemporary context differs in significant ways from the past, however. New—but limited—political, educational, and employment

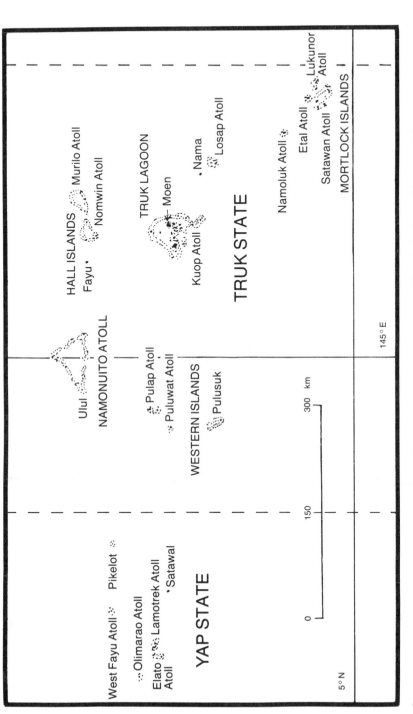

Map 3. Truk State and the eastern portion of Yap State, Central Caroline Islands, Federated States of Micronesia. Drawn by Diana Breneiser-Renfro.

opportunities are becoming available. As the island's young people pursue secondary education and then college degrees and jobs, the volume
of migration from Pulap and the average length of absence have
increased. Patterns of interaction with other islanders have shifted as
well, especially with the growth of Moen, Truk's administrative center,
and the American emphasis on formal schooling. Cultural beliefs about
past relations with other islanders, perceptions of contemporary cultural differences, and the constraints and opportunities of this modern
political and economic context interact to shape Pulapese formulations
of identity.

Pulapese and other Western Islanders lagged behind others in Truk in
pursuing education, wage labor, political offices, and other opportunities. From their perspective, as well as that of others in Truk, they are
the most traditional people in the area. They still sail canoes and navi-
gate with traditional lore. Men still wear loincloths, and women wear
lavalavas. Sisters still bend low and speak respectfully for their brothers. Pulapese today contend for a position in a modernizing Micronesia
in a context in which they and others view them as among the least
modern participants.

Instead of accepting an image of themselves as backward and primitive, however, Pulapese transform these potentially negative attributes
into positive aspects of their identity. Yet to do so, they have to resolve
an apparent paradox: they present themselves simultaneously as former
warriors, fierce and brave, and as peaceful, respectful, modest, and
caring. They do so by manipulating two levels of nested cultural identities (cf. Cohen 1978; Linnekin, chapter 7). On the one hand, through a
Western Islands identity they can refer to their past and an alliance with
a belligerent neighbor, but through a Pulapese identity they can both
disclaim the past and dissociate themselves from other islanders and
their perceived faults. These people may be Pulapese in some instances
and Western Islanders in others; aspects of both contribute to formulations of Pulapese cultural identity.

Defining Pulap Identity: Kinship and Customs

Decisions about whether or not a given individual is a citizen of Pulap
can be made in ways similar to those found on other atolls of Micronesia
(Marshall 1975; Nason 1975; Poyer, chapter 6) and are based on such
criteria as residence, behavior, kin ties, descent, and rights to land. For
many individuals, the decision is unproblematic; they are people of
Pulap, with no claims to citizenship elsewhere. For others, such as those
married to or adopted by other islanders, the situation is more ambigu-

ous, especially when they have land rights on more than one island. For example, someone married to a Pulap woman and living with her descent group may in some contexts be considered Pulapese and in others a citizen of his natal island.

But who is and who is not Pulapese is not yet a pressing question for Pulap islanders. They are not usually preoccupied with making categorical distinctions about an individual's citizenship, nor are they much concerned with the question of how a person can become Pulapese. They ask different questions. What kin relationships do people have? How do they fulfill kin obligations? What rights to land do they have and how are they exercised? How do individuals behave? Is that behavior good or bad? Instead of asking who is Pulapese, or how one can become Pulapese, a more appropriate question is how a good Pulapese behaves. The answer is based on their notions of being a good person, and to be a good person one must first and foremost be a good relative. This is consistent with Lieber's contention that cultural conceptions of the person structurally resemble characterizations of larger social categories (chapter 4), and further, that for Pacific Islanders in general, a person is above all someone with a network of relations with other persons. And Pulapese are concerned with how one behaves toward those others, particularly kin. Since kinship is demonstrated by and contingent on behavior (cf. Howard, chapter 12), being a good relative involves exhibiting respectful and nurturant behavior. Like the Kapingamarangi, Pulapese focus on interpersonal interaction to demonstrate character. For Pulapese the archetype of nurturant behavior is sharing food. The primary referent of *mwéngé* 'food' is cooked, starchy staples grown on land, and Pulapese commonly speak of "eating" from a particular plot of land. In other words, sharing food both demonstrates kinship and symbolizes the sharing of land. In this way Pulapese are typical of Pacific Islanders, for whom kin relations and land are fundamental to identity (Howard, chapter 12).

Pulapese are concerned with the related question of how the behavior of other islanders differs from that of Pulapese. Pulapese cultural identity is formulated in contrast with and in relation to other islanders. In general Pulapese view themselves as superior to other islanders because they behave as good people and practice valued customs and traditions —especially those having to do with respect and sharing among kin— that others have either already lost or may soon lose. Losing traditional customs, being ungenerous, showing bad character, failing to act as good kin—all are related concepts for Pulapese. Other islanders are characterized as having lost their customs, as evidenced by behavior demonstrating that they do not behave as good kin. Furthermore, when Pulapese establish relationships with other islanders, they do so by activating or creating kin ties. In other words, a cultural "other" who behaves appropriately can become a relative.

The Pulapese word for custom is *ééreni*, which also means 'be accustomed to, be used to', and is derived from *é* 'be learned, learn' (Goodenough and Sugita 1980, 63–64). The term is important in relation to beliefs about how children learn who their kin are and how they should behave toward them (cf. Thomas 1978, 81–90). This usage also sheds light on Pulap beliefs about acquiring attitudes and patterns of behavior through the process of "accustoming." Children learn to feel an emotional bond with kin through becoming familiar with them, and they learn how to behave properly by getting used to or familiar with what is expected of them. The belief is "that individuals develop a predilection for that to which they are accustomed" (Thomas 1978, 68–69). Furthermore, the way in which a cultural "other" can become a relative is through the same process of accustoming. When two people, even from different communities, become accustomed to each other, they may form the emotional bond necessary to become kin. This process requires considerable interpersonal interaction.

Pulapese contend that many of their customs emerged on Pulap itself. In the words of one informant, Pulap was a cultural warehouse for other islands, the source of many customs and ceremonies, the most important of which was the art of navigation. Even their name for the island, *Pwollap*, supposedly means the center or origin of navigation, from *ppwo* 'to be initiated as a navigator' and *lap* 'big' or 'important'. This belief is a source of considerable pride for the island, and Pulapese derive self-esteem from other islanders' acknowledgment that navigation originated on Pulap.[2]

In fact, the myth Pulapese most eagerly tell concerns how Haakúr, the first navigator and a Pulap god, obtained the secrets of navigation from a bird. One of the names given to Pulap, *fanútóópw* 'misty, or gray island', refers to Haakúr's ability to protect Pulap by making it invisible to the giant predatory bird that had previously eaten the people of other islands. This bird eventually revealed the secrets of navigation, and Haakúr was soon accepted, with the spread of navigation, as a god by the navigators of other islands. Honor was—and on occasion still is—accorded Pulap as a result. For instance, Pulapese say that no one should pass a Pulap canoe, and if one from Pulap and another from elsewhere are both visiting an island, the Pulap canoe must be allowed to leave first, or the other canoe risks developing problems at sea. Pulapese tell a recent story of a renowned Puluwat navigator who left the turtle island of Pikelot while a Pulap canoe remained; a storm caused him to drift far from his course.[3]

Other names for the island and associated myths are cited with pride by the people of Pulap today: *fanehoomeh* 'ghost island', *faneyanu* 'spirit island', and *fanirah* 'holy, or sacred island'. Pulapese contend these labels reflect the belief that strong and powerful magic has existed on the island, and a lack of respect for Pulap has caused people to sicken and die. Even today navigators should select one of these alternative names for Pulap as a sign of respect when approaching the island or risk falling ill.

Pulap believed Haakúr to be a powerful god, capable even of defeating a Yap magician, the most powerful and feared of sorcerers. When a foreign ship's cannon frightened the Pulapese, the god is said to have sunk it. And during World War II, Haakúr reputedly protected Pulap, shielding it from bombs. Another label for the island has been *fanekut* 'small island', which Pulapese interpret to mean that despite its size, the island is dangerous. Pulapese abandoned their former religious ceremonies with conversion to Catholicism, but these myths and beliefs remain part of their heritage and a source of pride, especially with respect to people of other islands, both within and beyond the Westerns.

Tribute, Trade, and Warfare

Beliefs about their past and oral traditions regarding relations with other islands shape Pulap attitudes, identities, and stereotypes. Pulapese often interpret contemporary events and social contacts, especially among Western Islanders, as reenactments or continuations of previous patterns of behavior. Conceptions of past interisland social, economic, and political relations continue to have relevance in many contexts, since Pulapese use the past to explain, justify, or interpret the present. Being more traditional than other Trukese is particularly asserted as a virtue. An overview of Pulapese views about their historical relations with other islands thus contributes to an understanding of their cultural identity in the modern context.

Yap

The widest system of tribute and trade in which Pulap participated once extended from the high, volcanic island of Yap through all the coral islands and atolls east to include the Westerns and the Namonuitos. Yapese domination linked the islands, including Pulap, which were all ranked relative to one another (Alkire 1965, 1970; Lessa 1950, 1956, 1966). Orders for tribute traveled from Yap through a chain of authority from the highest- to the lowest-ranking island, beginning with Ulithi. In general, rank decreased with distance from Yap, with the Namonuitos, Pulap, and Pulusuk lying at the bottom (see Map 3). The order proceeded eastward through the Central Caroline atolls; Puluwat received the order from Satawal and passed it on to the other Westerns and the Namonuitos (Lessa 1950, 39). As the lowest in rank, these latter islands embarked first on the tribute voyage to Yap. Thus Western and Namonuito canoes carrying tribute met at Puluwat and continued from there to Satawal and Lamotrek.

Despite their low rank relative to Yap, the atoll dwellers benefited from the tribute system because they received food and shelter while on Yap, and they left with canoes full of timber, turmeric, betel nut, yams, and other items scarce or lacking on their own islands (Lessa 1950, 43; Lessa 1956, 71). How Yap achieved its domination over the tributary islands is unknown, but the system persisted both because of the economic advantages to the outer islanders and because of their fear of Yapese sorcery (Lessa 1956), especially the reputed ability to send disease, famine, and typhoons.

Today, Pulapese remember fears of sorcery, rather than economic benefits derived from the Yap tribute system.[4] They claim to have avoided trade with Yap precisely because of this fear. Nonetheless, the situation may have been more advantageous in earlier times if Western Islanders stopped at Yap when traveling to Guam (Lessa 1956, 72). Yapese could have provided them with food, shelter, and advice, and may also have acted as middlemen in trade with islands beyond the Central Caroline atolls.

In the middle of the nineteenth century the Westerns and Namonuitos stopped participating directly in this system and began to send tribute indirectly through Satawal rather than through their own representatives (Lessa 1950, 42). Even this minimal participation ceased during the German era (Alkire 1965), although the rest of the system did not completely fall apart until the late 1940s.[5]

Despite the years that have elapsed since the collapse of the Yapese empire, Pulapese still speak freely of the fear they had of Yap in the past and of the bitterness they still harbor. Many point out that even though they believe the people of the outer islands of Yap are more similar to them than are the people of Truk Lagoon, they prefer to be associated politically with Truk. Although Pulapese never had a choice in the matter, since the administrative boundaries were externally imposed, a few politically active men wistfully mentioned an ideal arrangement whereby the outer islands of Yap State would join with the Westerns, separate from both Yap and Truk.

Pulapese refer to the atolls of Yap State as *fanúwen hottiw* 'islands to the west'. The closest and most frequently visited is Satawal, and the two places have some close clan ties. Men sailing west to Pikelot to catch turtles take the opportunity to visit Satawal, carrying gifts such as food and sleeping mats, and they receive hospitality and goods such as turmeric and cloth.

In addition to structuring exchange with Yap, the tribute system also facilitated informal exchange among the coral atolls themselves, linking them not just to Yap but also to one another. Alkire (1965) has described the precarious position of these islands if they remained socially and economically isolated from one another. These small coral islets support only a limited range of agricultural products and are also vulnerable to tropical storms that regularly sweep through the area. With a network of established ties, people could, in times of disaster, turn to unaffected islands for assistance. Even in normal times, systems of regular exchange considerably expanded each island's resource base. Food and other materials scarce in one place could be obtained from another. Consequently, even when the Yapese no longer dominated the area, smaller systems of tribute and exchange persisted. Alkire has described an intra-atoll system at Woleai (1970) and an interatoll tribute and exchange system involving Lamotrek, Satawal, and Elato (1965).

The Western Islands: Puluwat

A similar small-scale tribute system existed in the Western Islands into the Japanese era. According to Damm and Sarfert (1935), all the Westerns and Namonuitos once paid tribute to Puluwat, although by the German era only Pulap and Tamatam continued to do so.[6] In return for tribute, Puluwat was to protect its subjects from other islanders. Pulapese do not consider the relationship to have been a benevolent one, however, and they speak today with resentment of the tribute system, and especially of Puluwat's arrogance and belligerence. Pulap informants claim, in fact, that Puluwat warriors occasionally arrived in fighting garb to demand tribute and then proceeded to raid the island, appropriating what they pleased and indiscriminately destroying property. The relationship between Pulap and Puluwat was—and still is—a very ambivalent one; Pulap could rely on its neighbor for aid and protection yet lived in constant fear of Puluwat raids.

The men of Puluwat were renowned as fierce fighters and feared throughout the area, even as far away as the Halls, Namonuitos, Mortlocks, and atolls to the west. Even Lamotrek, a higher-ranking atoll in the Yapese system, feared Puluwat, and Western Islanders could therefore freely exploit Pikelot, which belonged to Lamotrek. To further illustrate Puluwat's reputation, Pulapese cite a recent case. When a Lamotrek man took the wife of a Puluwat man living on Lamotrek, Puluwat reacted by preparing to fight the offending island. Since

Lamotrek feared Puluwat and wanted to prevent a battle, the islanders sent indemnity gifts.

When the Germans entered Truk, they insisted that the islanders stop their warfare. Pulapese remember German threats of reprisals and claim that they complied out of fear. Although the Western Islands were included in the interdiction, at least one incident violated the order, and Puluwat was punished by the Germans for raiding Pulap (Damm and Sarfert 1935). The incident occurred when Pulapese took back food they had given Puluwat visitors for their voyage home after learning that some food had been stolen. When the Puluwat men returned home, they reported to their chief that Pulapese had stolen their oars and ropes, and to retaliate, Puluwat decided to raid Pulap, plundering their houses and seizing several canoes. The raid did not go unnoticed, and the governor arrived in November 1908 to punish Puluwat by removing some men to Saipan.

Stories of warfare remain alive today and contribute to contemporary stereotypes and relationships. Pulapese retain ambivalent attitudes about Puluwat and believe its people to be violent and aggressive islanders who want to resurrect the days when they ruled the area. To prove their point, Pulap informants cite a recent confrontation when a Protestant mission boat visited from Puluwat. Pulapese are Catholic and adamantly maintain that the island should be of one faith. Thus Pulap did not extend its customary hospitality to the visitors, although a few individuals brought food to Puluwat relatives. Insulted, the Puluwat visitors returned home and prepared to raid Pulap. When the fleet of canoes and motorboats arrived, however, Pulap elders managed to assuage the anger of the Puluwat men and thereby avoided a fight.

Pulap attitudes and resentment toward Puluwat have surfaced in other contemporary situations and have colored their interpretation of events. For example, Pulapese are convinced that Puluwat voters were responsible for the defeat of a Pulap candidate in a recent election. Pulapese contend that Puluwat voters will unite in support of a Western Island candidate only if he is from Puluwat. Moreover, Pulapese claim that Puluwat elders resist new ideas and are reluctant to allow young people to hold power. In sum, Pulapese place a high value on unity and cooperation and deride Puluwat as an island divided both by religion and by politics.

Pulap's resentment also manifested itself at interisland athletic games held on Puluwat in 1980. Pulapese expressed annoyance even before the games began because the event had originally been scheduled for their own island. They complained that Puluwat could get whatever it wanted; Puluwat claimed it was their turn to be hosts even though the games had been held there the previous year. (Puluwat apparently maintained that the year before had been Tamatam's turn, but Tamatam leaders had asked that the games be held on Puluwat since they had no playing field.) In any event, Pulap resented Puluwat's arrogance in the matter, and when the contestants returned to Pulap after the games, they accused Puluwat of having fumed whenever Pulapese cheered for their own athletes. Pulapese were gleeful at winning the games—and defeating Puluwat—especially in the canoe races, an event for which Puluwat had supposedly allotted a high number of points in anticipation of winning themselves. Considering Pulapese pride in navigation and their belief that it originated on their island, that event was particularly significant to them.

Pulapese define Puluwat people as behaving toward others in ways that belie good character. For example, they are supposedly inhospitable toward visitors and assault foreigners. They often fail to offer food and shelter, and they cannot cooperate over religious issues. Rather than show concern for others, the people of Puluwat are said to focus on selfish, personal concerns, making large war claims, for example, and voting for a political candidate simply because he promised to provide them with motorboat fuel. In other words, they do not behave as good people, good kin, or good Pulapese. Valued behavior such as generosity, respect, humility, and loyalty to tradition characterize Pulapese, whereas greed, arrogance, and aggression—traits scorned by Pulapese—are attributed to Puluwat. The context is one in which Pulapese perceive Puluwat as attempting to reassert control and domination over them. Pulap's response is to assert superiority; the behavior of Puluwat people is seen as making them unworthy of such authority. Implicit in these assertions is the notion that Pulap deserves respect, and other islanders, such as the people of Pulusuk, should side with Pulap in any sort of confrontation. In the past Puluwat may have reigned as chief, and in the present may continue attempts to reassert that position, but Pulap need not meekly submit.

Although Puluwat did indeed reign as chief island of the Westerns in the past, Pulapese do not believe they played a completely subservient role. In fact, they maintain that they served as the strong right arm of Puluwat, and cite as an example an unsuccessful raid Puluwat made on Magur in the Namonuitos, when Pulap's assistance was necessary for victory. Pulapese maintain, in fact, that Puluwat could not have achieved or maintained its position without them as allies, and they believe they continue to provide support to Puluwat. Their health aide, for example, saved a Puluwat twin, a feat Puluwat people supposedly respect and appreciate. Moreover, Puluwat is said to have obtained many of its customs and ceremonies—especially those having to do with navigation—from Pulap. Pulapese contend they not only retain traditional customs today but provided them to others in the first place. Pulapese are particularly proud that Puluwat acknowledges that navigation originated on Pulap. Puluwat may have had armed power, but Pulap had supernatural power. Thus Pulapese assert their past in the present, incorporating it into their modern cultural identity.

The Western Islands: Tamatam

Tamatam, across the atoll, is the closest inhabited islet to Pulap and engages in the most economic exchange. Pulapese dismiss Tamatam, however, as a poor and unimportant place with only a small population, and they contend, without resentment, that they give far more to Tamatam than they receive. Once or twice a year they send food to their neighbors, and canoes and motorboats frequently arrive from Tamatam for goods such as sugar, kerosene, and cigarettes. The name of the place itself reflects the uneven relationship: *taam* means 'outrigger float', and the islet is said to be nothing more than Pulap's outrigger.[7] The exchange relationship is not completely one-sided, however, because Tamatam shares with Pulap any turtles it catches at Pikelot and sends occasional gifts as well. For example, in 1980 after Pulap had sent its neighbor preserved breadfruit and swamp taro, Tamatam reciprocated with cigarettes as a gesture of thanks. Each islet occasionally sends the other a gift of fish from an unusually good catch, the receipt of which can be an occasion for a feast when the women of the receiving islet prepare vegetable dishes for the visiting men.

The Western Islands: Pulusuk

The island the people of Pulap claim to be fondest of and most similar to is not Tamatam but Pulusuk, the southernmost of the Westerns. In comparison to the people of Tamatam, the people of Pulusuk are considered more the equals of Pulapese. Moreover, the two places share a history of resentment toward Puluwat and some ability and inclination to resist. Before the German era, Pulusuk even stopped paying tribute to Puluwat and allied itself instead with Namonuito, an atoll north of the Westerns, to fight against Puluwat. On several occasions Pulusuk offered payments to Namonuito and Pulap, encouraging them to kill some Puluwat men. Today Pulap claims a bond of solidarity with Pulusuk against Puluwat's domination and aggression, and the virtues Pulapese attribute to themselves they also assign to the people of Pulusuk, who are said to be modest, unassuming, generous, peaceful, and respectful. In other words, "they" are like "us," not like the people of Puluwat.

In statements supporting Pulap contentions about Pulusuk, food again emerges as a symbol of solidarity and kinship. Giving food is evidence of generosity, hospitality, and fulfillment of kinship obligations. When describing Pulusuk, Pulapese fondly recall the generous amounts of food they have been given when visiting the island and the many people who summoned them to eat. Moreover, Pulusuk visitors to the 1980 athletic games on Puluwat shared their provisions with Pulapese contestants because Puluwat allegedly slighted Pulap when distributing food. Pulapese in general perceive the people of Pulusuk both as trusted friends and as allies against the possible animosity of Puluwat.

Although Pulap bears resentment toward Puluwat and has developed an identity that affords a sense of self-respect and even superiority over Puluwat, a high degree of solidarity prevails among the Western Islands as a whole. In particular, the islanders feel they can rely on one another; resources are shared both among islands and among individuals, and any Western Island can ask another for aid. Even in normal times a shortage of anything from food to cigarettes in one place can be alleviated by turning to another. And if stranded for some reason, a visitor can request the use of a canoe to return home. Communication through interisland visits, and in recent years through walkie-talkies, also serves to bind the area together. Interisland relationships based on clan, marriage, adoption, and created siblingship are also more numerous and extensive for Pulap within the Westerns than beyond. Students at the secondary schools and migrants working or visiting in Moen interact primarily with other Western Islanders, though virtually all Pulapese express particular fondness for the people of Pulusuk. A Western Islands identity thus emerges in addition to a Pulap identity.

Namonuito Atoll

Pulap's closest neighbor beyond the Western Islands is Namonuito, but despite this proximity, relations between Pulap and Namonuito are far more strained than between Pulap and atolls to the west in Yap State. Although the Namonuitos are geographically, culturally, and linguistically close to Pulap, the history of warfare and enmity between the two affects their relationships and contemporary attitudes. Four of the five Namonuito islets are considered poor and lightly populated "islands of hunger" like Tamatam, but the islet of Ulul is another matter. Because of an Ulul raid on Pulap sometime before the 1880s, Pulapese attitudes toward Ulul are particularly bitter. When Ulul warriors raided Pulap, they killed a large portion of the population; according to Damm and Sarfert (1935), only thirty people survived. Although Pulapese today attribute no motive to Ulul other than their base nature, Damm and Sarfert recorded the raid as vengeance for a previous Western Island attack against the Namonuito islet of Magur. When people of Tamatam, just a few miles across the lagoon, witnessed the battle on Pulap, they notified the people of Puluwat, who decided to retaliate since they were responsible for Pulap's welfare. When the Western Islanders arrived at Ulul, however, only one woman, originally from Pulap, remained on the island, the others having fled on a foreign ship.[8] Ulul was later resettled, and today's inhabitants are considered the heirs of the former residents.[9] Although the raid on Pulap took place in the nineteenth century, animosity toward Ulul persists and surfaces in contemporary situations.

Pulap attitudes toward Ulul, like those toward Puluwat, reflect the notion that the islanders are deficient in traits and behavior valued by Pulapese. In particular, they claim that Ulul people no longer observe the requisite customs of hospitality. As one Mwóóř clan member put it, "Mwóóř people from Ulul visited us here, and we took care of them, but Mwóóř on Ulul won't take care of us." In general, Pulapese maintain that Ulul islanders no longer care for visitors, rarely offer gifts to other islands, and are stingy with food. A former student, for instance, described her surprise when she helped prepare food with an Ulul household, which then failed to send any to other relatives. In an area where nurturing behavior evidenced in the giving and sharing of resources is not only highly valued but essential for survival, these statements are intentionally both insulting and demeaning.

Pulapese also contend that Ulul islanders are "losing their customs," such as navigational skills, canoe construction, and respect behavior toward siblings. Ulul residents are supposedly becoming more violent and are bringing in knives and guns from Truk Lagoon. Pulapese also resent Ulul politicians, both at the local and the state level, claiming, for instance, that Ulul leaders attempted to have a Pulap teacher at the junior high school fired. In elections, Pulapese refuse to vote for an Ulul candidate, even one not running directly against a Pulap man. They seem particularly indignant about an Ulul politician who supposedly failed in his responsibility for years to help the area select a legislator. The political system the Americans were attempting to introduce remained in essence a secret to Pulap at a time when the Ulul politician presumably was to have explained it to them.

Like Puluwat, Ulul is a potential threat to Pulap and has already acquired access to power and newly available resources. Ulul became a subdistrict center under the United States administration and the site for Weipat Junior High School serving the Western Islands. This brought increased status to Ulul as well as other tangible benefits such as more frequent and regular visits by the government ship bringing supplies to the school. Perhaps more important, however, is the fact that Ulul produced a highly respected and powerful politician. Rather than accept an inferior position, however, Pulapese assert moral superiority and the value of tradition in the modern context.

Truk Lagoon

Traditional relations with Truk were based primarily on trading, and even into the late 1960s Pulap continued to sail canoes to Truk Lagoon. Although they still have the navigational skills, today they prefer the government ships. Tobacco, a prized commodity, formerly provided the primary motivation for sailing to Truk, but now Pulapese can more easily buy cigarettes from the ship. The impact of the old trading relationships still persists; for example, adult children of elderly navigators occasionally send food and gifts to relatives of the old Trukese partners, although usually only when members of both kin groups happen to be in Moen.

Relations with Udot Island in particular were strong during World War II, because Pulapese in Truk Lagoon took sanctuary there. Pulap men had befriended Udot men while working together for the Japanese on Dublon and later went to Udot to escape the bombing. A son of one of these men later married an Udot woman, and Pulapese have supported political candidates from the island, even against other outer islanders. The established kin ties outweigh the more diffuse outer-island solidarity.

The reputation of Trukese as a whole, however, is one of a violent people. Pulapese say, "They hold you up for money, and if you have no money, they may knife you; they tie people up, they rape women, they cut people in the face, and they steal." Trukese are also said to be skilled in malevolent magic. Suicidal and prone to drunken fighting, Trukese men are also accused of deserting unmarried, pregnant women and of being faithless even when married.

Furthermore, the people of Truk Lagoon increasingly rely on a cash economy, and Pulapese assert retention of a traditional way of life as superior to the modern ways Trukese have adopted in their stead. Implicit in such assertions is pride in their own self-sufficiency. Imported foods are luxuries Pulapese enjoy, but they are proud to have retained their subsistence economy on the atoll and the patterns of sharing traditional foods. Buying and selling food is viewed as a foreign intrusion. By adopting foreign ways, Trukese have abandoned traditional customs and behavior. Pulapese do not wish to be relegated to the status of unimportant, backward outer islanders, however. They want the prestige, power, money, and luxury items available in the modern context. They want college educations for their young people, political offices, and prestigious jobs. Yet Truk Lagoon is far more acculturated than Pulap, with more immediate access to resources and positions. Pulapese have responded by deriding the acculturation of the Trukese, asserting themselves as culturally superior and therefore a force to be reckoned with.

In sum, Pulap beliefs about trade and warfare with other islanders influence relationships and attitudes today. Former enemies still present potential threats and Pulapese have formulated an identity of themselves as superior because they follow valued patterns of behavior, whereas cultural "others" violate those standards. Pulapese demean the ways of many other islanders and assert their own self-worth in the process. Pulap is not only the origin point of valued customs but the place where traditional customs and values can still be found.

Education and Migration

Although Pulapese beliefs about past relations with other islands bear on contemporary relations and attitudes, so does the contemporary context of interisland interaction. Some negative attitudes based on perceived cultural and behavioral differences have recently developed in these new settings. New patterns of population mobility have encouraged more contact between Pulapese and other Trukese, necessitating choices about how and with whom to interact in the new social settings.

Some key settings are the secondary schools. Schooling has also played a crucial role in what is primarily a pattern of circular migration,[10] because education beyond the elementary level is not only a common motive for migration but also a prerequisite for most employment opportunities, especially the preferred government positions. In January 1980, for example, 13 percent of the total Pulap population was away attending school. In comparison, the total number of those employed off the island, together with their wives and children, amounted to only half the number away at school. Pursuing a secondary education, which necessitates leaving the atoll, has recently become the norm for all Pulap young people who pass the entrance exam and maintain the necessary grade-point average. Students first attend junior high school on Ulul, in Namonuito Atoll, and then high school on Moen, in Truk Lagoon. Schooling brings together young people from throughout Truk, providing key arenas for formulations of identity. Greater numbers of people are involved than in previous eras, and the length and intensity of contact far exceed those of the trading days, since these students spend months at a time over a period of years with one another.

Students are also a major component of the Pulapese community on

Moen, the port town of Truk. Moen attracts migrants from throughout the area, making it a major site for negotiation of identities. Education is a resource, an essential ingredient for access to money, goods, and prestige; thus high school graduates and returned college students look for jobs on Moen. Together with their families, the high school students, and Pulapese temporarily visiting the port town for medical or other personal reasons, they form a small community in the village of Iras on Moen. There, they participate in Moen activities and interact with other islanders, while retaining and asserting a Pulap identity. Determined to avoid the acculturation plaguing other islanders and to find for themselves a secure and valued position in modern Truk, they assert the value of tradition.

Interisland interaction at the schools and on Moen reveals the Pulapese emphasis on tradition and the moral superiority of their customs. A set of nested identities also emerges because Pulapese may assert a specifically Pulap identity, a wider Western Islands identity, or an even more inclusive outer-islands identity. Selection depends primarily on structural oppositions of the setting, that is, the specific islanders involved and their relationships with Pulap. In addition, past relations and current perceptions of political and economic realities structure much of this intergroup interaction and assertion of identity.

Education

Since 1965 Truk has been experiencing an "education explosion" (Hezel 1978). For example, the total number of high school graduates from Truk in all the years before 1965 is exceeded today by the number who graduate in a single year. Although formal schools existed before that time, far fewer students attended them. Western Islanders attended at even lower rates than other people in Truk. Pulap young people did not attend missionary schools set up in Truk during the Spanish and German administrations, and only about half a dozen Pulap boys (no girls) attended Japanese schools.

The advent of the American administration brought about a significant change, beginning with the establishment of a system of elementary schools throughout the district, including one on Pulap. Until about 1967, however, Pulapese did not as a rule leave the island to pursue postelementary education even though the American administration transformed secondary education in the early 1960s by replacing the single Trust Territory public high school with six separate district schools. Academically oriented secondary education became available to all young people, rather than a select few. Truk High School opened on Moen, and secondary school enrollment for Truk as a whole increased. In 1970, when academic junior high schools were established in Truk, enrollment increased once again (Hezel 1978).

The forerunners of these junior high schools were postelementary vocational schools set up in 1967. Students from the Western Islands began at that time to attend Weipat School on Ulul in the Namonuitos. This opening of Weipat encouraged Pulap students to begin leaving the island for secondary education. Most Pulapese failed the entrance test for Truk High School in those years, but they could still attend Weipat, then a vocational school, and subsequently continue on to Truk High School. Thus in the early 1970s Pulap began producing high school graduates. In 1970 Weipat became an academic junior high school open to students from the Westerns, Namonuitos, and Halls. Weipat graduates attend Truk High School on Moen, which serves the entire state. Today, in fact, it is unusual for either girls or boys not to continue through the secondary school system, and many are now studying at United States colleges.[11]

At Weipat Junior High School on Ulul, island group identities and distinctions come to the fore in a number of areas, particularly dormitory organization, social activities, work groups, and occasional student fights. Here two levels of structural opposition operate. On one level, Pulapese view themselves as separate from people of Tamatam, Puluwat, and Pulusuk. At another level, however, they claim a bond of solidarity with other Western Islanders, in contrast to those from the two other island groups at the school: Namonuito Atoll and the Hall Islands. Pulapese contend that the Western Islanders share a cultural unity that distinguishes them from other areas of Truk. Namonuito peoples are considered to be more like them than the Hall Islanders, but unlike the Namonuitos, the Halls supposedly did not engage the Western Islands in warfare, "or at least not big or bad wars," in the words of one young man.

Contemporary dislike for the Hall Islanders is primarily expressed by students who have attended school with them, an attitude derived from perceived behavioral and cultural differences. The Hall students are labeled *lamalam tekiyah* 'conceited, arrogant' (literally 'high thoughts'), the opposite of *méhónóhón* 'quiet, modest, unassuming' (Elbert 1972, 89), which also implies respectfulness and concern for other people. In other words, someone who is arrogant is aggressive and rude to others; he disregards their feelings and deliberately refuses to accord them the respect they are due (Caughey 1977, 28–30). Hall students are also accused of being *nemaayki* 'insolent' and *sikippwach* 'lecherous', because they flirt and openly show an interest in sex. In the same vein, they use language considered in the Westerns either vulgar or inappropriate in mixed company.

Pulapese themselves believe the stereotype of the Halls developed

since students began attending school together in relatively large numbers. Memories they have of schooling in the Japanese and the early
American years dwell primarily on antagonisms between Truk Lagoon
and the outer islands, when solidarity was strong among outer islanders
as a defense against the Truk Lagoon students. Once the school on Ulul
began accepting Hall Island students, however, and after Truk High
School was established and student enrollment dramatically increased,
the situation changed. Pulapese at the high school even began to resent
being classified together with Hall Islanders, complaining that they
gave outer islanders a bad reputation. Hall Island students were characterized as being sneaky; former students claim, for instance, that Hall
Island boys often went around at night peeping in the girls' dormitories.
Hall students were also accused of not studying seriously, being interested only in *wurumwot* 'play'.

Students from throughout the state, including Mortlockese from the
outer islands southeast of Truk Lagoon, attend Truk High School
together on the island of Moen. Like the Halls, the Mortlocks did not
historically engage in intense warfare with Pulap, but neither were they
ever in a position of structural opposition to the Westerns as are the
Halls at Weipat. Attitudes about them are more favorable. At Weipat,
Hall Islanders contrast more strikingly with Western Islanders, whereas
in Moen, Lagoon Trukese are considered the most different. Pulap high
school students, for instance, claim a bond with Mortlockese as fellow
outer islanders. In other words, at one level of contrast, the Mortlockese
are absent: at Weipat, the structural opposition includes the Halls, the
Namonuitos, and the Westerns, and the Halls are the most different
from the Pulapese. At Truk High School, however, the highest level of
opposition and contrast is between Truk Lagoon and the outer islands,
which include both the Westerns and the Mortlocks.[12]

Thus three levels of nested identities emerge: Pulap, Western Island,
and outer island. The school even has an organization, ABC (Always Be
Cooperative), specifically for outer-island students, reflecting a sense of
unity and common purpose. Pulapese describe a degree of outer-island
solidarity, especially in opposition or contrast to Truk Lagoon. They
express pride in this solidarity and maintain that lagoon students followed their initiative in forming similar organizations; in the words of
one student, "They learned cooperation from us." Cooperation, sharing, unity, and mutual respect are related concepts in their thinking.

Pulapese in Iras Village, Moen

A number of Pulapese have found employment on Moen, the administrative and commercial center of Truk. Together with their families, the
high school students, and Pulapese temporarily visiting the port town

for medical or other personal reasons, they form a small community on Moen. A strong identity as Pulapese emerges in this context.

This community is geographically centered around land in the village of Iras that some Pulap men purchased in the 1950s from fellow clan members. Their land has enabled the Pulapese to develop a strong community base on Moen, since it serves both as an extension of Pulap and as a part of Moen. Since Pulapese obtained full ownership, not merely use rights, the land is seen as belonging to people of Pulap. In a sense, this land is a part of Pulap itself. Pulapese own the land, live on it, and attempt to follow a way of life similar to that on the atoll. Participation in community affairs is one avenue migrants have for retaining ties with home, and therefore rights to land and residence.

Since Pulap now extends to Iras Village in Truk Lagoon, the islanders can leave the atoll for Moen and yet not really leave Pulap, even if they abandon permanent residence on the island. This provides migrants with a sense of security and psychological support. Most Truk High School students from Pulap live in the dormitories, but they spend weekends and afternoons "at home" in the Pulap community of Iras. Iras also represents home for sailors and college students who can visit briefly in Moen but do not have time to return to the atoll. For people temporarily in Moen on personal business, living in Iras provides access to the excitement and diversions of Moen together with the security of kin ties and identity as Pulapese through participation in Pulap community affairs. They can enjoy the company of kin to explore Moen and not have to face the unknown alone. The Iras Village land is perhaps most valuable, however, for migrants residing for long periods of time in Moen, because they do not have to abandon Pulap even though they have left the atoll itself.

Pulapese in Iras specifically attempt to recreate aspects of atoll life. They consciously retain their customary style of clothing, changing from dresses or pants to lavalavas and loincloths when returning from shopping, work, or school. Saturday activities are especially intended to duplicate those on Pulap. Women prepare traditional food in large quantities to last several days, and the men go fishing.

Nested Identities

A specifically Pulap identity is primarily asserted with reference to the migrant community on Moen and in contexts where only other Western Islanders are involved. In other situations at the schools and on Moen, the Western Islands identity is salient, with other islanders often perceiving the Western Islands as a unit. When describing students from various areas of Truk, for instance, teachers and staff at the high school describe the Western Island students as a group, emphasizing their shyness, consideration, and respectfulness.

At another level of nested identities, Pulapese distinguish themselves as outer islanders from the people of Truk Lagoon. This is clear at Truk High School, and the outer-island identity is also appealed to in political elections with the contention that outer islanders have shared interests because of their similar atoll environments. Furthermore, when Pulapese reflect on the "old days," they describe how Truk Lagoon people looked down on outer islanders and frowned on intermarriage with them. Those who attended school in the Japanese and early American periods comment that outer-island students had to unite in the face of Truk Lagoon antagonism.

In constructing and presenting a cultural identity Pulapese thus differentiate themselves from other Western Islanders in certain contexts, and in other contexts categorize themselves as Western Islanders in contradistinction to others. Similarly, they at times distinguish themselves as outer islanders from the people of Truk Lagoon. The contrast between "them" and "us" persists, but the content of the categories shifts.

Beyond the Westerns, Truk is perceived as the major power, the center of commercial, political, and social activity for the state. When making invidious distinctions between "us" and "them," Pulapese tend to describe "them" as being "just like Truk." Truk in essence becomes the opposite of "us." "We" still follow traditional customs and retain navigational skills; Trukese have abandoned them. "We" take care of visitors and share our food; Trukese care only about themselves. "We" work hard, grow good taro, and have little need for money. "We" are peaceful, religious, and caring of other people; Trukese practice sorcery and ignore church rules. "We" are concerned with navigation, Trukese with fighting. Other islanders are either "like us" or "like Truk," but the personnel in these categories may vary according to context. At times all outer islands are "like us," but in other contexts only the Westerns are "like us." In opposition to Truk Lagoon, for instance, the Halls are "like us," but at Weipat School they are "just like Truk."

Being Pulapese in a Modernizing Truk

The art of navigation, production and exchange of local foods, respect behavior toward kin, and traditional dress are the major traits that Pulapese invoke to conceptualize their culture, and this process appears in its most pronounced form on Moen. Pulapese present these cultural characteristics as evidence of their worth in a context in which others are abandoning tradition.

Pulapese have thus transformed what others may consider negative attributes into a positive aspect of their identity. The male *yafittitá* 'loincloth' in particular has become a symbol of their traditionalism, especially in Moen, even though the contemporary loincloth is made from imported fabric. Stories concerning the early years of the American public educational system, for instance, assert that Trukese used to be afraid of them when catching sight of the loincloth, evidence that the Western Islanders were powerful and fierce. The male loincloth represents both ferocity and caring because it symbolizes Pulap's fierce past through the alliance with Puluwat and their retention today of traditional customs, especially those having to do with navigation and with respect and sharing among kin. To the Trukese it may represent primitiveness, but to the Pulapese it is a symbol that they remain close to their roots, unlike other islanders who have chosen acculturation. Gladwin and Sarason described Trukese attitudes in the early American years: "They . . . look upon the people of Puluwat, and of the other outer islands, more or less as country cousins whose speech is odd, although at the next moment the Trukese reveal their awe and anxiety in the presence of the esoteric lore and power they have left behind them but do not entirely disbelieve" (1953, 39).

Skilled both at magic and fighting, Western Islanders were respected by others, who refrained from violence against them, and the attributes of savagery and backwardness were transformed in the eyes of the Pulapese into a sense of power and strength. Pulapese speak with pride today of how Trukese used to fear them, and yet they maintain an image of themselves as both a powerful and a peaceful people. By assuming the identity of Western Islanders, Pulapese look to the past and their alliance with Puluwat and thereby portray themselves as fierce, brave, and powerful. Bravery, though still valued, can no longer be manifested in warfare, but the reputation of having been great fighters in the past remains a source of pride. Through an identity as Pulapese, however, they can disclaim the aggression and violence of Puluwat and present themselves as peaceful, respectful, modest, and caring. Moreover, they can build a nonviolent but powerful image through the belief that Pulap was the origin of navigation. Pulapese have no need to fight others in order to earn respect because skilled navigators remain the most respected men in the atoll.

Although Pulap is one of the least modernized places in Truk and its people among the last to seek educational and employment opportunities, they have formulated an identity affording them self-esteem vis-à-vis the cultural others around them. Pulapese pride is specifically based on the assertion that they are the closest to their cultural roots and least contaminated or changed by the outside world. They point to aspects of their heritage to interpret and explain contemporary relations and differentiate themselves from others on the basis of specific cultural differences. Both as Pulapese and as Western Islanders they integrate aspects of their past to project an image of proud, powerful, yet modest islanders. They seek a place in contemporary Truk and the Federated States of Micronesia not as naive or backward country hicks but as islanders with a rich cultural heritage.

NOTES

Most of the material presented in this chapter is based on fieldwork conducted from January 1980 to March 1981 on Pulap Atoll and among Pulap migrants in Moen, Guam, Saipan, and the United States. The research was supported by a grant from the National Science Foundation (BNS-7906640), a National Science Foundation Graduate Fellowship, and a Stanford University research assistantship. I also collected data while teaching at Weipat Junior High School on Ulul, Namonuito Atoll, as a Peace Corps volunteer from 1974 to 1976. I am particularly grateful to Jocelyn Linnekin, Lin Poyer, and Michael Lieber for their valuable comments on early drafts of this chapter.

1. Pulapese stereotypes and attitudes toward other islanders do not preclude formation of individual relationships across perceived boundaries. As an alternative to asserting a separate cultural identity when interacting with other islanders, Pulapese can choose to relate on the basis of kinship ties, such as common clan membership or created siblingship.

2. Other islands recognize Pulap's claim. Burrows and Spiro, for instance, confirm that Ifaluk attributes the beginning of navigation to Pulap (1953, 90, 346).

3. Motorboats are not exempt from this etiquette. A few years ago when Pulap men attended a meeting on the Truk Lagoon island of Woley, an elderly and otherwise respected Uman Island man who wished to leave early asked permission of the far younger Pulap men because they could speak for Haakúr. Later, when the Pulap men and the other visitors left the island, faster motorboats that drew ahead of the Pulapese developed engine problems because of their disrespect.

4. Fischer in 1950 discovered a similar attitude among the people of Puluwat, who claimed that they, too, had failed to benefit economically from Yapese domination (Lessa 1956, 72). Both Pulap and Puluwat, for example, claim to have obtained turmeric from Truk, not Yap, and sent it together with other tribute goods out of fear of Yapese sorcerers.

5. Pulapese today do not recall Namonuito participation in the system, although one elderly man remembers carrying tribute to Yap on a foreign ship.

6. Pulap informants recall the Namonuitos sending tribute to Fananu, in the Hall Islands.

7. Krämer, too, commented on the arrogance of Pulap with respect to Tamatam (1935, 251).

8. They went to the Marianas, taking with them a captured Pulap woman whose descendants live on Saipan today.

9. Ulul was resettled by people from Tamatam and Piserach. Tamatam is the smaller islet of Pulap Atoll, and Piserach is part of Namonuito Atoll, closer to Ulul. Although people from both places would have had kin ties with people of Ulul, today's Ulul inhabitants are not the direct biological descendants of those who raided Ulul. That appears to be irrelevant to the Pulapese, however, illustrating Watson's (chapter 2) notion of Lamarckian inheritance. Settling on Ulul land made the new residents people of Ulul and heirs of the previous inhabitants.

10. For a discussion of circular migration in Africa, see Mitchell (1969); for a variety of Third World societies, see Prothero and Chapman (1985); and for Oceania, see Bedford (1973), Chapman (1970, 1975), Chapman and Prothero (1985), and Ritter (1980).

11. Although most Pulapese attend the public schools in Truk, a select few have attended private Catholic schools on Moen, Pohnpei, or Saipan.

12. The only major exception to this diffuse sense of solidarity is some resentment that Mortlockese were the first in Truk to reap the rewards of education and obtain lucrative government positions. Mortlockese taught in the Pulap elementary school, for example, because of a lack of qualified Pulapese or other Western Islanders. And one of the early Pulap high school graduates complained he was unable to find a job because Mortlockese either had them already or gave them only to fellow islanders.

6

Being Sapwuahfik:
Cultural and Ethnic Identity
in a Micronesian Society

LIN POYER

In 1837 the adult male population of Sapwuahfik (formerly Ngatik Atoll)[1] was massacred in an attack by European sailors and Pohnpei warriors. The atoll was subsequently repopulated by some of the attackers who settled there, a few surviving Sapwuahfik women and children, and deliberate and accidentally voyaging immigrants from Pohnpei, the Gilbert Islands, and the Mortlock Islands. Despite the diverse origins of their ancestral population, Sapwuahfik people today see themselves as a single cultural community. In this chapter, I describe the people of Sapwuahfik undergoing a shift in the form of their community identity as they develop into a politically active ethnic group.

Sapwuahfik personal identity is hierarchically nested, situationally variable, and potentially changeable over a person's lifetime. I shall outline the characteristics that identify an individual as Sapwuahfik and discuss the implications of that ascription. At a more inclusive level is the identity of the Sapwuahfik community as a unit. The identity of this community is variable only in the sense that its salient characteristics may shift over time, and that it appears different to members and outsiders. Unlike personal identity, community cultural identity is semiotic in the elementary Saussurean sense that it has meaning only in the context of the set of regional identities of which it is a part (Poyer 1988a). In the second section of this chapter, I present the Sapwuahfik perception of the distinctive character of their community in the context of other Eastern Caroline populations, paying special attention to relations with their nearest and most important neighbor, Pohnpei.

The third section describes the maintenance of Sapwuahfik identity by atoll people residing permanently on Pohnpei Island. In this multicultural situation identity comes to be a topic of conscious reflection and action. Self-conscious recognition of a Sapwuahfik culture, including processes that Linnekin (chapter 7) discusses as the objectification and politicization of tradition, paves the way for the development of a

Sapwuahfik ethnic group in the social-structural sense. In conclusion, I argue that Sapwuahfik people on Pohnpei, by participating in local, state, and national politics, are in the process of creating an ethnic group understood in terms of similarly organized groups competing in a pluralistic political arena for mutually valued resources.

Sapwuahfik is a Micronesian atoll eighty-eight miles southwest of Pohnpei Island in the Eastern Caroline Islands.[2] Nine small islets enclose a nine-mile-square lagoon; the nearly six hundred permanent residents of the atoll live on the largest islet, Ngatik. Taro, breadfruit, coconuts, and bananas are major crops; fish and other seafood, pigs, and imported foods complete the diet. Cash income is earned through copra sales and government wage labor.

The atoll's modern social organization is a result of Pohnpei import and indigenous development in the culturally mixed community established after the destruction of aboriginal society in 1837. Traditional social organization in the Eastern Carolines persists in matrilineal, non-localized, exogamous clans and in a two-line chiefly title system based on the Pohnpei model. Atoll life today, however, is determined more by the organization of colonially introduced elective positions, households, and sections (named geographical units that elect municipal councilmen and share in atollwide work or windfalls).

Sapwuahfik is a municipality of the State of Pohnpei, one of the Federated States of Micronesia (see Map 2). Pohnpei State comprises the five districts of Pohnpei, the Micronesian atolls of Mokil, Pingelap, and Sapwuahfik, and the Polynesian outliers of Nukuoro and Kapingamarangi. The small outer islands of Pohnpei State have a precontact history of only sporadic interaction (through trade, accidental voyages, and military expeditions) with one another and with Pohnpei. The grouping of Pohnpei Island with nearby atolls into a colonial administrative district effectively began in the nineteenth century. It was as a result of Spanish and subsequent German, Japanese, and American administrations that the people of these islands entered into sustained interaction. In the Eastern Carolines, as elsewhere in the Pacific, colonial policies and racial ideas made island populations explicitly aware of their cultural and physical differences from one another and from Europeans, and tended to freeze these differences into bounded units (see Howard, chapter 12).

Sapwuahfik Identity

On Pohnpei and on Sapwuahfik, *Ih mehn ia?* 'He (or she) is a person of where?' is a common question when someone is being identified. This means not only, as an English speaker would say, "Where is he from?" but more to the point, "Where is he *of*?" A person's place of origin tells where his land and his kin are, what titles he is eligible for, where his language was learned, and where his physical and social skills were developed. To be *mehn Sapwuahfik* 'one of Sapwuahfik' is to hold to certain attitudes and behaviors, to know certain things and be ignorant of others, to be related to others of Sapwuahfik, and not to be "one of" somewhere else. For various reasons, perhaps at different times of life, a person may very much want, or not want at all, to be identified as one of Sapwuahfik. How it is determined who is or is not Sapwuahfik, or how an individual decides whether to claim this identity, is itself part of being Sapwuahfik.

Minor phenotypical distinctions, variations in clothing style, dialect, food customs, and material culture are seen by Sapwuahfik people and other Eastern Caroline Islanders as distinctively Sapwuahfik. But individual identity does not rely on these traits, which are recognized as potentially misleading indicators of group affiliation. Criteria of Sapwuahfik citizenship, listed below, consist predominantly of sorts of individual behavior, so personal identity is not necessarily unique or unchangeable. Sapwuahfik people share the notion of consocial personhood described by Lieber (chapter 4). Consistent with generalizations about regional variation presented in the introduction to this volume, the sense of personal identity formed in the matrix of atoll life is explicitly concerned with social relations rather than with the ingestion of local food or water, or with supernatural relations with the local environment.

Cultural identity reflects local ideas of personhood. Important to Sapwuahfik concepts of both individual and group identity is the contrast of *loleh* 'inside' and *liki* 'outside'. Applied to persons, the contrast refers to intentions versus actions, or words versus deeds. Likewise, many differences among population groups are seen as outside, but Sapwuahfik also recognize invisible differences among peoples in their *lamalam* 'belief, way of thinking', which is inside. These concepts are similar to the ethnographic concept of cultural differences.

External differences among peoples, in Sapwuahfik thought, are variations in physical appearance, material culture, and custom or social behavior. Some of the perceived differences are value neutral (e.g., fishing techniques, clothing styles); others are value ranked (e.g., skin color, relative industriousness). They outline a scheme by which cultural affiliation can be identified by both outside and inside criteria.

Attention to inside differences is illustrated by one woman's comment that members of a certain matriclan have "a different way of thinking" from the rest of the community. A young person with an American education may be accused of trying to "think like" a white instead of an islander. Adults adopted onto Sapwuahfik from other islands as children are said to "think like" Sapwuahfik people. Behavior that is difficult for people to understand or approve of is attributed to a different way of thinking. For example, the Kapingamarangi propensity to give up children for adoption to other islands is incomprehensible to people on Sapwuahfik. "They have a different way of thinking," the Sapwuahfik say. That "ways of thinking" are not mutually exclusive is suggested by a schoolteacher's comment on Western education: that it is best if students can learn to hold and use "both ways of thinking."

The criteria people use to assert their own or determine another's identity as Sapwuahfik are, in this local theory, outside. Although, as I discuss below, Sapwuahfik people do perceive themselves as sharing inside qualities such as an ethos of egalitarianism and strong Christian belief, adherence to these values is not a diacritic marking community membership.

In some Pacific communities, and this might have been more widely true before the colonial era, group membership criteria are not elaborated. For example, on Kapingamarangi (Lieber 1977a), Nukuoro (Carroll 1977), or Rotuma (Howard and Howard 1977) there seems to be no question of defining who is, for example, Kapinga. The island population is coterminous with the cultural community (except for a few visitors, inmarried spouses, and adoptees). Only when these people come into close, sustained contact with other cultural groups—such as Kapinga people on Pohnpei (Lieber 1977a; chapter 4)—or with an externally imposed colonial system that freezes differences (such as Southwest Islanders on Palau, McKnight 1977) does identity come to be of overwhelming concern for the individual or the community or both. In other cases, such as Namoluk (Marshall 1975) and Etal (Nason 1975), diversity of origins, a high rate of immigration, or other local circumstances make identity potentially problematic even in the absence of continual contact with other populations. These last examples demonstrate that the Sapwuahfik case represents a wider Micronesian or even Pacific pattern of how identity is determined.

The population of Namoluk Atoll is descended from immigrants from throughout the Central Caroline Islands. Marshall writes that "this heterogeneity of background . . . is ignored by the islanders who maintain the fiction that Namoluk is an ethnically distinct population" (1975, 165). Though I would not use the word *fiction* to describe the sense of identity shared by Sapwuahfik people, Namoluk provides a similar case wherein diversity of biological origin does not impede the development of singular identity. Marshall lists the criteria of Namoluk citizenship (that is, membership in a community) as mother's citizenship (matrilineal clan affiliation), marriage, adoption, government records, and employment. Namoluk citizenship is fluid, depending "not on characteristics that a person is born with, but rather on a set of contingent relationships in which an individual may or may not participate" (1975, 173).

Nason describes how the first settlers of Etal Atoll deliberately sought out immigrants from other islands of the Lower Mortlocks; ties with these islands have been maintained by trade, marriage, warfare, mutual assistance, and kinship. Citizenship is attained through birth to an Etal mother or through "naturalization" by establishing an enduring relationship with an Etal lineage through adoption, marriage, or clientship. Land ownership does not suffice to establish citizenship, and citizenship can be lost if a person fails to "establish residence and permanent social relationships in the community" (1975, 155). The Etal community has a positive attitude toward increasing its population by immigration, and so it is relatively easy for an alien to become a citizen of Etal.

Determining who is Sapwuahfik involves many of the criteria used on Namoluk and Etal. Genealogy or descent, residence, language, lifestyle, and access to land all figure in establishing personal identity. The criteria are flexible in action; situational factors both within and beyond individual control play a part in determining identity. A person has a certain limited freedom to push his or her identity one way or another (given enough of a genealogical or situational base on which to make an argument). In the same way, the community has some leeway in ascribing citizenship to its putative, or potential, members.

Genealogy is the basis for most people's identification as Sapwuahfik, though no Sapwuahfik person today is fully descended from indigenous Sapwuahfik ancestors. Sixty-four percent of adults (in 1979) describe both their mother's parents and father's parents as Sapwuahfik. Genealogical claims to community membership depend on whether one's parents are considered to be Sapwuahfik—and that classification involves criteria of identity other than the parents' ancestry.[3]

There is some patrilateral bias in assigning identity, as there is in inheritance and postmarital residence, but assignment through the father is not a rule and is often offset by other factors determining citizenship. For example, an elderly man who knew his family's genealogy well told me that his grandfather was *uhdahn* 'truly' Sapwuahfik, because his grandfather's mother was Sapwuahfik (though he identified his grandfather's father as Pohnpeian). It is interesting that this informant, while describing himself as Sapwuahfik, has a mother whom he identified as Pohnpeian—her father was Pohnpeian. Furthermore, the idea that members of a matrilineal clan share some sort of identity is common. During conversation about a family's unorthodox handling of a funeral feast, one woman complained about the behavior of members of the deceased's clan: "They're people of Tarawa" (the matriclan ancestor was a Gilbertese immigrant), "they have a different way of thinking from Sapwuahfik people."

Possessing an ancestor identified as Sapwuahfik is a powerful claim to Sapwuahfik identity. But, although a foreigner with a Sapwuahfik ancestor can come to the atoll with that claim and be treated as an honorary community member during the visit, the tie does not automatically include rights to land, kinship obligations, or involvement in local affairs. A genealogical link must be accompanied by appropriate social behavior if a person is to be considered truly Sapwuahfik. Nonetheless, descent links are important to situation-specific claims of Sapwuahfik identity, for example in initiating a request for personal assistance. Some people with no genealogical ties to the atoll come to be considered Sapwuahfik by appropriate social behavior following adoption or marriage into the Sapwuahfik community.

Long-term residence on the atoll is also important but not sufficient to constitute Sapwuahfik identity. Several people adopted onto Sapwuahfik as babies, who have lived there all their lives, are still frequently referred to as "those of *Kirinis*" (Kirinis is from the former English name for Kapingamarangi, Greenwich Island). On the other hand, some Sapwuahfik people who were born and have lived on Pohnpei all their lives, save perhaps for occasional brief visits to the atoll, are Sapwuahfik without dispute by selective application of other criteria of identity.

Access to land on Sapwuahfik does not seem to play the central role in determining identity that it does elsewhere in Micronesia. By no means do all those considered Sapwuahfik have rights to atoll land. In particular, many Sapwuahfik people residing permanently on Pohnpei do not. Others have sold their land rights. But all plots of land on Sapwuahfik, with a single exception, are held by those considered to be Sapwuahfik. (Some people with rights to land are nonetheless not considered Sapwuahfik in every context; for example, the Kapinga people adopted as babies have rights in the land of Sapwuahfik adoptive kin but may be commonly identified as Kapinga.) Access to land is closely related to maintenance of personal ties with the atoll for Sapwuahfik people living elsewhere.

Using the Sapwuahfik dialect of the Pohnpei language is one identifying mark of a Sapwuahfik person. On Pohnpei, or on Sapwuahfik when dealing with government officials of any background or other foreigners, most Sapwuahfik people speak Pohnpei, considered the more formal language. On the atoll, Sapwuahfik people may use Pohnpei's "high" or respect language (described in Garvin and Riesenberg 1952) in church and in formal public speeches, though only a few atoll people are comfortable with it. Ordinary conversation and school classes are held in Sapwuahfik dialect. The use of the dialect when away from the atoll is a self-conscious distinguishing characteristic of those who consider themselves to be Sapwuahfik. Men and women who speak both Pohnpei and Sapwuahfik dialects fluently are interlocutors (in several senses) between the two populations. Sapwuahfik men use among themselves an English "pidgin" (as they call it) modified from nineteenth-century sailors' speech. They see this language as distinctive of their community, and until the American introduction of English-language schooling (as a result of which many other Micronesians speak English more fluently than most Sapwuahfik men), it was a source of pride.

Given that a person has some claim to being Sapwuahfik, certain choices of action will confirm this identity and others will invalidate it. An individual chooses to maintain or drop personal ties with the atoll after moving away, to consistently identify himself as Sapwuahfik or to use some other identification. One must decide in each conversation whether to speak Sapwuahfik or Pohnpei; a man chooses whether or not to use pidgin. He must also decide whether or not to use the respect form of the Pohnpei language to high-titled people, and whether to strive to advance in Pohnpei's traditional title system or to pay it little attention. When planning a feast, he must decide if it will be held in the Sapwuahfik or Pohnpei style. The most important of these social behaviors, which are also those that explicitly contrast Sapwuahfik identity with that of Pohnpei, involve titles and feasts and are described more fully below.

This option of active choice in being Sapwuahfik is distinct from Barth's discussion of "performance" in an ethnic identity (1969, 28). Barth states that an ethnic identity (in his structural definition) does not depend on a person's control of specific resources, but on the person's origins (presumably biological) and "commitment" (presumably self-ascription). An individual's performance in that identity, though, does depend on possession of particular assets, such as wealth, kin ties, and personal ability. The identity of Sapwuahfik individuals as I am discussing it here is not graded in terms of performance. With increasing interaction among islands in the region, several locally meaningful identities could now be attributed to a person. Someone behaving in a non-Sapwuahfik way is not thereby judged to be acting improperly as a Sapwuahfik person, but instead is taken to be (more or less seriously, depending on the person's biography and the situation) not Sapwuahfik at all, but some other identity. Sapwuahfik people do not speak of someone being "un-Sapwuahfik" as a moral evaluation (as an American might be judged "un-American"). Rather, saying that someone is not Sapwuahfik explicitly ascribes an alternative identity to that person, based on criteria of affiliation allowing such a reclassification. This is because to be Sapwuahfik is not a moral choice, but a behavioral one; and, following the Lamarckian model described by Lieber (chapter 4), a person's behavior is seen as resulting from his or her group identity. Thus, the reasonable explanation for Joe's actions is that he is behaving as his people behave—and so his identity is recategorized to explain his behavior. As the examples below demonstrate, recategorization may be an effort to control behavior, as well as to explain it. This potential for alternative classification based on social behavior is most evident in sorting out problematic Pohnpei and Sapwuahfik identities. Because of the dichotomizing criteria that identify individuals as one or the other, to act as though one is not Sapwuahfik is by definition to act as a Pohnpeian.

Only with the development of political-action ethnic alliances (discussed in the conclusion of this chapter) does it become possible for a person to act in a non-Sapwuahfik way and yet maintain Sapwuahfik identity. In this situation, ethnic community membership is only one attribute of personal identity. In addition to being Sapwuahfik, for example, the resident of Kolonia is a town dweller, part of a neighborhood group, an employee, and a church member. As identity becomes differentiated and multivalent, evaluation of identity shifts from objective categorization of behavior to subjective evaluation of performance in these roles.

Ascriptions of identity frequently serve as personal commentary— especially, as in Lieber's description of similar phenomena on Kapingamarangi (chapter 4), in joking situations. Adults teasing children and friends joking with each other will call on the other's foreign ancestry (which everyone has) to make their jest. So a noisy child is laughed at: "What is that, a Mokilese girl?" This is not simply a reference to the reputed rowdiness of Mokilese women, for the child does have a Mokilese ancestor. As another example, a man whose biological parents are Mortlockese but who came to Sapwuahfik as a small child is subject to teasing about Mortlockese customs, such as wearing ear decorations.

Such teasing heightens awareness of the critical importance of gossip and public opinion in small-island communities and is part of a wide Oceanic pattern of socialization through teasing and shaming, aimed at adults as well as children. A woman who married onto Sapwuahfik as a girl and has lived there for fifty years is invariably referred to as "that Kapinga woman." A younger woman, whose father and mother's father are Sapwuahfik, but whose mother's mother is Mokilese, is often called "the woman of Mokil." Both women have set themselves apart from the community by their outspokenness and eccentricity. In contrast, a thirty-year-old man from Pohnpei, of Mortlock/Filipino descent, who married a Sapwuahfik woman and has lived quietly and worked diligently on Sapwuahfik for less than a decade, is seldom pointed out as foreign. "Of him, people would say, you are truly 'one of Pohnpei,' but now you are 'one of Sapwuahfik,' " one man told me. Didactic ascriptions of identity encourage people to adhere to Sapwuahfik standards of behavior: to be generous, helpful and loyal to kin, to work hard in crafts and food production, to foster positive feelings in the community and dampen jealousy or ill-will, and to avoid displays of pride.

Public ascriptions of identity are potentially serious and damaging. At times of intense political activity—during an election campaign or when a conflict arises over community resources—they are one of many weapons available to the skilled gossips and orators of the atoll. The reason once given for not reelecting a chief magistrate was that he was not truly Sapwuahfik—a reference to his ancestry. Political infighting for weeks preceding the decision actually involved questions of family status, personal effectiveness, ties with the Pohnpei political establishment, and the distribution of favors. The ascription of identity as a political weapon, however, is not consistent. One young man was removed from his position as radio operator with the public excuse that he "isn't truly Sapwuahfik"; he had been adopted from Kapinga as a baby. His replacement, however, had also been adopted to Sapwuahfik. These references to someone being "not truly Sapwuahfik," unlike the didactic comments described above, are not attempts to stem behavior contravening community norms. Instead, they seem to be *ex post facto* genealogical explanations for decisions actually having nothing to do with citizenship.

Reference to the genealogical aspect of identity may also be used without political intent to explain personal traits, in a way appropriate to the Sapwuahfik idea that both inside and outside characteristics are associated with certain groups and are inherited. As an explanation of his physical appearance, one man is sometimes referred to as a "Negro" —which puzzled me until a check of his genealogy showed a Black American sailor as a nineteenth-century ancestor. Similarly, the fishing skill of a man raised on Sapwuahfik from babyhood is attributed to his Kapinga parentage. Of course, the potential of such innocent explanations influencing people's behavior is always present. Since all are Sapwuahfik (and this must go without saying for the comments to work), community members deliberately use genealogical aspects of a person's self to shape social situations. Ascribed identity that is neutral or humorous in one context can readily become a weapon when circumstances change.

It is evident from this discussion that no consistent rule defines Sapwuahfik citizenship. To be "one of Sapwuahfik" is to an extent to choose to be so through one's social acts (providing the community is willing to accept that choice). Unlike ethnicity in Barth's definition, Sapwuahfik cultural identity is not superordinate; ascription of Sapwuahfik identity is not the dominant factor controlling an individual's social activity. Of course, being Sapwuahfik exists only in contrast to being some other identity. Sapwuahfik people are conscious of their place in the geographic and political setting of the Eastern Carolines and define a regional set of equally marked identities of which Sapwuahfik is but one.

Regional Cultural Identities

Eighty-eight miles northeast of Sapwuahfik lies Pohnpei Island, a high (volcanic) island of about 130 square miles, with a population of over twenty thousand. The city of Kolonia, with more than five thousand people, is the largest urban concentration in the Eastern Carolines and is the capital of both Pohnpei State and the Federated States of Micronesia. Pohnpei and Sapwuahfik people share the same language and also many customs and values. Sapwuahfik people recognize their close similarity to Pohnpeians but see themselves as quite distinct. Because of the importance of the Pohnpei contrast to Sapwuahfik identity, relations between these two groups will be discussed separately.

East of Pohnpei are the Micronesian atolls of Mokil and Pingelap; south of Sapwuahfik lie the Polynesian outliers, Nukuoro and Kapingamarangi. Immigrants and visitors from all these islands meet on Pohnpei, especially in the urban area of Kolonia. Since the establishment of foreign political control, and especially since the 1960s, these populations have come into ever more frequent contact with one another, with consequences for each group's perception of itself and its neighbors.

Sapwuahfik people distinguish themselves from neighboring populations as *mehn Sapwuahfik* 'those of Sapwuahfik'; they speak of *tiahk en Sapwuahfik* 'Sapwuahfik custom' and of a canoe or dance as *stylen Sapwuahfik* 'Sapwuahfik style'. This self-defined group identity has no absolute content, but takes its meaning by contrast with nearby Eastern Caroline and other identities.

Sapwuahfik people participate in a set of nesting identities at different levels of inclusiveness. They recognize a common identity with all Pacific Islanders as distinguished from European and Asian foreigners. *Tohndeke* 'inhabitants of islands' share a common subsistence life-style, close family ties, and patterns of gift giving and resource sharing not found among nonislanders. Sapwuahfik people also share with the other atolls in the region a feeling of distinction from Pohnpei Island. The lifeways of the people of these "little lands" are seen as nearly the same. There is a sense of alliance—and I believe the political implications of this word are increasingly appropriate—with the citizens of Pohnpei State's outer islands as conceptually opposed to Pohnpei proper.

Sapwuahfik people think of these outer islands in two sets of dual categories: one, the Micronesian/Polynesian outer-island distinction, is reinforced by perceived differences in physical appearance, language, and custom; the other, seen as a difference in frequency of contact (and signaled by the routing of the interisland supply ship linking Pohnpei with the atolls), is that between Mokil and Pingelap to the east of Pohnpei, and Sapwuahfik, Nukuoro, and Kapingamarangi to the south. These outer-island subsets are less important in reference and behavior than either the key outer island/Pohnpei distinction or the specific characterization of each island population.[4]

Sapwuahfik generalizations about their neighbors were elicited from a series of interviews in 1979–1980.[5] My field notes and eight lengthy interviews produced fairly consistent stereotypes of the populations most familiar to Sapwuahfik people. The descriptions tend to support Lieber's conclusion (chapter 4) that Kapinga and Pohnpei ethnic imagery reflects current sociopolitical concerns of each group. More explicit symmetry between Sapwuahfik political concerns and descriptions of other cultural groups would probably be given by Sapwuahfik permanently residing on Pohnpei, who were not included in my interviews. Descriptions of their neighbors by atoll Sapwuahfik people highlight attributes that Sapwuahfik consider important in social interaction. About their neighbors, Sapwuahfik people comment on the following features: (1) subsistence work, the sexual division of labor, the productivity of land; (2) clothing and personal appearance; (3) sociability (how peaceful, or prone to fighting, people are; hospitality customs); (4) distributive and feasting behavior; (5) presence or absence of sorcery practices.

Sapwuahfik people identify their atoll as very productive (in contrast to neighboring atolls) and list local food specialities. Atoll women are noted for fishing and weaving; Sapwuahfik canoes are "beautiful" and the fastest in the area because of their sail and hull shape. Sapwuahfik people describe themselves as kind to visitors, generous, peaceful, not given to speaking ill of other populations. They also mention the argumentativeness of Sapwuahfik people, the boys' and men's drinking, and the women's laziness. And they note what others say of them: that they eat cat and shark, like to fight because of their "Gilbertese blood," and are expert sorcerers (this because of the renowned magic of the ancient

Sapwuahfik people). Sapwuahfik people have an ambivalent view of themselves as peaceful folk and as fighters. They often express their sense that they are people of goodwill, cooperative and helpful; but they also relish the fear others may have of their fighting ability and supposed (but denied) skill as sorcerers (cf. Pulapese, chapter 5).

Accompanying the traits that Sapwuahfik people see as distinctive are shared values regarded as unique to the community. The most important of these are an ideology of economic and political egalitarianism and a rejection of sorcery in favor of adherence to Christian teachings. These values are expressed most explicitly when Sapwuahfik is contrasted with Pohnpei.

Sapwuahfik and Pohnpei

As Flinn demonstrates for the Central Carolines (chapter 5), "metropole" high islands are of great importance to the inhabitants of neighboring atolls. Sapwuahfik's relationship with the island of Pohnpei is subject to continual reconsideration. Pohnpei plays a central political and economic role in the Eastern Carolines, and many outer-island immigrants live permanently on the high island (the same factors affect Kapinga-Pohnpei relations, described in chapter 4). But no Pohnpeians live permanently on Sapwuahfik, and marriage and adoption between Pohnpei and Sapwuahfik Atoll are infrequent.

In addition to political-economic ties, Sapwuahfik and Pohnpei are linked by history and descent (since Sapwuahfik's modern population is in part descended from Pohnpei immigrants) and by shared language and culture. This historical relationship has profoundly shaped modern Sapwuahfik culture, which could be seen as a localized version of Pohnpei's. While recognizing the significant historical dimension of any Pohnpei-Sapwuahfik comparison, this chapter is limited to a synchronic consideration of the modern Sapwuahfik sense of distinction from Pohnpei.

At different times I was told, occasionally by the same people, that Sapwuahfik and Pohnpeians are just the same, are similar but not identical, or are completely different. Naturally, the judgment depends on the context of the situation. When an informant made a schematic drawing of the layout of a Sapwuahfik feast, I asked him if it was also valid for Pohnpei. He said it was, since "we are truly Pohnpei people"— adding that Sapwuahfik and Pohnpei have the same traditional stories and so on. Atoll people refer to their identity with Pohnpei in terms of shared language, folktales, clans (five of Sapwuahfik's eleven clans are traced to Pohnpei immigrants and exist also on Pohnpei), physical descent from Pohnpei immigrants, and a shared title system. The sameness is a recognition of material, historical ties; it is not phrased in kinship terms or other metaphorical expressions of shared social identity.

But other Sapwuahfik ideas about Pohnpei sharply distinguish the two populations, and here we see the primacy of a sociological definition of group identity. The Sapwuahfik distinction from Pohnpei is a good ethnographic example of Barth's path-breaking argument that it is not objective cultural differences that separate two self-defined populations; rather, their felt distinctiveness is marked by selected diacritics validating the dichotomy. Pohnpeians are closest, both geographically and culturally, to Sapwuahfik people; and this very closeness seems to call for the cultural implication of difference. Because of the great similarity, the minimal contrast pairs that Sapwuahfik people select and express as distinctions are critical to maintaining their separate identity.

The attributes that most clearly evoke assertions of what it means to be Sapwuahfik take their power from critical contrasts drawn between Sapwuahfik and Pohnpei. These are discussed in Poyer (1988a) and can be summarized as (1) values and behavior involving titles, feasting, and respect etiquette, which Sapwuahfik people deemphasize in favor of an ideal of egalitarianism; and (2) the Sapwuahfik sense of themselves as true Christians, rejecting sorcery.

Pohnpeians are thought to value high status in the traditional political system; Sapwuahfik see themselves as less knowledgeable about and less concerned with traditional rank. Sapwuahfik's title system is a simplified version of Pohnpei's, introduced by whites and Pohnpei immigrants after the 1837 massacre. Beyond the few highest titles in the primary and complementary lines (see Riesenberg 1968), titles and respect etiquette are not important in Sapwuahfik daily life and are seldom used apart from formal feasting occasions. This contrasts with their continuing importance on Pohnpei, despite severe depopulation in the nineteenth century and a long history of European, Japanese, and American rule (Fischer 1974; Hughes 1982; Petersen 1977, 101–105).

The people of Pohnpei appear to be concerned that Sapwuahfik do not know proper respect language and behavior, going so far as to send a delegation of high-status men from Pohnpei to the atoll to instruct Sapwuahfik in these things. "No one told them to come," an old woman told me, "they came to say that we should do what *mehn Pohnpei* do . . . none of us went to listen! . . . [They] said we should bow to the Nahnmwarki, in giving anything to the Nahnmwarki, even a cigarette, to put it on a banana leaf. *Mehn Sapwuahfik* refuse, because we are truly not going to do that, for we are going to follow our own ways, not [those of] Pohnpei. We don't like their customs."

Sapwuahfik also distinguish the style of their feasts from those of

Pohnpei (see Petersen 1977 on Pohnpei feasting). Pohnpei men strive to advance in the title system in part by participating in feasts; since title advancement is less important to Sapwuahfik men, feasting has a different role on the atoll. A Sapwuahfik feast, though based on the Pohnpei model, is less formal in organization and conduct and does not include kava (a vital element of social events on Pohnpei). Both Sapwuahfik and Pohnpei people identify the allotment of feastgoods as the key difference in feasts. Sapwuahfik people identify their custom as egalitarian, with all contributors sharing equally in the distribution of feastgoods. In contrast, they describe Pohnpei feasts as benefiting high titleholders at the expense of the common people.[6]

While agreeing that aboriginal Sapwuahfik possessed the most powerful sorcery in the area, atoll people today unanimously claim to possess no magic of their own, saying it was discarded after Christian conversion (Poyer 1988b). *Wini suwed* 'evil magic' (which can cause sickness, death, sexual infatuation, destruction of property, or misfortune) is always spoken of in the context of Pohnpei use. (My concern here is with Sapwuahfik ideas, not with the existence or nonexistence of local magical practice. On Pohnpei sorcery, see Riesenberg 1948; Ward 1977.) Sapwuahfik describe Pohnpeians as using sorcery freely and often, and see them as serving "both sides"—the Christian church and traditional magic—while they themselves have abandoned sorcery.

The Atoll Community and Pohnpei

The discussion of traditional status, feasting, and sorcery outlines critical distinctions drawn by Sapwuahfik people between their customs and way of thinking and those of Pohnpei. This sense of distinction is being increasingly challenged by contact, as Sapwuahfik people find themselves more frequently involved with Pohnpei (and to a lesser extent with other islanders and foreigners). Visiting, doing business with, marrying, adopting and being adopted by, going to school with, being governed by, working with, and living in the midst of Pohnpei people and others provides constant opportunity for asserting, evaluating, and compromising the separateness of Sapwuahfik ways.

Sapwuahfik's nineteenth-century population history is largely one of immigration. Today immigrants arrive not in waves, but as individuals, who may *wiala* 'become' Sapwuahfik through adoption and marriage (though, as we have seen, some spouses retain a foreign identity). Sapwuahfik individuals living on Pohnpei or on other islands may similarly "become" other ethnic identities. When asking about distant relatives, I was sometimes told that the informant knew nothing about those people; they had "become Pohnpeian" or Pingelapese. The history of interethnic marriages, of course, extends back to the massacre, but recently there has been a consistent increase in outmarriages. Most of these marriages are between Sapwuahfik people permanently residing on Pohnpei and non-Sapwuahfik people. Decreasing atoll endogamy with increasing commitment to Pohnpei is part of the thinning out of identification with the Sapwuahfik cultural community seen in people of Sapwuahfik descent residing elsewhere. The shift in identity can be abrupt, as when an islander marries a foreigner and moves far away, forcefully and dramatically breaking all ties except those of occasional communication and gift exchange. But most transformations from being Sapwuahfik to becoming members of another group occur over a number of years, requiring a generation or more to pass before ties with Sapwuahfik are matters of genealogical record and memory only.

Those who live on Sapwuahfik are not isolated. They go to Pohnpei for medical treatment at the hospital, to deal with government, legal, or church business, to make major purchases, to visit family, or to accompany a relative doing any of these things—or simply for the pleasurable novelty of travel. "Pohnpeians are another sort of people," a man told me as we stood on the deck of the supply ship leaving the lagoon. "I don't want to see only Sapwuahfik people." A few Sapwuahfik youth attend the regional high school in Kolonia, and others like to visit Kolonia for the excitement of movies, cars, fights, alcohol, and the bustle of the town.

Sapwuahfik people living permanently on Pohnpei do not form a distinctly bounded physical community, as do the Kapinga people in Kolonia (Lieber 1977a and chapter 4) and the Pulapese on Truk (Flinn, chapter 5); nor are they as dispersed as Nukuoro on Pohnpei (Carroll 1977). Several Sapwuahfik families live near one another in two parts of Kolonia known as Sapwuahfik areas. A larger cluster owns land in Sokehs, another part of Pohnpei. Sapwuahfik living on Pohnpei work for Pohnpei people or for the government; they may operate a small store, do some fishing, or, if they live outside Kolonia, keep gardens.

Among families permanently resident on the high island, marriage with Pohnpeians (and in Sokehs with neighboring Mortlockese) is frequent, and there is a constant small movement of people who shift from Sapwuahfik to Pohnpei identity. I did no formal research among Sapwuahfik residents of Pohnpei, but my impression is that those who wish to do so have little difficulty in becoming Pohnpei (at least from the Sapwuahfik point of view; I do not know the Pohnpei opinion of them) by obtaining land, establishing ties of adoption, employment, marriage, and assistance with Pohnpei people, and by participating in Pohnpei custom (for example, contributing to feasts in their section and chiefdom or taking a Pohnpei title). Other Sapwuahfik people living permanently on Pohnpei keep up relationships and behavior that maintain Sapwuahfik identity.

Casual meetings help maintain personal ties among atoll people on Pohnpei, but feasts sponsored and attended by Sapwuahfik are the only formal occasions that encourage Sapwuahfik solidarity. Funerals and commemoration feasts (marking the first anniversary of a death) of people with Sapwuahfik ties who die on Pohnpei are the most frequent and well attended of these. At such a death genealogical ties are traced for the privilege of attending, and so the ties are maintained. It is said that everyone, including non-Sapwuahfik people, likes to attend Sapwuahfik feasts because of the egalitarian distribution of feast goods.

Yet in feasts given by Sapwuahfik (as in nearly every aspect of their lives on Pohnpei), Pohnpei customs have entered into the usual way of doing things. When kava is found at a Sapwuahfik feast on Pohnpei, Pohnpei customs of preparation and presentation accompany it. On Pohnpei, a Sapwuahfik family sometimes holds a very large death commemoration feast; on the atoll such feasts are as a rule small, confined to near relatives. Sapwuahfik people recognize that things are done differently on Pohnpei and on the atoll and comment on the prevalence of Pohnpei-style behavior among Sapwuahfik people on Pohnpei. Opinion about this is mixed, though most find it unacceptable to transfer Pohnpei ways to the home atoll. This belief was demonstrated vividly when one family with extensive ties to the high island held a Pohnpei-style death feast on Sapwuahfik. Their actions were roundly and explicitly criticized as inappropriate.

A brief description of one large feast will demonstrate the mix of Sapwuahfik and Pohnpei ways in the lives of Sapwuahfik on the high island. The feast marked the anniversary of the death of the daughter of a Sapwuahfik man and a Pohnpei woman from a high-ranking family of Net. Some five hundred people attended the commemoration, held in the feast house belonging to the mayor of Kolonia (a Sapwuahfik man permanently residing on Pohnpei), located in a Sapwuahfik area of the city. The Nahnmwarki of Net and other Pohnpei titleholders sat in a place of honor in the feast house; most Sapwuahfik people were outside. Quantities of cloth and tables piled high with food were prominently displayed. The mayor alone had spent $500 (he was the dead girl's father's father's sister's son); I was told that more than $1,000 had been spent on food.

Compared with most Sapwuahfik feasts, especially those held on the atoll, this one was very large, but it was not remarkably so by Pohnpei standards. Sapwuahfik people explained the size of the feast by saying that many Net people joined in because of the deceased's ties to the family of the Nahnmwarki of Net. Yet the bulk of the work and expense was borne by Sapwuahfik. It was they who had brought the gifts of food and purchased goods, which, following Pohnpei custom, would go to the Pohnpei family of the deceased. Some people who attended the feast brought food, but others came and ate without contributing, which would not normally happen on Sapwuahfik. A pig was brought to be killed in a rush because of the Nahnmwarki of Net—atoll men explained that it is Pohnpei custom that an earth oven must be made if a Nahnmwarki is present; the pig was owned by a Sapwuahfik person. Pohnpei custom was followed for the distribution of the feast goods: the Nahnmwarki was to receive half of the pig, and the group of high-titled men of Pohnpei received much of the food.

This feast, then, essentially followed Pohnpei practice. In addition, on the morning of the feast a Pohnpei ceremony was held at the grave of the dead girl (who is buried on the mayor's family's land "because her father is Sapwuahfik"), which involved prayers and a giveaway of cloth goods at the gravesite. Sapwuahfik people expressed particular dislike of this giveaway ("That's a stupid custom," an elderly Sapwuahfik woman who has lived on Pohnpei for years asserted forthrightly) and in general commented negatively on the Pohnpei style in which the entire affair was conducted. Referring to the high titleholder receiving a large share of the food, one Sapwuahfik man who had helped said, "Why should I do it? I do the work and the Nahnmwarki gets it all. I'm like a slave, eh?"

The reasons Sapwuahfik people gave for being involved in this costly and elaborate feast centered on their ties with the mayor. They were "just helping him," they said. The mayor in turn was "helping" the dead girl's father (his mother's brother's son), who is cash poor. He said he was doing it "for his mother," out of his duty as eldest son and as the most cash-rich person in the family. The mayor's family mentioned the importance of such a large feast to the Pohnpei people, who (they told me) say it is done "for your name" so that a family's honor is not lowered. The father of the dead girl was pleased with the show of support from his family; it was perhaps more than he expected, since he himself is not a person of wealth or high status and his ties with the Sapwuahfik community are not particularly strong (his mother is Marshallese, and he was adopted by a Pohnpeian).

The details of this feast indicate both how willing Sapwuahfik are to conform to Pohnpei customs of feast giving to make a point (in this case, to underscore the cohesiveness, wealth, and pride of the Sapwuahfik community, with political undertones related to the mayor's ambitions and the Sapwuahfik community's support of them), and how they nevertheless retain ideological distance from those customs and assert the uniqueness and preferred status of their own ways.

Conclusion: A Nascent Ideology of Ethnicity

Several chapters of this volume describe situations in which aspects of culture are objectified by members of a social group for broadly political ends. Although the atoll Sapwuahfik community's cultural identity currently serves no clear instrumental purpose, I believe that Sapwuahfik people on Pohnpei are in the process of objectifying characteristics that they regard as distinctively Sapwuahfik and are using them to forge an explicitly identified Sapwuahfik ethnic group.[7]

The emergence of a Sapwuahfik ethnic group is indicated by the increasing involvement of Sapwuahfik people on Pohnpei in local, state, and national politics. Because of the interest and activity of several men who hold or aspire to positions in local and state government, a Sapwuahfik constituency is developing. Flinn (chapter 5) describes voting activity of certain Central Caroline Islanders as determined by bonds of kinship and history. While this has been true of Sapwuahfik and other Eastern Caroline outer islanders in the past, and continues to be an important factor in explaining voter patterns, I believe that voting behavior in the past two decades has become more politically purposive.[8]

Much of Pohnpei politics is played out in the context of that island's traditional political system, centering on the title complex (Fischer 1974; Hughes 1972, 1982; Petersen 1979, 1982a). Pohnpei people, being greatest in number and—importantly—already organized for political action, have long dominated the state (formerly Trust Territory District) government and controlled its part in the national administration. Until the last decade, Sapwuahfik has lagged behind Pohnpei, and Mokil and Pingelap as well, in Western education and in the political lobbying activity that results in status, power, and authority on the supralocal level. As the concrete benefits of such political activity become evident—showing that participation in elections, legislatures, and the judiciary results in schools, new housing, health services, loans, and wage labor—outer islanders living on Pohnpei have begun to organize for action.

For Sapwuahfik people, such organization is barely underway. The Sapwuahfik community on Pohnpei has only recently begun to have a sense of itself as such, and has only in the past few years initiated activities that may eventually create an ethnic group in the political and structural sense. The feast described above is one example. What is happening among Sapwuahfik on Pohnpei, who are linked to the atoll community, is the creation of an ideology of ethnicity that goes beyond simple identification with a group to include political obligations to that group, the establishment of adversarial and alliance relations with other groups regarding resources to be shared, and mobilization of the group for specific ends to be achieved through political activity.

In order for Sapwuahfik leaders to create a coherent constituency, which implies political loyalty and a unified front, from what is by no means a tightly knit community on Pohnpei, several rifts must be bridged: between Sapwuahfik on the home atoll and on Pohnpei, between people in Kolonia and those scattered across the high island, between Sapwuahfik people who identify themselves as such and others who are beginning to drift (through marriage, adoption, or choice) into becoming something else. I witnessed one such effort at unity in 1980, when a group of Sapwuahfik women went on an overnight fishing expedition from Kolonia. Women visiting from the atoll and women from families permanently residing on Pohnpei took part in the trip, the appeal of which was partly based on the self-conscious ideal that Sapwuahfik women (unlike women of most neighboring populations) know how to fish and enjoy fishing. On their return, a large part of the Sapwuahfik community on Pohnpei met them for feasting and celebration. A major purpose of the occasion, expressed only obliquely by the women but openly by the politically influential man whose sister had organized the trip, was to draw together Sapwuahfik people on Pohnpei. The event was underwritten by several politically important Sapwuahfik men.

In recent years, then, growing political sophistication has increased local politicians' awareness of a useful constituency of minority groups. Although it cannot yet be said that Sapwuahfik people on Pohnpei vote as a bloc or see themselves as a political action unit, there are signs that such intentional activity lies ahead. The mayor of Kolonia in 1980 was Sapwuahfik and his Sapwuahfik father had been mayor as well; the political savvy of these and other leaders has helped to create a sense of potential political power. The ideology of ethnicity, which can be seen developing also in other minority communities of Pohnpei, is a way of reaching that potential by drawing on Sapwuahfik awareness of shared history, descent, and custom, and on the Sapwuahfik sense of distinctiveness.

Sapwuahfik people today appear to be in the initial stages of a process of political mobilization. An obvious element of this process is the selective emphasis on certain aspects of Sapwuahfik culture (such as history, the Sapwuahfik dialect, egalitarian distribution of feast goods), which begin to be objectified as tradition, perhaps eventually to play the role of unifying symbols for a Sapwuahfik ethnic group. The emergence of an ethnic identity in the sense discussed in the introduction (chapter 1) entails the dominant importance of self-ascribed group membership on three levels: (1) identity as *mehn Sapwuahfik* becomes increasingly important in shaping and constraining an individual's social action; (2) Sapwuahfik people as a group begin to interact with other groups (reified as political entities) as a positioned element in a multiethnic social organization; and (3) Sapwuahfik identity becomes objectified and instrumental for Sapwuahfik individuals. Despite the development of the organizational characteristics of an ethnic group as a politically salient entity, I see no evidence that Sapwuahfik people are adopting the Euro-American biological theory of personal identity implicit in the Western popular concept of ethnicity. To be "one of Sapwuahfik" is still very much to act as a Sapwuahfik person and to be formed as a Sapwuahfik person in the matrix of atoll life or the life of the Sapwuahfik community on Pohnpei.

NOTES

Twenty months of fieldwork (1979–1980) on Sapwuahfik and Pohnpei were funded by a National Institute of Mental Health grant. I thank Jocelyn Linnekin and Michael Lieber for useful comments on early drafts of this chapter.

1. At the time of my fieldwork, and for a century before that, the atoll was called Ngatik Atoll. In 1986, the community officially revived the aboriginal name, Sapwuahfik, to apply to the atoll, reserving Ngatik for the name of the main inhabited islet. I have replaced Ngatik with Sapwuahfik in quotations from my fieldnotes.

2. Ethnographic information on the Eastern Caroline Islands is in Fischer (1957) and in the *Civil Affairs Handbook* for the Islands (U.S. Navy, 1944); on Pohnpei social organization and politics, see Bascom (1965), Riesenberg (1968), and Petersen (1977, 1982a, 1982b). Sapwuahfik social organization and history are discussed in Fischer (1957) and Poyer (1983).

3. Of 278 adults considered *mehn Sapwuahfik* in residence on the atoll in 1979, all but 31 have parents considered to be Sapwuahfik. Of those 31, 10 have a non-Sapwuahfik mother, 11 have a non-Sapwuahfik father, and 10 are non-Sapwuahfik individuals adopted onto the atoll.

4. There are even finer distinctions of local identity in this nested series. Outer islanders often distinguish among inhabitants of Pohnpei's five chiefdoms or districts (Pohnpei people consider district affiliation critical and no doubt make much finer area characterizations). On tiny Sapwuahfik, people draw distinctions of emotional character and habitual activity among residents of the five sections of the largest islet, and some sections have localized legends explaining the origins of these microlevel attributes. Howard and Howard (1977) note this also for Rotuma. People assume that clan members also share characteristics; since Sapwuahfik clans are associated with their places of origin, I cannot tell if the sharing is thought to be through kinship or through common geographic origin (see discussion of consocial personhood in the introduction and Lieber, chapter 4). This chapter discusses island-level distinctions.

5. The interview format, based in part on the *Ethnocentrism Field Manual* (LeVine and Campbell 1972), included direct questions, a task of ranking populations on a set of opposing qualities, and provision for undirected commentary.

6. I cannot judge whether the Sapwuahfik assertion of redistributional inequity on Pohnpei is empirically true. While Petersen describes unequal shares of meat at a feast, he nonetheless asserts the essentially redistributive nature of the event (1977, 140, 104; also Hughes 1982, 10; Petersen 1982a, 137).

7. If a typological category is necessary, Sapwuahfik on the home atoll, and until recently those on Pohnpei, fit Howard and Howard's notion of "ethnic aggregate" (1977, 165), which they distinguish from an ethnic group. The latter requires development of an ethnic community and ethnic consciousness, and describes a situation in which ethnic distinctions are superordinate in individual and group identity.

8. A report on the 1983 plebiscite on the future political status of the Federated States of Micronesia discusses the voting solidarity of outer islanders in explicitly ethnic terms (Schwalbenberg 1984).

7

The Politics of Culture
in the Pacific

JOCELYN LINNEKIN

In the ethnographic cases described in previous chapters we have seen the cultural identities of Pacific Islanders defined mainly according to Lamarckian premises. The social boundaries thus constituted have been permeable with, in most cases, minimal ideological emphasis on ancestry as the unambiguous determinant of an enduring cultural affiliation. In contrast, the chapters that follow describe situations where Oceanic cultural identities are becoming (or have become) institutionalized along the lines of the Western model of ethnic groups, largely for political reasons. In Vanuatu, cultural issues are salient in the negotiation of local and national identities. In Hawaii, New Zealand, and Australia, native peoples have been transformed into subordinated minorities of the Fourth World. In each of these cases the colonial society's categorization and treatment of the indigenous people has been founded on Western biological criteria and openly racist assumptions. In each case, indigenous groups have long struggled to assert their own cultural identities in opposition to the life-style of the dominant colonial society.

The remaining chapters in this volume deal with cultural identity in the context of contemporary nationalism. At issue is how the theory that we have called Lamarckian fares in the encounter with global political movements. In the Pacific today we see indigenous cultural identities apparently transformed into ethnic identities (see chapter 1). The principles of alignment espoused by politically emergent groups seem to share with the Western concept of ethnicity the premise that a culture is coterminous with a bounded social unit (cf. Howard and Howard 1977, 191). Increasingly prevalent is the notion that cultural affiliations are rooted in descent. Nationalist ideologies, in other words, have much in common with "primordialist" ethnic theories in anthropology. For anthropologists and indigenous nationalists alike, the most problematic issue is whether the adoption of ethnic strategies is merely an instrumentality employed at a particular political level, or a sign of thoroughgoing change in Oceanic conceptual modes.

I hasten to add that I cannot provide a definitive answer to this question here; indeed, there may be no generally applicable yes-or-no answer. My present aim is somewhat more modest. This chapter offers an ethnographic and theoretical overview of the politicization of culture in the Pacific, by way of a backdrop for those that follow. I focus particularly on a process that Richard Handler (1984, 1985b) has called "cultural objectification" (see also Clifford 1988). Keesing (1982a, 300) describes this phenomenon as "the externalization of culture as symbol": a process whereby culture becomes a thing outside the individual, to be contemplated, discussed, and reflexively modified. In this chapter I examine various modes and contexts in which Pacific Islanders externalize culture to achieve political ends, and I emphasize the use of a model of the past to define cultural identity. The approach employed here is comparative, drawing on the current literature and pointing out parallel processes at work in my area of fieldwork, Hawaii, and in other Pacific societies.

One caveat before proceeding: this chapter is programmatic and may represent a more relativistic position on cultural identity than other contributors to the volume wish to embrace. But if my admittedly contentious treatment of ethnicity sparks some disagreement, then I may have helped to fulfill the primary purpose of our work, which has been to poke, prod, and stretch conventional assumptions about cultural identity.

The Politics of Tradition

Long important in Western scholarship and European nationalist ideologies (see Handler and Linnekin 1984; Hobsbawm and Ranger 1983; Worsley 1964, 69–74), the concepts of culture and tradition are politically salient today in the Third and Fourth Worlds. In contemporary nationalism the concept of cultural identity—so often manipulated by regimes to undermine unity among the powerless and perpetuate stratification (Vincent 1974, 378)—has been turned against colonial powers and even against governments of the new states. Whether called ethnicity, nationality, or even "race," cultural identity is a potent basis for political mobilization among peoples disenfranchised under colonial rule. Almost invariably, this identity is explicitly held to derive from common origins and a shared cultural heritage.

The terms *culture* and *tradition* are not interchangeable here. I use *culture* in the holistic, comprehensive sense familiar in anthropology. I use *tradition* to refer to a conscious model of past lifeways (Linnekin 1983). For the moment I beg the question which of these terms most aptly describes current Oceanic conceptualizations such as *kastom* (variously *kastam* or *kastomu*) and *fa'aSamoa*, although I will return to this point below. As suggested in the introduction, Lin Poyer and I believe that there are significant differences between these Oceanic models and the analogous Western concepts despite years of interaction between them.

Invoking the cultural past to validate and solidify group identity is a common practice in modern nationalism. Indeed, the use of tradition to define cultural identities has become an international political trend (Keesing 1982a, 297). As many social scientists have noted, the past is commonly used to validate the present, and particularly to justify or "ratify" contemporary political relations (Williams 1977, 116). Appeals to tradition have this conservative function because they convey the mandate of the past, "a sense of *predisposed continuity*" (Williams 1977, 116, emphasis in original). It is this "normative" quality (Shils 1981, 23–24) that differentiates tradition from culture, as I use the terms here. As kastom, Hawaiiana, Maoritanga, and fa'aSamoa, tradition is a subject of public debate in the modern Pacific. Categories that objectify culture in this way can usually be traced to Western concepts, but they have been incorporated into the conceptual framework of non-Western peoples.

An entire anthology (Hobsbawm and Ranger 1983) has recently been devoted to making the point that tradition is not so much received as creatively and dynamically fashioned by the current generation. Many other writers have suggested that the past is never objectively given, that traditions are always selective (e.g., Eisenstadt 1973, 21; Linnekin 1983; Marcus and Fischer 1986, 173; Shils 1981, 26, 213; Wagner 1981; Williams 1977, 115). And this assertion does not apply only to societies where oral transmission is the norm; Western written history is no more a set of unambiguous, objectively given facts than the oral histories of nonliterate peoples. Immanuel Wallerstein may seem an unlikely authority to cite in an essay that stresses the symbolic nature of cultural identity, but he has provided eloquent support for the position that the past is created in the present: "The past can only be told as it truly *is*, not was. For recounting the past is a social act of the present done by men of the present and affecting the social system of the present . . . everything is contemporaneous, even that which is past" (1974, 9, emphasis in original).

As Williams (1977, 115–116) and others have noted, cultural transmission is a directed and intentional process. Changes may be introduced in response to situational contingencies or to bring current practice into line with what is believed to be authentic tradition. When cultural identity is a means of structuring political relations, as it is today in the Pacific, the pressure to reflect upon and redefine one's life-

ways is intensified. The modern international context dictates a reexamination of one's own culture in contradistinction to others as Pacific
Islanders sort out their cultural, national, regional, Third and Fourth
World interests. Inevitably, this ongoing "self-reflexiveness" (Keesing
1982a, 298) is a process of culture change.

My emphasis on the contemporary use of the past should be understood as part of an argument that culture is symbolically constituted.
There are parallels here with other problematics in anthropology. The
recent concern with reconciling structure and history (see, e.g., Comaroff 1985; Sahlins 1981, 1985), for example, is but the latest theoretical
attempt to resolve a long-standing anthropological dilemma: the discipline's seeming inadequacy when confronted with the unpredictability
of "human action in the world" (Sahlins 1981, 6). My assertion that tradition is the contemporary interpretation of the past, rather than something passively received, is a crucial element in a theory of culture
change. If we do not allow for the efficacy of interpretation and "invention" in the present (cf. Wagner 1981; see also Sahlins 1981 on the
notion of symbolic revaluation), we are left to conclude that culture is
static and change necessarily originates from outside. My point is that
like culture, cultural identity must be understood as creative, dynamic,
and processual, and such an understanding is only possible with a dog-
gedly symbolic concept of culture.

This position is not particularly new. Saussure laid the foundations
for symbolic analyses of culture with his famous dictum that the sign is
arbitrary, that is, it "has no natural connection with the signified"
(1959, 69). The interpretive position has been elucidated by Geertz
(1973), Schneider (1968), and Wagner (1981) most prominently and by
Rabinow (1977) perhaps most eloquently (for recent discussions see
Clifford 1988; Marcus and Fischer 1986). Whether as scholars or as citizens, however, we are often reluctant to apply the premise that culture
is not in our genes to ethnicity. Surely ethnic identity must be a matter
of parentage; such a truth seems self-evident, common sense. But whose
common sense? The creative reflection and redefinition that characterize the use of culture as "political symbol" (Keesing 1982b, 298) call into
question certain presuppositions behind the Western notion of ethnicity
—particularly the premise that biological ancestry is the primary criterion of ethnic affiliation.

To admit that cultural transmission is creative is not to undermine the
reality or legitimacy of modern cultural identities, however. To think
otherwise is to accept that contagious Western separation of thought
from so-called objective reality. My suspicion (expressed by many before
me) is that this division, so pervasive in Euro-American thinking, is not
indigenous to Pacific Island cultures. But that is not my bailiwick.

Westerners—as well as many Pacific Islanders caught up in political struggles with the West—find it hard to admit that thought is real and, indeed, is quite potent in producing real-world effects. The biologically based notion of an objectively definable, unchanging cultural (and personal) identity is part of an ideological conquest that began with missionization and continues in the arena of international politics.[1] The conquest is not complete, but certainly its impact is discernible in the politicization of culture in the Pacific as well as in other regions of the world.

Ethnicity in Hawaii

Preceding chapters (see also Larcom, chapter 8) have made the point that social context and environment are more important than ancestry in the construction of cultural identities among native Pacific peoples. This is not to dispute the adamant insistence of many indigenous political activists that their identities are "in the blood." Contextual variation in the perception of cultural identity is particularly evident where ethnicity is highly politicized at the national level. The situational contrasts can be striking. Ascriptions of identity made by rural villagers may differ from those of urban intellectuals, who are typically in the vanguard of ethnic political movements (Smith 1981, 97–112). Even in highly politicized situations ethnicity is more imperative and more likely to be asserted in some contexts than in others.

The issue of cultural identity is particularly acute for peoples such as Hawaiians and Maori (see Sinclair, chapter 10; Dominy, chapter 11), who are minorities in their own lands. Because of a long history of intermarriage with foreigners, there are conflicting definitions of what a Hawaiian is. Most legal and institutional definitions have been based on the proposition that being Hawaiian is a matter of degree—a premise that is increasingly seen as untenable by Hawaiians and non-Hawaiians alike. Census treatment of Hawaiians over the past few decades has been woefully inconsistent. In 1960 the federal census distinguished between the categories "Hawaiian" and "part-Hawaiian." The combined total for these two groups in 1960 was approximately 102,400, or 16 percent of the state's population (Schmitt 1968, 120). When the 1970 federal census eliminated the category "part-Hawaiian" and based classification on "self-identification or race of father," the result was 71,000 "Hawaiians" (State of Hawaii 1974, 28, table 11)—a figure obviously far too low. The 1980 federal census once again revised the instructions on ethnic classification, this time to read "self-identification or race of mother." Meanwhile, the state of Hawaii uses a somewhat different method to determine ethnic category and continues to differentiate between "Hawaiian" and "part-Hawaiian" (Kanahele 1982, 1). Thus the 1980 federal census arrived at 115,500 "Hawaiians" (approximately 12 percent of the state's population), while the state counted 175,453, or nearly 19 percent of the state's population (Kanahele 1982, 1–2).

Although the bureaucratic confusion may seem humorous, determining one's degree of Hawaiianness is crucial for claiming land under the major homesteading program available to Hawaiians. Under the provisions of the 1920 Hawaiian Homes Act, the Hawaiian Homes Commission uses the criterion of 50 percent Hawaiian ancestry to limit eligibility for homestead leases. Until the law was amended in 1986, this requirement occasionally resulted in the disenfranchisement of homesteaders' children if they were less than half-Hawaiian in legal terms. Now lessees' offspring may inherit the homestead if they have 25 percent Hawaiian ancestry.

The 1978 state constitutional amendment establishing the Office of Hawaiian Affairs (OHA) similarly stratified the beneficiaries of OHA's trust into two categories. OHA is mandated to serve primarily Native Hawaiians, who are defined as those with 50 percent or more "aboriginal blood." Those categorized simply as "Hawaiians," who have less than a 50 percent quantum of Hawaiian ancestry, do not share equally in OHA's services. Recognizing that the number of 50-percent Hawaiians will inevitably dwindle through the remainder of the century, OHA trustees have proposed eliminating the ancestry differential. The definition favored by many Hawaiians today holds simply that a Hawaiian is anyone descended from those who inhabited the archipelago in 1778 (the year of Cook's arrival). This definition is more in tune with social realities, and was incorporated into the 1980 federal law mandating the Native Hawaiians Study Commission. In the fall 1988 elections OHA sponsored a referendum on the issue, and Hawaiians voted overwhelmingly in favor of a single definition of "Hawaiian."

Outsiders and newcomers typically use the term *Hawaiian* to refer to any state resident. Most local people consider this usage uninformed, and many Hawaiians view it as an offensive appropriation of their identity. The following discussion attempts to analyze the categorical ascriptions made by Hawaiians in the rural taro-growing community where I did fieldwork. When I refer to Hawaiians in this context, I mean a self-ascribed identity: those who define themselves as such. Certainly at a logical, categorical level ancestry is a limiting factor in the attribution of Hawaiian identity; no Hawaiian will call someone Hawaiian if it is pointed out that the individual referred to has no Hawaiian ancestry. Nevertheless, in everyday interactions being Hawaiian is primarily a matter of social rather than biological criteria (Gallimore and Howard

1968, 1). Ethnicity in this context is not completely arbitrary in the sense that any conceivable association is possible; Hawaii does, after all, have a two-hundred-year history of colonization by societies that viewed the world in racial terms. But neither is ethnicity predictable a priori from alleged facts of ancestry.

Few residents of the community where I worked claim to be pure Hawaiian but most nonetheless consider themselves to be Hawaiian, and other islanders (and I) agree with this characterization. The village is widely regarded as a quintessentially Hawaiian place and a font of traditional cultural practices (see Linnekin 1985). In this community, both kinship and ethnic categorical ascriptions are contingent on partic- ipation in reciprocities and on observing egalitarian protocols. Judging from nineteenth-century land records and court cases, the Hawaiian theory of familial affiliation has historically been extremely flexible. Households easily incorporated new members through adoption, mar- riage, and land tenancy. Only after the introduction of private land titles did families begin to debate whether kinship was demonstrable or stipulated, close or distant.

Today, one can be called a relative whether or not there is a known genealogical tie, if one meets the behavioral expectations for a relative. The genealogical knowledge of most Hawaiians in this community is elaborated horizontally rather than vertically. While they could detail contemporary affinal and collateral relationships of dizzying complex- ity, most informants could name their forebears no further back than two generations, and they were hazy about the surnames of women in ascending generations. But the lack of precise knowledge of past lineal relationships makes for great flexibility in the present. It may be impos- sible to cite the links that make someone a cousin, but ruling out some past relationship is just as impossible. The point is, as one informant said, "You never know."

Similarly, ethnic designations such as Hawaiian, Chinese-Hawaiian, *hapa*-haole 'half-white', Portuguese, and haole are used to describe qualities of behavior and relative social status as much as supposed national origin, and they form a gradient of social distance from Hawaiians, measured in quality of reciprocities. Overt diacritics such as dress and speech (speaking pidgin) enter into the categorization, as well as physical cues: someone with dark hair, skin, and eyes is more likely to be called Hawaiian or Portuguese than haole. As commonly used in Hawaii, Portuguese is a category distinct from haole and is a more sym- pathetic epithet. What, then, marks someone as Hawaiian rather than Portuguese when an individual has both kinds of ancestry? Of para- mount importance is the way one conducts social relationships: one's behavior in friendships, casual associations, and particularly gift exchanges. Certain behaviors are regarded as characteristically Hawaiian: generosity, gift giving, humility, observing symmetry in exchange. If one engages in long-term, symmetrical, in-kind exchanges, one is more likely to be called Hawaiian. Social categorization is therefore vulnerable to actions and may change over time as the quality of a relationship changes. Pretentious behavior and social climbing, identified as "acting high," are considered un-Hawaiian. Social isolation may befall a peer who violates the egalitarian ethic of relationships; such a person is *maha'oi* 'bold, brazen, uppity'.

If the social distinctions made by Hawaiians were primarily about parentage, the offspring of Hawaiian-haole unions would be called hapa-haole. But not everyone with one white parent is called hapa-haole, and people with less than half Hawaiian ancestry are nonetheless commonly considered Hawaiian. Ben Finney (1973) similarly points to a "cultural and behavioral" definition for *Démi* 'half-European', the Tahitian analogue to hapa-haole. I never heard a Hawaiian in the community where I worked refer to a close relative or a neighbor as hapa-haole; the term was applied rather to distant kin, relatives by marriage, and family friends living in town. The categorical distinction between Hawaiian and hapa-haole involves the recognition of subtle behavioral cues that mark someone as not fully or not comfortably Hawaiian: not speaking pidgin or speaking it in a forced manner, being the best-dressed person at a luau, self-consciously using the Hawaiian language or telling tales about the spirits. Hapa-haoles are those who cultivate their Hawaiianness, and for precisely this reason they are often the guardians of traditional knowledge, the intellectuals.

Alan Howard has pointed out (pers. comm., 1984) an important characteristic of Hawaiian (and perhaps more broadly, Polynesian) categorical ascriptions, noting that Hawaiian kinship and ethnicity emphasize inclusion rather than exclusion: "The attempt is to facilitate kinship bonding and categorical inclusion rather than to restrict it." Inside the community and within the stratum of Hawaiian social relationships, the Hawaiian identity is dominant and encompassing: it is the marked ethnicity that is stressed above Chinese, Japanese, Filipino, Portuguese, and haole ancestry. The Chinese plantation laborers who settled in rural villages during the late nineteenth century married Hawaiian women but their children were categorically Hawaiian. Although most villagers will admit to mixed ancestry when questioned by an outsider such as an anthropologist, qualifiers such as "Chinese-Hawaiian" are rarely used in casual conversation, except when referring to someone little known or unfriendly to the speaker. Part-Hawaiian relatives and friends are always called Hawaiian in casual reference. The grandchild of a family will be called "Hawaiian with a Japanese father," for example.

Maori ethnic categorization—as applied by Maori, that is, not necessarily Pakeha (white New Zealanders)—is similar to that of Hawaiians in its inclusiveness. Joan Metge (1976, 40) writes that "in practice [Maori] usually accept as a Maori anyone with a Maori ancestor, if he or she desires acceptance." Since Maori have intermarried extensively with Pakeha, the primary criterion for social acceptance as a Maori is self-definition. Physical criteria such as hair and eye color are more important to Pakeha in making ethnic ascriptions (see Metge 1976, 40–42) than to Maori themselves; many Maori have fair skin and blue eyes. At a conference on historic preservation held in Hawaii, a Maori representative said that the Maori are preparing themselves for demographic and political ascendancy in New Zealand. By the inclusive definition of Maori outlined above, they are "outbreeding" the Pakeha and look forward to attaining a numerical majority early in the next century.

In practice the Hawaiian category is not yet so inclusive as this, revealing at least in part the historical impact of American affiliative criteria, which emphasize physical markers, biological descent, and exclusiveness. The Kamehameha Schools, supported by the Bernice P. Bishop Estate for the education of Hawaiian children, are open to children with any quantum of Hawaiian ancestry. But students who are fair report experiencing some unease about their Hawaiian cultural identity because they "look haole," and this ambivalence is intensified if the student is also middle-class and does not speak pidgin. Even Princess Abigail Kekaulike Kawananakoa, who would probably be the rightful heir to the throne if the Hawaiian monarchy were restored, reported in a newspaper interview that some have questioned her Hawaiian identity because of her blond hair and blue eyes. She responded that she has "always felt Hawaiian" in outlook (Bowman 1985).

The similarity between the Hawaiian and Maori models of cultural identity raises the question whether the tendency to categorical inclusiveness is characteristic of Polynesian modes of ascription in general as opposed to European. An alternative possibility is that categorical inclusiveness is a product of colonial history, since it is a particularly functional strategy for the social and cultural survival of indigenous peoples who have become minorities in their own lands. It is also possible, of course, that categorical inclusiveness is both a cultural precedent and a historical necessity. The Maori political vision may foreshadow a similar destiny for Hawaiians. If the inclusive definition of Hawaiian—as anyone descended from the aboriginal inhabitants of the islands—is applied, then Hawaiians are the most rapidly increasing ethnic group in the state. But their future political ascendancy may well hinge on whether Hawaiians can reject criteria of blood quantum.

Key Symbols and Traditional Enactments

In the introduction to this volume we suggested that flexibility and contingency characterize indigenous Oceanic modes of formulating identity. But it is also quite clear that because of their political history and the nature of the political present, Hawaiians and Maori must formulate and use their cultural identity in the context of a struggle for power. In this section I explore some of the implications of politicization for Oceanic cultural models—that is, for the ways in which Pacific Islanders conceptualize their own cultures. I return here to the theme of objectification: what happens to a people's model of themselves as they solidify and mobilize group identity?

As many writers have noted, the self-conscious formulation of cultural models is inherently a selective and creative process (Barth 1969, 35; Blu 1980; Clifford 1988, 217–218, 277–346; Handler and Linnekin 1984; Landsman 1985, 1987; Smith 1981; Trosper 1981; Wallerstein 1973, 169–180). This selectivity is a key characteristic of culture as an externalized symbol, rather than as an all-inclusive compendium of traits in the Tylorian or Boasian sense. Sherry Ortner (1973, 1340) identifies "summarizing symbols" as those which condense or "synthesize a complex system of ideas" and thereby come to stand for the system as a whole—analogous to the rhetorical device of metonymy. Summarizing symbols focus, draw together, and catalyze emotions: their function is "a crystallization of commitment" (Ortner 1973, 1342). For European and American cultures, they include such sacred symbols as the flag and the cross. For our purposes, summarizing symbols are thus particularly significant as icons of collective identity.

Land has been the focus of Hawaiian political organizing at least since the late nineteenth century (see McGregor-Alegado 1980), when the process of Hawaiian land alienation culminated in the overthrow of the monarchy. In the late 1970s the island of Kaho'olawe became a summarizing symbol of the desecrated Hawaiian land, and it is particularly the land's sacredness that has been emphasized in the drive to halt the U.S. Navy's use of the island for bombing practice. The taro plant has come to symbolize the traditional Hawaiian life-style and to connote Hawaiians' link to the land. The acronym OHA evokes the word 'oha 'sprouts or shoots of the taro plant', which is part of the agency's logo. For ni-Vanuatu 'Vanuatu born' in the era of independence, the slit-gong has become "an icon of the country" (Larcom 1982, 332). For the

Maori, Metge (1976, 48–50; see also Dominy, chapter 11) identifies land, tribe, the *marae*, and *tangihanga* (see Sinclair, chapter 10), among others, as particularly central to Maori self-definition.

Symbols such as these draw on the cultural past but acquire new meaning and become emotionally weighty in the present. Keesing writes that "such symbols do not *carry* meanings: they *evoke* them" (Keesing 1982a, 299; emphasis in original). The taro plant in Hawaii and the slit-gong in Vanuatu are often held up as examples of a return to prior times, and it is specifically their traditionalism that is invoked as the basis for a collective identity. Particular artifacts and customs are not inherently icons of the past, however, but are dynamically infused with such meaning in the present. In this sense, the taro plant, the slit-gong, and the Polynesian voyaging canoe are "traditionalized" phenomena, to borrow a term from Dell Hymes (1975, 353–355). Lindstrom similarly uses the term *kastomized* to mean legitimized by reference to the past (1982, 319).

Enactments of traditional performances, rites, and art forms are common in Oceania today. One has only to leaf through the pages of *Pacific Islands Monthly* to find numerous examples of Pacific Islanders seeking to preserve their culture by reviving and reenacting it—and their efforts are formulated precisely in terms of the preservation of tradition. These invocations of the past are not simply motivated by nostalgia for its own sake, but must be understood within their social and political context. Traditional reenactments function somewhat differently for Hawaiians, Maori, and Australian Aborigines than for Pacific Islanders who have won political autonomy. Subordinated Pacific Islanders invoke traditional culture in contradistinction to that of the dominant colonial society; for the new nations of the Pacific, traditional reenactments play a crucial role in constructing a national identity out of indigenous diversity. On the eve of Vanuatu's independence in 1980, for example, Film Australia produced a film about the first national arts festival to be held in that country. It bore the revealing title *Taem Bifo —Taem Nao* (Time Before, Time Now) and was associated with the slogan *ol pipol blong Niu Hebridis*, which could be glossed as 'we are all citizens of the New Hebrides' (PIM 1980, 51, no. 7:25).[2] A representation of the past was thus juxtaposed with an appeal for national solidarity.

One aspect of the Hawaiian cultural renaissance has been the effort to rescue the hula, the indigenous dance form, from its appropriation by the tourist industry (see Barrère et al. 1980). Hula schools have enjoyed a resurgence of interest from young Hawaiians as well as from admirers who have no Hawaiian ancestry. Evidence of the significance of past customs for modern identities is the fact that in recent years interest in the *kahiko* 'ancient' hula style has burgeoned. We now expect to see large men's and women's companies performing dramatic, technically difficult ancient dances in the kahiko segment of the annual Merrie Monarch Hula Festival. But this popular success has been accompanied by increasing concern that authenticity has lost out to entertainment and creativity (the Merrie Monarch is, after all, a competition). Some *kumu hula* 'hula masters' are troubled by the fact that the choreographies performed are newly created, and that some of the teachers have slender links to the older, more rigorous forms of hula training. The inventiveness of traditional enactments is nowhere so evident as in the creation of art for public performance and competition.

But artifacts and customs need not be indigenous to be identified as traditional. Larcom (1982, 333; see also chapter 8) and Lindstrom (1982, 324) both point out that in Vanuatu kastom as locally defined includes imported artifacts and performance elements. In Vanuatu, conforming to kastom may mean readopting traditional dress such as penis wrappers, but exchanges may still be identified as kastom even when they include modern commodities (Lindstrom 1982, 325, 328). Certainly this is true in many societies, such as Samoa, where customary exchanges are regarded as no less traditional—by anthropologists as well as by the participants—for the fact that they incorporate foreign goods.

A Samoan-style kava ceremony marked rites for the first launching of the Hawaiian voyaging canoe *Hōkūle'a* (Finney 1979, 31; Kane 1976, 482–483), since the details of the Hawaiian *'awa* custom have been lost. Whether one finds such borrowings objectionable depends on one's paradigm of cultural identity. The Western commonsense view assumes that ethnicity is exclusive, that one can belong to only one ethnic group. But particularly in the context of the *Hōkūle'a's* voyages Hawaiians have recognized a broader, Polynesian ethnicity. To adumbrate the conclusion of this essay, an overview of modern Oceanic constructions of cultural identity suggests that we are dealing not with single, but with multiple potential ethnicities. And traditions can be called upon to ratify all of them. Whether these levels of identity remain dormant or are actively mobilized depends on the contemporary political context.

The inclusion of a borrowed ritual procedure in Hawaiian canoe-launching rites does not detract from the canoe's overall importance in crystallizing a Hawaiian, Polynesian, or, more broadly, pan-Pacific cultural identity. In fact, the ceremony enhances the power of the canoe as a cross-cultural symbol precisely because the kava custom is found in varied forms throughout the Pacific. A Micronesian navigator guided the *Hōkūle'a's* first voyage to Tahiti because Hawaiians had lost the skills of deep-water canoeing. He has since trained a Hawaiian, Nainoa Thompson, in the art of celestial navigation (see Babayan et al. 1987; Finney et al. 1986). A Marquesan lead dancer with Tavana's Polynesian Revue sought a full-body tattoo "in the style of his ancestors" (PIM 1982, 53, no. 1:23–24). Since tattooing had not been done in the Marquesas for 120 years, a Western Samoan tattoo artist was hired to perform the job after studying pictures of Marquesan body tattoos. Tavana, asked whether the Marquesans should be offended by this cross-cultural effort, replied, "Why should they? We are all Polynesians and we all originated from Savaii in Western Samoa."

Cultural revivalists frequently face the quandary of seeking to revive old practices in the absence of living practitioners (see, e.g., Tonkinson 1982a, 311). Without firsthand knowledge or resident experts, people may attempt to construct an approximation or look to a cognate culture for appropriate models. The fact that this version does not correspond precisely to previous custom does not undermine its significance or its power as a symbol of collective identity. We might say colloquially, "the idea is the same," and that is precisely my point: the custom *is* an idea.

By emphasizing that culture is symbolically constructed in the present, I do not mean to suggest a cultural tabula rasa for every generation, nor am I implying that the identities so constructed are insincere or inauthentic. Certainly there are more and less consciously constructed cultural practices. When Hawaiians take children in adoption or participate in exchange-in-kind (see Linnekin 1985), they are engaging in practices with demonstrable links to the past, and they are not consciously doing so to prove that they are Hawaiian. And yet, even in these examples, one cannot say that the custom has been inherited passively, without reflection. Even in these examples of customs apparently passively received, there is an awareness of significance, a knowledge that such practices differentiate Hawaiians from cultural others. An inauthentic or false culture would be one in which no such symbolic reflection takes place. Such a culture is an illusion.

The view of cultural identity that I assert in this chapter rests upon the proposition that culture is not like a rock, which ostensibly can pass through many hands and remain unchanged, but is rather like a story that is tailored and embellished in the process of transmission. One raconteur feels that certain details should be amended to make the point clearer; another perhaps emphasizes a different part of the story to reveal its true meaning. False cultures—static and passively transmitted —are produced by tourist industries, by nationalists, and by scholars, both Western and indigenous. The process of cultural transmission described here is dynamic, creative—and real.

Kastom and Culture

Perhaps the clearest example of the objectification of culture by Pacific peoples is the Melanesian category of kastom. Keesing (1982b) points out an important characteristic of the concept of kastom on Malaita: it is not equivalent to the comprehensive anthropological notion of culture. "*Kastom* canonically denotes ancestrally enjoined rules for life. . . . Genealogies, lands, and shrines, all closely associated with ancestors, are *kastom*," as opposed to "a mundane realm that is part of 'culture' to an anthropologist but not *kastom* to a Malaitan" (Keesing 1982b, 360). On Malaita kastom, if not culture, is very much tradition as I use the term—a conscious model of the past.

Categories analogous to kastom can be found in other Oceanic societies. Although these named conceptions of culture vary in the comprehensiveness of their content, they are similar in that they generally define native-born people in contradistinction to foreigners. According to Larson (1977), the Tikopia have an indigenous concept of tradition that is equivalent to culture in the comprehensive Tylorian sense. Tikopia see themselves as different physically, linguistically, and in custom from the Melanesians who surround them. Interestingly, Tikopia roots are said to be autochthonous rather than foreign, "the original ancestors emerging from the land of Tikopia itself" (Larson 1977, 258).

The category *Maoritanga* differs from kastom in that it denotes Maori identity, literally "Maoriness"—the state of being Maori (Metge 1976, 48)—rather than culture in the comprehensive sense. But Maoritanga also means "an acknowledgement and pride in one's identity as a Maori" (Walker 1975, 32). Metge (1976, 48) notes that Maoritanga emphasizes "Maori ideas and values." Maoritanga thus seems comparable to kastom in its normative aspect. Anne Salmond (1975, 210) describes Maori values as contradictory to the European in several ways. But she sees Maoritanga as compartmentalized; Maori solve the problem of conflicting ideologies by activating Maori culture in restricted social contexts, primarily ceremonial gatherings.

Samoans refer to their culture as *fa'aSamoa* 'the Samoan way' in contrast to *fa'apalagi* 'European style' (Pitt 1970, 7). Hawaiians similarly use the phrases "Hawaiian style" and "haole style." Pitt states that the concept of fa'aSamoa is primarily a political tool, invoked in political contexts and aimed at achieving "power rather than the retention of traditional custom" (1970, 8; see also 113–126). But I suspect that in the years since Pitt's 1970 study, the concept of fa'aSamoa has become more current, both in Samoa and among expatriate Samoans, in the sense of kastom, as the category of indigenous Samoan culture. Fa'aSamoa and fa'apalagi are used in casual speech to contrast different ways of doing things, the Samoan and the European. In some contexts, for example, the terms may be used to contrast in-kind and monetary exchanges.

I know of no single, all-inclusive term by which Hawaiians refer to their culture; the category Hawaiiana is less comprehensive and is not politically focal in the way of kastom or fa'aSamoa. But Hawaiiana has been important in the Hawaiian cultural renaissance because the category includes crafts and performance arts that are identified with the past. Hawaiiana denotes traditional skills that have been revived and is a way for Hawaiians who do not otherwise take part in nationalist activities to assert their identity.

Keesing (1968, 1982b) offers many examples of Melanesians codifying and adjudicating custom—that is, constructing a model of their own culture. The conservative, pagan Kwaio adopted "chiefs," who were "traditional-style big men" with new titles, during the Maasina Rule movement (Keesing 1968, 277). Later, a "Tuesday culture" arose around the Tuesday meetings of a committee entrusted with the task of codifying Kwaio custom. The Kwaio chiefs, who are recognized only on Tuesday, have the right to adjudicate questions such as the size of opening bridewealth payments—matters previously decided by haggling and situational factors (Keesing 1968, 278–279). The effect of codifying custom was thus to standardize cultural practice. Interestingly, the adjudication of custom is associated here with an imported political ideology.

In these examples culture has become something to be contemplated and publicly discussed (Keesing 1982a, 300). This externalization is also a process of culture change. Redefined as authentic culture, casually observed customs may become obligatory. Keesing writes that kastom on Malaita has become "codified law" and is clearly used in an effort to gain local political autonomy (1982b, 361; cf. Larcom, chapter 8). Debates over kastom law and kastom courts in Melanesia aptly illustrate the encounter between indigenous norms and a Western-style legal system (see Larcom, chapter 8). Cultural and social boundaries may become less permeable as people attempt to realize sectarian political goals. And culture itself may acquire "thinglike" properties—rigid boundaries, unchanging attributes—as it is debated.

Writers on kastom emphasize its use as a political symbol (see, e.g., Tonkinson 1982a). In Vanuatu, kastom is a basis for national unity even though—or precisely because—its content reflects a variety of localities and eras (Larcom 1982, 332; Larcom, chapter 8; Institute of Pacific Studies 1980). Indeed, Lindstrom (1982) and Tonkinson (1982a, 310–312) point out that as an amalgam kastom can be used to invoke solidarity at various levels. At a national level, the ambiguity of the content of kastom empowers it as a symbol of unity for various cultural identities (Lindstrom 1982, 317).

In his pioneering analysis of ethnicity, Barth (1969, 35) pointed out that the processes by which politicized ethnic groups emerge are much the same, and that they tend to become "structurally similar" in whatever cultural milieu they are found (for variations on this theme see Bourgois 1988; Castile and Kushner 1981; O'Brien 1986; Rothschild 1981; Smith 1981; Vincent 1974). The objectification of culture in Oceania today reflects shared premises about what constitutes culture and cultural identity; the diversity of indigenous paradigms appears to be giving way to a single mode of self-perception. Invocations, reenactments, and recreations of the cultural past are catching, which is to say that they represent an evolving global system of categories and distinctions.

The Politicization of Culture

Contemporary nationalist movements in the Pacific resemble like movements elsewhere in their organizational efforts to transcend local divisions while emphasizing cultural distinctiveness "at a particular level of scale" (Cohen 1978, 396). The strategic imperatives of national and international political struggles foster similarity of group structure and method. Without attempting to review the voluminous literature on millenarian movements in this section, I will point out ways in which the late cargo cults of Melanesia prefigured modern political uses of tradition to crystallize cultural identity in the Pacific. Peter Worsley (1959, 1968) sees the later millenarian movements as "embryonic nationalism" (1968, 178), part of a "transition to completely orthodox politics" in the postwar period (1968, 182). Peter Lawrence (1964, 256 and the following pages) cautions that cargo movements were not predominantly nativistic or revivalistic. But both nationalist and millenarian movements can be seen as attempts to wrest autonomy—indigenous political control—from a context of subordination (Keesing 1978, 242; Worsley 1968, 168, 273).

Keesing traces the use of kastom as a "political symbol" to the rise of anticolonialism (1978, 58; 1982a; 1982c). Contemporary nationalism, which particularly links cultural identity to traditionality, has replaced millenarianism as the dominant form of political activity in the Pacific. Certainly the chronology, with millenarian activity declining after World War II and in the postcolonial period, suggests that nationalism has assumed some of the political functions of the cargo cults, particularly that of integrating diverse and previously divided groups. In the following excerpt from Worsley (1968, 228), "nationalism" or "national identity" can equally well be substituted for "millenarian cult"; the par-

allel between the two as political forms is striking: "The main effect of
the millenarian cult is . . . to weld previously hostile and separate
groups together into a new unity. . . . Since the people have developed
new common political interests where previously they had none, so they
must create new political forms of organization to give expression to this
new-found unity."

Worsley sees the Marching Rule or Maasina Rule movement in the
Solomons as less a cult than "a proto-nationalist political party" (1968,
182) that successfully garnered popular support from diverse groups.
The movement's emerging doctrine sought to unite Christians, pagans,
and different linguistic groups (Keesing 1978, 50), and Keesing (1978,
57) notes a precedent for such unity in regional anticolonial cults of the
late 1930s. Keesing too sees such movements as the predecessors of
nationalism and traces them to an opposition that is both economic and
political. He writes that these ideologies reflect "the emergence of a
class consciousness whereby kastomu was externalized as a symbol and
anticolonialism came into focus" (1978, 58).

The content of these movements draws selectively on cultural precedent. Although cultural revival and a return to the past are part of some
millenarian ideologies, Worsley stresses that they also contain many
new elements: "Only certain of the features of the traditional order
. . . are revived, and, since these are revived or perpetuated under
changed social conditions, they may have changed significance" (1968,
273). Keesing (1978, 51) relates how, late in 1946, the Maasina Rule
chiefs presented the colonial administration with a plan of "custom
chiefs," a form of leadership unprecedented in the indigenous social
organization. The creation of chiefs by people who aboriginally had
none (see also Keesing 1968) suggests structural relativity at work: faced
with the more complex European political organization, the egalitarian
Melanesians opposed analogous leaders of their own to the colonial
authorities. Social organization is thus reconstructed dynamically as
people pursue political goals.

Some millenarian movements challenged colonial authority with
codification of custom, foreshadowing contemporary evocations of culture by ethnic nationalists. In both contexts, indigenous culture is put
forward as an alternative to that of the alien power elite. The Maasina
Rule movement on Malaita was particularly concerned with defining
custom as a realm over which the local people, not the colonial administration, should have authority: the movement demanded jurisdiction
over customary matters, which were defined as those "related to ancestors, taboos, lands and the sex code" (Keesing 1978, 50; see also Worsley
1968, 170–183).

In spite of repression by the colonial government, the movement succeeded at least to the extent that in 1953 the protectorate recognized custom as applicable to civil cases (Keesing 1978, 53). Even Christians, for whom allegiance to custom presented inescapable contradictions, found this externalized concept of indigenous culture a potent symbol of an essential identity, a link to a heritage shared by both pagans and Christians: "Codifying and preserving a kastomu they could but partly follow became for Christians a symbolic and political commitment, a link to ancestors, to the past, to the land" (Keesing 1978, 57). Keesing notes (1978, 54) that concern with codifying custom and settling disputes according to customary rules have been part of Kwaio politics to the present day.

Nested Cultural Identities

The Western model of ethnic politics is so internationalized at this point that shared political goals are widely presumed to imply cultural units, however broadly these are defined. However, just as there are various levels of political interest, cultural identity in the Pacific consists of several nested identities, and these are by no means mutually exclusive. The idea of nesting affiliations is an adaptation of Ronald Cohen's definition of ethnicity as "a series of *nesting* dichotomizations of inclusiveness and exclusiveness" (1978, 387, emphasis in original). Barth (1969) redirected the focus of ethnicity studies to contemporary interactions and the process of self-ascription. Even so, as Cohen points out (1978, 376–377), much of ethnicity theory has continued to overemphasize the unitary, unambiguous quality of cultural identity. Implicit in many works is the premise that only one enduring affiliation constitutes ethnicity (see, e.g., De Vos 1975; Enloe 1973; Keyes 1981). Indeed, this assumption seems inescapable if one adopts the "primordialist" approach. In contrast, Vincent (1974, 376–377) warns against "a too stolid perception of ethnic groups as permanent component units" and calls for an awareness of situation: "the articulation of ethnicity is seen to be contingent." Peter Worsley similarly criticizes conceptions of nationalism that posit only one allegiance as constituting national identity: "Men . . . belong to no *single* cultural community . . . social and cultural memberships are always multiple" (1964, 79, emphasis in original).

In contemporary Pacific politics local identities alternate with regional identities, such as Pacific Islander, and with a wider, Third or Fourth World identity. Prime Minister Walter Lini of Vanuatu, for example, in his keynote address to the 1982 Australia and the South Pacific Conference, identified a regional, pan-Melanesian culture. He spoke of a "renaissance of Melanesian values, principles and expectations," and painted a somewhat idealized portrait of *"the* indigenous culture" (Lini 1982, 27, emphasis added), citing characteristics such as "Melanesian socialism" and "a sustained awareness of the need for communal discipline." In traditional Melanesian societies, he noted, " 'Giving' was based on one's ability to do so. 'Receiving' was based on one's need." It is of course appropriate for a speaker at a regional conference to stress regional commonalities, but what is particularly interesting here is the emphasis specifically on *cultural* commonalities: the appeal is not to shared economic interests or to a common political history of colonization, but to common roots, a shared traditional past.

One may note that there is precedent for Lini's enterprise in anthropology and the other social sciences. We anthropologists regularly make similar statements in our "Peoples of the Pacific" courses and monographs (see, e.g., Belshaw 1954, 1 and the following pages). And such generalizations are not necessarily invalid. What is striking about the contemporary political scene in Oceania, however, is the extent to which Pacific Islanders are making use of Western disciplinary models to achieve their own current political goals. In effect, they are turning the colonialists' models back on them—a fitting denouement to the colonial saga in the Pacific. Some Pacific Islanders feel ambivalent about the resulting cultural concepts, however. At least one has expressed skepticism about the notion of Maoritanga precisely because it is not indigenous: "I have a faint suspicion that Maoritanga is a term coined by the Pakeha to bring the tribes together. Because if you cannot divide and rule, then for tribal people all you can do is unite them and rule. Because then they lose everything by losing their own tribal histories and traditions that gave them identity" (Rangihau 1975, 233).

The evolution of the Polynesian voyaging canoe as a political symbol in recent years encapsulates the move from less encompassing identities to broader levels of association, and illustrates the cross-fertilization of ideas that characterizes contemporary Oceanic politics. The 1976 voyage of the *Hōkūleʻa* from Hawaii to Tahiti was a focal event for the Hawaiian cultural renaissance (Finney 1979; Kane 1976). In a message directed to Hawaiians, Herb Kane, the *Hōkūleʻa*'s designer, called the voyaging canoe "the spaceship of your ancestors" and "the central artifact of Polynesian culture" (Finney 1979, 29).

Since the *Hōkūleʻa*'s first voyage, the canoe has evolved into a summarizing symbol of identity not only for Hawaiians but for Polynesians and all Pacific Islanders. Construction began on a Maori voyaging canoe in 1981 (PIM 1981, 52, no. 2:25). Rodo Williams, a Tahitian navigator who had sailed with the *Hōkūleʻa*, later joined the project (PIM 1981, 52, no. 11:28). Commenting on the significance of this endeavor in a letter to *Pacific Islands Monthly,* Herb Kane invoked a pan-Pacific cultural identity: "To all Pacific Islanders whose ancestors explored and settled this ocean world, the voyaging canoe is a common symbol" (PIM 1981, 52, no. 3:7–8). The growing power of this common symbolism culminated in the *Hōkūle'a*'s ambitious two-year voyage in 1985–1987, when the canoe completed a transit of the South Pacific, visiting Tahiti, the Tuamotus, Raiatea, the Cook Islands, New Zealand, Fiji, and Samoa (Babayan et al. 1987). Pacific Islanders met the canoe with tremendous enthusiasm wherever it landed, and the encounters were portrayed as contacts between long-separated but related peoples.

Pan-Pacific interests (see, e.g., Tupouniua et al. 1980) and a pan-Pacific identity also crystallize in regional gatherings such as the South Pacific conferences and in the movement for a nuclear-free Pacific. In 1980 the Nuclear-free Pacific Conference was attended by delegates from Vanuatu, Tonga, Fiji, and Belau, among others, as well as by Hawaiians and Native Americans (PIM 1980, 51, no. 11:37). In this context, a young islander wrote an impassioned letter calling for all Pacific peoples "to begin to perceive ourselves as Pacific Islanders full stop" (PIM 1981, 52, no. 1:9). Appeals to such supranational affiliations as bases for action illustrate how local and regional identities may logically and easily grade into a wider identity when it is politically advantageous.

Particularly revealing are instances of "networking" among Pacific Islanders, Native Americans, and other peoples formerly or presently disenfranchised, confirming that the common historical experience of colonial subjugation founds a commonality of political interests (Worsley 1964, 77). In the newsletter of the Protect Kaho'olawe 'Ohana (1981, 16), the movement formed to stop the U.S. Navy from using the island of Kaho'olawe for bombing practice, a Hawaiian wrote: "Whoever they are: Maori, Hopi, Iroquois, Dineh, Tahitian, Samoan, Puerto Rican, Arab, Filipino or African, all are experiencing the same pressures of American colonial policy." Formal meetings between Hawaiian and Maori representatives have at least a twenty-five-year history (M. Jocelyn Armstrong, pers. comm.). In 1981, the secretary of New Zealand's Department of Maori Affairs met with the nine trustees of the Office of Hawaiian Affairs (Burris 1982). Hawaiian nationalists have attended American Indian conferences and have noted the parallels between their fight for Kaho'olawe and Puerto Rican activism over the island of Vieques. Vieques has also been used for target practice by the U.S. Navy, and the Crusade to Rescue Vieques is directly analogous to the Protect Kaho'olawe 'Ohana (Protect Kaho'olawe 'Ohana 1981, 17, 19). At a conference held in San Juan for "all indigenous native peoples from U.S. possessions," Hawaiian delegates noted similarities between Puerto Rican and Hawaiian petroglyphs. A Hopi leader also described the petroglyphs as "'the same as those of the Hopi nation'" (Protect Kahoʻolawe ʻOhana 1981, 17).

Ideological opponents have attempted to dismiss appeals to Melanesian, Pacific Islander, Third and Fourth World identities—what Worsley calls "Pan" affiliations (1964, 69)—on the grounds that they represent a politically motivated and even metaphorical denial of cultural boundaries. Should not this political use of culture be distinguished from a more basic, elemental identity? Does not one fundamental, "primordial" ethnicity underlie these modern redefinitions? Hawaiians may find unexpected affinities with Hopi and Puerto Ricans, but are they not really Hawaiian? Walter Lini may speak of Melanesian socialism, but his primary identity is ni-Vanuatu—or is it?

The Western commonsense view of ethnicity calls for such distinctions. Certainly today, most people of Hawaiian ancestry are Hawaiian first and foremost: this is their basic, encompassing identity. But even this identity—as salient and imperative as it is today—has a history of reconstitution and change. We can only speculate how the aboriginal inhabitants of the archipelago defined themselves before European contact (cf. Dening 1980). But before the coming of foreigners they saw themselves as "people of " an island, a land district, or even of a particular chief. And anciently, the settlers of the islands must at some point have categorically distinguished themselves from the people of Kahiki, their myth-historical point of origin.

Identities emerge and change historically in the context of salient social and political oppositions. From an indigenous point of view Walter Lini's primary ethnic affiliation might equally well be based on his birthplace or his linguistic group, for such ties are also significant in Melanesia (Bonnemaison 1985; see Pomponio, chapter 3, and Watson, chapter 2). My point is that the question cannot be decided a priori. The ni-Vanuatu identity is no less legitimate than these other possibl affiliations; it simply illustrates an identity in the process of definition, one that is coming to be, in response to changing historical circumstances and political imperatives. Moreover, the processes by which these various levels of identity are constructed—the externalization of culture, the use of tradition as a political symbol, the conscious formulation of cultural models—are very much the same, and are indicative of the inherent dynamism and flexibility of cultural identity.

Conclusion: Deconstituting Ethnicity

If, in Barth's (1969, 29) well-known phrase, "people's categories are for acting," then cultural identity is not given, fixed, or immutable, but is dynamically ascribed in the present. If cultural identity is created in the present, then—contrary to the Western notion of ethnicity—vertical factors such as putative ancestry, territorial origin, and parentage are less important in determining cultural affiliation than are factors we might call horizontal: interactions with social others, the political environment, prevailing categorical distinctions. Such familiar diacritics as how one behaves and how one speaks and dresses are the stuff of cultural ascriptions, but so are the criteria of tradition—which custom one embraces, which version of the past one invokes to validate one's identity. And today's models of the past can never be isomorphic with prior cultural practices and interpretations.

The objection can be made that these remarks about the conscious construction of cultural models and cultural identity apply only to politically and ethnically complex situations, that is, to people operating in the context of nation-states. The point must remain moot because no anthropologist has ever worked in a precontact society, and none ever will. But Rabinow (1977) and others have expressed the opinion that the un-self-conscious pristine society is a myth, that people everywhere and in all times have thought about their culture as they have lived it. Models that assume fixed boundaries and a static, passively transmitted culture seem inadequate when confronted with the dynamics of categorization and action.

The processes of social differentiation, self-ascription, and ratification that enter into the construction of cultural identity are largely the same whether the identity is local, tribal, linguistic, national, or regional. For that matter, the same processes enter into the formation of other kinds of group identity, such as professional and political. In a witty and heretical broadside at our disciplinary boundaries, Bernard Cohn outlines the different traditions adhered to by anthropologists and historians, thereby demonstrating that ethnic nationalists and social scientists often engage in a similar enterprise, "the objectification of social life" (1980, 217). Scholars too invent traditions, even about their own identities.

The range of identities espoused by contemporary Pacific Islanders suggests that there is no inevitable or primordial group attachment. Yet, however stubbornly we anthropologists assert the malleability of cultural identity, recent events in the Pacific have called into question the relevance of our theories. The Fiji coups of 1987 and the 1988 hostage battle in New Caledonia, where twenty-four people died, erupted as this volume was in the final stages of preparation. These events seem to herald a new era of ethnic conflict in the Pacific—a time of hardened boundaries and violent confrontations more characteristic of Northern Ireland and the Middle East than the island Pacific. The Fiji and New Caledonia conflicts have their own complexities, which I will not attempt to analyze in depth, but the two sets of events also seem to illustrate the inevitable outcome of advanced ethnic politics. I use the term *ethnic* advisedly here, for in both Fiji and New Caledonia the operant model of cultural identity, at least as promulgated by prominent political leaders, has more in common with classic Western ethnicity theory than with the Lamarckian affiliations described in earlier chapters. As the introduction to this book suggests, the experience of colonialism can be expected to alter notions of cultural identity.

In both Fiji and New Caledonia indigenous Melanesians make up just under half the total population. As an independent nation, Fiji represents the postcolonial Pacific, while New Caledonia remains a French colony. As portrayed in the international media, the current situation in New Caledonia is disturbingly familiar: an indigenous people struggles to wrest land and political power from European colonial domination. The native Melanesians of New Caledonia espouse the label "Kanak" and have become known as such in the international media. The phrase "Kanak tribes" appears occasionally in reports in *Pacific Islands Monthly;* the difference in cultural labels encapsulates a political struggle. There are twenty-eight Melanesian dialects in New Caledonia (PIM 1987, 59, no. 9:21). The Kanak Socialist National Liberation Front (FLNKS), the indigenous liberation movement, seeks to polarize the population into Kanak/non-Kanak segments and to establish an independent nation called Kanaky. Their dilemma, familiar in the new nations of Melanesia (see Larcom, chapter 8), is to forge political unity from diversity (a task faced by other groups elsewhere, for example, by American Indians; see Trosper 1981). The French in turn attempt to undermine Kanak unity by appealing to the "true diversity of races" in New Caledonia (PIM 1987, 59, no. 9:21).

Land alienation is a crucial issue for the Kanaks of New Caledonia. In Fiji, customary land rights have long been protected by law and most land is held by Fijians; thus before the May 1987 coup there was no present danger that Fijians would lose their lands to the Fiji-born Indians, who dominate business and commerce. Nor does Fijian culture appear to have been at risk. Nonetheless, fear of Indian political ascendancy has been a reality for several years (see Lal 1986). Although the coup was phrased as a nationalistic move to ensure "Fiji for Fijians," close observers have noted another agenda: the coup was an attempt by a circle of established chiefs to restore their authority over commoner Fijians as well as Indians (Lal n.d.; Rothwell 1987). According to a University of Hawaii historian's assessment, "The emergence in an incipient form of class-based multi-racial politics . . . posed a grave threat to the politics of race . . . and thus had to be nipped in the bud" (Lal 1987).

Like many indigenous nationalists, Brig. (formerly Col.) Sitiveni

Rabuka justifies his actions by invoking a romanticized vision of the past —in this case precolonial but post-Christian society (Rothwell 1987, 13). According to Rabuka, the missionaries turned "cannibal land into paradise," but this paradise was contaminated under British rule by the importation of Indians, whom he calls the "immigrant race" (Dean and Ritova 1988, 11). Invocations of "race" permeate Rabuka's rhetoric. Indeed, the use of "race" as a mobilizing tool is becoming increasingly common in Pacific nationalist movements. This is not surprising because, as described in the introduction, the Western concept of ethnicity lends itself readily to racial ideologies: Mendelian identity is fundamentally a matter of biological descent—egg, sperm, and genes. This premise is implicit in scholarly definitions of the ethnic group as "biologically self-perpetuating" (e.g., Barth 1969, 10–11; De Vos 1975; Enloe 1973, 17; Keyes 1981, 5; Reminick 1983, 8–10).

The recent use of racial ideologies in the Pacific appears to contradict my argument against primordial or Mendelian attachments. But one point of this chapter has been that contemporary Pacific nationalists are adopting international political strategies. Racial ideologies and invocations of tradition in the Pacific are modern, non-native forms of political action, and as such they must be distinguished from indigenous social theory. Even in the West, the historical salience of ethnicity as culture theory has been inextricably tied to its political uses (see Rothschild 1981). The ideologies promoted by political leaders do affect local theory. Rabuka's call to the Fijian race may be a political instrumentality of the moment, but Fijians are thereby encouraged to perceive and define themselves in unprecedented ways.

The adoption of Western-style racial rhetoric by Pacific nationalists highlights ethical quandaries faced by contemporary anthropologists. For example, the group working most actively for Hawaiian sovereignty today is *Ka Lāhui Hawai'i* 'the Hawaiian nation'. *Lāhui* is most often translated as 'nation' or 'people', but some activists gloss the term as 'race', and see the two meanings as synonymous. The difference in translation indexes a shift in emphasis: *nation* is an argument for political sovereignty, while *race* advances an exclusivist ideology. Anthony Smith (1981, 1) points out that one of Western liberalism's quixotic hopes was the disappearance of nationalism. Liberal scholars are typically sympathetic to the political struggles of indigenous peoples but discomfited by the racial ideologies and invented traditions that may be asserted to promote the cause. The Fiji case aptly demonstrates that such ideologies lend themselves to discriminatory policies in the hands of whatever group is in power. The ethical quandary persists despite a sense of tit-for-tat justice: the concepts of race and ethnicity were used by colonialists against Pacific Islanders, and perhaps it is only fitting that indigenous peoples now use the same tools to reaffirm their rights. But given the violent potential of ethnic conflicts I think it preferable that scholars retain a liminal status as questioners and critics, of native nationalism as well as of their own society's common sense. Anthropologists must continue to assert the contingent and symbolic rather than "natural" constitution of cultural identity.

NOTES

I wish to thank M. Jocelyn Armstrong, Alan Howard, and Lin Poyer for their critiques of earlier versions of this chapter, as well as the other members of the ASAO symposium, Cultural Identity in Oceania, for their comments. Fieldwork in Hawaii from 1974 to 1975 was supported by grants from the National Science Foundation (GS-39667) and the National Institute of Mental Health. The point of view expressed in this chapter owes much to my experiences living and teaching in Hawaii since 1984, and I wish to thank my students and colleagues at the University of Hawaii for many instructive dialogues.

1. It would be intriguing to trace the spread of Western models of ethnicity as accompanying the expansion of the capitalist world economy (see Wallerstein 1974). To date, "political economy" theorists have focused on economic stratification rather than comparative ideologies, however. Their argument is that ethnic conflict is founded in economic inequities of the world system (for discussion see Bourgois 1988; O'Brien 1986; Rothschild 1981, 52–60; Smith 1981, 26–44; Wallerstein 1973).

2. Brief news items from *Pacific Islands Monthly* (abbreviated as PIM) will be cited in the text.

8

Custom by Decree:
Legitimation Crisis in Vanuatu

JOAN LARCOM

As parliamentary debate on a successful recent bill to establish island courts in Vanuatu was concluding, a member of parliament commented that the concept of unlawfulness—on which the new courts would be based—was not found in past custom usage. His seemingly inconsequential observation, while it does not directly address controversies about the content of authentic custom in this newly independent nation, does relate to another issue, that of Vanuatu's current legitimation crisis. The term *legitimation crisis*, title of a book by Jurgen Habermas (1975), refers to a stage in late capitalism when the state fails to "maintain or produce effective normative structures to the extent required." Putting it more simply, Habermas explains that at this stage "there is no administrative production of meaning. . . . 'Meaning' is a scarce resource and is becoming ever scarcer" (quoted in Dallmayr 1981, 190).

Independent only since 1980, Vanuatu is by no means a late capitalist state. It had been governed by France and Great Britain since 1906 in a joint administration called the Condominium, yet nicknamed the Pandemonium because of the inefficiency of the arrangement. Though newly self-governing, the country has already been troubled by difficulties in "the production of meaning" at the national level. The meaning at issue for this new island nation surrounds *kastom* 'custom', which is rapidly being redefined by the national government as a concept that explains essential differences between Vanuatu and the West, or between indigenous linguistic groups (Larcom 1982). Although the preindependence concept of kastom had no bearing on issues of law or illegality (as the member of parliament suggested), some local courts are now preoccupied with issues of true and false customary rules. In their search for authentic cultural precedent, they are newly concerned with cultural identity as it is defined in contemporary international politics rather than with kastom as it was employed prior to independence.

This chapter will explore the construction of cultural identity in Vanuatu through current legal processes at the local level. I will argue

175

that the preindependence notion of kastom, at least as defined by the Mewun, a group of 550 people living on South West Bay, Malakula,[1] is being transformed into culture in the anthropological sense (Wagner 1981), and that this transformation is discernible in the proceedings of local courts. The organization of the chapter follows roughly the route by which I came to observe the changing meaning of kastom for the Mewun. I look first at Mewun models of the person, as evinced in court cases during 1973–1974, and then at Vanuatu nationalism, which was taking shape during my second visit in 1981. Last, I will address the problem of negotiating national and local cultural identity as it became apparent in 1983 in the context of changes in the legal system.

Since 1980 the national government has identified a composite of artifacts, including slit-gong drums, pigs' teeth, decorative leaves, and others as true national kastom symbols, even though this assortment is not significant for all the islands of the archipelago. These recent efforts to create a national culture as a rallying point for diverse indigenous groups have not yet proven broadly convincing. And the task of building national meaning, even if eventually successful, will proceed slowly. Meanwhile, local troubles highlight the need for a viable system of national control.

As it seeks to authenticate a national identity, the government must reconcile national concerns for the creation of meaning with the power of Melanesian localism, by which I refer to the predilection of ni-Vanuatu 'Vanuatu born' and numerous other Melanesians to recognize the consensus of their local coresidents as the most authoritative influence on dispute settlement and values. The recognition of local authority is particularly evident in the island courts bill discussed in this chapter.

The passage of the Island Courts Act in April 1983 was a crucial step in the government's attempt to construct and solidify a national cultural identity. The act was intended to grant decision-making authority over most local jural matters to local institutions. Apparently recognizing the inability of national legal codes to regulate social order in the villages, the government now sought to hand issues of law and justice back to village courts. The act authorizes village custom courts to determine custom laws to settle many of the land and social disputes that threaten to deteriorate into serious conflicts throughout the new nation. Islandwide courts and even the country's Supreme Court will be employed mainly as appellate courts for village disputants dissatisfied with local justice. But more is at stake here than law and order, for cultural identity itself will be negotiated by these village courts. Effectively, the Island Courts Act pushes each village kastom court to create a discrete culture as it legislates. I will suggest below that the decision to endow local institutions with this power stems from the failure of national efforts to accomplish the creation of meaning.

At the time of my initial fieldwork in 1973–1974, kastom was something akin to a commodity. It referred to sculptured artifacts and special actions (songs, dances), the performative rights that belonged to a distinct social group associated with a locality. Another group could acquire rights to replicate kastom by exchanging goods (usually pigs) with the inventors of a specific kastom. If the term *group* seems ambiguous here, that may be because the exchanging groups were often transitory and indefinite, created by and distinguished from other such groups by means of transactions such as kastom exchanges.

Until recently, particular kastom was not sacrosanct to a group. Indeed, it was often invented precisely to exchange or distribute. The secrecy that surrounded the invention and production of kastom artifacts and performances did not signify an essential identification with a particular group's tradition. Rather, secrecy was maintained to prevent the diffusion of kastom prior to its formal exchange. Systems of kastom exchanges and reciprocity defined group boundaries. Unique performances and artifacts (which are conventionally understood in the West as markers of different cultural groups) *derived from* rather than *determined* spheres of exchange among the Mewun.

Encouraged by the national focus on kastom, however, the Mewun have begun to substitute culture—a holistic concept of lifeways unique to a group—for exchange in the system of local order. As Wagner (1981, 32) has noted, "Culture extends the significance of technique, mode, and artifact to human thought and relationship." Mewun kastom, which once referred to a repertoire of transferable performances, techniques, and artifacts, is now used to denote a unique culture identified with the Mewun as a group. This new notion of Mewun kastom is defined by inalienable material items and practices as well as by the exchange relationships they signify.

Mewun Village Courts in the Colonial Setting

In many ways the Mewun aptly illustrate the role village courts play in negotiating both personal and cultural identity. Typical of Vanuatu's other citizens, this small population of subsistence agriculturalists engages in some cash-cropping of coconuts and cocoa and speaks an independent language. As Presbyterians, the Mewun belong to the largest religious denomination (40 percent of the total population); they are also loyal adherents to the leading political group, the Vanuaaku Pati. If the Mewun are atypical in any way, it is perhaps in the extent of their political zeal: as the first local group to displace a European from an adjacent plantation, they accelerated agitation for independence.

Although the Island Courts Act gives them authority to reinstitute kastom law, the Mewun have been missionized and colonized for nearly a century and thus remember little of precontact dispute settlement. The argument has been made that traditional communities such as pre-mission Mewun "could not be described as legal bodies" (Ngwele 1981, 12). In general, criminal behavior in such communities was not deterred by the threat of specific laws and sanctions, but by the positive power of social ties. A recent comment on the power of this traditional mode of order seems applicable also to the situation for the precontact Mewun: "In Vanuatu, . . . the most important reason for which custom is obeyed is that we know we have to live in the same community and we need help and security from one another" (Ngwele 1981, 12).

Most older Mewun concurred that Mewun disputes were avoided in this fashion; if not, they were settled by consensus. The aims of settlement were to make peace between the disputants and to repair or replace damages. If consensus was not reached, *muskat nomo i wok* 'the gun alone could settle it'. As Ngwele has noted generally for ni-Vanuatu, Mewun who were recurrent troublemakers among their kin and coresidents quickly lost support. As one Mewun man described it, they soon found themselves in Paradise.

Precontact disputes most frequently arose over adultery, slander, swearing, and murder. Most of them were between villagers, and disputes were usually settled through fines, reparations, or exchanges. Even if arguments were settled appropriately, miscreants were wise to keep out of the way of the offended, who might give way to rage and bloodshed when faced with a reminder of grievances. While there was no chief or central authority to settle disputes, big-men had a predominant influence through their control of pigs, which were often used as indemnity payments. People with fewer resources attached themselves to a related big-man who might assist their peacemaking efforts and loan them pigs to pay fines. The power of a particular big-man was limited to his own wealth in women and pig resources. In turn, these resources were also linked. The big-man's porcine wealth was often connected to his plural wives. Pigs were used in bridewealth and in return, extra wives tended a man's pigs and increased their numbers.

The big-man's wives were often essential to peace negotiations between villages. A general rule of village exogamy, coupled with another restriction on marriage into a village into which a coresident had married within living memory, encouraged a village's affinal links with diverse villages. Wives who had come from the village in dispute were allowed safe conduct to make peace between their affines and their natal villagers. Because he was likely to have several wives, the big-man often controlled most peacekeeping networks with other villagers. Inspired by movie Westerns he had seen, one Mewun narrator compared the traditional big-man to the American *kaoboe* 'cowboy', whose power depended on his control of women and guns.

Colonial agents replaced the musket as the court of appeal when fighting was suppressed in the early twentieth century. The degree and kind of force employed by district agents varied as colonial personnel changed. Most early colonial administrators are described by the Mewun as impatient and often unfair. During this administration, troubles in the bay were unceasing. In 1962 the colonial government instituted a system of assessors, men nominated by local people and appointed by the British district agent (BDA) of each region. These assessors were to serve as links between indigenous people and colonial justice. For Mewun the BDA appointed a strong and talented arbitrator who held the position until independence. This assessor worked well with the last BDA, who remained in this post until the country was on the verge of nationhood. The assessor was schooled in the delegation of cases: which he should decide and which should "go to the hand of the Master [the BDA]." When they first began working together, the BDA carefully pointed out to the assessor those cases that should be saved for his arbitration. These included assault (or any other crime involving bloodshed), statutory rape, and adultery. Other grievances could be handled by the assessor unless the participants were dissatisfied with his decisions; in that event the BDA would act as an appellate judge.

By the time I began fieldwork in Mewun in 1973, the division between local and colonial justice had settled into a stable system, with expectations and results relatively clear to both the Mewun and the BDA. Colonial law was enforced by Native Court, a meeting of a colonial official and local Mewun leaders held every other month. Between colonial court sittings, Mewun leaders were allowed to hold their own courts. By this time, European paradigms and expectations—that chiefs were essential to tribal government—had influenced and reshaped Mewun political structures to include chiefs as titular liaison positions. Each of the four Mewun villages had a chief, chief's assistant, and a headman who settled internal village disputes. Trouble between villages or cases that village chiefs could not settle were brought to the assessor for resolution or referral to the agent.

The BDA was well regarded by the Mewun for his consistency and his reliable support of local courts. Although he was not thought to be cruel or erratic, as were his predecessors, he still wielded sufficient force to deter local offenders who feared the agent's infamous prison cell, *namba sikis* 'number six'. This cell, which was reserved for the worst offenders, assumed almost mythic proportions as the worst of punishments. A few Mewun claimed to have peeked inside it. According to them, this tiny solitary confinement cell was lined with shards of glass. Imprisonment there was made even worse by a diet of heavily salted rice and too little water. Prisoners remained in number six until tractable, and Mewun leaders used it as the ultimate threat for unruly villagers. Defendants appearing before the BDA did make attempts to impress him favorably and thereby receive reasonable sentences. As one man noted, "We keep our hands out of our pockets and look him straight in the eye."

Mewun chiefs and the assessor used the agent's power as a symbol but settled most disputes themselves. Some of the cases earmarked for the BDA (adultery cases in particular) never reached his court. Only when the litigants were too "hot" and irreconcilable did they insist on retrial from the BDA. The Mewun retained control of their disputes in other ways as well. On several occasions the assessor and the chiefs manipulated the evidence they disclosed to the agent so that he would give them the judgment they felt appropriate for a village troublemaker. Even when the BDA presided, most legal cases were in effect settled according to Mewun rather than European standards of justice.

With the departure of European justice, which occurred before official independence, the Mewun lost the power of force that had supported social order; in exchange they gained little additional autonomy in their dispute-settling process, which they had effectively controlled for quite some time. They lost—temporarily at least—the final sanction of force lent by the BDA's presence. But the familiar precolonial alternative known as "musket justice" remained forbidden; those who took it up again during the Coconut War rebellion (discussed below) learned at great cost that the new independent government would not embrace this particular aspect of tradition. After the initial government crackdown on the rebels, however, the national leaders retreated from the use of force and left the villages to handle justice on their own.

The Justice of Emotions

The process of colonial justice and dispute settlement is worth further exploration for its impact on the emergence of an abstract concept of custom law. I suggest that justice as the Mewun enforced it in the colonial period was relative and relational. In this it departed widely from Western notions of justice, which emphasize impartiality, consistency in the enforcement of justice, and social criteria—the judgment of right-minded peers—for what is right (Morris and Read 1972, 292). Western definitions of justice rest on the assumptions of individual rationality and responsibility. In contrast, Mewun court judgments took into account the defendants' emotions and the causes of the emotions motivating offensive behavior. To an outsider, this Mewun recognition of feelings may seem to offer a justice that is highly contextual and based heavily on what Western justice calls extenuating circumstances. Outsiders may feel that a consistent code of justice would be impossible with such contextual guidelines. On the contrary, a closer look at Mewun concepts of emotion and personhood will reveal a consistency that is not necessarily alien to courts of justice as we know them.

The emotions referred to here were those regularly revealed and discussed in Mewun court cases: anger, jealousy, malice, passion. In most instances Mewun courts appear to have regarded these feelings as similar to states of enchantment, summoned up by another person's actions. Just as some social groups view all deaths as unnatural, as caused by sorcery, so the Mewun believed that the feelings of a defendant could usually be attributed to another person who intentionally or unintentionally caused them. This view of emotions explains the way justice was accomplished in those cases settled without the district agent's presence. Although people who committed misdemeanors were punished, individuals who caused any ill feelings inspiring asocial acts were also penalized, often more heavily than the offender. A short example from my 1974 field notes will illustrate this:

Three men had been working all day on a house. Corrugated iron was piled up inside so they could finish the roof the next day. After dusk, the three of them began drinking beer. Masing drank so much that he fell asleep inside the house. His two companions decided they should take their sleeping friend back to his own house so that his sharp-tongued wife wouldn't come looking for him. But when they tried to move him, Masing awoke and got so angry that he kicked out in all directions. This sent the corrugated roofing flying around the house and its noise awoke and disturbed other villagers.

This case of disturbing the peace never reached Native Court. A local court was held that, contrary to my expectations, did not limit its punishment to the noisemaker. One man was fined six pounds because it was his idea to move the sleeper, thus making him angry. The other one was fined four pounds because he had said something to Masing that made him still madder after they had awakened him. Masing, whose anger and noise disturbed the peace, was fined two pounds, the lightest of the three penalties.

The verdict in this case was typical of Mewun courts at the time. People who became angry and did disturbing things were punished in court cases, but those who made them angry were thought to be even more responsible for the anger and its consequences. While the man who disturbed the peace was punished, those who induced his anger, even though unintentionally, were penalized more. It is important to note here that intentionality had nothing to do with the fines set. In case after case, innocent remarks or actions with destructive results were fined without consideration for the perpetrator's intent. Sometimes a case was brought to the chiefs and assessor on the basis of hurt feelings alone, although no official wrongdoing (assault, disturbance of the peace, or adultery) had resulted because of it. The accused were fined just as if their acts or remarks had resulted in illegal acts.

The role of emotional states in court cases highlighted important characteristics of Mewun personal structure and the justice designed to deal with it. First, troubled emotions were not presumed to be the product of a person's inner psychological life. Second, these emotions were usually attributed to someone else, to a relationship gone awry and requiring a court hearing to straighten it out. In the Mewun courts, justice was not only contextual but dependent on relationships for its guidelines. Maintaining amicable personal ties was regarded as crucial; emotional slights were regarded more seriously and brought to court more frequently than property damage.

Concern with emotional equity between villagers meshes with a consociate (cf. Lieber, chapter 4) rather than individual conception of personhood, as other researchers in Melanesia have recognized (see, e.g., Burridge 1978; Battaglia 1984; Fajans 1986; Leenhardt [1947] 1979). Conspicuously absent from discussion in these court examples from 1973 to 1974 is any acknowledgment of kastom law, which the village courts have now been asked to establish.

The parameters of Mewun personal structure are suggested by similarities with the outline of the Melanesian person described by Maurice Leenhardt ([1947] 1979). Drawing on his forty-two years of mission work in New Caledonia, Leenhardt proposed that for the indigenous Melanesians, the self and body were not a unit. Rather the body was simply the support for a wider sense of person, which Leenhardt preferred to call "personage": "The notion that the human extends beyond man's physical image . . . explains why the [New Caledonian Melanesian] needs to find authenticity in the people around him" (Leenhardt [1947] 1979, 22). Leenhardt went on to explain this "authenticity" more specifically: "[The personage] knows himself only by the relationships he maintains with others. He exists only insofar as he acts his role in the course of his relationships. He is situated only with respect to them." When ostracized, a New Caledonian "no longer has any relationship through which to find himself again. . . . Feeling he is no other than a social being, he suffers from not being" ([1947] 1979, 153, 155). Leenhardt, then, outlined a concept of personhood very similar to the notion of the consociate (see Geertz 1973, 364–367; Lieber, chapter 4).

Although my research with the Mewun does not equal Leenhardt's lengthy experience with other Melanesians, his description of the Melanesian person or "personage" fits well for the Mewun (see also Larcom 1980). In particular, the essential link he postulates between person, identity, and relationships can explain the great concern with relationships and emotions evident in Mewun court decisions, both in the past and, to a certain extent, nowadays. If relationships are presumed to constitute identity, then breaches in relationships would be regarded as a serious matter indeed.

Missionaries and others have attempted to change the Mewun into individuals with a "capacity to deliberately step outside custom, tradition, and given social rules, rights and obligations, scrutinize them, formulate a moral critique . . ." (Burridge 1978, 15). But Mewun court cases tried outside of European supervision indicate that the participants, defendants and adjudicators, saw themselves as consociates rather than individuals in the sense familiar in European law. For the Mewun, social relationships and their emotional markers were the focus of the proceedings.

While European justice tends to relegate emotions to extenuating circumstances, colonial Mewun courts did not. For them, emotions were central; as noted, courts were sometimes summoned for the sole purpose of settling troubled feelings. Verdicts in Mewun courts sought justice, but a justice based on personal relationships and their emotional connections. These relationships were supported by the symbolic importance of place and locality; members of Mewun communities talked about their relationship in terms of contiguity rather than consanguinity. Although a locality might be populated chiefly by agnatic relations, principles of kinship were subordinate to stronger loyalties to location, a relationship inspired by living in the same place. Residents who were not kin could, through their presence and participatory actions, be permitted to join a new place (see also Larcom 1980, 1983). The mix of relational justice and potential colonial force worked well for the Mewun. The assessor once confided that he too, like the big-man and the kaoboe, was a rough type who accomplished things. When he was not able to settle a court case successfully, the British district agent stood by with cell number six, a modern replacement for the bygone big-man with his musket justice.

With independence and the departure of the BDA, the Mewun expected the big-man's role to be assumed by Walter Lini, the new prime minister. When Lini visited South West Bay in 1980, local men carried him aloft on a special platform, a recreation of one used to carry the big-man in earlier times. But the Mewun were perplexed by the national government's call for a nationwide return to kastom law. They themselves had no clear idea of this concept and wanted the government to guide them. Although police were still stationed on Malakula, they were apparently reluctant to employ force against miscreants at a time when law and custom were still being negotiated.

A year later, Mewun were complaining frequently that they needed clear laws defined from above: that trouble wouldn't "die" as it had in the past. The same conflicts flared up repeatedly. They reiterated a need for forceful police to support village leaders. While unlawfulness may not have been a concept in Vanuatu's custom past, Mewun concern with law and order was certainly increasing at this time. This was evident from the talk about kastom rules and from new distinctions being articulated between their laws and those of others. A new word was coined to describe this categorical opposition. Again drawn from Western cinema, the word *bondi* 'outlaw', from the French *bandit*, was used to refer not only to lawless people (such as those in urban areas) but also to groups with characteristic differences from the Mewun, such as the Small Nambas people from Malakula's interior. Mewun confusion over kastom law was not surprising in view of national government policy after independence. This policy remained murky as to the letter of the law and the locus of legislative authority. National leaders vacillated between decentralization and centralization throughout their first three years in office. The next section explores some of the valid reasons for the seemingly quixotic changes in government policy.

The Aftermath of Rebellion: Issues of Decentralization

Although preindependence discussions at the national level favored a decentralized mode of government, this plan was later set aside in favor of a more centralized administration when independence sparked rebellions at either end of the nation. In December 1980, three months after the end of colonial rule, this change of policy inspired the Decentralization Act. Decentralization was a misnomer in this instance for what was effectively a centralization act. While this law established and authorized island governments, it stripped them of any effective independent power, placing them under the complete control of the National Ministry of Home Affairs. While the curtailment of regional power was perhaps warranted by the circumstances surrounding Vanuatu's traumatic independence, the act nevertheless launched an abrupt change of course, steering the nation away from preindependence intentions to a highly centralized government structure. Passage of the Island Courts Act suggests the government has again swung back toward an acknowledgment of local autonomy.

The new government's actions regarding island governments have been greatly influenced by recent French actions in Vanuatu. At the 1979 Constitutional Committee meetings, attended by major political interest groups in the Anglo-French colony, members essentially agreed on the issue of decentralization (although there were differences about the extent and establishment of this policy). While pro-French representatives pushed for confederation, with strong regional councils and a weak central government, the pro-British Vanuaaku Pati argued in favor of a federal system with a slightly stronger central government. The Constitutional Committee finally came to the consensus that each elected regional council (some governing only a single island, others controlling island clusters) would negotiate with the national government about its particular powers (Constitution of the Republic of the New Hebrides, chapter 13, section 81-2). This solution seemed to satisfy all participants and the constitution was signed. Subsequent French-inspired (but probably not instigated) rebellions resulted in the reversal of this policy and sent the national government moving rapidly to consolidate control of its far-flung local administrations.

The French had good reasons for supporting confederation. They were more reluctant than their British partners to relinquish the colony. Since the time of Charles de Gaulle (under whose leadership France lost Algeria), this colonial power had emphatically asserted that it was in the Pacific to stay (Molisa et al. 1982, 83). Had Britain not insisted on withdrawal, France may well have postponed independence indefinitely, for their loss was to be much greater than that of their British counterparts (cf. Molisa et al. 1982). When independence became inevitable, the French government sought to make the best of the situation by retaining close ties with those islands known to have large French populations or pro-French sentiments. Their encouragement of these ties may have gone too far, for Santo and Tanna—large and economically important islands located at opposite ends of the new nation—became sites of pro-French rebellions. Ni-Vanuatu affiliated with the French attempted to secede from the national government; fighting and bloodshed resulted. This Coconut War, as journalists nicknamed it, began in late May, two months before the scheduled independence date of July 31, 1980. Fear and fighting continued on through independence celebrations while the last rebels were not captured until the end of August. During that time, two men were killed, stores were looted, and many people were evacuated from the rebellious islands. The French perhaps received more than their fair share of blame for the disturbance and, in the aftermath, a large part of the French population left or was deported.

In the following months, the national government quickly moved to empower itself to change the country's constitution without a referendum. This permitted parliament to pass the Decentralization Act, which altered the constitution's structure for island governments, not only removing much of their anticipated power but also changing the titles of regional councils to island governments. Having taken potential power from these decentralized councils, the national government then handed some of this power over to the villages (admittedly less threatening entities than island governments) when it passed the Island Courts Act two years later.

Persistent local problems persuaded the national government to give the village courts unrestricted authority to settle disputes with the support of the national police force. This power was given without qualification because of the strong belief in custom. As the prime minister himself noted in debate over the Island Courts Act, local courts "did not need a formal law because they had existed for many years; if a law was drafted, it would interfere with custom" (Lini, First Ordinary Session of Parliament, April 11, 1983). For the Mewun at least, this is not precisely the case, unless precontact consensual decision making can be called a court. Nevertheless, national government settled its "legitimation crisis" by giving decentralized authority to the village and custom courts. What and where was the "custom" invoked by this decision?

Culture on Trial

At both the national and the local Mewun level, kastom is becoming "culture" in the anthropological sense. Previously, the Mewun readily referred to kastom but employed it to mean commodities, things that could be manufactured, bought, and sold. As noted above, kastom was used to refer to concrete artistic creations, but it could also apply to the nonmaterial, such as a song whose words were in a language unknown to the purchasing group (Guiart 1963). Kastom, however, was never invoked as law or used to justify behavior.[2] While kastom was the product of creativity, it was not at that time a part of what authenticated a social group. Rather, authenticity (a concept remotely—if at all—familiar to Mewun before independence) rested on relationships created through commensalism, contiguity, and exchange. Mewun cultural identity was not derived from pristine forms exclusive to them and differentiating them from their neighbors. Although such cultural forms might have been distinct in the eyes of an anthropological observer, they did not shape, condition, or monitor identity for the Mewun themselves.

But kastom as culture now refers to customary actions and beliefs. Recently, the *Wunderkammer*[3] of Mewun kastom—a collage of symbolically colored leaves, masks, puppets, war clubs, spells—has become the object of conscious reflection. As Wagner (1981, 29) has written, culture in this narrow anthropological sense is an invention of Tylor and others who brought it out of museums (ordered versions of the Wunderkammer) and claimed to find it (with the same characteristics) in living human societies: "Because this invention . . . took place in the context of museums and of an historical self-identification, the resulting notion of culture assumed the characteristics of a museum assemblage. It was finite, discrete, and unequivocal; it had peculiar 'styles' and 'usages' that could be determined with great precision." It is this sort of culture that village courts have been asked to crystallize into custom law. With this precedent established, they may legislate from a locally established custom code—different from colonial law but a code nonetheless. At the present time, Mewun identify themselves increasingly with this custom law and as a result court cases tend to focus on cultural abstractions as well as on the emotional dynamics that have characteristically brought plaintiffs to court (Larcom 1982).

This far-reaching mandate has already caused disputes in Mewun about the validity of various past practices and correct kastom behavior; each point is hotly debated. The best example of the impact of the recent law was the village decision to divest three men of their land. (See Larcom 1982 for a more detailed discussion of this case.) A court case brought by their cousin claimed that they were not true members of his place or clan. He argued that they were descended from outsiders who moved in and had acquired membership two generations earlier. Prior to this, the cousin and the three disinherited men had recognized the same food restrictions, used the same garden magic, known the same spirit ancestors, and farmed the same stretch of land. Essentially, they had behaved like brothers and regarded one another as such. Yet the cousin, made freshly aware of kastom as cultural essence, claimed that the three others were in effect imposters and should return to their own land. As evidence he cited gong beats, each of which was unique to a clan and used to summon members to gatherings in precolonial times. It was noted that the "imposter" cousins were linked with a different gong beat than the cousin. He won his case against them, thus demonstrating the triumph of kastom as inherited culture over rights deriving from a lifelong relationship (cf. Watson, chapter 2, for recognition of the same distinctions in social action).[4]

The new debates can lead to arcane claims and appropriations. Courts recently debated whether affinally related women should continue to have water rights at a local river when they had been forbidden by taboo to draw water there two generations ago. More recently, a younger man tried to convince others that limestone building material (used to build cottages in the early mission days at South West Bay) was really his relatives' invention, *kastom simen* 'custom cement'. Older men persuaded him that he was mistaken and that the manufacture of this lime had been taught to them by Scottish missionaries. In this drama of active and ongoing negotiation, one month's custom rules are sometimes eclipsed by those of the next.

The irony of this process of cultural definition is that by encouraging local village courts to decree true custom to distinguish the nation from the West, Vanuatu may unwittingly be replicating the West. By endorsing a museum culture of its own, the nation implicitly challenges a most distinctive aspect of Vanuatu social life—its emphasis on relationships, creativity, and exchange. For many local groups, including the Mewun, the unabashed invention of artifacts as emblems and invitations for relationships may come as close as possible to an authentic ni-Vanuatu culture (if I may be permitted to use a word in a context for which it has just been discredited). For both the person and the group, relationships have been more salient features of identity than any inherent essence or characteristic. Until recently, ni-Vanuatu concern with relationships as personal identity included kin and coresidents, while affiliations with more distant persons could be negotiated by means of the purchase and sale of invented kastom performances or artifacts. These inventions were important, but only for their role in transactions. Power resided in the knowledge of manufacture, dance, or song (rather than in the item or act itself), and in the relationship such an item could create if sold to someone else.

Fundamentally, most Mewun court negotiations in the colonial era were about relationships—the social ties that Leenhardt saw as emblematic of personal identity. Cultural identity, on the other hand, if used to refer to the authenticity of a group based on a unique repertoire of values and artifacts, is new to the Mewun. To be sure, from the anthropologist's vantage point the Mewun have had a cultural identity for as long as they have been known to Westerners. Earliest visitors noted them as distinct from their neighbors in beliefs, customs, and language (Deacon 1934; Layard 1928).

But the significant point here is that the Mewun have not perceived themselves as a separate cultural entity until recently. Their authenticity—if such a concept ever crossed their minds—was instead entwined with the land on which they lived and the relationships in which they participated. This home, their sociomythic place, gave them a common frame for social connections and a joint history defined by inhabited space. Growing Mewun consciousness of the power inherent in cultural distinctions has arisen with their awareness of national politics and kastom. Moreover, the two forms of identity—personal and cultural—are at odds. The first is fluid and relational; the second is a recent conversion of purchased artifactual creations into discrete custom or tradition for the anthropologist to catch in her net. The Mewun and other local groups in Vanuatu must now negotiate between these systems of identity.

In returning these issues to the villages, the national government has at least situated its legitimation crisis in the appropriate place. In the village courts the scale of the debate ensures that localism will remain strong and that the primacy of personal relationships will not soon be set aside. As for the Mewun, their hopes for the newly strengthened local courts remain high. Nowhere is this optimism more evident than in their name for the group of chiefs who will adjudicate the courts. They are called *nikikinau* 'linchpin of a fence', that strong and straight piece of wood that holds all the other pieces in place.

NOTES

I wish to thank Jocelyn Linnekin for her encouragement and editing on this project. Any weaknesses and errors are, of course, mine.

1. Since the country's independence the official spelling has been changed from Malekula to Malakula.

2. Concepts that the Mewun formerly referred to as *fasin* 'manner, custom, way of doing things' are now called kastom. Fasin had also been extended to the phrase *fasin blong bifo* 'a traditional way of doing things'. The new use of kastom to represent that which was formerly called fasin shows the change from earlier (1973–1974) uses of kastom described in the first section of this chapter.

3. An early modern precursor to the museum (and perhaps also to the sideshow), the German Wunderkammer was, quite literally, a chamber of wonders. "Providing a kind of humanist counterpart to medieval treasures of holy relics, the *Wunderkammer* displayed both the wonders of creation and the works of man" (Honour 1975, 30). Otherwise, collections were eclectic: narwals' horns, Brazilian rattles, ostrich eggs, dried flowers, and Egyptian "idols." Brought back from European voyages of exploration, such items found their way into the uncategorized bricolage of these chambers. They were apparently included in the display simply because they were curiosities, and not because they were critical to systematic knowledge of the material world.

4. Although this may seem to fit neatly into Watson's (chapter 2) distinction between inherited cultural identity (Mendelian) and acquired cultural identity (Lamarckian), I have found a different distinction more accurate for the Mewun experience. In my view, changes occurring in Mewun should not be characterized as different kinds of cultural identity. Instead I see the Mewun as choosing between culture and exchange/reciprocity as alternate modes of defining social identity.

9

Is It in the Blood?
Australian Aboriginal Identity

MYRNA EWART TONKINSON

Who are Australian Aborigines and what are their distinguishing characteristics? These questions have been posed in a variety of ways and have evoked a variety of responses over Australia's two-hundred-year colonial history. The question of Aboriginal ethnicity is certainly a postcolonial one. The British created "Aborigines" as an ethnic category based on European notions of culture and heredity and imposed Aboriginal ethnicity on the indigenes. In establishing the Australian nation, the British settlers and their successors defined Australianness in essentially racial terms and excluded the indigenous people from that category.

Ethnographic evidence clearly indicates that before the arrival of Europeans, numerous distinct groups existed on the Australian continent. Although they shared physical and cultural features and had ties of affinity, trade, and religious cooperation, these societies were distinguished by geography, language, and culture. There is no evidence that the indigenes perceived themselves as a homogeneous group in the way that Europeans perceived them. Indeed, given the size of Australia, the antiquity of Aboriginal occupation and dispersal over it, and the economic adaptations they had made, homogeneity would have been impossible. Aboriginal ethnicity is most evident in the Aborigines' interaction with whites in Australian society (cf. Cohen 1974a, xi). Certainly, Aborigines in precolonial Australia were not without self-conscious group identities, but power relations were of an order different from the politics of the modern nation-state, and this difference heightens the significance of ethnicity.

From the earliest days of colonization, white Australians assumed the prerogative of defining and classifying Aborigines. They did so largely by contrasting Aborigines with themselves. Aborigines came to be defined as "others" (cf. Tatz 1979), lacking the physical and cultural characteristics valued by their colonizers. Nineteenth-century European notions about culture and nature helped shape the whites' perceptions of Aborigines. It was believed that culture was carried "in the

191

blood," that color was the external indicator of both biological ancestry and culture, and that cultural characteristics, hereditary and immutable, separated human groups from one another. According to this model, Aborigines were at the bottom of an hierarchical scale and Europeans, particularly those of British stock, were at the top. Although such notions have been rejected or refined by scientists and scholars, they remain in popular theories to varying degrees and continue to be invoked.

Ethnographic evidence suggests that in determining identity, Aborigines traditionally attributed greater importance to culture and genealogical ties than to heredity. Groups were differentiated on the basis of the presence or absence of certain beliefs and behaviors, and of spiritual ties between people and land.[1] Ethnocentrism led to the attribution of negative characteristics to other groups, but this seems to have been understood in cultural rather than hereditary terms (see, e.g., Meggitt 1962, 34–35, 41, 43–49). Personal identity and group affiliation are only partly accounted for by parentage; other important factors include place of conception, the actual rearers of the child, affiliations to land, rights in ceremonies and religious paraphernalia, and language "ownership" as well as use.[2] All these factors are linked to the Dreaming, the spiritual essence and beings that preceded and continue to give life and meaning to the landscape and everything in it, including humans (Stanner 1979, 23–40).

Despite their cultural diversity, Aborigines share a history of exclusion from white society, subjection to special laws, and a subordinate and powerless status relative to white Australians, though not within their own groups and communities. Today, Aboriginal leaders seek to build upon the notion of an Aboriginal ethnicity originally imposed upon them.[3] Aboriginality is a tool of contemporary Aboriginal political struggle and is viewed by its proponents as a positive force. Yet this identity was in the past defined negatively, institutionalized, and legally codified and enforced by the dominant European society.

Although cultural and other differences persist, most Aboriginal activists emphasize the essential oneness of all people of Aboriginal descent. They assert that Aborigines share a common cultural heritage as well as a history of oppression by white society, and seek to wrest from whites the prerogative of defining Aboriginal people. They are working to transform their status from that of a powerless and despised minority to one fully participating in Australian society, or even to a sovereign Aboriginal nation. The identification of common cultural themes and the maintenance of traditions—or their revival (and invention) where they are moribund or absent—are all part of the process. Changes within Australian society and global changes in the position of indigenous peoples have contributed to a modern notion of pan-Aboriginal identity, which is being institutionalized in political movements, evocative symbols, and personal action.

At least two aspects of Aboriginal identity must be considered here. One aspect is the identity of specific local or regional groups sharing history, culture, and social organization. The other is a more inclusive pan-Aboriginal Australian identity. For many Aborigines both identities are equally important; for some, one or the other takes precedence.

Local Identity

Describing Aborigines in the Cape York Peninsula region, von Sturmer (1973, 21–22) remarks on the "high degree of group segmentation and personal individuation." Despite many cultural similarities between groups, it is the differences that are most conspicuous and significant from the Aboriginal viewpoint. This finding is not unusual in Aboriginal Australia, where people often invoke their uniqueness of language, traditional territory, and kinship in asserting their identity. They do not usually refer to abstract values as distinguishing features, but those values are nonetheless implicit. Color is recognized and labeled, just as blindness or size is, when individuals are being described, referred to, or even addressed. But it is culture that is paramount in establishing identity.

Aborigines among whom I worked at Jigalong describe their group membership at several levels. They are members of language groups whose distinctiveness they emphasize, although these are technically dialects of one language. The dialect label also indicates specific areas of land in the Western Desert, "countries" from which they originate and which they traditionally owned: for older people especially, identification with their country, from which they have long been separated, is laden with intense emotion. In their dealings with other Aboriginal groups in the wider region where they have ties of kinship and religion, they are the "Jigalong mob," both to themselves and to those others (Tonkinson 1974). At another level they are *mardu*, a word that has multiple meanings (discussed below). As a cultural label it refers to Western Desert people, a dispersed regional group that shares a body of cultural practices labeled by the Aborigines in English as "the law" ("the Dreaming" is a more common gloss). "The law" is what distinguishes them from whites, from Aborigines with whom they do not share this code, from "others"; it is what makes them unique (see Stanner 1979, 23–40; Tonkinson 1978, 14–18). While they recognize affinities with other Aboriginal groups, Jigalong people emphasize their cultural differences from those groups. Similarly, groups throughout the continent draw cultural (as well as kinship and territorial) boundaries between themselves and others (cf. Berndt and Berndt 1985, 91–106; Meggitt 1962, 34–46).

Mardu has a wide range of meanings. At its most general level it means people among whom the speakers include themselves. Thus the term can mean human being or person, though it is seldom used in this way. In some situations, it means black people in a generic sense, in contrast to white people. Thus, black American actors in a movie may be referred to as mardu. However, Jigalong people do not use this term inclusively when shared culture is a salient factor. Thus, although I am black, Jigalong people never called me mardu; in fact, they often called me "whitefella." When I questioned people about this they explained that I spoke English, lived as white people do, and came from a country (Jamaica) unknown to them. Similarly mardu may be applied to other Aboriginal people in Australia when only physical appearance is significant, but not when culture and behavior are considered (cf. Poyer, chapter 6). Mardu is also contrasted with *mardamarda*, a color term for people of mixed white-Aboriginal ancestry, and others such as Japanese. Jigalong people of mixed descent are called mardamarda in a descriptive but not exclusive sense; they are also mardu, unlike people of mixed descent who are strangers to Jigalong people and are mardamarda in contrast to mardu (cf. Sansom 1982, 135–137). Aborigines of mixed descent may also be classified as whites by Jigalong people, based on their behavior. For example, I once heard a Jigalong woman refer to an urban Aboriginal woman as *mijiji* 'missis' (white woman). It is not that Jigalong people have no concept of inherited characteristics (they do, although I am unable to provide an account of this here), but that they are most concerned with relationships and identifiable behavioral features. Lieber's exposition (chapter 4) on Lamarckian identity in the Pacific suggests a useful direction for exploring Aboriginal people's understandings about identity.

Jigalong Aborigines' ideas about conception and development of children also differ sharply from European scientific explanations (discussed below). Conception occurs when a spirit child finds and enters its mother. While both parents are important in establishing the identity of the spirit-child (its assumed animal, plant, or mineral form becomes the child's conception totem), much of what the child "inherits" is determined from the site from which it emerges and the ancestral creative beings (Dreamings) associated with that territory (Tonkinson 1978, 1984). In this scheme, biological endowment is of far less significance than in the European worldview. Jigalong people place great importance in their links with their ancestors, biological and spiritual, back to the beginnings of their world. Yet genealogical time is shallow, so notions such as atavism and the racial ideology that gave rise to it would be inconsistent with their beliefs concerning the origins and development of persons. For people like the Jigalong group, Aboriginality is not a self-conscious identity; there is no evidence of a pan-Aboriginal consciousness, nor of the notion of being Australian. With access to modern transportation and communication, however, Jigalong Aborigines have increasing contact with people outside their customary arena of relationships. They are aware of Aboriginal groups in distant parts of the continent and are curious about them. They are becoming involved as a community in regional Aboriginal politics, which links them to ever-widening circles of Aboriginal interests. The efforts of those working to forge a pan-Australian Aboriginal identity will have a growing impact on the consciousness of Jigalong people and others like them.

Aboriginality

What I have called local identity has a long history. In this section I discuss the development of pan-Aboriginal identity, a process that is relatively new, so new in fact that some observers do not acknowledge its existence. The controversy about pan-Aboriginality will be discussed later. Jones and Hill-Burnett (1982, 214–246) have described the development of Aboriginality as a process of "ethnogenesis." This is a political process involving the construction of a common culture out of a situation of cultural diversity. Ethnogenesis is in its early stages in Australia. A tension between local identities and pan-Aboriginal constructions results from "discontinuity between a politically motivated ethnic elite and the rest of the ethnic population who are culturally diverse . . ." (ibid., 229).[4] This process resembles similar political and intellectual processes occurring among indigenous peoples elsewhere in the Pacific (cf. Linnekin, chapter 7).

Sansom (1982, 117–138) attempts to explain why ethnogenesis is such a difficult process for Australian Aborigines. He describes what he calls the "Aboriginal Commonality," a set of shared cultural characteristics, and asserts that Aborigines in widely divergent regions and conditions adapt in distinctively Aboriginal ways to changed circumstances, resulting in remarkably similar structures and behaviors. But, Sansom argues, these very "commonalities" serve to sustain barriers between Aboriginal groups because among them is a tendency to limit group membership to a narrow range of persons and to maintain boundaries between groups (ibid., 136, 137).

The term *Aboriginality* is being increasingly used to denote Aboriginal identity, usually in the broadest sense. Its meaning remains imprecise. The notion of Aboriginality has emerged in a climate of political change among Aborigines, and among white Australians as well. It is perhaps not a coincidence that official policy shifted from assimilation to self-determination about the same time a self-conscious promotion of Aboriginal identity by Aboriginal people (and their white sympathizers) was taking place. Aboriginality has more in common with Maoritanga than with kastom, although it shares some features of both (see Linnekin, chapter 7; Larcom, chapter 8). It is an important political symbol at a time when Aboriginal people are demanding recognition of their uniqueness as descendants of the original Australians, as well as rights appropriate to that status.

A number of symbols, themes, and activities can be identified among Aborigines who espouse Aboriginality as the basis for national unity, if not nationhood. Foremost among these is the focus on land. Since the early 1970s the demand for land rights has become a potent rallying cry for Aboriginal people across the continent. As dispossessed people, most Aborigines share the desire for the restoration of land, secure tenure, and compensation for the loss of land. These wishes and demands have been made implicitly and explicitly by Aborigines at many stages of Australian history since white settlement. However, the struggle took on new dimensions in the early 1970s with the emergence of a strong, highly visible Aboriginal protest movement.

A major political impact in the land rights campaign was made by the "Aboriginal Tent Embassy," which itself became a symbol of Aboriginal identity and solidarity (Gilbert 1973, 27–32; Miller 1985, 195). The embassy was set up outside the Federal Parliament House in 1972. Participants came from all over the country and considered themselves to be representing the interests of all Aborigines. They drew up a list of demands, including land rights, protection of sites, and compensation. This protest attracted enormous publicity and the then-opposition Labour party promised to take up the issues the protest raised. Although by no means entirely successful, the movement gained momentum when, on winning government in 1972, the Labour party began to implement new policies on land rights and in other areas of Aboriginal affairs (Lippmann 1981, 51–54; Newfong 1972, 4–6). "Land Rights" continues to be the slogan most often used by Aborigines to encapsulate their demand for equity in Australia. Even the most liberal land rights policy benefits only a minority of Aborigines, but the willingness of governments to confer such rights is seen as a symbol of reparation to all Aborigines for past dispossession (cf. Miller 1985, 194).[5]

In their political struggle, Aborigines emphasize the antiquity of their habitation of Australia. They cite archaeological findings, firmly establishing Aboriginal presence on the continent for at least forty thousand years. Although most white Australians do not concede any prior right of land ownership to Aborigines, many find this record impressive in a new country where people are anxious to establish their Australianness by claiming generation depth through their settler/immigrant ancestors. But even that status is not unconditionally granted; those most likely to achieve such recognition are those who can claim with some credibility that their cultural practices are rooted in antiquity. Those who cannot make such claims are often described as detribalized or as having "lost their culture" (cf. Chase 1981) and are sometimes accused of attempting to benefit by claiming Aboriginality.[6]

Aboriginal people have developed or modified a number of symbols and events to mark their separate and unified status. The most successful of these has been the Aboriginal flag—a golden sun on a red and black background. It first appeared around 1972 and has featured prominently in land rights and other campaigns since then. For some the flag is probably an indicator of desired sovereignty, while for the majority it is a powerful and easily recognized way of marking things and events as Aboriginal. Its power as a symbol may be demonstrated by the fact that in 1982 the mayor of a small town burned one such flag in protest when it was flown during Aborigines Week.[7]

Throughout the country a National Aborigines Day of Celebration (NADOC) is observed each year. This celebration originated from a Day of Mourning and Protest held by Aboriginal activists in Sydney in 1938 on the 150th anniversary of colonization of New South Wales (Aboriginal Newsletter 1983; Lippmann 1981, 48–49).[8] Over the years the celebration has widened in scope and softened in tone. It is now a week of cultural activities, during which national attention from both Aborigines and whites is focused on Aboriginal heritage and achievements.

Rowse (1985, 45) points out that the notion of Aboriginality "has some pertinence to the mobilization of Aborigines as a national interest group" and points to areas in which Aborigines have succeeded in establishing national bodies and in getting governments to deal with them (cf. Jones and Hill-Burnett 1982, 230). Aboriginal voluntary organizations and representative bodies have proliferated over the past fifteen years or so. Some serve local needs for health, legal aid, and housing; others have regional or national constituencies. Many of these bodies attract government funding. Some have statutory authority, having been established by government to administer Aboriginal land or perform other functions. Individuals hone their skills as leaders, negotiators, and lobbyists in such organizations, which have important lobbying functions. There are no Aboriginal representatives in the Australian

Parliament (though there was a senator until 1983) and only one elected Aboriginal state politician.

The closest thing to a national Aboriginal representative body was the National Aboriginal Conference (NAC), which was disbanded in 1985. The NAC had little power, being only an advisory body answerable to the federal minister for Aboriginal affairs and subject to criticism from many quarters. But its demise has left a void, for the NAC at least acted as a high-profile national body that could lobby governments on behalf of Aborigines, offer comment or criticism of government policies, and generally act as a watchdog body.[9] It was also an important if controversial symbol of Aboriginal unity (Weaver 1983).

Aboriginal delegates have attended sessions of the United Nations Sub-Commission on the Elimination of Discrimination, and Aboriginal representatives sit on the World Council of Indigenous People (WCIP). Through these bodies, Aborigines have aired their grievances and demands in international forums, where they interact and establish links with other members of the Fourth World (NAC Newsletter 1980, 9, 25). The term *Fourth World* denotes indigenous minorities who are structurally if not numerically subordinate in their homelands; this is the status of all members of the WCIP (Manuel 1974).

The Aboriginal political movement that emphasizes the unity of all Australians of Aboriginal descent uses rhetoric similar to the independence movements and postindependence nation-building ideologies of the developing countries (cf. Jones and Hill-Burnett 1982, 217). In this respect, the concept of Aboriginality has similar meaning and function to the concept of kastom (see Larcom, chapter 8). Some Aboriginal leaders actually speak of an Aboriginal nation, either metaphorically (Gilbert 1973, 193) or as a potentially separate state within Australia (ibid., 189). Some proponents of the latter even suggest that there was an Aboriginal nation before Europeans arrived. The demand for Aboriginal sovereignty is not generally supported by Aborigines and is rejected by Australian governments. But Australian Aborigines as a national constituency are represented on several international bodies.

As a result of the recent focus on Aboriginal identity, some Aboriginal people have been impelled to revive traditional culture or to embark upon a quest for personal historical and cultural information to establish their Aboriginal heritage. Miller carried out documentary and oral research on his own family and concluded that the "destruction" of Aboriginal identity was a deliberate policy of governments (1985, 138 and the following pages). He asserts that "the most important thing that I received by tracing my family was a new sense of identity" (ibid., 227). A concern with "loss" or "destruction" of Aboriginal identity recurs in the writings of many Aborigines and whites (e.g., Berndt 1977, 1; Colbung 1979, 102, 103; Gilbert 1973, 115, 130, 150–152).

The theme of recovery is summed up in the slogan "Cultural Revival
Is Survival," which appeared on a NADOC poster a few years ago. It
affirms the link between the local and national, the cultural and political aspects of Aboriginal identity. Those who are conscious of their
Aboriginality in the inclusive political sense often seek genealogical and
cultural details from their past or borrow them from existing groups
with strong traditional features (Gilbert 1973, 184; Miller 1985, xvi).
This trend resembles the prescription offered by Berndt for the successful forging of a "*real* Aboriginal identity [that is] composed of two features": aspects of traditional culture, which are "transferable," and
"that part of the Aboriginal heritage which is derived from the long and
painful process of Aboriginal-European contact" (1977, 11–12, emphasis in original).

Defining Aboriginality

Although the terms *Aboriginality* and *Aboriginal identity* are widely
used, they are seldom defined. The meanings are usually assumed to be
self-evident. The past ten years have seen a proliferation of writing by
Aboriginal people; books, articles, pamphlets, and from 1971 to 1982 a
national magazine called *Identity*, have been published by Aborigines.
Despite this increase, there is little in published form that specifies the
components of Aboriginal views of Aboriginality.

Some Aboriginal writers speak in terms of a shared experience of
oppression and discrimination as the basis for pan-Aboriginality (e.g.,
Gilbert 1973, 7, 193). Others refer to a common heritage or to cultural
continuities (e.g., Perkins 1974, 28, 29). Aboriginal writers sometimes
mystify Aboriginality as something unique and inscrutable that all Aborigines share and non-Aborigines cannot understand (e.g., Langton
1981, 1). A few Aborigines go even further and refer to "race memories"
shared by Aborigines (e.g., Gilbert 1973, 1–11; Willmot 1982), suggesting a biological component of culture. There is a tendency to emphasize
spiritual qualities and to idealize the Aboriginal past. When specific
traits are mentioned they are broad and, at least implicitly, they are
contrasted with white Australian values and attitudes (e.g., Gilbert
1981, 34–35; cf. Gilbert 1977, 1).

Social scientists specializing in Aboriginal studies have debated the
concept of Aboriginality. Opinion on all sides recognizes both cultural
similarity and cultural diversity in the Aboriginal population, but disagreement arises as to the relative weight to be given to differences and
continuities. Von Sturmer, for example, argues that Aboriginality simply does not exist: " 'Aboriginality' is a fiction which takes on meaning
only in terms of white ethnocentrism. . . . This identity can be nothing

more than an expression of faith. It represents an ideological position far removed from the concrete situation from which it is presumed to have drawn its substance" (1973, 16–17). Berndt (1977) suggests that "pan-aboriginality" is a "mirage" that can nevertheless take on "reality" by the self-conscious adoption of aspects of traditional and post-European Aboriginal heritage. Thiele (1984, 173–177) has accused fellow political scientist Tatz, a proponent of the concept of Aboriginality, of having made a political decision to " 'talk up' Aboriginality" (and " 'talk up' white guilt") when there is no empirical basis for its existence.

Tatz argues that the concept of Aboriginality accurately describes an Aboriginal reality that is at least emergent if not fully fledged. He speaks of recognizable cultural generalities among all people of Aboriginal descent wherever they are in Australia, even though they may not recognize or assert this common endowment. But he does not define Aboriginality in any specific terms; indeed, he declines to do so, implying that such definition is an Aboriginal prerogative: "I wouldn't presume to define the essence of Aboriginality" (Tatz 1979, 86). Tatz sees Aboriginality not only as a cultural actuality but a political potential, an emergent Australia-wide form of Aboriginal identity that must be fostered by Aborigines themselves. He argues that Aborigines are "collectively *other*" in Australian society (1982, 13, emphasis in original) and that this is a basis for unity.

Langton, an Aboriginal scholar, argues for the legitimacy of an "urbanizing Aboriginal culture" that demonstrates the "Aboriginality" of adjustments to city life (cf. Sansom 1982). She sees this adaptation as continuous with indigenous Aboriginal culture, which displays certain common features.

> There were pervasive commonalities in aboriginal life across the continent. The most important of these is the Dreaming. . . . [Also important are] a simple but highly efficient material culture, the complex social organisation and its acephalous nature and the "metaphysical emphasis on abidingness." The result has been social organisation as the source of the dominant mode of Aboriginal thinking. (Langton 1981, 21)

She accuses "mainstream social scientists" of failing to comprehend "the inside story of Aboriginality" (1981, 19).

Coombs, Brandl, and Snowdon (1983) have presented the most detailed description to date of Aboriginality. They identify the following characteristics as common to all Australian Aborigines: descent from the original inhabitants of Australia; a shared historical and cultural experience, particularly that arising from relations with non-Abo-

rigines; the Dreaming, or Aboriginal worldview; intimate familial relationship with the land and with the natural world; social interaction
based predominantly on the mutual obligations of kinship; observance
and social importance of mortuary rituals; and bi- or multilingualism
(1983, 21, 62). Coombs et al. (ibid., 62–63) argue that the "particular
synthesis of these elements constitutes Aboriginality." They offer a long
list of Aboriginal values, such as reciprocity, individuality, and competence, while conceding that these are not unique to Aborigines.

The question of what constitutes Aboriginality will not be resolved in
the short term. Perhaps a definition will emerge from continuing
research and debate among and between scholars and Aborigines. Similarities appear in aspects of Aboriginal culture throughout the continent, despite obvious variation in language, life-style, and socioeconomic circumstances. Certain similarities in speech styles, emphasis on
kinship, forms of dispute settlement, and patterns of generosity also
endure among Aboriginal people, but these have not been thoroughly
documented on a continentwide basis. I can say with confidence that in
contemporary Australia Aboriginal people share the consequences of
colonization and oppression and are building political unity by identifying common values, characteristics, and goals.

Racial Ideology and Policy: Origins and Impact

Available ethnographic evidence indicates that in precolonial times the
indigenous people of Australia constituted a number of small societies.
Despite interaction and cooperation across boundaries, there was no
overarching organization (see Berndt and Berndt 1985, 28–45; Hiatt
1965; Maddock 1974, 42–43, 183). Aboriginal reaction to their invaders
was therefore localized. The British, on the other hand, perceived the
indigenes as an undifferentiated mass; what mattered was how they differed from Europeans rather than whether they differed from one
another. Aboriginality was imposed on the native inhabitants. English
labels were applied to the indigenes instead of the names they had for
themselves: "natives," "aborigines," "blackfellows," and more-deroga-
tory labels like "niggers." Today "Aborigines" or "Aboriginals" is most
commonly used by whites and Aborigines. The latter also use a variety
of regional and local names. Derogatory labels, such as "coons" and
"boongs," are still used by many whites.

An emphasis on race, color, and national ethnic origin has always
characterized Australian society. Not only Aborigines but other nonwhites such as Melanesians, on the basis of their physical and cultural
features (actual or assumed), have often been victims of discrimination,

hostility, and violence (Evans, Saunders, and Cronin 1975; Lippmann 1973; Stevens 1971–72. To a lesser extent whites of non-British origin, especially those from southern and eastern Europe, have also been labeled as "others."[10] Even now, the unmarked label "Australian" usually denotes a person of Anglo-Celtic background (although in some contexts Irish ancestry is also labeled); all others are usually marked further (as Greek, Dutch, etc.) and Aborigines are always marked. Aborigines also tend to identify themselves as Aboriginal rather than Australian when questions of nationality arise. Aborigines and other nonwhites (notably Asian immigrants) continue to be the objects of hostility from segments of white society (Blainey 1984; Collins 1985; Lehmann 1983). Since these factors have all contributed to the development of Aboriginal identity, I will briefly outline the history of contact and relations between Aborigines and whites in Australia.

The British colonizers of Australia were confident of their superiority to the Aborigines and of the rightness of their colonizing actions. They were not universally hostile to the indigenous inhabitants, however. For example, Capt. James Cook, who first claimed New South Wales for the King of England in 1770, was influenced by images of the noble savage and wrote admiringly of the Aborigines. Many early settlers and administrators, too, were sympathetic in their portrayals of them (Reynolds 1987, 93–97; Woolmington 1973, 13). While there were always some whites kindly disposed to the native inhabitants (though seldom seeing them as equals), their views did not prevail during the intensification and expansion of colonization (Broome 1982, 47–48; Reynolds 1987, 97). There was a natural tension between benign attitudes and the exploitation of the land and its people.

Within a few decades of the first British settlement, relations between newcomers and indigenes greatly deteriorated. Colonial expansion began in earnest by the 1820s and continued for a century, as more colonies were established and exploration for land and resources spread into more remote parts of the continent. Inevitably these developments brought increasing numbers of indigenes into contact and conflict with the colonists. By 1852 most of the Australian colonies were self-governing and had the power to make laws, including the regulation of relations with Aborigines. This development was not, however, beneficial to the Aborigines, since the rights and aspirations of the whites were paramount. The whites wished to ensure their economic success unimpeded by the indigenous people (but when necessary assisted by their labor). To do this they perpetrated, usually with impunity, acts of dispersal, murder, and massacre (Rowley 1972a, 23). Resistance by the Aborigines engendered harsh retaliation (Lippmann 1981, 16–21); Rowley 1972a).

Justifications for colonization and domination of the Australian Aborigines, and even of their extinction, were usually couched in racial terms, based on theories developed in Britain.[11] Whether the prevailing racial theories were based on biblical notions of one origin for all humans with the degeneration of some groups (or God's curse on them), on biological or environmental determinism, or on popular versions of Darwinian evolution, as black people Aborigines fared badly, invariably being placed at or near the bottom of a hierarchical scale of humans.

Fear of the indigenes was strong, since many whites believed that the Aborigines were innately violent and treacherous. This belief justified whites taking violent action and instilling fear in the blacks (Reynolds 1987, 42–44). Few questioned their right—as white, Christian, agricultural, "progressive" people—to dominate black, pagan, hunting-gathering, "backward" people. In newspapers, fiction, cartoons, scientific works, and official reports, Aborigines were usually depicted as apelike, indolent, unintelligent, improvident, depraved, untrustworthy, childish, and filthy. Aborigines were seen as embodying the antithesis of all that whites thought (or wished) themselves to be, and the differences were accounted for in racial terms.

A dramatic decline in the indigenous population of Australia began in the early postcontact period and continued into the 1930s. Disease, violence, starvation, and other factors attendant on colonization decimated many groups (Reynolds 1972, 71). This pattern supported the belief, widely held and influential in policy making for many decades, that the Aborigines were biologically as well as culturally inferior to whites and were destined eventually to disappear (Woolmington 1973, 144). However, concomitant with this decline was a steady rise in the numbers of people of mixed Aboriginal-European descent (Rowley 1972b, 7, 9, 19). This discovery added a new dimension to popular debate and official action.

There was a great preponderance of white males on the frontier, and they often found sexual partners among Aboriginal women. Some unions were stable and lasting, though seldom entailing social equality. White men who married or lived openly with black women risked ostracism (and, later, legal sanctions). Most liaisons were fleeting or casual; prostitution was widespread, and coercion was common (Reynolds 1972, 27, 29, 32; Stone 1974, 63, 89; Woolmington 1973, 64–67).

As the frontier expanded, the progeny of these unions increased rapidly all over the continent. The reaction of Aboriginal groups to miscegenation is very poorly documented. However, many violent incidents in which Aborigines were the aggressors seem to have been provoked by white men forcibly taking Aboriginal women or reneging on agreements with men (Evans 1975, 103–104; Reynolds 1972, 28–32; Rowley 1972a, 78). There are reports of Aboriginal mothers or their relatives killing or rejecting babies of white fathers (Stone 1974, 113, 116; Woolmington 1973, 71). The frequency of such incidents is difficult to estimate. What is certain, however, is that thousands of children of mixed descent survived, they were rarely acknowledged or supported by their white fathers, and their mothers and Aboriginal relatives (including their mothers' husbands) cared for them, often concealing them from policemen or welfare officers (Cole 1979, 120, 133).[12]

For many whites the presence of people of mixed descent was a moral outrage, incontrovertible proof that the social taboo on intimacy between blacks and whites was being repeatedly broken. Whites expressed fear that a "mongrel" race was developing in Australia, that the children inherited the worst features of both groups and were a menace to society. There were calls for strict legal controls to stop the growth of the mixed-race population (Broome 1982, 93; Evans 1975, 108–109). However, opinion as to what should be done was not unanimous. Some whites thought that an admixture of "white blood" made for greater intelligence and malleability in "half-castes," who therefore would more successfully acquire European values and behavior than "full-bloods" (Reece 1974, 90–93). Some holding this view advocated policies to encourage miscegenation (at least between white males and "part-Aboriginal" females) and the consequent absorption of nonwhites into the white population. Segregation according to color of those who could not be absorbed was also advocated (Rowley 1972a, 139).

Although Australia was influenced by European ideas, it developed unique—though inconsistent and even contradictory—policies and practices in the area of race relations. There are parallels and contrasts with other new nations where Europeans colonized indigenous people and/or introduced African slaves, but the Australian system does not mirror any of the others. The American principle that classifies any person with known Negro ancestry as Negro regardless of phenotype (called "hypodescent" by Harris 1964, 37, 56), with its concomitant concerns with the preservation of racial purity among whites, is discernible in modified form in Australia. At the same time, efforts to classify people of mixed descent on the basis of color and other phenotypic features also occurred in Australia, although categories and terms were relatively few and did not persist. Although legally mixed-race people were differentiated from both blacks and whites, they were not accorded any intermediary socioeconomic niche as a category comparable to "free half castes," ladinos, mulattoes, or creoles in Brazil and other parts of the Caribbean and Latin America—somewhere between black slaves/Indian peasants and white owners/managers (cf. Harris

1964, 86–87; Hoetink 1967, 35–49; Smith 1980, 6).[13] This might be due to demographic factors as well as prejudice. Whatever the reasons, Australia has traditionally relied on new (usually white) immigrants to fill gaps in the labor force, rather than training and employing Aboriginal people in any significant numbers, except in the pastoral and agricultural areas. There was ambivalence about incorporating people of mixed descent into white society and opposition to their remaining in black society.

The views of two men who guided and enforced government policies in Aboriginal affairs illustrate some of the ideas white Australians held about Aborigines, heredity, and culture. Although J. W. Bleakley and A. O. Neville subscribed to different theories, there was little difference in the policies they implemented. Bleakley, for many years Chief Protector of Aborigines in Queensland, was commissioned by the federal government in 1928 to carry out a study of "aboriginals including half-castes" in the Northern Territory. In his report Bleakley repeatedly invoked the theme of the deterministic power of "blood." He was far more radical than many of his contemporaries, advocating that Aborigines, especially those of mixed descent, should all be trained, educated, and afforded certain basic rights in society. But he felt there were limits on what could be achieved: "With appreciable exception, the half-caste of 50 percent or more aboriginal blood, no matter how carefully brought up and educated will drift back to the aboriginal, where naturally he finds the atmosphere most congenial to him . . ." (1929, 17).

For those with less than 50 percent Aboriginal blood, Bleakley advocated quite different measures. They should be separated from Aborigines to "avoid the dangers of the blood call" and placed in institutions run by whites where they could be prepared to "take their place in white society on as equal a footing as possible" (ibid., 17, 28–29). This included the possibility that "some of the superior half-castes or quadroons may help solve the sex question [i.e., the shortage of white women] by marrying men in the outback not able to get wives of their own colour" (ibid., 28).

Bleakley's policies suffered a high rate of failure. For one thing, the placing of children in institutions had disastrous effects for them and their families. However, failed attempts to civilize people of Aboriginal descent were commonly explained as their succumbing to the force of their "Aboriginal blood" (Rowley 1972a, 139).

A. O. Neville spent twenty-five years (1915–1940) as Western Australia's Chief Protector of Aborigines and later was Commissioner of Native Affairs. He argued that culture was more important than "blood": "There is no marked difference between the blood of the native and ours, all human blood being fundamentally alike. Difference between the 'bluest' blood and the lowest in the land are due to tradition, environment and habit, not to blood variations" (1947, 55).

But, like Bleakley, Neville was very concerned about color and he seems not to have been convinced by his own arguments. His writings are replete with references to the redemptive quality of "white blood" and to the undesirable behavioral traits of nonwhites being transmitted genetically. Neville was certain that "full-blood" Aborigines would die out, and he strongly advocated assimilation, entailing the "breeding out of color" as well as the inculcation of European ideas, values, and behaviors. Neville believed that Aborigines would not "throw back," and color could be "bred out [of them] in three generations"; therefore, white men could marry light-skinned part-Aborigines without fear of atavism (1947, 59, 63; cf. Tindale and George 1979, 62). Unlike Bleakley, he could not countenance any mating of "full-bloods" with those of part-European ancestry; he also thought that white women found black men repugnant, so there was no danger of such unions occurring.

In the debate about the mixed-race population, the "law of atavism" played an important part (Evans 1975, 109; Markus 1982, 90). According to this view the physical (and assumed concomitant behavioral) characteristics of Negroes and Asians were so tenacious that even after generations of interbreeding with whites, people with a nonwhite ancestor, though seemingly white themselves, could produce a "throwback," a child with dark skin or other nonwhite characteristics. Those who advocated miscegenation as a method of assimilation were anxious to allay fears that this would be the case when whites interbred with Aborigines (Neville 1947, 58–60). In 1938 a team of researchers from Adelaide and Harvard universities undertook a study of the feasibility of absorbing "part-Aborigines" into the white population. In a report on this question, Norman Tindale, a member of the team, stated, "Complete mergence of the half-castes in the general community is possible without detriment to the white race. . . . Two successive accessions of white blood will lead to the mergence of the aboriginal in the white community. . . . A low percentage of aboriginal blood will not introduce any aberrant characteristics and there will be no fear of reversions to the dark aboriginal type" (1941, 67).

The policy of assimilation (and absorption) at least implied miscegenation, which had some vocal advocates, including Neville, who again were influenced by scientific developments, especially Mendelian population genetics, as well as by folk theories (Jacobs 1986). Australia appears to be unique in its consideration of a policy of miscegenation as a way of completing the process of colonization. However, a miscegenation policy was never implemented, perhaps because the regulation of marriage and sexual relations required for its success were beyond even the draconian controls placed on Aboriginal people. In any event, even the advocacy of miscegenation was short-lived. On this as on many other race-relations questions, Australian policymakers were ambivalent and self-contradictory.

Policies devised to deal with people of mixed ancestry have had lasting impacts on Aborigines and on race relations in Australia. In keeping with the prevailing notion that color corresponded with inherited behavioral proclivities, whites perceived persons of mixed descent as both culturally and genetically mixed. Because the Aboriginal component in such mixtures was undesirable, it was measured and marked. The term *half-caste* was applied to persons with one black and one white parent, but it also became a generic term for people of mixed descent. Terms such as *quadroon* (or *quarter-caste*) and *octoroon*, derived from Spanish for Negro-white admixture, were also used for a time but did not persist, unlike the situation in colonies such as Brazil, Cape Verde, Jamaica, and Surinam, where color terms and their related social categories proliferated and endured (Harris 1970; Hoetink 1967; Meintel 1984). The term *part-Aborigine* found wider acceptance and is still in use, although along with terms like *half-caste* it is rejected by many.

Skin color is not irrelevant for Aborigines, although they do not accord it the same prominence as whites do. As noted in the foregoing discussion of local identity, Aborigines apply color labels but do not attribute any necessary behavioral concomitants to color, though there are individual exceptions (e.g., Matthews 1977).[14] Sometimes Aborigines privately question the claims of those who do not look Aboriginal and do not have the family credentials that make appearance unimportant; and Aborigines sometimes use "black" as an epithet in teasing and quarreling in the same way that whites might (Eckermann 1977, 300). All this is at least partly the result of the influence of European ideas on Aboriginal thinking (cf. Jordan 1985).

When they were not removed from their Aboriginal families, people of mixed descent usually enjoyed acceptance and full participation in their Aboriginal communities (e.g., Palmer and McKenna 1978). Even if they were removed, many were aware of their links to Aboriginal relatives who strived to maintain contact. Contact was rarely maintained by white relatives. Furthermore, life in institutions did little to integrate Aboriginal inmates into white society. It is not surprising that most people of Aboriginal descent today prefer to be known as Aborigines and identify with other Aborigines. Some Aborigines adopt the label "black" to apply to all people of Aboriginal descent, whatever their skin color (cf. Dominy, chapter 11). This defiant symbolic rejection of white society and values coincides with an embracing of Aboriginal heritage.

As one activist, Paul Coe, put it: "We've never been part of the white Australian mainstream. . . . The only way we could join is by becoming imitation white men. . . . [We are] better off maintaining . . . separate identity" (quoted in Gilbert 1973, 188).

Current Aboriginal ideas about race and identity, at least among those who air their views publicly, show both European and Aboriginal influences. The Aboriginal emphasis on kinship and behavior in determining identity is apparent in their analysis. But so too are European notions of biologically determined behavior and hence identity. Many Aborigines seem to be saying that "Aboriginality" persists through generations, regardless of the degree of genetic inheritance, socialization, and experience (cf. Berndt and Berndt 1985, 547; von Sturmer 1973, 19).[15] Thus contemporary Aboriginal views on race show similarities with the American notion of the endurance of Negro characteristics referred to above, and with nineteenth-century European ideas about blood and its cultural concomitants (cf. Lieber, chapter 4).

Many white Australians, while regarding most people of mixed ancestry as outside white society, also deny their claims to being Aboriginal (e.g., English 1985). For them, authentic Aborigines are black, live in remote areas, and have exotic languages and cultural features. Persons lacking these characteristics cannot be "real Aborigines."[16] At the very least, as Jordan (1985, 33) points out, in both legal and popular definitions, "real Aborigines were those with negative attributes, segregated from white society, located in a negative world." People who do not fit these physical, social, and cultural stereotypes are rejected by many whites as opportunists or imposters if they claim to be Aboriginal or to speak for Aborigines (see, for instance, English 1985, 93–109). Whites' antagonism toward people of Aboriginal descent is greatest where the distinguishing physical and cultural features are blurred, probably because Australian policies toward Aborigines have given some validity to the color-culture equivalency view. A kind of self-fulfilling prophecy has been at work (cf. Palmer and McKenna 1978, ix). Thus those Aborigines who are most genetically distinct from whites also tend to be most culturally distinct. It is useful then to briefly review some of the policies that have led to this situation, and some of the ideas informing those policies.

By the end of the nineteenth century, the expectation that the indigenes were dying out was proving false. This view had served to justify neglect, but now pressure on governments to intervene was mounted from several quarters (Franklin 1976, 49–72). Renewed humanitarian efforts, along with demands for the Aboriginal "nuisance" to be removed and calls of alarm at the rapid increase in numbers of people of mixed descent, resulted in legislative action by colonial governments throughout Australia. Rather than ensure that Aborigines were granted the rights and obligations of British subjects, the laws passed for their "protection" formally stripped them of the rights of citizens (Franklin, 1976, 40–44; Rowley 1972a, 20–21, 35). Hasluck, writing in 1942, remarked that protective legislation diminished rather than enhanced the position of Aborigines by "[confining] the native within a legal status that has more in common with that of a born idiot than of any other class of British subject" (1970, 160–161). This was virtually inevitable because, as Rowley has cogently argued, whatever its aims legislation of this type is necessarily discriminatory: "The very attempt to protect the 'native' British subject in such rights as are left to him involves a separate status in law which places him at the mercy of the protecting agencies" (Rowley 1972a, 20). (See Dominy, chapter 11 and Sinclair, chapter 10 on the Maori.)

Not only did the laws apply exclusively to Aboriginal people, but they also differentiated among perceived types of Aborigines. Officials had the power to recognize descent by color and apply the appropriate labels and restrictions to individuals on that basis. Their judgment would override the wishes or opinions of the individuals to whom the labels were applied. A notion of contagion was implicit in these legal definitions so that, despite physical features, a person who lived or associated with one category of Aborigines could be included in it. This system usually placed individuals in the more restricted group rather than the reverse (Rowley 1972a, 354–355; 1972b, 46–47).

Each Australian state or territory had its own statutes relating to Aborigines; these laws present a bewildering array of definitions, distinctions, and regulations. (See Rowley 1972a, appendix A, for an extensive discussion of legal definitions of Aborigines.) Each state's laws included a definition along these lines: "Every person who is a) an aboriginal inhabitant of Australia, or b) a half-caste who lives with an aboriginal as husband or wife or c) a half-caste who, otherwise than as wife or husband habitually lives or associates with aborigines, or d) a half-caste child whose age does not apparently exceed sixteen years, shall be deemed an aboriginal within the meaning of this Act . . ." (Western Australia Aborigines Act of 1905, Section 3).

This act was superseded by the Native Administration Act of 1936, which established an even more complicated definition. It had wider application than the earlier laws, imposing regulations (with some exceptions) upon "quadroons" and "persons of less than quadroon blood." In 1963 the Native Welfare Act superseded the 1936 act. The 1963 definition of "native" expressly excluded persons who are "only one-fourth or less than one-fourth of the original full-blood" and some other persons as well.

The laws provided for the creation of reserves, areas of land set aside for Aborigines, mostly in remote areas of northern Australia, in rural parts of the south, or outside the city or town limits of urban areas. A regulation in each state empowered the minister to remove Aborigines to reserves, to keep them there, and to transfer them from one reserve to another; unless issued with permits, the Aborigines were virtual prisoners. This power was often used punitively; for example, reputed troublemakers could be taken from their familiar surroundings and families and sent to live among strangers (see Massola 1975; Read 1982; Reynolds 1972, 165–167).

Children were the particular focus of efforts to change Aboriginal people and their cultures. On the reserves children were often placed in dormitories, and their interaction with parents and other adults was controlled. More drastic separation occurred when children, especially those of mixed descent, were taken from their parents and placed in special institutions, usually far from their places of origin and with others from diverse areas. The reserves and children's homes were run by missionaries or government employees, who imposed strict regulations on the inmates. Strenuous efforts were made to break down Aboriginal traditions and replace them with ideas and behaviors acceptable to white Australians. For example, in many places indigenous religious ceremonies were prohibited and Christianity was promoted; the use of Aboriginal languages was often banned or discouraged (Miller 1985, 159–170; Rowley 1972a, 1972b). Today few would argue that these efforts were successful, though their repercussions are still being felt. Much was destroyed or changed, but the outcome was not as intended.

Marriage and the choice of sexual partners was regulated. The Western Australian laws, paralleled in other states, prevented the marriage of a "female aboriginal with any person other than an aboriginal" without the consent of the chief protector and made it an offense for a non-Aboriginal male to cohabit or travel with a female Aborigine unless the couple was married. Also, a person classified as "quadroon" (or "less") would be committing an offense by marrying or cohabiting with a "native." Laws everywhere distinguished between male and female Aborigines (especially those of mixed ancestry). Females were deemed to require greater protection and control than males, and at the same time they were considered to be more redeemable. Those who hoped to whiten the Aboriginal population expected to do so through unions of white men and women of Aboriginal descent. This plan went beyond the common colonial incidence of men of the dominant (white) group having ready sexual access to women of the subordinate (nonwhite) groups, despite legal sanctions or social disapproval (cf. Meintel 1984, 112–114). As noted earlier, those who advocated miscegenation did so in the context of a relative shortage of white females, and expressed horror at the thought of dark-skinned men having sexual relations with women of lighter color. Women were encouraged (expected) to marry men of similar or lighter phenotype. This expectation contrasted sharply with Aboriginal traditional marriage rules, which placed greatest emphasis on kinship and country (land) affiliation, without reference to physical characteristics.

The laws relating to children were particularly harsh and had disproportionate effects on females as both mothers and children. Removal of children from their families did not depend on evidence of neglect; the policy was imposed largely on the basis of color. It was assumed that children who were partly white, especially girls, were in "moral danger" (Read 1982, 15–16) if they lived among black people, including their own mothers. For Aboriginal children, placement in the care of white people was seen as beneficial, a necessary prerequisite to their assimilation into white society. But the expectations for these children were limited: girls were destined for domestic service, boys for farm labor (Miller 1985, 146–148, 167–170). These practices continued until the 1960s in many parts of Australia.

The application of these restrictive discriminatory policies wreaked havoc in the lives of many Aborigines. Among people of mixed descent, especially, few families escaped the direct impact of the regulations. In recent years numerous books and articles have recounted the personal experiences of Aborigines and address aspects of the question of Aboriginal identity (Edwards 1982; Gilbert 1973, 1977; Matthews 1977; Miller 1985; Morgan 1987; Palmer and McKenna 1978; Read 1984; Tucker 1983).

The laws that defined also provided for exemptions: a kind of honorary white status could be conferred on Aborigines. In the Northern Territory, for example, any Aboriginal woman "legally married to a person who is of European origin or descent and living with her husband" was exempted from the status of "native" (Northern Territory Native Administration Act of 1940). The New South Wales Aborigines Protection Act of 1943 (section 18c) allowed the issue of a certificate of exemption to "any aborigine or person apparently having an admixture of aboriginal blood, who in the opinion of the board ought no longer be subject to the provisions of this Act. . . ." Aborigines seeking exemption had to make written application, and the certificate could be canceled.

Under the Western Australian Native (Citizenship Rights) Act of 1944, applicants for citizenship (exemption) were required to make a statutory declaration that, for two years prior to the date of the application, they had "dissolved tribal and native association" except with their closest relatives, and that either they had served in the Army or Air

Force and had received an honorable discharge or were otherwise "fit and proper" persons to receive citizenship certificates. Also required were two recent references from "reputable citizens certifying as to the good character and industrious habits of the applicant." The certificate could be revoked if the holder was deemed to be failing to "adopt the habits of a civilized life" or to have contracted syphilis, leprosy, or yaws (Broome 1982, 170). This act remained in force until 1971, when it was repealed after citizenship had been extended to all Aborigines by the federal government.

Officials authorized to grant exemptions/citizenship used their power cautiously, and few certificates were issued. Gaining a certificate conferred privileges such as access to alcohol, but other controls, over the holder's property, for example, remained (Rowley 1972b, 48). Although exemption was used by some Aboriginal people, usually those of mixed descent and living in towns or cities, for many its benefits were not worth the costs. They had to prove their eligibility to be granted what white people enjoyed as rights; only whites had the authority to give and withhold the exemptions and holders were obliged to carry certificates, which could be revoked at any time. The term *dog license*, in popular use among Aborigines to refer to the citizenship/exemption certificate, probably sums up their attitude (Broome 1982, 171; Miller 1985, 174–176; Rowley 1972b, 48).

Some people of Aboriginal descent took the more extreme step of passing as white. For obvious reasons estimating their number is difficult. Successful passing could rid some Aborigines of a handicap, and it might be seen as a logical outcome of assimilationist policy, the triumph of color over culture. However, as Rowley notes, persons who have passed as white "may be sensitive on the point," while those unable (or unwilling) to do so view it with scorn and resentment (Rowley 1972a, 396). Moreover, the risk of losing the security of kin and the familiar for an uncertain future would have been an inhibiting factor. Many who could pass as white have chosen not to (Barwick 1964; Beckett 1964, 35). Eckermann states that the people among whom she worked considered it unthinkable to forsake their Aboriginal identity in this way (1977, 300–301). Nevertheless, some researchers have estimated that in some parts of the country, notably Queensland, where assimilationist policies were most vigorously promoted, the number of people of Aboriginal descent who have passed as white is very high. Certainly a high frequency of intermarriage between whites and Aborigines has been reported in Queensland, particularly during the past twenty years. These unions involved Aboriginal men as well as women, although the latter are more likely to marry whites (Eckermann 1977, 295–297; Gale and Wundersich 1982). Marriage to whites has doubtless been a reason to deny or reject Aboriginality and to disappear into white society (cf. Smith 1980, 8).

Some Aborigines express sympathy and understanding for those who have "escaped" into white society rather than suffer the hardships of Aboriginal life. Similarly, views are divided about "new identifiers," people who have chosen to reveal their Aboriginal ancestry in the less restrictive, but still difficult, conditions that now prevail. Some Aborigines are welcoming, but others are suspicious of possible opportunism. Gilbert records a range of Aboriginal views on these issues (1977, 96, 184, 203–204, 210). Recent census figures indicate a larger increase in the number of Aborigines than can be accounted for by natural growth alone. It is not clear to what extent those who now choose to identify themselves as Aboriginal also participate in Aboriginal communities and adopt a public Aboriginal profile. Some of the new identifiers were undoubtedly taken away as children and encouraged to conceal their Aboriginal origins, or else discovered them only recently.[17]

In the late 1930s policies shifted significantly from those aimed at protection of Aborigines to those emphasizing assimilation. Initially the two policies overlapped, as assimilation at first applied only to part-Europeans among the Aboriginal population. Although experiments in assimilation were already taking place, the policy of assimilation was first explicitly adopted in 1937 at the first Commonwealth Conference on Aboriginal Welfare, which was attended by representatives of each state of the federal government.

According to this policy assimilation was to occur gradually; for some officials it meant "absorption" or the elimination of color as well as complete cultural change to make people of Aboriginal descent indistinguishable from white Australians (Reynolds 1972, 172–174). This process was considered impossible for those Aborigines who were "tribal" and "full-blood," and who were in any case still expected to die out; protection policies continued for them until 1961 when the Commonwealth Native (changed from Aboriginal) Conference extended the assimilation policy to all Aborigines: "The policy of assimilation means that *all Aborigines and part-Aborigines are expected* to attain the same manner of living as other Australians, and to live as members of a single Australian community enjoying the same rights and privileges, accepting the same customs and influenced by the same beliefs as other Australians" (quoted in Reynolds 1972, 175, emphasis added). The 1965 Native Welfare Conference modified the wording: "The policy of assimilation seeks that *all persons of Aboriginal descent will choose* to attain a similar manner of living to that of other Australians" (Reynolds 1972, 175, emphasis added).

Cultural change rather than physical absorption became the official goal. While still assuming that assimilation was the best policy, the 1965 statement also acknowledged that some Aborigines might not wish to follow it. The policy of assimilation was abandoned in the 1970s in favor of self-determination, which was temporarily displaced by self-management but has recently been reinstated.

As a result of a national referendum in 1967, citizenship was extended to all Aborigines. Special legislation for Aborigines adopted since then differs from earlier laws in being somewhat responsive to their wishes. Legal definitions of Aborigines have been broadened; for example, the federal government's Aboriginal Land Rights (Northern Territory) Act of 1976 states that " 'Aboriginal' means a person who is a member of the Aboriginal race of Australia" (section 3 [1]). The word *race* is not defined in the legislation, probably deliberately. The vernacular rather than any scientific meaning is probably what is intended. (In Australia *race* is commonly used to denote ethnicity or nationality, e.g., the Irish or Italian race.) The Western Australian Aboriginal Heritage Act defined Aboriginal as "pertaining to the original inhabitants of Australia and to their descendants" (section 4). The emphasis has shifted to self-definition and Aboriginal community acceptance for membership of the category "Aborigines."

Policy changes have not put an end to controversy in Aboriginal affairs, and there has been something of a turnabout in reactions to special legislation for Aborigines. Such legislation, especially with regard to land rights, is advocated by most Aborigines and their supporters. It is opposed by many individuals and organizations, including several highly vocal if numerically small racist groups, who argue that Aborigines should not be awarded special benefits unavailable to other Australians. There are slogans such as "One Land, One Law," and accusations that Aborigines who call for separate services and control of Aboriginal affairs—and any government that supports them—are promoting apartheid. The more extreme antagonists cast Aborigines as privileged intruders who, like nonwhite immigrants and various others, pose a threat to (white) Australian society (see English 1985; Lehmann 1983; McDonald 1982). Yet despite their relatively high profile on the news and on the political agenda, Aborigines remain by far the most disadvantaged group in Australia by all socioeconomic indicators. Aboriginal identity still entails struggle—for equality, for respect, and for acceptance as the original Australians.

Conclusions

The experiences of Aboriginal people and hence the formation of their personal and cultural identities have been in contexts created largely by white Australians. Those experiences have been marked to a great extent by color prejudice, segregation, and legalized discrimination. This I believe accounts in large measure for the concerns, the aims, and the rhetoric of the current Aboriginal political movement based on the notion of Aboriginality as an identity and an ideology.

The assertion of Aboriginality is part of a political process. Although the legal and social status of Aborigines has changed significantly, they are by no means equal participants in Australian society. They still suffer severe social disadvantage and de facto discrimination; in the eyes of many whites, being Aboriginal is still a social stigma. Against this background, many Aborigines are consciously and actively working to establish positive images of themselves and their cultures. This involves the rejection or reversal of white people's definitions; the promotion of color as a desirable feature rather than a taint; and the revival, invention, or adoption of distinctively Aboriginal cultural behaviors and symbols—in short, the construction of a new identity in which all Aboriginal people can share and that will evoke acceptance and respect from the rest of Australian society (cf. Berndt and Berndt 1985, 528–532; Jordan 1985, 32–34).

Aboriginality, however, is still a new concept that does not fully describe identity as it is perceived by many Aboriginal people. The emphasis on nationwide common bonds and shared characteristics almost requires an outside view. This view is essential in building solidarity among a minority population and endowing it with political force in the Australian nation, but it downplays the great emphasis placed by many Aborigines on the uniqueness of their own small community, language group, or extended kin group. Of course, as Poyer (chapter 6) points out for the people of Sapwuahfik, people can simultaneously hold inclusive and exclusive views about themselves and their neighbors (cf. Sansom 1982, 137). While Aboriginality is developing as a political force, local and regional Aboriginal identities continue to have salience and provide, though not exclusively, some of the content of Aboriginality. And there are reciprocal influences on local attitudes. The two forms of identity help to sustain each other and are therefore likely to coexist well into the future.

It is perhaps most useful to see Aboriginality as a concept that is still being defined, a label for an emergent reality. I agree with Anderson that "to assert 'Aboriginality' is not to assume that Aborigines form a wholly coherent, unified body," and that what is important for the scholar interested in this issue is not so much to state whether or not Aboriginality exists as to "account for the fact that people think it does, argue that it does and act as though it does" (1985, 42). Those who talk and act as if there is a unitary self-conscious Aboriginal constituency both signify its existence and promote its development.

NOTES

For their careful reading and helpful comments on early drafts of this chapter I thank Lin Poyer, Jocelyn Linnekin, Bob Tonkinson, Betty Stoate, and Nancy Williams. Thanks also to Rina Fiorentino and Susan O'Connor, who typed the manuscript and patiently dealt with numerous revisions.

1. There is a large body of literature on Aboriginal cultures. Berndt and Berndt (1985) provide a comprehensive account of the range of Aboriginal cultures plus a useful bibliography. Another general work is Maddock (1974). There are numerous ethnographies with relevance to the issues of identity raised in this paper; they include Goodale 1971; Hiatt 1965; Meggitt 1962; Myers 1987; Tonkinson 1974; Warner [1937] 1958. (See note 5 for works on land ownership; several historical works are cited throughout this chapter.) Since this chapter was written, Keen (1988) has edited a volume on Aborigines whose contact (physical and cultural) with whites has been most intense and prolonged; many of the papers in Keen cover themes treated or referred to here.

2. The role of language in establishing Aboriginal identity cannot be discussed adequately here. Note, however, that in many parts of Australia language name is the primary label for a group, that language is often linked to a specific area of land, and that in the modern context the language label indicates language ownership, but not necessarily language use (Sutton and Palmer 1981, 30; see also Merlan 1981). Eades (1981) discusses the importance of Aboriginal English as an identity marker among Aborigines whose only language is English.

3. The "ethnic" label is rejected by Aborigines because they see it as including them with immigrant groups from non-English-speaking countries to whom that label is usually applied (McKellar 1981). As one Aboriginal man said to me, "We are not new Australians." ("New Australian" was until recently in common use to refer to non-British/Irish European immigrants.)

4. The diversity of which Jones and Hill-Burnett speak is evident in many forms among Aborigines and coexists with the push for Aboriginal unity. There are, for example, factions based on kin-group affiliation resulting in conflict and even protracted feuding in some areas. There are also divisions between Aborigines who identify as Christians—often fundamentalists, some of whom oppose land rights—and those who maintain traditional religious beliefs and practices.

5. Under British common law Australia was declared *terra nullius:* despite the presence of the indigenous people the land was considered empty, and despite active resistance from the Aborigines in many areas, the country was deemed to have been settled rather than conquered. One result of this view was that no treaties were made with the Aborigines and virtually no attempts were made to reconcile their interests in the land with the interests of the white newcomers. Recent publications on various aspects of this issue include Gumbert (1984); Maddock (1983); Peterson and Langton (1983); and Williams (1986). Since this chapter was written Australia has been celebrating the bicentenary of British settlement in 1788. Massive publicity and special projects and events have been mounted to promote pride in history, a sense of nationhood, etc.

Understandably, most Aborigines have reacted negatively to what is essentially a celebration of the British invasion of their land (Australia did not gain independence from Britain until 1901). Aborigines have responded with a variety of antibicentennial actions and protests, which have heightened the essential cleavage between white (especially Anglo-) Australian interests and priorities and those of Aboriginal Australians. On Australia Day, 1988, Aborigines from all over the country staged a march in Sydney to express their solidarity, and much emphasis was placed on the diversity of Aboriginal representatives present. As part of an attempt at rapprochement, the federal government has promised to negotiate a "compact" or form of treaty with Aborigines. Although its content is still to be determined, and it is unlikely to have great material significance, it is nonetheless proving very controversial.

6. In the 1980s, the issue of Aboriginal land rights has steadily lost public support, partly as a result of aggressive anti–land rights campaigns by mining companies and farming lobbies. As a result, no government, federal or state, and only one small political party currently espouse land rights. While Aborigines still see land rights as a priority, the opportunities to air their concerns have dwindled.

7. In 1988 an Aboriginal passport was devised. Although it has no diplomatic status, it was presented by a delegation of Aborigines visiting Libya. On the delegates' return to Australia, immigration authorities refused to stamp the Aboriginal passports and detained their bearers until they presented their Australian documents.

8. As noted in note 5, however, a similar but much larger protest took place in January 1988.

9. The NAC was created by the federal government, and any viable replacement will need government backing. In 1985 a new "consultative" Aboriginal body was expected to replace the NAC (O'Donoghue 1985). This did not happen. A new minister for aboriginal affairs, appointed in 1987, announced plans for a major restructuring of his portfolio, and extensive consultation with Aboriginal communities ensued. Among the matters being considered is a representative body, but the enabling legislation has not yet been passed.

10. In 1896 the colonies unanimously adopted a "White Australia" policy, which became law soon after federation in 1901 (Crowley 1974, 273–274; 1980, 488–489). This policy was directed against foreigners and particularly Chinese (who had been the first to be excluded in the 1880s), but it effectively denied the existence of the indigenous nonwhite peoples as part of Australia. In 1988 there has been a resurgence of the debate concerning nonwhite (specifically Asian) immigration. In times past, southern European and other immigrants have met with similar hostility, arising from convictions concerning their "unassimilability."

11. Folk concepts influenced the development of natural and social scientific theories and were in turn influenced by them. The colonial experience in Africa, the Americas, Australia, and elsewhere also provided data that contributed to changing ideas. Banton (1987) provides a useful analysis of the complex history of the concept of race. He makes it clear that the interaction of folk and scientific ideas has influenced the development of racial thought. Husband

(1982) also provides a useful account of the development of racial thinking in Britain, showing the convergence of ideas about race/blood with ideas about color in the attitudes of the British toward Africans and other nonwhite people. The major impetus for these theories has come from Britain, the Continent, and the United States, and they have influenced Australian popular racial ideas from the earliest days of settlement to the present (see Broome 1982, 25–26; Evans 1975, 16, 74–75; Reynolds 1972, 109).

12. My own observations, life histories I have collected, and various anecdotal and documented accounts suggest that children of mixed descent are usually accepted as the offspring of their mothers' Aboriginal husbands. This is in keeping with the emphasis in Aboriginal societies on the rights of pater over genitor (see Goodale 1971, 137–141; Meggitt 1962, 97; Tonkinson 1984, 120).

13. All these situations are complex and cannot be explored here. I am not suggesting that any of these systems is preferable to any other, as both Harris (1964) and Hoetink (1967) are emphatic that racism was present in all the places named, though it took different forms.

14. Trigger (1988) has taken issue with this argument. He claims that Aborigines do accord skin color considerable social significance, along lines similar to those held by whites.

15. In terms of the interpretations put forward by some other authors in this volume (cf. Lieber, chapter 4 and Watson, chapter 2), it might be argued that traditional Aboriginal notions of local identity are Lamarckian. White Australians, on the other hand, have Mendelian notions of identity, as evidenced in the historical section of this chapter. In promoting a national pan-Aboriginal identity, Aborigines are shifting from a Lamarckian to a Mendelian emphasis. While I cannot take this approach further here, it may be a useful way of analyzing changes in Aboriginal cultural identity.

16. This attitude is codified, for example, in the Northern Territory land rights legislation, which has enabled Aborigines to recover sizable areas of (mostly marginal or barren) land. This act requires applicants to demonstrate, as descent groups, that they are the "traditional landowners." Several legal tests of traditional ownership must be proved, such as "primary spiritual responsibility" and "strength of traditional attachment."

17. The history of the enumeration of the Aboriginal population is extremely complicated and displays many of the inconsistencies in policies and their implementation that arose in other areas. Since 1971 the census has permitted self-identification for Aborigines, rather than empowering the census takers to assess "race" (see Smith 1980 for a thorough examination of this topic).

10

Tangi: *Funeral Rituals and the Construction of Maori Identity*

KAREN P. SINCLAIR

In contemporary New Zealand, Maori funeral rituals, known as *tangihanga* 'mourning ceremonies', have become an important constituent of Maori identity. These rituals punctuate the round of daily life by marking extraordinary events in a distinctively Maori manner. All that is positive in being a Maori is exhibited and celebrated on these occasions. More important, the Maori maintain—and in this they receive some support from anthropologists and historians—that tangihanga have not changed dramatically over the two centuries of European contact. Viewed as immutable and unchanging, tangihanga stress continuity with the past, the celebration of tradition (which is defined as authentic rather than putative), and hence Maori legitimacy in a social world dominated by Europeans.

Maori have had to renegotiate their identity on many occasions since the arrival of Captain Cook in 1769.[1] As it became clear in the early nineteenth century that Maori culture would not survive unaltered, a tension developed between the requirement that Maori accommodate themselves to European society and the countervailing quest for a distinct Maori identity, maintained apart from the encroaching domain of the *Pakeha* (the New Zealand term for individuals of European ancestry). Maori identity has, then, been redefined and reformulated during two hundred years of dramatic social change.

With New Zealand's growing awareness of itself as a multicultural society in the late twentieth century (see Dominy, chapter 11), the issues of cultural uniqueness and integrity have become critical. As indigenous inhabitants, Maori are not sanguine about their position; the realities of dispossession and discrimination are not easily ignored.[2] The situation in New Zealand, unlike that in Melanesia or Micronesia, can best be characterized as postcolonial. Pakeha are firmly entrenched, their dominance reaching into most areas of New Zealand life. In this context the formulation of Maori identity has been especially complex. Despite two centuries of exposure to metropolitan influences, Maori identity continues to be based upon tribal affiliation (Rangihau 1975). Tribal histories

219

locate individuals in terms of land and ancestral achievement, while tribal canons of etiquette provide guides for behavior. The *marae* 'ceremonial courtyard', the major ritual arena, in almost all cases is attached to and commemorates the specific history of a local group (see Salmond 1975; Tauroa and Tauroa 1987). While these identifications are profoundly satisfying, they are also divisive. Faced with Pakeha prejudice and stereotypes, Maori have found in the tangihanga a ritual that facilitates the expression of unity. In this context, harmony may be asserted while the distinctive features of Maori culture, such as reciprocity and commensality, are also on display. Therefore, in a situation characterized by often conflicting nested identities, the tangihanga, often abbreviated to tangi, provides a context for asserting a positive, unified conception of Maoriness.

Maori distinguish themselves by the quality of their interpersonal relationships. Here the contrast with Europeans is marked and explicit. While in the Maori view Pakeha remain committed to solely instrumental social relations, Maori vest profound importance in mutuality and empathy, best expressed in the notion of *aroha* 'love, empathy'. In no instance are the Maori unaware of Europeans; Maori identity and distinctiveness have always been created against a background of European technological superiority and Pakeha political and social institutions. In twentieth-century New Zealand, the most salient political fact about the Maori is their minority status. In a variety of contexts Maori take the opportunity to proclaim that Maoritanga is a political issue and a social force in New Zealand.[3]

While ceremonial activities are one component of Maori identity, more mundane aspects of social life also serve to set the Maori apart from the European establishment. Commitment to land, obedience to the demands of kinship, preference for certain foods identified as Maori, *hui* 'gathering defined by Maori etiquette', mastery of oratory and Maori language are all seen as contributing to Maori distinctiveness and would all be readily acknowledged by Maori as part of Maoritanga. The ritual occasions enacted on marae around New Zealand today no doubt depart from ancestral performances (see Salmond 1975). Nevertheless, in the contemporary context they have come to signify the differences between Maori and Pakeha. They are now imbued with new, but no less significant, meanings. Such events do more than mark differences—these ceremonial occasions symbolically define the social situation of contemporary Maori.

Present Maori formulations of identity depend to a large degree on a reexamination of the past. If Maori are not comfortable with their present position, they are far from content with the impulses, however well intentioned, that led their ancestors to derive satisfactions from the

European social order. Early settlers and missionaries urged the abandonment of ancestral deities and, at the turn of the twentieth century,
Maori leaders hastened the demise of Maori as a first language. The
contemporary interest in Maori religion and language as well as the
revival of putatively traditional arts and crafts (such as action songs, see
below) indicates the uneasy dispensation that remains when a group
turns its back on its heritage. This heritage is recalled today in Maori
funeral rituals, which serve to emphasize the continuity of the past with
the present. Such ritual occasions assert that there has been no fragmentation in Maori experience, while providing an arena in which Maori
identity can be formulated and sustained.

Although Maori funeral rituals have undergone changes (Beaglehole
and Beaglehole 1945; Best 1924, 1926; Phillips 1954), Maori nevertheless view them as consistent with traditional Maori culture. By asserting
that tangi are immutable and unchanging, contemporary Maori
become party to the invention of tradition (see Linnekin 1983 and chapter 7; Ranger 1983). A tangi remains a time set off from ordinary experience. For its duration, the bereaved decline to engage in mundane
activities; mourning and its social consequences dominate their lives.
The liminal status of the mourners, expressed by their suspension of
ordinary activities and their proximity to death, reflects the condition of
the deceased who, in like fashion, resists classification. The conclusion
of the tangi reincorporates the bereaved into the world of the living,
while burial effects the transformation of the corpse into the category of
the dead.[4] In the shifting and complex currents of New Zealand political life, Maori have found an anchor in the tangi. Death has become not
only a time to mourn an individual who goes to join a collectivity of
ancestors, but also an opportunity to pay tribute to all that is positive in
Maori social identity. Roger Oppenheim writes of the tangi: "The
dynamics of the *tangi* then are those of the sense of mutuality and
dependence upon the good will of others, on their sense of proper and
'Maori' way to act. The *tangihanga* symbolises 'defensive solidarity': it
closes the ranks of Maoris vis-à-vis the world which Maoris know to be
the one in which they *must* live in favour of one in which they *can* live,
if only for short periods" (1973, 23).

Background

In two hundred years of contact with Europeans, Maori political for-
tunes have undergone dramatic fluctuations. During the first century
after contact the Maori were transformed from proud landowners who
suffered the presence of the intruding colonists into an apparently

defeated, virtually landless minority. In the twentieth century Maori health has improved, and their population is once more increasing. Nevertheless, they are an underprivileged minority (a scant 12 percent of the New Zealand population) who must come to terms with a social order defined by a powerful and alien majority. The Maori position in New Zealand has therefore been regularly reevaluated and redefined; the formation of Maori identity has varied accordingly with changes in historical and social contexts (see Keesing 1982b; Linnekin, chapter 7).

By the time of Captain Cook's arrival in 1769, Maori had been in residence for almost one thousand years. Their first contacts with Europeans did not augur well: "Being forthright people most Maoris struck back when the first visitors massacred a few of their fellows and they thus acquired reputations for savagery" (Oliver 1975, 171). First missionaries, then colonists, failed to be discouraged by these early skirmishes. The temperate climate and economic possibilities of the country soon overcame whatever reservations might be occasioned by the natives' behavior. For their part, Maori were clearly interested in the material arsenal brought by the Pakeha and impressed by the apparent potency of their god. But their enthusiasm turned to dismay and bitterness as their own traditions failed to resist the onslaught of the newcomers' social innovations.

The annexation of New Zealand began in earnest as more settlers arrived from Great Britain. In 1840, after more than forty chiefs signed the Treaty of Waitangi, New Zealand was formally placed under England's sovereignty and Maori interests ceased to be the dominating force in the definition of the emerging social order. In the ensuing century and a half there has been much debate about the meaning and intentions of those party to the treaty (see especially Orange 1987). But it quickly became apparent that the nominal rights provided to Maori by the document could be readily circumvented by clever colonial lawyers:

> The annexation Treaty of Waitangi turned out to be a document of noble intent but of impossible application. It confirmed the Maoris in possession of their lands and granted them "all the rights and privileges of British subjects"; but it did not take long for the lawyers, acting on behalf of the British colonists, to interpret these treaty guarantees out of existence. For a few years, however, the unsuspecting Maoris were too busy acquiring the new civilization to realize their true predicament. (Oliver 1975, 171)

The introduction of European material goods affected all levels of Maori society. Tribal stability and cohesion were undermined as Maori became more involved in a market economy. Tribal leaders and religious specialists yielded to men equipped with the new prerogatives of power (Parsonson 1981; Sorrenson 1981; Ward 1974; Williams 1969; Wright 1959). By the time Maori realized their land was lost, in the last third of the nineteenth century, they had to go to war to regain it. In the end, with thousands of casualties on both sides, the British colonists won and the Maori retreated into defeat and decline.

By the late nineteenth century Maori numbers had declined so drastically that it was assumed in several Pakeha quarters that within decades Maori would no longer exist in significant numbers. This assumption was probably wishful thinking on the part of less than enlightened legislators who wanted the "native problem" to disappear. The disappearance of the natives promised a quick solution. However, as these dire predictions were being set forth the Maori population was on the increase. A subsequent Maori population and cultural revival at the turn of the century reversed these trends. Maori leaders such as Sir Apirana Ngata and Sir Peter Buck provided a bridge between the two populations and cultures of New Zealand, with the result that the condition and prestige of the Maori improved considerably (King 1981). As Maori were drawn into a rapidly expanding New Zealand economy before World War I, their population and material prosperity increased. Traditional art forms were resurrected and Maori dances were merged with European music to produce the action songs still heard today. The past was cast in new terms; a romantic and idealized image emerged that "appeared admirable in European eyes and a proper object of pride for the modern Maori. This pride was encouraged by the new leaders who encouraged the fostering of this remodelled Maori culture" (Schwimmer 1966, 124).

In the 1940s Maori rural life had reached a high point of coherence, "with the government accepting a bicultural situation founded on a degree of social separation" (Butterworth 1973, 15). The distinction between Maori and Pakeha was reinforced by the fact that Maori lived predominantly in rural areas, while Europeans had progressively become more urban. Strong tribal and local leaders were often responsible for the crystallization of Maoritanga. Moreover, the success of the Maori Battalion in World War II and the passage of the Maori Social and Economic Advancement Act in 1946 enhanced the prestige and pride of most Maori (B. J. Kernot, pers. comm.). In the 1950s the burgeoning Maori rural population had begun to emigrate to the urban areas of the North Island. Maori youth, especially, were drawn to the employment and social opportunities offered in the cities. Soon overcrowding, crime, and alcoholism typified the Maori experience in urban centers. As Maori increasingly came into contact with Europeans, they confronted discrimination and prejudice. The problem of identity reasserted itself once more: "Once in town they found new problems and the need for a reaffirmation of their Maori identity. A new synthesis had to be found that would allow Maoris to remain Maori while participating in a Pakeha world" (Butterworth 1973, 15). Indeed, feelings of distinctiveness in contrast to Pakeha promoted solidarity among otherwise disparate groups of Maori. Such an impulse led to the formation of a variety of clubs and voluntary associations (Walsh 1973a, 46).

Existing policies could not deal adequately with the problems Maori encountered. A public study was commissioned that resulted in the Hunn Report, which in essence championed a unicultural (Pakeha) model of New Zealand.[5] Despite the report's critics, evidence indicates that it has dictated government policy (Dunstall 1981). For Hunn, Maori would do best to abandon any distinctive traits and readily conform to European standards.[6] Implicitly, cultural differences have been interpreted as Maori deficiencies. B. J. Kernot (1981, 140) has described this situation:

> Instead of being taken on his own terms, a Maori must experience the invidious comparisons of Maoris with Pakehas, and added to this are the indignities of discrimination. The end result of so much effort and striving is an unacceptably high casualty rate measured in terms of school failures, prison population, mental hospital admission rate, the loss of identity and self respect, and a growing alienation of a considerable section of the Maori population from the mainstream of cultural and social development in New Zealand.

Differences between Maori and Pakeha have been reinforced as the Maori population has become increasingly urban. Thus Dunstall (1981, 424) has written that

> Maori selfconsciousness had been present for generations, but intensified as the interaction between the races grew. Post-war urbanization reduced social separation. As the material conditions of Maoris began to converge towards those of Pakehas, the quickening pace of social change heightened the awareness of disparities in housing, educational attainment, employment and income. In the late 1950s the increasing appearance of Maori youth in city magistrate and children's court seemed symptomatic of social dislocation. Culturally, questions of identity were raised anew.

Compared to Europeans, Maori are overrepresented in unskilled and semiskilled labor and underrepresented in professional occupations.[7] Such economic disparities will continue to have an impact on the social and political position of Maori in New Zealand society. As a marginal, underemployed segment of the population, they are becoming an underclass. Such a process is accelerated when rising aspirations exceed earned income. The availability of installment payments and credit cards leaves many Maori both indebted and impoverished. The social disadvantages of Maori are manifest on many levels: higher mortality rates, lower levels of educational achievement, more domestic violence, poorer living conditions, and higher crime rates all reflect the under-privileged status of most Maori. In the face of such evidence, European complacency should be hard to sustain. In fact, most Pakeha know very little of the Maori or of Maori traditions and are content to allow stereo-types to guide them in their intermittent contacts.

Maori-Pakeha relations in New Zealand are not nearly as harmonious as official public statements on the matter would have the rest of the world believe. Both physical and symbolic barriers separate Maori from Pakeha. Stereotypes reinforce this separation, further eroding any chance of intercultural communication. Europeans view Maori as shift-less, improvident, unreliable, and happy-go-lucky. For their part, Maori see Pakeha as selfish, grasping, individualistic, and concerned with material advantage to the exclusion of more important spiritual values. What is more poignant, Maori appear to accept the negative stereotypes of themselves (Archer and Archer 1970). Such negative images not only create and maintain barriers, they contribute to the persistence of low self-esteem and feelings of worthlessness.[8]

Maori leaders have been "almost unanimous and even more impor-tant, vocal and assertive in claiming a right to be Maori" (Butterworth 1973, 27). But what it means to be a Maori and the mode chosen to express Maoritanga have not met with ready agreement. If anything, disagreements over these matters tend to emphasize the divisions in Maori society. Rural elders assert Maoriness in ways that are not always acceptable to younger urbanites (see Dominy, chapter 11), who in gen-eral favor more innovative and even more militant tactics.[9] Schisms in Maori society often become wider over these issues and thereby limit the possibility and effectiveness of concerted action. The divisions that exist in contemporary Maori society, aggravated by the shifting currents in Maori-Pakeha relations, are to some extent superseded in the tangi-hanga. In funeral rituals differences are overcome as attention is turned to the much larger issues at hand. Ritual symbols permit the partici-pants to define the situation to lend credence to Maori claims of conti-nuity and legitimacy.

The Tangi: Historical Considerations

Before the introduction of Christianity in the first third of the nine-teenth century, attitudes toward death and rituals of bereavement were consistent with the shape of the Maori cosmos. This was a universe bounded and ordered into distinct domains (Salmond 1978; Sinclair 1983). The corpse, no longer living but not yet fully incorporated into an ancestral category, was viewed as polluting and dangerous. Numerous ritual restrictions signaled the contamination of both the deceased and the principal mourners. Oppenheim (1973, 14) writes, "The manifest function of the *tangihanga* was to give proper burial to the dead according to the prestige that they had in life. It was intended to offer comfort to the bereaved, but more importantly, the aim was to control by rigidly prescribed practices the dangers which were thought to arise from the state of ritual contamination that death brought about." Mourning was often violent, marked by bloodshed, tears, and mutilation. The liminality of the situation was reinforced by the belief that the *wairua* 'soul, spirit of the dead' of the deceased lingered about the proceedings. Thus in the days of oratory preceding burial the corpse was addressed directly in the present tense.

The transition to ancestor status required several steps after the tangi. Bones were exhumed, cleaned, and ultimately reburied in a secret area. Restrictions on mourners paralleled the fate of the corpse; as the deceased moved toward ancestor status, mourners were progressively released from their restrictions. Funeral rituals, then, affirmed order and meaning in the midst of disorder and death.

There were of course political consequences to the form and duration of the tangi. Unity was asserted not only in the face of loss but in light of the complex structure of alliances that characterized Maori society. Tribal pride was reflected in high-flown oratory linking the deceased to lofty ancestral accomplishments,[10] and in the elaborate feasts provided for visitors. Maori funerals have always been vehicles for the dissection and celebration of social life; the nature of the social group, its boundaries and its distinctive characteristics, has insinuated itself into the most solemn and sacred of ritual occasions.

Missionaries introduced an ideology that was from the very beginning at odds with Maori premises. "The introduction of Protestant Christianity, with its values of suffering, vicarious atonement, sin and forgiveness and its customs of moderation, thrift, prudence and deferred gratification—above all its nonviolence and sexual prudishness—presented the antithesis of almost everything that Maoris valued" (Oppenheim 1973, 19). But the overwhelming success of European technology made the religious ideas of the newcomers far more attractive than they might otherwise have been. Moreover, missionaries were responsible for Maori literacy; conversion was a small price to pay for the social advantages conferred by the ability to read and write (Owens 1968; Parr 1963).

For a time, introduced Christianity coexisted with traditional Maori beliefs. But eventually (and the chronology varied considerably from one tribal area to another) Christianity seems to have superseded Maori religious conventions. Missionaries no doubt underestimated the tenacity of traditional ideology, which reasserted itself prominently in the nineteenth and twentieth centuries, while tribal leaders probably overestimated their groups' abilities to withstand the Pakeha onslaught. At no time was Maori confidence in Christianity complete. The land wars served to highlight the inconsistencies in the missionary stance. The readiness of the missionaries to fight contradicted their presentation of themselves as men of peace. While Maori were willing to overlook some troubling theological inconsistencies, the paradox of Christian fighting Christian—with each side seeking the same divine guidance and assistance—was especially difficult once the Maori clearly began to lose. Since the land wars many Maori prophets have argued for the separation of Maori from Pakeha and have resurrected traditional beliefs. Religious ideology and ritual symbols have therefore become a means of proclaiming a distinct Maori identity. In a similar manner the contemporary tangi celebrates ideals that Maori continue to view as important and sustains a world view that is still, today, profoundly satisfying.[11]

The Contemporary Tangi

The modern tangi removes the Maori from a world grounded in European rules and places them in a context that is entirely Maori. But it does far more than provide temporary relief from European hegemony; by lending form and shape to Maori experience, it also legitimates Maori as social actors. The Maori community moves into action as soon as news of a death has an opportunity to spread. Relatives and friends are notified and elaborate arrangements made. In the days that follow, the deceased's community will play host to hundreds, perhaps thousands of mourners who have traveled long distances to pay their respects. Usually a marae committee (in most instances composed of members of the deceased's extended family) organizes the tangi: the marae is prepared, stores are brought in, the minister is notified, food is organized, sleeping arrangements are made. A traditional division of labor according to sex and age means that in very broad terms all individuals know their sphere of responsibility. While death is always disruptive, it is nevertheless familiar enough that the response is efficient and automatic.

The body arrives on the marae as soon after death as possible[12] and is greeted by the wailing of old women, the principal mourners, who initially welcome the corpse home for the final time and stay with him or

her through the last hours. That the tangi customarily takes place on a
marae is significant, for "the *marae* is the major arena left in New
Zealand where European culture stands at a disadvantage—the rituals
are unknown and the speeches are unintelligible" (Salmond 1975, 180).
Moreover, few concessions need be made to European sensibilities; for
once, Maori are free to flout European conventions: "You can wail,
chant, orate, talk Maori and eat Maori food as much as you like and
everyone else will join you. The atmosphere would naturally be ham-
pered if the dominant members at a hui came to be European and not
Maori" (Salmond 1975, 180).

Dissension is likely to occur in the early stages of the tangi. Existing
rifts in the community may erupt as the details of the funeral, the place
of burial, and the selection of officiating clergy become subjects of long,
often vigorous debate. Most people are not uncomfortable with this initial rancor, for they know that hostility will not linger. The tangi ultimately asserts the unity of the social group, in the face of considerable
evidence to the contrary. Individuals can depend, then, on the timely
resurrection of goodwill and the resolution of differences.

Frequently a canvas tent is set up and serves as the *whare mate* 'the
house of death' for the corpse and the major mourners.[13] Flax mats and
mattresses are laid on top of the canvas, the tent is adorned with pictures of the deceased and his ancestors, and family heirlooms (such as
greenstone adzes and feather cloaks) assert the continuity of living and
dead (Metge 1976, 261). Once the coffin is placed in the tent and the lid
removed, the body is never left alone. Old and middle-aged women and
any younger close female relatives remain with the body until burial,
usually two or three days later. These women, called *pani*, are polluted
by contact with death and are therefore restricted in their activities during the tangi. They may not eat with other visitors, nor should they
leave their vigil for any but the most necessary of reasons. These spatial
arrangements, in addition to the restrictions placed on pani, indicate
the continuing relevance of pollution beliefs and the persisting importance of rituals designed to control the effects of contamination.

As visitors come onto the marae over the next few days the etiquette is
unvarying. Men remove their hats, women place wreaths or scarves
about their heads and enter the marae with a traditional *poroporaki*
'farewell' to the deceased. The female elders of the home marae and the
visitors exchange greetings, and the guests are seated. Speeches by the
men allow both visitors and hosts to send the deceased to the land of the
ancestors. Speeches of welcome unite visitors and kinsmen and as the
ritual ground over the marae is traversed, so social distance is decreased. As in the past, the corpse is addressed directly in the present
tense. Here, as in all other aspects of the tangi, the traditional division

of labor between the sexes asserts itself; men are preeminent as orators, while women lend support by chanting and singing. Women organize the kitchen and marae, men handle the woodchopping and preparation of the *hangi* 'earth oven'. Yet, unlike other traditional rituals on the marae, the tangi draws attention to women. Their call welcomes the dead and greets arriving mourners, and it is they who maintain a watch over the deceased. Their presence links them irrevocably to the pollution of death.[14] But equally clearly, their importance in funeral rituals also connects them to the persistence of Maori tradition in the contemporary social order. The centrality of women in mourning, no doubt a liability in the past, has been turned to advantage as women become focal points in this most important of Maori rituals.

When the speeches are over the visitors remove their shoes and enter the tent where they *hongi* 'press noses' with the mourners. Often two individuals will stand with their noses pressed together, weeping copiously for several minutes. Such evidence of profound emotion expresses both sympathy with the mourners and a personal sense of loss. No attempt should be made to hide or avoid an emotional display. Tears should be unrestrained and mingle freely with those of the bereaved. All of this is evidence of aroha, of empathy, sympathy, heart, and sadness and is viewed as a major distinguishing feature of Maori.[15] Before leaving the tent, women drop their wreaths at the foot of the coffin and in so doing "leave something of themselves behind" (Salmond 1975, 184). Visitors then wash their hands and are ushered into the dining room where young girls serve food specially prepared for the occasion. Delicacies that are considered peculiarly Maori (such as eels and fermented corn) are in evidence whenever possible.

Both the ritual and physical space surrounding death are demarcated and bounded. While the marae contains Maori (as opposed to Pakeha) elements, there is a division within the marae between the sacred and polluted on one hand, and the ritually unmarked on the other. The body is placed away from other living areas. Its main attendants, the pani, are isolated and restricted in their movements and activities. Wreaths are shed and hands are washed when mourners leave the immediate vicinity. There is, then, a distinct effort to control the pollution associated with death and to maintain its separation from the ritually undefiled areas of social life.

When visitors are not being welcomed onto the marae, people talk, argue, and sometimes joke. At this time major issues (such as the place of burial and the form of the religious service) are likely to be resolved. On the nights preceding burial there is often a religious service. Hymns are sung and prayers are recited, often without the leadership of an ordained member of the clergy. Should a minister or priest be present, he seldom stays the entire evening, unless he is a Maori. However, many visitors and mourners remain awake until daylight. On the last night it is customary to stay up with the corpse, discussing his life, singing his favorite songs. In the talks that go on through the night, unity (of the family, of the tribe, and often of all Maori) is exhorted; as the deceased becomes an ancestor, harmony among his survivors is urged.

The final stage of the tangi is a religious service and burial. Close kinsmen dig the grave in either a private family plot or in the graveyard of a church.[16] Quiet weeping accompanies the lowering of the coffin. It is not uncommon for individuals to spend a few minutes at the foot of the grave in silence before they turn to wash their hands and depart for the marae. Younger women and one or two middle-aged matrons will have stayed at the marae to prepare the feast that traditionally signifies the end of the tangi.

At the marae, the elders lift the *tapu* 'ritual restriction' from the place where the body rested by reciting prayers and consuming a small amount of liquor or food (Metge 1976, 263). A similar ceremony, the *takahi whare* 'purification of the house', is also performed over the home of the deceased. Prayers and sacred water are used conjointly to rid the house of evil spirits. Survivors are now permitted to return and are welcomed back to their house with speeches.[17] A festive air is likely to prevail once the purification, accomplished with great solemnity, is completed. The purification of the house is therefore simultaneously a cleansing, a sanctification, and a ritual by which mourners are reincorporated into the ongoing social life of the community.

The tangi is formally concluded by a feast. In some cases this involves feeding hundreds of people, who, no longer restricted by conventions governing mourning, are free to depart from their previous gravity. At this time oratory is cheerful, often ribald. Music and alcohol turn the end of the tangi into a festive occasion. The intensity of mourning often requires a powerful release that is frequently misunderstood by Pakeha.[18] In some areas, the pani are present at the feast. In more conservative tribes, however, their isolation ends in the evening following the burial. They are reintegrated into the group, reintroduced to mundane concerns. At this time a husband's family may release his widow from her obligations. They will exchange her black veil for one with a lighter hue, thereby signifying that her ties to them need no longer restrict her.[19]

Within a day or so, the funeral is over, the marae is cleaned, accounts are paid, and life returns to normal.[20] The process of normalization requires several steps and is both more intricate and longer the more intimate an individual was with the deceased. Thus pani are more isolated and restricted than are those casual mourners who need only wash their hands before eating. Exhausted yet refreshed, most participants are ready to resume their lives again. Harry Dansey (1977, 132) writes, "For me, this is still my way of farewelling the dead and comforting the living. It is proper, satisfying, comforting, leaving me when all is over with no more tears to shed and fit to take up the business of life once again. In a strange way I feel emotionally drained and at the same time emotionally refreshed."

In the weeks that follow small tangi are held as groups of relatives from the home marae visit other areas for a *kawe mate* 'carrying of the dead'. Oratory commemorates the deceased's achievements and the bereaved give thanks for the support, financial and emotional, that they have received. The social fabric is once again woven together. "The significant thing about a *kawe mate* is that grievances are settled and signs of esteem and solidarity are exchanged between groups" (Salmond 1975, 191). The completion of the mourning sequence comes a year or so later when the close kin of the deceased unveil a gravestone at a hui. Several writers maintain that this second step apparently replaces the pre-European exhumation ceremony. Salmond (1975, 193) writes:

> In precontact times the body was buried for a period, then exhumed, and the bones were scraped and coated with red ochre. A second mourning ceremony was held before the bones were finally hidden away. . . . With contact this custom was discarded, and Maori people began to erect gravestones over their dead instead. The unveiling ceremony is not as a rule used by Europeans in New Zealand . . . and it seems in this case, elements of European ceremonial have been transformed during the period of contact into a peculiarly Maori event.

Once again a feast marks the occasion and celebrates this final transition. Mourners, especially widows, are now released from any remaining restrictions, and the deceased has been firmly incorporated into another category, that of ancestor or *wairua* 'soul, spirit of the dead'. This gradual transformation, incorporation, and reincorporation of both deceased and bereaved would appear to be faithful to the traditional Maori conception of mortality and society. The unveiling is the last and final step in a sequence triggered by death.

A distinctly Maori ritual, the tangi retains much of its traditional form. Of all Maori ceremonials, it has made the fewest concessions to modern pressures. It is a time set apart, an event governed almost exclusively by Maori rules and conventions. Its temporal and spatial boundaries demarcate it clearly from the mundane concerns of Pakeha-dominated social life. As such, it is viewed as an occasion of great moment and power. In the contemporary situation, this liminality confers an

obvious advantage: ritual transformations are effected in an atmosphere free of European intrusion. Rituals declare solidarity and unity
not only in light of the chaos introduced by death, but in the face of
pressures that have fragmented the Maori community. The tangi provides an arena in which Maori may proclaim their autonomy and unity.

Discussion

In the European social world there is widespread ignorance of things
Maori. Quite literally, Pakeha do not know who or what Maori are.
Europeans who have lived in small New Zealand towns all their lives,
who have worked with Maori, and who no doubt would consider themselves enlightened, rarely visit Maori communities. If town festivals or
bingo games take place on Maori land, they are governed by European
rules. Most Pakeha have no understanding of events such as the tangi,
and even less sympathy for them. In European eyes the ceremonies are
empty rituals, devoid of all meaning except as another forum for Maori
drunkenness. For many, Maori are no longer "real"; they are caught in
a netherworld between their illustrious but all too distant past and their
immediate, but none too glorious present.[21] Pakeha blindness to the cultural integrity of contemporary Maori makes it much easier for them to
pursue policies of discrimination. European ignorance of Maori lends
support to their view of Maori as moral outcasts and justifies the marginal esteem that Maori are accorded as social actors (cf. Braroe 1975).

The tangi and the values associated with it arm its participants with a
moral counterchallenge, for this is an arena that is subject to Maori, not
European, definitions.[22] At a tangi, Maori virtues are implicitly and
explicitly opposed to European ways. For once, Europeans come up
lacking. Pakeha materialism loses ground to assertions and demonstra-
tions of Maori spirituality. Maori generosity and hospitality emerge as
superior values when compared to rigid Pakeha politeness that, in
Maori eyes, masks a lack of caring. The tangi vindicates Maori definitions of themselves as morally superior. While Pakeha are seen as motivated by self-interest, the tangi provides a conclusive demonstration
that Maori are concerned with their family, their near and remote kin,
and with anyone who has a lien, however indirect, on their affections.
The tangi provides both a refuge from European encroachment and an
opportunity to redefine the Maori position in New Zealand society.

In New Zealand today Maori identity is formulated in a variety of
contexts and is invoked differentially, according to the situation (Fitzgerald 1977; Salmond 1975). The tangi and other ceremonial events are
exclusively Maori occasions, with spatial and temporal boundaries that

exclude Pakeha. By making claims about the nature of society, such rituals permit participants to form conceptions about themselves and to behave accordingly. In times of rapid change and upheaval, attendance and participation in such events become effective strategies for defining the situation and creating an identity. This identity is undoubtedly self-conscious, and this awareness is perhaps predictable in a colonial situation. Fernandez (1972, 43) has written that the Fang of central Africa have been forced by circumstances to become self-conscious about their behavior and about their culture:

> An almost inescapable reaction in Fang villages as they have undergone acculturation, is a greater selfconsciousness, a greater awareness of their patterns of behavior: this consequence of acculturation is probably inescapable. Acculturation means a widening of the scale of relationships and hence a diversifying of the kinds of information. Particularly in a situation of domination and subordination after colonial conquest do the ways of life of a dominant culture make the members of a subordinate culture, such as Fang, selfconscious about their own way of life. They become anxious to explain it to themselves.

Maori are particularly anxious to explain the past to themselves. Tangi make clear assertions that authority is still to be found in ancestral traditions. Invocations bidding the dead return to the night, to Hawaiiki, do not necessarily contradict missionary instruction but do proclaim the value of traditional teachings. The emphasis on continuity with the past is an intense refusal to relinquish their heritage and become part of the Pakeha world. By looking to their ancestors, to their past, they reaffirm the value of being a Maori in the present. Their heritage has thus been vindicated, its value undiminished.

In many ways tangi posit continuity with the past, for if the burial permits disposal of the time-bound individual, the unveiling and the 'carrying of the dead' recreate a permanent order on which traditional authority is based (Bloch and Parry 1982). The categories and classifications evident at tangi affirm the permanence and value of the traditional Maori cosmos. Thus women continue to be associated with death and pollution, men with ritual purity and transcendance. Similarly, the distinction between *tapu* 'ritually restricted' and *noa* 'unrestricted, profane', between the chapel and the kitchen, persists in Maori social life. In the tangi we see this separation in the isolation of the corpse and the pani, in the boundaries that are so carefully maintained between different spheres. As a rite of passage there are prescribed stages not only for the deceased but for the bereaved. As in the past, the fate of the soul and the fate of the social body mirror each other. Of course, there have been transformations and reversals, but there is, as well, significant continuity. This continuity offers an important rebuttal to the fragmentation that mars the contemporary experience of most Maori.

Above all, tangi address the troubling contradiction in Maori life between the sacred authority of ancestral traditions and the secular yet definitive dominance of the New Zealand political order. Past endeavors now lend meaning to the present. The tangi is upheld and specifically contrasted to the quick burials accorded Europeans; the Maori value of sharing is juxtaposed to Pakeha acquisitiveness. Rituals such as the tangi reconstruct the Maori social universe and provide alternatives, so that Maori can now see that the superiority of Europeans need not be axiomatic. The implications of this are not lost on most Maori. They realize as does Keesing (1982a, 240) that "following the rules of the ancestors is a mode of political struggle as well as a way of life." Indeed, the symbolic constructions and manipulations of identity are profoundly political acts (see Dominy, chapter 11; Linnekin, chapter 7; Poyer, chapter 6), acts that are essential in an increasingly political world.

NOTES

Research was conducted from 1971 to 1973 under the auspices of the Fulbright Program and the National Science Foundation. In 1982 research was supported by a sabbatical leave from Eastern Michigan University. My most recent research, from January to May 1987, was conducted under the auspices of the National Endowment for the Humanities (grant FE-21005-87) and an Eastern Michigan University faculty research grant. During the combined period of fieldwork, I probably have attended more than one hundred tangi.

1. The term *maori* means ordinary, commonplace. Only after European contact did the term and its connotations acquire any further significance.

2. Some anthropologists question the contemporary effectiveness of Maori culture. James Ritchie (1973, 69) writes,

> This dismal collusion of deception offers young Maori a "Maori identity" putatively based on the frankly ridiculous proposition that a separate and viable Maori culture does exist to which the young have full access and in which they've been socialized. There is a Maori culture of the based kin group and their *marae*, lands, ceremonies, customs and tradition. There is a Maori culture of an occasional kind, to which young people gain access in their spare time through youth clubs, sports, and church hui, and similar activities. There is a Maori culture in terms of scholarship and the academic pursuit of things Maori. There may be other Maori cultures yet to be defined and described. But there is *no* Maori culture as a unified pattern, no universal Maori traits or behavior patterns, no traditions borne by all who claim or protest Maoriness.

On the other hand, Joan Metge (1976, 46) has written, "Most Maoris intuitively reject this view of Maori culture with its emphasis on the past and a few occasional activities. For them Maori culture is a matter of present experience, a living and lived in reality either for themselves or for others well known to them."

3. The reader should bear in mind the distinction between tangihanga, the Maori funeral ritual that is the subject of this paper, and Maoritanga or "Maoriness," the state of being Maori.

4. This analysis of death rituals owes much to Durkheim ([1912] 1965), Hertz (1960), and Turner (1967). Recently Bloch and Parry (1982), Danforth (1982), and Huntington and Metcalfe (1979) have all reexamined Hertz' work on double burial and used it to elucidate the symbolic significance of mortuary rituals.

5. The Hunn Report was completed in 1961. Criticism of it has continued through two decades.

6. Walsh (1973b, 27) writes, "Hunn, according to John Booth, made the word 'integration' an unpopular word on the *maraes* of New Zealand. This was because the whole tenor of the report was patronising. Hunn saw no intrinsic value in *Maoritanga* and sought to put pressure on Maoris to conform to Pakeha standards. In short he saw integration as a process leading to assimilation."

7. In a preliminary report of the 1981 census, 10 percent of Pakeha men were classed as professional/administrative, while slightly over 2 percent of Maori males fell into that category. Similarly, less than a third of European males were laborers, while almost half the Maori men were so labeled. The life expectancy for Maori males was almost ten years lower than for Pakeha males, and more than three times as many Europeans as Maori had attained at least a school certificate.

8. Ranginui Walker (1973, 115) describes the effects of stereotypes:

The emergence of the Maori in the post-war years and the migration to urban centres has brought about a new confrontation between Maori and Pakeha. The Maori wishes to participate on an equal footing with the Pakeha but his ability to do so is being continually eroded by the ethnocentric and patronising attitude of the Pakeha who is insensitive to his need for approval, for acceptance and for success. Instead the Maori is reminded on all sides that he's fat, lazy, cunning, promiscuous, happy go lucky, lacking in ambition, apathetic, shiftless, improvident and unreliable.

9. Similarly Dunstall (1981, 426) writes that "to the extent that Maoritanga implied the existence of a homogeneous culture, a united Maori nation, it was a myth. Young articulate urban Maoris showed impatience with the outlook of their elders whom they saw as being 'too accommodating to Pakeha pressures.' "

10. At funerals the accomplishments of individuals and their kin groups often merged. Traditional chants suggest that the accomplishments of the deceased redounded to the glory of the tribe.

11. Oppenheim (1973, 22) views the tangi as a major exemplar of Maori identity: "From being the predominant symbol of a world view expressing the man/nature relationship however, it has become representative of a group attitude toward bereavement and of the solidarity of Maori culture. The *tangihanga* thus no longer symbolizes an intact system, but rather the value which is

put upon personal relationships and which is thought of as being specifically Maori."

12. Today, most bodies are embalmed before they are brought to the marae.

13. In the center of North Island and on the west coast, the two areas in which I have done fieldwork, the dead were always housed in a tent. The size of the tent varied according to the importance of the deceased; the larger the tent, the greater the number of mourners anticipated. However, in other areas, the body may be placed at the back of the meetinghouse or on the porch (Metge 1976; Salmond 1975).

14. It is not unusual for women to be equated with death and mourning (Bloch 1982; Douglas 1970). It would be possible, but beyond the scope of this paper, to demonstrate that the structure of the double funeral has been retained in contemporary Maori culture. The relationship between the multiple parts of the funeral is a means of talking about the relationship between men and women, the individual and the social body.

15. B. J. Kernot (pers. comm.) indicates that this is a modern understanding. The proverb *Me nga roimata me te hupe ka ea ai te mate* 'By tears and mucus is death avenged' indicates another and older meaning to the nose pressing and weeping that takes place at tangi.

16. In the areas where I did fieldwork, this was considered a highly tapu responsibility. But Hohepa's (1970) discussion of Northland suggests that some of the purificatory rituals have been relaxed.

17. Salmond (1975, 186) writes, "Food or liquor may be served to complete the deconsecration ritual. If there are no expert elders in the community the tapu may be lifted by a beer party in the house that evening or several days later."

18. Beaglehole and Beaglehole (1945) report that drunkenness at tangi tended to occur only rarely among the workers. They drank, but tended not to become drunk. The revelry that I observed almost always occurred after the burial and can best be seen as a release.

19. The night after the burial was often a time of merriment and matchmaking. It is just as likely today to take place before the burial, while most visitors are still on the marae (Salmond 1975, 186).

20. The pattern for tangi described here is not followed in the cities. Not only are chapels and funeral homes substituted for the marae, but the event is governed by European rather than Maori conventions. As Salmond (1975, 186) writes, "this [European style burial] is regarded as inappropriate for someone of Maori descent." Whenever possible, individuals are brought home to their rural marae.

21. Jorgensen's (1972) description of the situation of the Utes and Shoshones is remarkably similar to the one given here for the Maori. Similarly, the attitudes of the surrounding whites are very similar to the attitudes of Pakeha New Zealanders.

22. Erik Schwimmer (1972) draws parallels between Native Americans and Maori. In both cases, minorities use rituals to assert their own superiority vis-à-vis the majority. He calls this process "symbolic competition."

11

Maori Sovereignty:
A Feminist Invention of Tradition

MICHELE D. DOMINY

Cultural identity, like constructions of gender, can be viewed as a product of social and cultural processes rather than as an extrapolation from
common ancestry or territory (see Linnekin, chapter 7). Since it is culturally constructed, cultural identity shifts over time with changing historical circumstances and social contexts. In New Zealand the processual and situational nature of cultural identity is reflected in the highly
variable definitions of Maoritanga. The formation of Maori identity has
involved continual interaction with, and reaction to, Pakeha (of European descent) identity (Archer and Archer 1970; Fitzgerald 1974; Mead
1976). Metge (1976, 46) highlights the creation of Maoritanga against
the backdrop of Pakeha culture as it sometimes incorporates, sometimes
rejects elements of that culture. In focusing on Maoritanga, "ways of
doing things and a manner of looking at the world that has become symbolic of Maori identity," theorists such as Metge (1976), Salmond (1975),
and Sinclair (n.d. and chapter 10) have focused on the adaptation of
Maori tradition to a new cultural context. They agree that Maoritanga
is not a simple concept but one with multiple meanings implying varying modes of action. Salmond (in Stirling and Salmond 1976, 167)
writes:

> I have seriously begun to wonder whether there is such a unit as "Maori
> society" in any case, or whether there ever has been. A closer look at what
> actually happens reveals a wealth of tribal and individual difference, and
> these differences are not accidental but critical to the way that Maori peo-
> ple interact in Maori contexts. "Maoritanga" seems to be built on these
> critical differences (of tribal history, contact experiences, marae eti-
> quette . . .) as much as it is on shared values, concepts and strategies, and
> this is something which has been consistently underestimated by its schol-
> arly interpreters.

Salmond focuses on particular expressions of Maoritanga. She does so
by adopting approaches from the study of life history—telling one

woman's life story and thus conveying her tribal and personal individuality—and by using a situational approach in analyzing the hui, a ceremonial context in which Maoriness is expressed (Salmond 1975; Stirling and Salmond 1976). Like Salmond, Sinclair (chapter 10) recognizes the significance of examining the ritualization of ethnicity—the revival of ancestral traditions and reaffirmation of Maori identity in contemporary New Zealand—for understanding the situational nature of cultural identity and the objectification of a culture in particular symbols such as tangihanga.

Maori women have played a significant role in formulating identity, sometimes defining and redefining Maori culture through the fostering of Maoritanga, sometimes bridging Maori and Pakeha cultures, and sometimes rethinking traditional Maori gender conceptions. They do not always agree on particular formulations of identity. In this chapter I focus on the construction of a highly politicized, self-conscious cultural identity by Maori activist women, and on a particular expression of Maoritanga called Maori sovereignty. I situate these women within the context of New Zealand feminism to illustrate how they draw upon two key identities, as Maori and as women. Their identities as Maori and as women share aspects with each other, and both identities at times join in opposition to white male-dominated culture. In particular, Maori activist women work to redefine and recreate their cultural tradition, rejecting certain aspects of Pakeha culture and the imposition of Western concepts of ethnicity; they explicitly reject a biculturalism that absorbs Maoriness.

Within a nation-state such as New Zealand, cultural identities are part of a larger set of social categories that provide varying possibilities for conscious affiliation and distinction. The Maori tradition these women seek shares a content with the women's culture that Pakeha lesbian separatists are in the process of creating, just as the white culture they reject shares a content with the male culture that Pakeha separatists reject. Consequently Maori activist women and Pakeha lesbian separatists have begun to forge alliances within the context of New Zealand protest movements. Maori identity is perceived by women as nested (Cohen 1978) within increasingly inclusive levels and crosscut by a shared identity with Pakeha women, Pacific women, and all women.

I begin by documenting the mediating role Maori women have played between Pakeha and Maori culture through their involvement in female-based associations such as the Maori Women's Welfare League and in *maramatanga* (a religious movement researched by Sinclair n.d.), which not only asserts a Maori identity in the postcolonial context but contributes to unique assertions of female identity and to female bonding among Maori women. While asserting Maori identity, women increasingly began to recognize the ways in which traditional Maori culture constrained women's position.[1]

Such voluntary associations express social identity (Parkin 1966), often in symbolic terms (Manning 1973). A focus on associations or interest groups, such as female solidarity groups, highlights the cross-cutting of identities as people are differentiated into particular groupings while at the same time they unite on the basis of other commonalities (Cohen 1974b; Warner 1959). Individuals may define their identity through membership in political groups and social protest movements (Kushner 1970). In this chapter I examine the protest activity of a younger generation of Maori activists who have begun to assert their identity as Maori women. Women's actions in the Maori Land March of 1975, the Bastion Point occupation of 1978, and the 1981 Springbok Rugby Tour protest have signaled the assertion of a radical Maori female identity, one that recognizes parallels between racism and sexism, colonialism and male culture. These women specifically invoke feminism as a model for Maori identity and suggest that sexism provides the model for racism; the primacy of sexism even for Maori women is evident in Donna Awatere's statement that "feminism is the black women's movement." A spokeswoman for the Black Women's Movement, Donna Awatere provides impassioned rhetoric that articulates the consciously constructed ideology guiding behavior in contemporary protest events.

Separatists and Traditionalists

In examining the range of Pakeha women's gender conceptions I have focused on the cultural representations of these notions in women's attitudes, actions, and beliefs (see Dominy 1983). The varieties of power available to and used by women in informal organizations and the complexity of their roles suggest considerable variation in women's gender conceptions. Not only do women and men in New Zealand have separate conceptual systems and standards of evaluation such that the meaning of women's activities may be different for women and men,[2] but the models held by Pakeha women also vary within what is ostensibly the same culture.

Two of the gender constructions emerging from my analysis of Pakeha women have parallels in modern Maori identity categories and share a cultural content with those categories. I call these traditionalist and separatist gender constructions.[3] Traditionalists work to preserve the social structures and cultural beliefs that prescribe their roles in society as women. Separatists work to alter fundamental cultural constructions of gender by upsetting those structures and beliefs. The source of value and purity for Pakeha traditionalists rests in their cultural transformation of the natural world. For these women the essence of femaleness lies specifically in their reproductive powers and in their roles as mothers and controllers of unrestrained male sexuality. As volunteers in the community, they work to preserve the domestic sphere, by which they mean the activities of mother and homemaker. They define themselves as carers and sharers with a special concern for social relationships and believe they can make unique contributions as women in New Zealand society. These contributions are seen as reflecting their primary obligations to family at the local and national level and are not dependent upon changing their role or the structures of society (see Dominy 1985 for fuller discussion).

In contrast, separatists promote an ethos of natural purity that rejects not only male sexual energy but also the products of male technology and culture. The separatists seek to generate a female-based culture modeled on aspects of female sexuality and claim spiritual unity with life, with nature, and with the earth. For these women, the essence of femaleness lies in their powers of reproduction but, even more important, in their sexuality; thus they expand the concept of sexuality, redefining it as an aspect of all interpersonal relationships. Women should not control and constrain the sexual dimension of their interactions, but use their sexuality as a model to structure behavior. They believe sensory perceptions such as instinct, intuition, and telepathy are among women's natural capacities. Structurally, separatists withdraw from society and create communities based around female alliances. They are creating an exclusive "women's culture."

Concepts of separation reinforced by pollution beliefs are important to both groups. Separatists promote a broader notion of sexuality than traditionalists, however, one that is not limited to reproduction and its connection to motherhood. Whereas traditionalists assert occasional separation from men in female solidarity groups that draw upon the distinctive skills of women, separatists assert complete separation from men in all spheres of social life. The contrast between the gender constructions of Pakeha traditionalists and separatists is paralleled by Maori women's construction of identity categories. Some women join Maori-based voluntary associations modeled on and affiliated with Pakeha associations and work through established political structures; they affirm their domestic roles and traditional authority as mothers. Other women, affirming notions of spiritual unity with the land, nature, and with their past, join the Maori sovereignty movement and work to upset and redefine Pakeha-based social structures and cultural beliefs.

Women's Adaptation of the Maori Tradition

Like gender conceptions, cultural identity implies the sharing of a set of symbols by which people interpret their relationships and structure their behavior with others while also situationally expanding and contracting categorical boundaries (Deshen and Shokeid 1974; Howard and Howard 1977, 166; Vincent 1974). Through their involvement in the religious movement of maramatanga and the Maori Women's Welfare League, a national voluntary association, Maori women have played a mediating role between Maori women and Pakeha traditionalist women. In maramatanga and the Pakeha-modeled League, women work to expand their role in redefining Maoritanga while drawing on the authority of their traditional roles as wives and mothers, and while working to preserve the primacy of their role in the domestic sphere.

Karen Sinclair's work (1984, 1985) on Maori women's involvement in maramatanga has focused particularly on the definition and formation of a distinctive Maori identity and on the rejection of European values. Maramatanga is a nominally Catholic, rurally based religious movement that draws extensively on the Maori prophetic tradition. While the rituals stress the continuity of tradition by upholding the importance of the Maori language, oratory, art forms, and the retention of the marae, the hui, and the tangi (see Sinclair, chapter 10), they also reflect the adaptation of the Maori tradition to a new, urban cultural context and the sustaining of present-day values (Sinclair 1984).

This dual process is apparent in Sinclair's analysis (n.d.) of a pilgrimage of maramatanga adherents to Waitangi, where some chiefs signed a treaty with representatives of the British government: "That the pilgrimage is to Waitangi, where rights to land were relinquished, is a symbolic attempt both to reexamine and reevaluate the actions of the ancestors and to express protest at the seemingly impious materialism of the Pakeha" (Sinclair n.d.). In addition, specific Pakeha concepts such as institutionalized, economically based hierarchy and individualism are rejected through a process of symbolic inversion in the pilgrimage in which that structure is absent. The pilgrimage is above all an assertion of Maori identity.

In particular, the extensive participation of rural Maori women in maramatanga reflects their increasing influence in postcolonial New Zealand. Sinclair attributes this to women's traditional ambiguity in Maori culture, which was evident in their life-giving but simultaneously polluting powers (Sinclair 1984, 127):

> The contingencies of the colonial situation have enhanced the authority and influence that Maori women were traditionally permitted to claim.

. . . By their continued involvement in [European] institutions and by
their enduring commitment to their children and grandchildren, women
have come to understand a social world dominated by Europeans. . . .
They are therefore willing both to uphold tradition and ease its passing.
Thus the colonial situation, which has so often diminished the stature of
Maori men, has enhanced the prestige of Maori women.

Not only is maramatanga a positive assertion of Maori identity, but it
also provides a context for female solidarity in their communities, an
involvement that extends to participation in nationally organized
groups such as the Maori Women's Welfare League. Such activity,
which particularly involves older women, demonstrates a "proficiency
in and understanding of Maori culture [that] allows them to be media-
tors between the two cultural traditions of New Zealand" (Sinclair
1985, 11). Patterned along the lines of the Mother's Union and Country
Women's Institutes for Pakeha women in New Zealand, the Maori
Women's Welfare League was founded in 1951 at a conference of delegates from women's welfare committees formed after World War II by
Maori welfare officers (Metge 1976, 144). The first organization to
explore the effects of Maori/Pakeha contact, especially racial discrimination consequent to postwar urban migration, the League contributed
to a renewed sense of Maoriness throughout the country (King 1983,
178). The 1946 Maori Social and Economic Advancement Act established tribal committees and positions for welfare officers within the
Department of Native Affairs. These tribal committees were dominated
by men and men's issues, such as land legislation and servicemen's reha-
bilitation. As King argues, the most severe problems confronting Maoris
were infant mortality, sanitation, hygiene, diet, and the trauma of moving to the cities (1983, 167). Clearly, a Maori women's organization was
needed.

In the 1950s the Maori Women's Welfare League established itself as a
powerful political voice for Maori concerns. Its first dominion president, Whina Cooper, visited almost every Maori community in the
North and South islands. Cooper was often opposed in districts where
she had no tribal ties, often for "taking a man's role" by standing up and
speaking in public. Many women thought her domineering. According
to her biographer (King 1983, 185), Whina Cooper's goal for the league
in her six years as president was to strengthen Maoritanga, especially
through supporting the building of marae, the teaching of Maori language in the schools and training colleges, and the recognition of Maori
arts and crafts. Of particular interest is Cooper's appreciation for the
significance of the league as a women's organization:

> We exist because of a need among our people, because they need such an
> organisation as ours. Remember, too, that we are part of the wider move-
> ment of the National Council of Women. We are also part of the Pan-
> Pacific Movement of Women . . . should we not try to establish our real
> independence, linking ourselves more closely with the women's organisa-
> tions as an autonomous body among our Pakeha sisters . . . ? (Cooper in
> King 1983, 185–186)

In New Zealand, as the demographics shift and as more Maori move
to urban areas, Maori identity is being interpreted differently by the
young, and its meaning is reformulated to cope with the changing social
context. There is no consensus on the content and meaning of Maoriness
as an ethnic identity. But the young radicals have totally rejected league
ideals. Rebecca Evans (1982, 13), a feminist activist, makes reference to
"beautiful women" like Mira Szaszy, ex-president (1973–1977), foundation member, and dominion secretary during Whina Cooper's presi-
dency. With her heightened awareness that traditional Maori culture is
failing Maori women, Szaszy reflects the concerns of young feminists:
"The League started mainly because the men on marae committees
weren't dealing with the problems of women and children. The League
was formed so that women could handle situations that concerned them
greatly" (Szaszy in Hawke 1983, 34).

An awareness of women's issues and of New Zealand's links to other
Pacific women unite league members and Maori activist women. While
members of maramatanga are older and rural, their social movement
also bears a resemblance to the protest movements of younger, more
radical Maori women. Both share concerns for the symbolic significance
of land, as well as for values that explicitly reject elements of Pakeha
culture such as materialism, individualism, and hierarchy. In contrast,
Pakeha traditionalist women support such values in their organizational
structure. Yet many young Maori break with rural values when they
become urban dwellers and radical activists (see Sinclair, chapter 10)
and advocate a more complete separation from Pakeha culture. Why
then do they share radical strategies with Pakeha lesbian separatists?

The United Women's Convention, April 1979

The alliance between Pakeha lesbian separatists and Maori women
activists rests on their perception of New Zealand culture as white and
male defined, and reflects the oppositional nature of identity formation. Their shared rejection of maleness (which is equated with white-

ness) results in a shared affirmation and equation of female and black. Both groups recognize this equation, asserting that the analysis of each informs and strengthens the other. Both identities share aspects of each other in conceptual and social structural terms. A shared ideology rejects hierarchy, individualism, materialism, spiritual detachment, and racism. Shared political strategies include the symbolic inversion of white male culture through complete separation and radical protest strategies that demand a rethinking of cultural systems of classification.

These groups publicly acknowledged their alliance for the first time in their shared protest activities at the fourth national United Women's Convention, held in Hamilton in April 1979. At the closing session of the convention, one of the keynote speakers, Charlotte Bunch, an American radical lesbian feminist, yielded five minutes of her speaking time to Rebecca Evans, a radical Maori woman activist. Evans argued that the "white women's convention" reflected racist exclusionary tactics by the organizers in its patronizing poster (a Maori woman holding a child beside a washing line), the lack of workshops for black women, the lack of a black speaker, and the complexity of organizational details. She said that the convention was a white, female replica of a white, racist male convention. Pakeha lesbian separatists vociferously supported her. Throughout the convention, lesbian separatists and Maori activist women together had resorted to graffiti, disruptive chanting, and loud behavior as the only ways to voice their objections to the convention's patriarchal (white) structure and middle-class (white) values.

As a self-ascribed label, "black," or occasionally "brown," is used by contemporary Maori activist women to assert a particular kind of Maori identity and to specify what one is not—not white (Pakeha) and not Pakehized Maori. The use of the polarizing "black" label reflects the highly politicized active creation of a new cultural identity. Given the occasional inclusion of all Pacific peoples or of activists from New Caledonia, French Polynesia, Hawaii, and Australia, the self-ascription "black" also underscores parallels in the experience of New Zealand Maori with other colonized peoples, although to my knowledge no one has made this connection explicit. In other words, these radical women use the category "black" symbolically, not as a racial ascription.

Lesbian-separatist ideology asserts that to be middle-class is to be male identified and male defined. To be middle-class and feminist is therefore a contradiction and implies co-optation. Thus to reclaim femaleness, middle-class behavior must be rejected. Politeness, tact, tolerance, respect, and niceness as female manifestations of middle-class distancing behavior are rejected in favor of behavior (anger, confrontation, and violence) that is sex marked as male by nonseparatists. The selective assumption of female and male attributes by women is an attempt to restructure gender categories by altering the content, the boundaries, and the actors. They are not trying to create an androgynous image, which they argue is based on male and female values and is thus modeled on current cultural stereotypes. For women to gain control of their own lives, gender for separatists must be defined by women. In the same way, lesbianism is redefined by separatists as a category and is broadened to include all women.

At the convention, separatist actions reinforced their commitment to female-based alliances and structures and simultaneously underscored their rejection of alliances with men and participation in male-dominated structures, including heterosexism, racism, class institutions such as universities, as well as consumerism and the mass media. Significantly, Maori activists protested with Pakeha lesbian separatists against these same structures.

Emerging Feminism in Maori Protest

Within Maori political movements, activist women have incorporated feminism into their construction of a Maori identity and their own expression of Maoritanga in the struggle for sovereignty. These women increasingly have asserted their female identity and expanded their role in protest movements. To do so, however, they have had to reject the authority of the male elders so intrinsic to Maori culture, where to be young and female is traditionally a liability. Reinventing tradition, Maori women cite the significance of their relatedness to the ancestors and to the land, simultaneously reinforcing Oceanic notions of personhood (see Lieber, chapter 4) and rejecting Western concepts of individualism; they also reject "sexist" elements of Maori culture. As "exercises in social engineering" (Hobsbawm 1983, 12), invented traditions typically characterize identity formation in the nation-state. Linnekin (1985, 241) writes that tradition "is interpreted anew in each generation. Every generation uses a model of the past to define itself, and this image is inevitably invented to some extent because it is formulated in the current social context. . . . Authenticity is . . . always defined in the present." Emerging schisms in Maori society reflect varying ways of reconstructing Maori tradition. Young radical women confront the double bind of either accepting traditional constraints or risking their old affiliations.

Whereas separatist culture is symbolically constituted in the cyclical and spiritual nature of female sexuality, indigenous Maori culture is symbolically constituted in a spiritual attachment to the land—that is, not the land per se, but rather the people's relationship to the land. Sep-

aratists incorporate the traditional metaphor slightly differently, inter-
preting the land not only as nurturing and female, but as having been
raped and subjugated.

The Maori Land March of 1975 led by Whina Cooper from Te
Haupua in the north to Wellington signified Cooper's belief that, for the
Maori, to be landless is to be cultureless (King 1983, 207). To hold onto
the land was a way to hold onto Maori heritage. The march was spurred
by a newly formed organization, Te Roopu Ote Matakite 'those with
foresight', which sought a gesture that might unify Maori and alert
Pakeha. The Maori Women's Welfare League and the New Zealand
Maori Council seemed not to be pushing issues of preserving Maori language, culture, and identity sufficiently.[4] Nga Tamatoa, formed in
Auckland in 1970 as an action group to preserve Maoritanga, and
the Wellington-based protest group, Maori Organisation for Human
Rights, formed to fight the 1967 Maori Affairs Amendment Act and
involved in detailing Maori grievances throughout New Zealand, were
also asserting Maori rights (Metge 1976, 177, 196).

Although all Maori support the land cause (Metge 1976, 112), many
opposed the march—as they opposed the later Bastion Point occupation
—because they preferred an appeal to Parliament through formal channels. For many, however, the march was unifying. Final fragmentation,
leading to the eventual dissolution of Matakite, occurred when some
protestors, mainly from Nga Tamatoa, refused to leave Parliament steps
in Wellington after the presentation of a statement of Maori rights.
Titewhai Harawira (1982, 27), who had supported Whina Cooper's
leadership of the march despite opposition against a woman leader from
some of the tribes, was one of the protestors who decided to camp at
Parliament. She writes: "But Whina believed Rowling when he said,
'You haven't marched in vain'. You can't ever believe the Pakeha. But
she did. Again a Maori struggle faltered because our old people are
unaware of Pakeha politics and do not have the courage to meet the
Pakeha and his tricks head on."

According to King (1983, 223), Harawira was the only Matakite exec-
utive member to camp out under the Matakite banner. Eventually,
Whina Cooper endorsed their arrest by claiming that the protesters did
not have Matakite's mandate and that internal fragmentation undercut
the strength of the land march statement (King 1983, 223). Harawira
interpreted the knighting of Whina Cooper and Maori Organisation for
Human Rights leader Graham Latimer the following year as a "sellout"
and as a sign that older Maori who get too close to Pakeha turn on other
Maori in their jealous guarding of power.

Not only age discrepancies between women, but also the increasing
involvement of Maori women in radical feminism, fostered this

fragmentation. Their emerging sense of a black female identity led to a rejection of the Maori Women's Welfare League and eventually to a rejection of male dominance in Maori organizations. Hana Jackson, a black feminist activist, writes (1982, 26): "I was first a member of the Maori Women's Welfare League 27 years ago when its aims were to help young Maori mothers. But when it came to making tea and cakes and doing these competitions I couldn't believe in it. After the first 10 years it changed. Now it's a sell out." Titewhai Harawira echoes her words and reflects on her emerging feminist consciousness:

> The League in my day was into positive stuff. Not this cup of tea stuff. Then . . . it was active in the Maori community in practical ways. I got nominated eventually to the New Zealand Maori Council. Well. What a shock. I was the only woman and the only one under 60. It was bloody disastrous. They just ignored me [behavior entirely consistent with Maori culture]. . . . At the third meeting they wanted to stop the meeting half-way through so they could listen to rugby. I couldn't believe it. All the important *take* ['agendas', 'causes'] that were coming through from all over the country from our people. And they wanted to stop it for a rugby match. (Harawira 1982, 27)

The feminist consciousness continued to emerge during the Bastion Point occupation when a group of Maori women challenged the sexism of Maori men. Hilda Halkyard (1982, 30), a Maori feminist activist, claims that those women are now the basis of the Black Women's Movement. In discussing the role of Whina Cooper in the Bastion Point occupation, Michael King (1983, 229–231) recapitulates the Auckland land dispute. In 1898 the Native Land Court decided to make the Ngati Whatua trustee owners of a 700-acre Orakei Block of land.[5] As owners of the land, both former trustees and their descendants began to sell the land to the Crown. By 1928 only 3 acres remained unpurchased. A 39-acre block of land in Okahu Bay, which the Native Land Court had declared inalienable, and a 4-acre site that included the Orakei community's church and cemetery, given to the Church of England in 1858, had also been sold to the Crown.

The early 1950s saw the relocation of the Ngati Whatua community at Orakei to a 10-acre site overlooking Okahu Bay. A marae was built late in the 1970s on adjacent Crown land; this site was offered as compensation for a Ngati Whatua site taken by the city council in 1953 and serves all Maori although the Ngati Whatua hold guardianship (Metge 1976, 242). In 1976 the government announced its plans to build a major upper-income housing development on 8.7 acres of Bastion Point, a site well situated over the harbor and part of the original Orakei

Block. In 1977 Joe Hawke, treasurer of Whina Cooper's Matakite activist group, led the Ngati Whatua to occupy Bastion Point. The protestors refused to leave until 180 acres of Bastion Point were returned to Maori ownership. The occupation lasted 506 days. On May 25, 1978, 222 occupiers of the Point were evicted by 700 police with the army offering backup support.[6]

While the occupation was supported by radical Pakeha and Maori alike, Maori elders were not unified in their support. Whina Cooper, for example, who initially had supported Hawke and supplied the protestors with a meetinghouse, eventually withdrew her support. King (1983, 230) writes that Cooper became disillusioned when the protestors stopped listening to her; she attributed this to the "communist" Pakeha influence.[7] She was also concerned about divisions within Matakite. She wanted sole focus on Maori issues and the obtaining of justice for the Ngati Whatua people.

Maori activist women argued that the occupation of Bastion Point in 1977–1978 was not only a struggle for land, but was also part of Maori women's struggle for equality within the movement in the face of traditional male dominance. While granting that the organizational structures used at Bastion Point drew on traditional Maori ways, Farr (1978, 21) argues that women must abandon such structures and increase their involvement in public life and in the marae. She argues that rural women's traditional organizing abilities led to their activity on committees, and in the case of urban Maori to their involvement in marches and in the courts. Women's activity in a protest movement as speakers, revolutionaries, challengers of chauvinistic attitudes, and as leaders in confrontations with the state (rather than traditional activities such as cooking and child minding) led to an "erosion of the accepted supremacy of the Maori male." Such involvement has persisted in more recent protest movements against the 1981 Springbok Rugby Tour and over land claims. On behalf of the Bastion Point women, Farr (1978, 23) wrote: "Men are the owners and perpetrators of oppressive institutions, governments, and systems. . . . Now we challenge, we fight, we dominate. It is necessary to be where the struggle is—for when it is won, the male-white-supremacist-power-oppression cycle will continue unopposed yet again—because we were not there." Maleness and whiteness become equated in her analysis, which demands a rethinking of traditional Maori gender relations.

Subsequent to the Bastion Point conflict and Rebecca Evans' speech at the United Women's Convention, Maori women held their first national hui in September 1980 at the Ngati Otara marae. The theme of the hui was "Black Women Unite" and a manifesto was issued: "Gonna share with all our black sisters/The right to be black/The right that was taken from us like the land." "Black" was meant to apply to Maori, Pacific Islanders, and Indians; in attendance were a number of antiracist, feminist activist groups, which had begun as all-women consciousness raising groups within larger organizations such as Nga Tamatoa (Awatere 1980). Much of the conference focused on new definitions of feminism, definitions that saw "feminism as the black women's revolution," a revolution rejecting sexism, racism, and capitalism.

The women strongly rejected relationships with whites (male and female) and argued that whites, not blacks, must change. Lesbian blacks had a central role and argued that just as blacks recognize the need for separation from whites to claim their identity, black women must recognize the same stance with respect to men. Again, *black* is used metaphorically here, as an oppositional marker rather than as a biological category. The term can include Maori women who "look" white and Pakeha women who behave as "black." In claiming a black identity, these women claim a cultural content in which mutable diacritics such as language and behavior (rather than the fixed diacritics of race) comprise the essence of identity.

Despite Maori separatist rhetoric, collaboration between Pakeha lesbian separatists and Maori activist women occurred in the winter of 1981 when radical protests against the Springbok Rugby Tour of New Zealand capped twenty-one years of protest against playing sports with South Africa. In 1960 the New Zealand Rugby Union (NZRU) chose to omit Maori from the national rugby team, named the All Blacks, chosen to tour South Africa. Widespread protest from all over New Zealand failed to prevent the all-white New Zealand rugby team from touring South Africa, and failed to add Maori to the team despite a national Citizens' All Black Tour Association that adopted the slogan "No Maoris No Tour" (Metge 1976, 298). The government refused to intervene with the private rugby union. In 1965 the NZRU would not send a team since South Africa refused to accept Maori participation, but in 1970 the South African government accepted a representative team. In 1975 Norman Kirk, Labour Prime Minister, canceled the tour of the South Africans to New Zealand to avert protest violence and in response to the nonrepresentativeness of the South African team. National Party Prime Minister Robert Muldoon, despite opposition from Maori and groups within New Zealand and the Commonwealth, permitted the South African Springboks to tour in 1981. As the tour progressed, with protest rallies in Gisborne and Wellington and despite a bloody confrontation in Hamilton when three hundred people stormed the fence and playing field to stop the game, women—especially Maori and Pakeha lesbian separatists—played a vital leadership role. Awatere (1981, 13) writes: "White dykes and blacks worked together during the Tour. . . . We didn't know them and they didn't know us—yet we had a parallel analysis of what was going on. . . . Was it because the leadership of the black group was all women, so that dykes felt more comfortable? Was it because giving up heterosexual privileges makes you vulnerable to attack from patriarchal power so you understand at a gut level, attack from white supremacy?"

In Wellington the participation of women in the antitour movement was evident by their positions in the front lines throughout the protests, by the number of them arrested, and by the vehemence with which women refuted Deputy Prime Minister McIntyre's assertions that "the leaders of the protest movement are using women" (Noonan and Aitken 1981, 16). Women were, however, absent from the official leadership.

Maori sovereignty as a particular formulation of cultural identity began to emerge in each of these events—the 1975 Land March, the Bastion Point occupation (1977–1978), and protests against the 1981 Springbok Rugby Tour. Its major proponent believes that "Maori women have built the strongest indigenous women's movement in the world. We have to step outside traditional Maori leadership's path to provide leadership for ourselves and for Maoridom as a whole" (Awatere 1984, 41).

Maori Sovereignty: The Black Feminist Perspective

Between June 1982 and February 1983, Donna Awatere published three articles—"The Death Machine" (June 1982), "Alliances" (October 1982), and "Beyond the Noble Savage" (January/February 1983)—in *Broadsheet*.[8] In 1984 the articles appeared as a book, *Maori Sovereignty*, which included a new chapter entitled "Exodus." Although *Broadsheet* has been attacked by radical Pakeha and Maori for not being radical enough, and by many Pakeha women for being racist and socialist in printing Awatere's work, it has the widest feminist audience in New Zealand. Awatere's views have elicited strong responses from all segments of New Zealand society. The following summary of Awatere's stance on sovereignty should be read as a highly conscious and politicized expression of her ideology:[9] "Maori sovereignty is the Maori ability to determine our own destiny and to do so from the basis of our land and fisheries. . . . At its most conservative it could be interpreted as the desire for a bicultural society. . . . It certainly demands an end to monoculturalism" (Awatere 1984, 10). Self-determination and the land are issues at the heart of Maori sovereignty. In Awatere's vision, Maori land is returned and she sees Waitangi and Bastion Point as symbols for fighting cultural imperialism embodied in racism, sexism, and capitalism. The signs of cultural imperialism are especially apparent in the areas of employment, justice, health, and mental health.[10]

Awatere's concept of Maori sovereignty is consistent with traditional Maori conceptions of Maoritanga, in which to be Maori is to make claims to land and ancestry (see Sinclair, chapter 10). Maori value *whenua* 'the land' for its emotional and social significance as the "land of our ancestors," a legacy linking contemporary Maori with their *whakapapa* 'lineage' (Metge 1976, 107). In Awatere's (1984, 69) rhetoric, "the love for the land, for one's loins, is a dialectic cementing one's links with nature. *At*taching, not *de*taching" (emphasis in original). References to primordial criteria of genealogy and locality resonate with Oceanic notions of personhood in which kinship—associated with common substance and shared roots and action—and locality—associated with ancestral spirits and legends—are concepts central to personhood (cf. Lieber, chapter 4).

But activist women are critical of the narrowness of traditional conceptions of Maoritanga. Their notion of Maori sovereignty demands a radical restructuring and rethinking of New Zealand's social institutions and values from the Maori perspective. In scope it extends beyond the issue of Maori identity and embraces New Zealand's identity as a nation: "The Maori people offer the Pakeha an opportunity . . . to establish an identity as New Zealanders which must be forged not in *opposition* to us, but for and with us. . . . The aim . . . has nothing to do with getting more 'education' or making more money. The aim is . . . [t]o forge a distinctive New Zealand identity from a Maori point of view" (Awatere 1984, 31–32, emphasis in original).

Ultimately Awatere claims Aotearoa (New Zealand) as Polynesian. Ironically the sovereignty stance—despite Maori protest against the "total" Pakeha culture—argues also for a selective fusion of Maori and Pakeha culture and the generation of a distinctive New Zealand identity reflective of the best of Maori and Pakeha cultures (the latter is differentiated from British culture). Awatere cannot completely advocate primordial criteria, since she argues here for the cultural construction of a new Maori (New Zealand) identity. Internal contradictions in her argument are not surprising, but as Howard notes (chapter 12), are only to be expected in rapidly changing cultural contexts.

Together, Pakeha lesbian separatists and Maori women activists reject reformism and compromise and call for structural change. Both condemn Pakeha New Zealand culture as male defined, and in equating male culture with white culture, Maori activists equate feminist issues with Maori issues. Ultimately, however, sexism assumes primacy as the fundamental opposition—"sexism was the first division," Awatere asserts. Female lack of autonomy suggests to her that women's bodies, like the land, were colonized by men. Maori sovereignty demands the rethinking of Maori traditions from a women's perspective; such a perspective speaks not only to the double oppression as Maori and as women confronted by these activists in Pakeha society, but also provides a challenge to Maori culture where women are "often rejected by our men as mates," and "often used as dogsbodies in the family" (Awatere 1984, 80).

With even broader concerns than their own cultural identity, Maori women are attempting to reconstruct Maori tradition. An article in the *New Zealand Listener* (McTagget 1984), for example, focuses on current tensions in the Maori community over women's rights to speak on the marae.[11] In November 1984 two Maori women, students at Victoria University in Wellington, brought a complaint to the Human Rights Commission because Maori women are denied access to speak at *paepae* 'formal occasions' at Te Herenga Waka, the university marae. The response of Professor Sidney Moko Mead reflects the more conservative voice among contemporary Maori. While arguing that women can learn other Maori skills, he says:

> They can also learn . . . the proper role of women. . . . The trouble with some of the radical women is that they're more interested in learning men's thing than their own. The thing about Maori culture is that the roles of men and women are complementary. Men cannot do some of the things that women must do. And there are things women cannot do—and will not be permitted to do, on the grounds of customary procedure. It is not as if we don't have any sympathy or aroha for the women. It is a matter of tradition. (McTagget 1984, 84)

Mead thus identifies the feminist intrusion of Pakeha culture. But some Maori women argue that the marae is a patriarchal institution mirroring the role of women in Pakeha society and supporting its oppressive structures. Mira Szaszy says, "Sexism is just as evil and damaging to the dignity of women as racism. Both have the same origins and both speak the same language" (cited in McTagget 1984, 84). She goes on to strike at the heart of the issue: "The denial of speaking rights to women on the marae appears on the surface to be harmless and acceptable to many women because it is said to be traditional. But in fact it reinforces the structures that dominate and oppress Maori women" (McTagget 1984, 84–85). For this reason Maori women had to create their own structures such as the Maori Women's Welfare League. In a speech, "Pay Heed to the Dignity of Women," given in 1983 at the national conference of the league, Szaszy turned to Maori cosmology and reinterpreted the Maori origin myth, suggesting that the creation of Hine Ahu One by Tane rendered the first human female.[12]

Maori women's cultural identity is crosscut therefore by a shared identity with all women, and alliances between Maori and Pakeha women are occurring in protest movements (see Awatere 1984, 44). Awatere outlines two elements of white culture that destroyed Maori sovereignty: (1) the spatialization of time, and (2) a concept of history as progress. Maori notions of spiritual unity with the land contrast with white colonialism, in which land is treated as a commodity. Furthermore, white concepts of time as mechanical and as a marketable commodity contrast with Maori notions in which past and present merge in the cyclic rhythm of nature and the ancestors' rhythm of life and death (Awatere 1984, 62).

In rejecting the Western view of history as progress Awatere presents three "illusions" necessary for colonialism: (1) capitalism and concepts of individualism and private property, (2) a confusion of artificial religion with natural spirituality, and (3) mechanical materialism, described as "mowed lawn mentality," a separation between the artificial (man-made) and the real (natural). For Awatere (1984, 74), Maori sovereignty rests on decolonization, in replacing "mechanical materialism with spiritual materialism rooted not in man-made artifice, but in land-based dialectic." Her concern for spiritual unity with the land and the cyclical rhythm of nature, and her rejection of white male mechanical materialism with respect to that land, resemble the cultural critique offered by Pakeha lesbian separatism. For Pakeha women female nature, like Maori culture, is cyclic and spiritually based while male nature, like white culture, is linear and measured. One of my Pakeha informants explicated the conceptual roots of separatism in a feminist publication: "I think sex is the key. And when I say sex I mean it in every sense of linking/harmonising one woman with another and with our environment. . . . I think the only way men can make a sexual 'connection' is by genital sex and even then they see it as blocking or plugging . . . that characterises men's conceptual ability; they think along straight lines and step by step (spurt by spurt). . . ."[13]

A concept of spiritual unity in which relatedness with the land, with nature, and with others presents alternatives to the spiritual detachment and individualism of male culture is the central value in the generation of Pakeha separatist women's culture. Pakeha separatist gender conceptions therefore share certain assumptions with Maori tradition as characterized by activist women: "The element forces of Maoridom are based on human connections, on the dynamics of human exchange, of pooling resources and pulling together, of mutual exchanges of thought and actions, of interweaving and interlocking patterns of human connections, of all skills, knowledge, talent and 'things' belonging to the group and not the individual" (Awatere 1984, 102–103).

With respect to Oceanic concepts of identity and personhood, Lieber (chapter 4) writes that relationships define the person, producing a sense of connectedness that defies Western individualism and materialism. Similarly, Linnekin (1985, 41) has written that the "meaning of Hawaiian lies in the wide and unknowable extension of relatedness, the mutual, enduring obligation established by kinship and the mandatory nature of exchange." These concepts of identity are equally essential to the recreation of Maori tradition and the creation of a women's culture.

Conclusion

With the global spread of ethnic politics, nationalist rhetoric and symbology have begun to assume predictable forms. In the case discussed here, however, while the concept of culture is being employed in a highly politicized and self-conscious way, gender is conflated with what Westerners would call ethnicity as the basis of a cultural identity. Attempting to reconcile received notions of Maoritanga with their own ideology about sovereignty, Maori activist women redefine and recreate their cultural tradition, rejecting certain aspects of Pakeha culture, such as colonialism and individualism, and incorporating other, newer aspects such as feminism. As radical women's movements, both have developed cultural critiques that privilege gender as a crucial basis of identity. The structure of their political arguments is markedly similar. Whereas lesbian separatists reject a synthesis of maleness and femaleness in androgyny, Maori activist women reject a synthesis of Maori and Pakeha culture in assimilation and biculturalism. The shared cultural values claimed by Pakeha lesbian separatists and Maori activist women are articulated in a Pakeha woman's words about Maori sovereignty and matriarchy: "There are strong parallels between the violation and subjugation of women in ancient matriarchal societies by white men and of Maori people in Aotearoa from the 1840's onwards. . . . The fight for the survival of Maori people is our fight as white women. It is the fight for the values which we have lost with the eradication of matriarchal society" (Mortensen 1983, 39). By this Mortensen does not mean that Maori culture resembles primitive matriarchies, but she is suggesting that the colonial process that has produced the dominance of Pakeha culture has violated matriarchal and Maori culture simultaneously and in similar ways. Both must reclaim a spiritual unity with the land and with nature that has been destroyed by a male-defined Pakeha culture.

Understanding an emerging Maori identity embedded in sovereignty depends on an analysis of the historical and cultural background against which that identity is created. Within the nation-state particularly, a cultural identity such as Maoriness is nested in increasingly inclusive levels and is crosscut by an identity shared with Pakeha and Pacific women. On May 24, 1983, International Day for Disarmament, Maori radicals joined Pakeha women and Pacific women in showing solidarity with the Greenham Camp women protesting the siting of American cruise missiles in the United Kingdom (Papali'i 1983, 21). Equating colonialism with male culture, feminist proponents of Maori sovereignty assert an alternative cultural identity that is fundamentally nonracial since it derives from a shared experience of oppression. This is perhaps best exemplified in Awatere's (1984, 86) statement that "white blood is not the problem. White culture is the problem." If gender and Maoriness are both equivalent to a metaphorical "blackness," then even in this highly politicized situation the Western ethnic/racial model proves to be not as inevitable—or as unambiguous—as one might expect. The formulation of cultural identity by radical Maori women is not simply an extrapolation from shared ancestry or territorial origin, but is clearly the product of cultural and social processes. Creative and ambiguous, that identity has the potential for expanding its boundaries past Aotearoa to the Pacific and beyond.

NOTES

I conducted fieldwork in Christchurch, New Zealand, for eighteen months from 1979 until 1980, funded by the National Science Foundation (Grant for Improving Doctoral Dissertation Research BNS 781063) and the Graduate School of Arts and Sciences and Center for International Studies of Cornell University. I am grateful for the comments and criticisms of Jocelyn Linnekin, Lin Poyer, and Karen Sinclair on earlier versions of this chapter.

1. Arapeha Blank (1980, 35) claims that women of her grandmother's generation were treated poorly, their lives defined by domestic chores and continual childbearing to increase their husbands' prestige. Of course Maori culture had already been shaped by colonial contact at this point. Amiria Stirling (Stirling and Salmond 1976, 86) recounts attempting to peek through the windows of the Hine Tapora meetinghouse during renovation to see how much of the interior carving had been completed by the men. When she was thrown off the veranda (women are *noa* 'profane' rather than sacred), she and the other women decided to go home and complete their *tukutuku* (flax weavings for wall coverings) and to stop cooking for the men.

2. Ardener's (1972) and Rogers' work (1975) in anthropology highlights differences between men's and women's conceptual systems and parallels Chodorow's (1978) and Gilligan's work (1982) in social psychology.

3. The data I use for Maori women are primarily written sources—Maori

words to Pakeha women—although I draw on firsthand field data in instances of Maori/Pakeha contact. I worked with a range of women's voluntary associations, many of which were working counter to each other, including traditionally based groups such as church groups and women's professional and special interest organizations, and various types of feminist groups (Dominy 1983, 1986).

4. The New Zealand Maori Council, composed of representatives of most tribes from Maori district councils throughout New Zealand, is a national organization that takes submissions on Maori issues directly to Parliament and to the Cabinet. Supported by government subsidies and district review, the council almost dissolved in 1970 from lack of funds (Metge 1976, 209).

5. The Native Land Court, established in 1865, ascertained Maori titles to land and issued freehold titles to owners. Freehold title effectively individualized Maori land-holdings and undermined the traditional authority of the Maori leaders (Keith Sinclair 1969, 146; see Metge 1976, 34). The 1967 Maori Affairs Amendment Act exempted Maori land with fewer than four holders from the supervision of the land courts. Maori land governed by special Maori land legislation is distinct from land owned by Maori with freehold title. Maori land is determined by the Maori Land Court in accordance with the Native Land Act of 1862 and other acts up to the Maori Affairs Act of 1953 and its amendments. The 1967 amendment effectively removed protections against individuals selling land to non-Maori. The 1974 amendment reversed this ruling retroactively. Maori support for each was mixed.

6. The Waitangi Tribunal serves as a commission of inquiry, investigating claims made by Maori that a statute, law, or action of the Crown violates their rights under the 1840 Treaty of Waitangi. On July 1, 1988, the New Zealand government announced its decision on the Orakei land claim case. The government accepted the tribunal's recommendation to restore to the Ngati Whatua most of the publicly owned remnants of the 280 hectares once owned by them, and to pay $3 million in reparations. This is the first major case in which the government has given back land as a result of tribunal recommendation.

7. Five months into the Bastion Point occupation in June 1977, I was in London investigating conceptions of cultural identity among young expatriate Pakeha New Zealanders. New Zealand Prime Minister Robert Muldoon, in Britain for the Commonwealth Conference, was the object of unabating protest rallies by these expatriate Pakeha, whose support for the Ngati Whatua was vehement. Support for the Bastion Point occupation was not limited to New Zealand nor to Maori.

8. In the United States, *Broadsheet* is on file in the Women's Collection, Special Collections Department, Northwestern University Library, Evanston, Illinois 60201. Two other publications, *Circle* and *Bitches, Witches and Dykes*, claim a more radical stance.

9. I heard Awatere speak at a Women's Day seminar while in Christchurch and I interviewed my Pakeha informants about her views, but because my primary focus was on Pakeha women, I never asked her for an interview. Other analyses of nationalism where identity is consciously constructed and tradition reinvented see such ideological statements (Handler 1984, 56) as "significant determinants of social behavior" (Linnekin 1985, 241).

10. In a 1971 report of Women for Equality, Maori women workers were the worst-paid group in New Zealand; 88 percent of all Maori women have no educational qualifications. From 1967 until 1971, 61 percent of all girls sentenced to Borstal (reformatory for the young) were Maori, and in 1975, 100 percent of all fifteen-year-old girls sentenced to Borstal were Maori. In 1973, 55 percent of all women in detention were Maori, and yet Maori women are only 12 percent of the female population. One-half of the Maori population is under fifteen. Life expectancy for Maori is eleven years less than for Pakeha. In South Auckland, Maori and Pacific Island children die of respiratory disease at twenty-eight times the white rate. Maori women have the highest death rate in the world from lung cancer and from cancer of the lower intestine. Between 1961 and 1974 the number of Maori women admitted to psychiatric hospitals trebled.

11. I would like to thank Jocelyn Armstrong for bringing this article to my attention and for providing me with a copy.

12. In exploring the ambiguities of the origin myth, Heuer (1969) and Sinclair (1983) also turn to it as a template for understanding the special roles of women and the restrictions on women rooted in Maori cosmology. Heuer, unlike Szaszy, stresses that Tane, breathing life into the figure, created woman from mud and earth. As Heuer (1969, 449) writes, "This account shows the culturally all-pervasive conception of man as both the provider of the creative fertilising elements, the life spirit; concomitantly woman is seen as the passive shelterer and nurturer, the receptacle, the *whare moenga*, of the life principle implanted by man." Sinclair (1983) points to the extraordinary complexity of Maori symbolism, citing Michael Jackson's (1968) contention that Hine as a feminine principle simultaneously signifies life and death, thus resolving their opposition and highlighting the ambiguity of women.

13. I have not identified the author and source of this quotation because it is in a "for women's eyes only" publication in New Zealand. The article, "I Believe Men Hate Women . . . ," (1979) is in my files.

12

Cultural Paradigms, History, and the Search for Identity in Oceania

ALAN HOWARD

The chapters in this volume attempt to come to grips with a phenomenon that would probably be unremarkable in most other regions of the world. The idea that the social world is composed of distinctive groups, each differing from one another in significant ways, is something most Americans take for granted, as it is taken for granted in much of Europe, Asia, and Africa. To be sure, there is not always agreement about the specific character of the groups involved, nor about the part they play in ordering social life, but that there are ethnic groups—peoples who recognize a common heritage and have special bonds with one another as a consequence of that common heritage—is part and parcel of societal perspectives in much of the world. Oceania is of special interest because the phenomenon of ethnicity is relatively new there; in many parts of the region it is still in the process of becoming. This provides us an opportunity to examine aspects of ethnicity we have been unable to study elsewhere, except in a few isolated instances. We have in Oceania the possibility of seeing people struggle for the first time with who they are—their cultural identity—in an increasingly complex social world. Change and transition are also taking place within developed ethnic traditions, such as in Australia, New Zealand, and Hawaii, that parallel changes occurring in other regions of the world. So we have a continuum to explore in Oceania, from indigenous notions of group differences and similarities (which generally emphasize open boundaries and flexibility) to institutionalized systems of ethnic discrimination.

One striking aspect of this comparative exercise is the wide range of features used to distinguish groups. Reviewing available materials made me realize, more clearly than ever before, that ethnicity ought not be looked at as a distinctive phenomenon, but rather as an instance of the human propensity to categorize experience according to sameness and difference. From this point of view notions of ethnicity belong to that broader class of phenomena concerned with individuals' identification with, or distantiation from, others. It has much in common, in other words, with conceptualizations of kinship, community, friendship, and other types of social relatedness.

Ethnotheories and Historical Events

To appreciate fully the developments reported in this volume it is necessary to take a dual view. On the one hand we must consider the ways in which various cultural groups conceptualize their social worlds and organize their experience. We must, in other words, examine their ethnotheories of similarities and differences. On the other hand are the historical contexts in which social action takes place. On a macro level these include such large-scale events as commercialization of economies, colonization, urbanization, mass migration, the emergence of national polities, and similar events. On a micro level are those events that mobilize groups along one set of lines or another, or that crystallize attitudes and emotions around collective symbols.

Before considering the interplay between cultural paradigms and historical events, I shall describe some features that distinguish Oceania as a culture area from the continents. Many of the inhabited islands are small, their populations limited to a few hundred or few thousand. Many are also rather isolated from their neighbors and interacted with them infrequently in the past. In Polynesia, for example, before Western contact the known social world consisted largely of people who were alike physically, linguistically, and culturally. In other areas, including large segments of Melanesia, terrain served to separate populations into small pockets, with intermittent warfare punctuating their isolation from one another. These ecological conditions had some important consequences for ethnicity, or rather for its de-emphasis. Perhaps most important, there were few instances in which people who were clearly distinguishable on the basis of physical appearance, language, or culture dominated another people for a protracted period. Thus one of the main conditions leading to ethnic consciousness on the continental land masses of Europe, Asia, and Africa was absent in Oceania. In addition, until missionization by Europeans, there were no universalistic religions serving to dramatize competing identities. Indigenous religions were localized, associated with particular places and kinship groups. It was in this context—one relatively uncongenial to a highly developed sense of ethnicity—that cultural theories of social groupings developed.

Ethnotheories may be thought of as consisting of three types of propositions (Howard 1985). First are those propositions that underlie conceptual distinctions (i.e., those that group phenomena as the same or distinguish them as different). Many, if not most, propositions of this type are encoded within the lexical and semantic structures of language and can be analyzed accordingly. Second are those propositions that relate concepts to other concepts, or to actions, events, thoughts, feelings, or other identifiable phenomena. Such propositions are often explicit and appear in statements of association, correlation, and causation, but they are just as likely to be implicit and unarticulated, requiring exposition by analysis. Propositions about types of people—what they are like, how they can be expected to behave, and why—are of this kind. A third type of proposition can be termed *metatheory*, which refers to propositions about the formation of propositions and about their acceptability, truthfulness, and the like. Considering metatheories is important because cultural paradigms are never static. They invariably have a generative aspect to them, as the ranges of possibility are explored and applied to new circumstances. As the chapters in this volume make abundantly clear, cultural templates for ethnicity in Oceania are far from static. Rather they are in a highly dynamic mode, as each of the peoples described strives to make sense of an increasingly complex world. The changes taking place are resulting in greater differentiation of social forms and functions, often leading to the dissolution of preexisting epistemological frameworks. Since uniformity is not expected under such conditions, it is as important to consider how people go about organizing and testing knowledge as it is to grasp the repertoire of principles they invoke to comprehend their experience. It may well be, in fact, that "culture" under conditions of rapid change is better conceived as an assemblage of propositions, many of which may be contradictory to one another, than as a neatly packaged coherent system.

For many of the same reasons issues of identity must be analyzed contextually—examining the ways in which individual actors label themselves and others within particular situations, and how this affects their thinking, feeling, and behavior. Although it would be impossible to exhaust the range of situations in which identity is at issue—new ones are continually arising—a judicious selection of certain types can be very revealing.

Personhood and Identity

It is apparent that we cannot make much sense of "ethno-ethnicity" in Oceania unless we examine notions of personhood. As Michael Lieber explicitly points out, and several other contributors acknowledge, the ways in which people generate ethnic descriptions are logically related to their views about "persons." What emerges from discussions of the topic (see, for example, White and Kirkpatrick 1985) is that notions of

personhood in Oceanic cultures are very much at variance with the
Western concept of the sovereign individual. Enough has been written
about Western individualism so that we need not belabor the point
here, but for contrastive purposes it may be useful to draw attention to
the underlying premise upon which the Western notion of personhood
rests. I am referring to the corpuscular theory of reality that formed the
foundations of Newtonian physics as well as other sciences, including
psychology. The central idea is that the world can best be understood by
looking at the qualities of individual entities, with only secondary attention to relationships between entities. This world view also came to per-
vade Western folk psychology and underlies our commonsense notion
of personhood—that persons can be thought of as discrete beings,
bounded by their skins, and *possessing* attributes. As the authors in this
volume make clear, personhood in Oceanic cultures is based upon a
quite different, indeed a contradictory, premise. As Lieber puts it in
chapter 4, "The person is . . . a locus of shared *biographies:* personal
histories of people's relationships with other people and with things.
The relationship defines the person, not vice versa" (p. 72).

Instead of being thought of as "individuals," persons are better considered to be *consociates* (Geertz 1973, 364–367). The social implications of this perspective vary from culture to culture, but Joan Larcom's
analysis of court cases among the Mewun in Vanuatu provides a nice
example (chapter 8). There, emotional outbreaks are regarded as the
product of social relations rather than a result of inner feelings, so a
man on a rampage is likely to be seen as less culpable than consociates
who angered him, regardless of their intent (indeed, since intentionality
is an aspect of the "inner psyche" it tends to be downplayed in cultures
emphasizing relational frameworks).

One suspects that this view of personhood emerged in Oceanic
societies as a result of people living in relatively small communities
based upon kinship, intensive face-to-face relationships, and a strong
attachment to locality. Correspondingly, it may have been the high
degrees of geographical and social mobility that accompanied industrialization and urbanization that led to the Western emphasis on individualism. Regardless, it appears that the processes leading to the objectification of individuals (qua individuals), and those leading to the
objectification of cultural groups (qua ethnic units), are similar if not
identical. In both instances boundaries come to be emphasized over
interpenetrating networks of relations. This concern for, or perhaps
more accurately, obsession with boundaries in Western thought is a
topic I will take up shortly.

Of the groups described in this volume, those least prone to objectification of cultural identities seem to be the Kainantu people in the High-

lands of Papua New Guinea. The Kainantu, as described by Watson, employ a cultural paradigm that presumes differences between individuals and groups of individuals, but accepts them in a rather unreflective way. Underlying their notion of difference is a view that the way people are is primarily a product of environment and place. Individuals are alike if they share a common history, if they are "people who have the same story." But the important point is that there is little concern for classification, and even less for explaining the behavior of others. Furthermore, the distinctions they do make are transient; as Watson puts it, it is "the process of differentiation, not the catalog of diacritics used locally as cultural markers" that is significant (p. 26).

Watson introduces a distinction between Lamarckian and Mendelian views of human nature, a contrast amplified by other contributors to the volume (especially Lieber). The Lamarckian view, which seems to be held in one form or another by most Oceanic peoples, emphasizes the importance of environmental contributions to group character, which is transmitted as legacy to subsequent generations until new environmental conditions prevail. This contrasts with the Mendelian model of inheritance, "whereby somatically fixed traits are transmitted in genetic succession from past to present generations and are impervious to the short-term change of surroundings" (Watson, pp. 36–37). While this distinction seems to elucidate a basic difference in worldview concerning the manner in which group character is formed, it leaves some important assumptions implicit. I will therefore summarize what I see as the main assumptions of each perspective and try to relate them to the case studies reported in this volume.

THE EUROPEAN (COLONIAL) PERSPECTIVE

Before contrasting the colonial and Oceanic perspectives in such summary fashion, a caveat is in order. There is obviously much diversity of opinion within European countries and the United States concerning ethnicity, so any depiction at this level must necessarily be overly simplified. It is problematic whether most contemporary Europeans and Americans still think of ethnicity in strictly Mendelian terms.[1] Still, I believe it is historically correct to say that the nineteenth-century colonial framework that structured interaction with Oceanic peoples was largely informed by a common perspective. Only recently has the framework been fundamentally modified to incorporate dissenting views.

Assumption 1: Genetic inheritance is the main transmitter of a person's vital substance. Given this assumption, a person's main attributes derive primarily from a condition, internal to the person, that is immutable. Experience can only superficially alter one's fundamental character. One can learn to behave in a way that deviates from inborn character and thus mask it temporarily, but in the long run, and through generations, genetically transmitted character prevails. This logic was applied at a group level insofar as it was presumed that people of the same ethnic stock (i.e., "race") shared the same pool of inherited genetic material.

Historically, this assumption was promoted in Europe by political aristocracies, who, in the process of institutionalizing their privilege, placed increasing emphasis on breeding, or bloodline, as the critical determinant of family differences, and by extension, of class differences. The logic, of course, was calculated to undermine attempts to overturn the order, for people could not alter their genetic makeup.[2] This same logic, along with its corresponding implications of moral right and political hierarchy, was extended to incorporate the whole known world during, and immediately following, the age of discovery. One result was the evolutionary perspective, formalized by anthropologists, which ranked peoples along a linear sequence from savagery to civilization.[3] Given the second assumption, discussed below, race thus became indexical of group character, including moral character; by logical deduction, social worth could be determined by race alone.

Assumption 2: Race, culture, and language strongly cohere with one another. This assumption, formed on the basis of relatively sharp boundaries between ethnic groups in Europe and the known world, was dramatically reinforced during the age of discovery. The scale of difference was such that it was convenient to employ ethnic labels to summarize the full array of distinctive features. Thus "Arab" came to summarize a set of features composed of a distinctive racial type, Arabic language, and a particular (and from a European point of view, peculiar) set of customs. Of importance for the contrast with Oceania, *place* was considered essentially independent of these three ethnic markers. That is, Arabs would always be Arabs, Jews would be Jews, Gypsies would be Gypsies wherever they might relocate. Increases in geographical mobility among Europeans accentuated this dissociation of place and ethnicity.

Assumption 3: Where race, language, and culture do not cohere, the character of individuals is determined primarily by genetic inheritance. The inevitable disentanglement of race from culture and language, theoretically heralded in anthropology by Franz Boas, created a major dilemma for Europeans. From the beginning of contact, Australian Aborigines, Hawaiians, and Maori interbred with Europeans, generating a group of individuals with "mixed blood." These people differentially learned European languages and customs, leading to a variety of combinations (e.g., light-skinned individuals who spoke only the indigenous language and lived in a "native" fashion, dark-skinned individuals who spoke only English or French and emulated European lifestyles, and everything in between). The net result was that, for an increasing proportion of the population, identity became a matter of degree. As categorical distinctions became more and more problematic, analogic language was introduced (individuals being described as more or less Aborigine, Maori, or Hawaiian) to talk about variability.

For a time, Europeans attempted to impose subcategories to keep boundaries clear and coined such categorical designations as "half-caste" and "Démi." But with time and further intermixtures, such stopgap measures failed to suffice, as did further elaborations like "quadroon" and "octaroon" (Tonkinson, chapter 9). In the face of such confusion, Europeans generally resorted to a fourth assumption, aimed at retaining the hierarchical presuppositions associated with racial distinctions.

Assumption 4: When mixing of races occurs, the character of individuals is most strongly affected by the "lowest" racial type in their genetic makeup. Inferior racial stock, to any degree, was therefore perceived as a "contaminant" that could not fully be overcome. It followed that an individual's fitness for participating in civilized (i.e., European) society was problematic if a racial taint was present. While mastery of language and custom might superficially prepare a person for participation, the possibility of atavism, if not the probability, was seen as ever present.[4]

THE OCEANIC PERSPECTIVE

Diverse viewpoints certainly existed among Pacific peoples in precontact times. Anthropologists have amply documented the rich variability of Oceanic cultural schemes. But by relative contrast with the Western colonial perspective, the underlying similarities in identity concepts strike our attention.[5]

Assumption 1: A person's vital substance is transmitted genealogically, but it is supplemented by the food from which one gains sustenance. Oceanic terms for kinship imply, in one way or another, notions of common substance, or derivation from the same roots. The fundamental conception is that kinsmen share substance through common ancestry, but substance can also be shared by virtue of individuals being fed or nurtured from the same source. If the people who feed a child are his or her genitors, and if they feed the child from ancestral lands, continuity of substance (and hence of character) is assured. If, however, the child is adopted by others, is fed from the land of other families, or moves to new locations, his or her substance is modified accordingly. Under these latter conditions children have different substance from their genitors. It follows from this assumption that physical appearance (or race) is not a particularly reliable indicator of character.

A corollary of this assumption is that kinship within Oceania is generally considered to be contingent, rather than absolute, as illustrated by studies of adoption and group formation (Brady 1976; Carroll 1970b; Feinberg 1981). Thus, on the one hand, kinship has to be validated by social action to be recognized; on the other, kinship status can be achieved through social action (i.e., by consistently acting as kinsmen even though genealogical linkages may be questionable or unknown). This means that although "we-ness" is commonly expressed in the idiom of kinship, its social reality is dependent upon acts of solidarity and reciprocal exchange. And so it is with ethnicity. The recognition of an us-them dichotomy is everywhere contingent to some degree, but in Oceanic societies it appears to be much more so than in Western cultures.

Assumption 2: A person's character, and by extension a group's character, is a product of one's specific relational history. Rather than being internally located, one's character is dependent upon an ongoing set of relationships that contribute to its formation (and continual reformation). Furthermore, it is one's *current* set of committed relationships that is primary for assessing character, not the set of relationships into which one was born. This means that a person's fundamental character can be modified by significantly altering his or her network of committed relationships. The salient attributes upon which identity is based in any given instance are thus a function of commitments between interacting parties instead of observable characteristics of the individual.[6]

The contrast with the European viewpoint, which subordinates social factors to genetics and generalizes from physical type, is stark. Since coherence is not assumed between physical type, language, and culture, differences and similarities between groups are open to interpretation, depending on context. In one instance linguistic variations may be important, in another not; on one occasion a minor difference in custom may promote differentiation, on another a major difference may be ignored. The result is that group boundaries are flexible and often indistinct.

Assumption 3: Places have character by virtue of their histories, and people who are raised in a place, or assimilate to a group occupying it, acquire its character. The prevailing notion is that places have spirits, ghosts, or magical powers that incorporate past history and infuse inhabitants with it. Thus, for Oceanic peoples the crucial question is not so much where one is "from" as where one is *"of"* (Poyer, p. 129). The logic is that successful adaptation to a place requires coming to terms with (being in the good graces of) the spirits, which requires acceptance of their character. In effect, this is the equivalent of being their genealogical descendants and acquiring their substance. In this sense, as the people of Kainantu put it, people from the same place "have the same story" (Watson, p. 39).

One's cultural identity is therefore often tied to a specific locality, to the place where one's ancestors' spirits dwell, but it may also be based on more generalized distinctions between forest and grassland (Watson, chapter 2), or bush and sea (Pomponio, chapter 3). The power that places have in relation to identity is well illustrated by Flinn's account of Pulapese attitudes toward the people from Ulul. Pulap was raided by men from Ulul in the 1800s, and the Pulapese maintain an animosity toward the Ulul islanders to this day. Yet all the original inhabitants of Ulul emigrated, with the except of one woman who was from Pulap, and the island is today inhabited by descendants of the Tamatam island- ers who resettled it (Flinn, chapter 5). The intense emotions generated over land rights, and their symbolic centrality in the political struggles of the Aborigines, Hawaiians, and Maori, also reflect this close associa- tion of place with identity in Oceanic societies.

Given these assumptions, the emphasis on situationally variable iden- tity documented in the preceding chapters is not surprising. Group dis- tinctions, whether ethnic or otherwise, are indeed cultural construc- tions, as Linnekin (chapter 7) and Dominy (chapter 11) point out, but in some cultures they are more subject to reconstruction than in others. In Oceania, continual reconstruction—process rather than structure— appears to be the norm.[7]

At the opposite end of the spectrum from the Kainantu, who are described by Watson as unreflective about cultural identity, are contem- porary Australian Aborigines, Hawaiians, and New Zealand Maori. As a result of European colonization they have been relegated to minority group status in their own homelands, where they are in the position of political and economic underclasses. Concerted, self-conscious efforts are being made in these part-societies to reformulate traditional identi- ties. In the face of political fragmentation, activists in each instance are seeking to redefine their heritage in a manner that will allow them to be more effective participants in the larger political arena. To quote Tonkinson, they "seek to wrest from whites the prerogative of defining Aboriginal people" (p. 192). But these people are in a bind. The most obvious way to achieve unity is to adopt European notions of ethnicity, to accept biological assignment in principle, but to invert the value loadings (which leads to such slogans as "Black is Beautiful"). Thus anyone with indigenous ancestors would qualify for membership in the ethnic community. Membership would be relatively unequivocal. Unfortunately this does not work in practice, in part because the people who are most indigenous culturally are least likely to accept group assignment in racialist (or biological) terms. If, however, a leader adopts traditional assumptions about identity, he or she is likely to receive support from only one faction—those who identify with the specific history (and current political interests) that the leader represents.

Events and Ethnicity

Of all the events that have implications for cultural identity in Oceania, none has been more important than the establishment of colonial regimes. Colonial administrations institutionalized ethnic categories as formal social entities, and generally prescribed rights and privileges accordingly. They brought to Pacific Islanders an awareness of social ethnicity as a phenomenon—one that was relevant to obtaining political power and economic well-being. It is therefore convenient to distinguish precolonial, colonial, and postcolonial periods to come to grips with issues of cultural identity.

During the early period of contact with Europeans many, if not most, Oceanic peoples responded to them less as a new category of people than as a special case of known types. This response was facilitated by a notion that chieftainship mediated between gods and humans, so that a continuum existed ranging from slaves, or individuals who were otherwise without social worth, to the creators—the highest of gods. The concept of *mana*, or its equivalent, provided a means of linking notions of personal worth based on genealogies to economic and political efficacy, so that exalted status could be achieved despite constraints of birth (see Goldman 1970, chapter 1, for a discussion of the principles of status in Polynesia). To further set the stage for Europeans, light skin was associated with godlike status in many parts of the region. The explorers were thus often greeted as chiefs or demigods, given their obvious wealth and power (especially the power to kill). However, they were not always treated with reverence, for the logic of such systems made gods, as well as powerful men, fair game for the intrepid. Sahlins' account (1981) of Captain Cook's fateful encounter with Hawaiians is a case in point. Further experiences with traders, missionaries, and beachcombers quickly altered any initial impressions the Islanders may have had of European godliness, but the evidence suggests that most were prepared to accept these peculiar outsiders fully into their social fabric provided they behaved appropriately. There is little evidence that the Islanders were preoccupied with matters of ethnic identity, despite confrontations with people so dramatically different in language, appearance, and custom.

Where colonial regimes were established, or where Europeans carved out territories over which they exercised economic control, issues of identity increasingly came into focus. In addition to the institutionalization of ethnic categories (including such classifications as "half-caste" or "Démi"), a we-they distinction was underscored by major discrepancies in economic and political prerogatives. Histories of the colonial period suggest an ambivalence on the part of indigenous peoples toward white domination. Despite occasional expressions of resistance (often in symbolic form) and attempts by Islanders to regain control of their own destiny, there was widespread submission to European hegemony. For the most part, social separation enforced by European colonists came to be taken for granted.

Historical trends in the postcolonial period (which I consider to have begun with initial steps to dismantle colonies following World War II) have created new conditions, with profound implications for the processes that concern us. Some of these conditions have nothing to do with decolonization per se, but are the consequence of better transportation, population growth, and a dramatic increase in commercial activity. Isolation has broken down almost everywhere, so that people are continually coming into contact with others who are culturally distinctive. Many have left their homelands and settled elsewhere, either in discrete enclaves (e.g., Kapingamarangi on Pohnpei) or dispersed throughout urban areas (e.g., Nukuoro, also on Pohnpei). Others have emigrated to multiethnic nations—especially to New Zealand and the United States —where they are lumped with other minority groups. The proportion of Islanders receiving advanced education has also dramatically increased, with many receiving graduate degrees at major universities. Such education almost invariably leads toward the objectification of culture, and in many instances to a conservative view of tradition. I first pointed this out over twenty years ago when writing about leadership in Rotuma (Howard 1963) and later indicated its significance for the genesis of Rotuman ethnicity in Fiji:

> Western-educated Rotuman leaders are likely to be more conservative than chiefs without Western education precisely because they have learned to make abstract contrastive judgments about social systems and cultural styles. . . . Western education . . . has helped to provide clear criteria for inclusion in a social unit of higher order despite the fact that the traditional system was characterized by groupings with highly permeable social boundaries. . . . [T]he emergence of an ethnic group is facilitated by the

presence of individuals for whom ethnic identity not only becomes problematic but is of ideological import. . . . [I]t is . . . often the case that
they are the products of isolation from their native cultural systems, with
the very isolation heightening their ethnic awareness. (Howard and
Howard 1977)

In the 1960s and 1970s ethnicity became a focal issue in Western universities, so that what might have been learned implicitly by previous
generations of Oceanic students has been explicitly encountered by students during the past twenty years. Part and parcel of the turn toward
ethnic consciousness in Western universities was a serious questioning of
the value basis for modern industrial society and a romanticization of
earlier, simpler social forms. The Vietnam War impelled violent criticism of power abuse by Western nations and thus provided a framework
for colonized, or previously colonized, peoples to reassess their own
values and bases for judging social worth. The radicalism of the 1970s
also raised ethnic consciousness among Hawaiian-Americans (Linnekin
1983), Australian Aborigines (Tonkinson, chapter 9) and New Zealand
Maori (Dominy, chapter 11; Sinclair, chapter 10).

The crux of the matter came to be defined as a question of alternative
values (or life-styles) on the one hand, and of political and economic
power on the other. The value issue led to discussions about "traditional" social forms and frequently opposed individualistic Western capitalism, based upon egoistic greed, and "native" cultures based on com-
munalism of one form or another. Marxist writings provided a
sophisticated rationale for this opposition, as well as a powerful critique
of capitalism, but they seem to have had less effect in Oceania than in
other regions of the world. Perhaps one reason is that, although Oceanic
societies are poor by world standards, economically based class differences have not been great. Even wealthy colonial Europeans rarely
lived in the lavish manner that characterizes elites in South American,
Asian, and some African nations.

However, Oceanic peoples have always struggled, in one way or
another, for greater control of their economic and political destinies,
and the radicalism of the 1960s and 1970s revitalized their quest. An
important part of such endeavors has been the need to define groups, to
distinguish "us" for political and economic purposes from "them." As
the chapters in this volume make clear, this is a tricky business. As once-
distinct peoples increasingly come into contact with one another, as
their lots are cast together within (culturally) arbitrary political units,
the possibilities for alliance and disengagement are multiple and shifting. Potential identities multiply and become "nested" (Cohen 1978;
Linnekin, chapter 7) in complex ways. Ethnic awareness—indeed,

what may be considered a preoccupation with matters of identity—has thus been given dramatic impetus by the processes of decolonization and nation building.

With this general framework of cultural paradigm and historical context in mind, let us move on to a consideration of some issues raised by the contributors to this volume.

Issues of Cultural Identity and Ethnicity

I begin this section by discussing general issues associated with constructions of identity and ethnicity, that is, problems related to the structure and content of categories. I then go on to consider issues that derive from macrostructural changes in Oceania, particularly in the economic and political domains. Finally, the way events relate to structures, and individual behavior to macrostructures, will be considered.

Ethnic Boundaries and Cultural Constructions of Identity

When ethnicity is talked or written about in the abstract it often seems to assume a kind of permanence and lack of ambiguity that is belied by the facts, especially in areas like Oceania. The archetype of ethnic distinctiveness involves at least two contrasting categories, the members of which can be clearly distinguished along several dimensions—prototypically physical appearance (or "race"), language, and custom. But even though colonial regimes attempted to introduce such a model, it simply did not take hold in Oceania, as the chapters in this volume make clear. In part this is the result of historical factors that have differentially affected the components of ethnicity, but it is also a consequence of alternative cultural ways of characterizing similarities and differences.

The issue is essentially one of boundaries, of how rigid or permeable they are. In a provocative article some years ago, Hallowell (1963) contrasted the exclusiveness of Western societies with the easy way in which American Indians absorbed foreigners into their communities and kin groups. The contrast could just as easily be made between Oceanic and Western societies, although boundary exclusiveness is not confined to the West (indeed, Japanese society is even more extreme in this regard). Precisely what conditions produce rigid or permeable boundaries remains to be determined, but it seems to involve propositions of all three types (categorical, theoretical, and metatheoretical). Thus rigidity appears to entail categories based on immutable characteristics, theories of differential worth that place relatively little emphasis on social action, and metatheories that minimize the importance of personal experience in relation to received information (i.e., that are based on acceptance of prevailing stereotypes). In contrast, permeable boundaries are associated with categories formed of mutable characteristics, theories of personal worth that emphasize social action, and metatheories that emphasize personal experience over learned stereotypes. That there are historical (particularly economic and political) circumstances that favor exclusiveness or inclusiveness is indisputable, but the translation of historical conditions into cultural paradigms remains a subject of debate (see, e.g., Sahlins 1981, 1985).

Where, as in Oceania, the diacritics of identity can be modified by social action, a prototypical *them* is likely to be defined in opposition to valued actions.[8] A nice example is provided by the Pulapese, for whom Trukese have become the prototypical other. The emphasis on action is striking: "When making invidious distinctions between 'us' and 'them', Pulapese tend to describe 'them' as being 'just like Truk'. Truk in essence becomes the opposite of 'us'. 'We' still follow traditional customs and retain navigational skills. . . . 'We' take care of visitors and share our food; Trukese care only about themselves. 'We' work hard, grow good taro, and have little need for money" (Flinn, p. 123).

There are several revealing aspects to this commentary in addition to the obvious emphasis on behavioral indicators. The notion, for example, that "they" (the Trukese) have abandoned traditional customs (which implicitly were similar to "ours") while "we" (Pulapese) have not is clearly a way of distancing; it is a way of saying that "they" have moved away from "us." Associated with this is a process of mystification, which expresses itself in views of the other as supernaturally potent, a theme that is expressed in several of the chapters. What seems to be involved here is a cultural sense of order that, when violated or transcended with impunity, generates anxiety and a sense of awe. Thus people who are perceived as consistently behaving in a contrary manner are likely to be characterized as dangerous, evil, or otherwise threatening, but also as extremely potent. This is often expressed in the benign form of seeking out healers from opposing groups in times of illness (see Golomb 1978, 1985). The emphasis on sharing food, which is so central to the Pulapese, is an interesting application of Oceanic principles of kinship, mentioned earlier, to attributions of cultural character.

All of this raises questions about the degree to which ethnic considerations order social and psychological experience in contemporary Oceania. After all, identity involves much more than simple assignment to a category. It involves emotional as well as cognitive components and may be superficial or profound in its consequences. Certain identities may come to the fore only in rare contexts, while others may have a continual social and/or psychological presence. Attachments may be single stranded, based on only one commonality, or multistranded, based on a number of likenesses. Commitments to solidarity may be ephemeral or long lasting. In other words, we simply do not know enough about what it means to belong to a social category unless we know a good deal about both its cognitive and affective parameters.

Dominy's discussion in chapter 11 is especially pertinent to this point. By placing the struggles of Maori women within the context of the women's movement in New Zealand, she has highlighted the crosscutting implications of two potentially powerful identities, that of women (in opposition to men) and that of Maori (in opposition to Pakeha). Both identities are joined, for some individuals, in opposition to an abstracted white, male-dominated culture. For others, a powerful tension exists as a result of dual commitments, while for still others there is no particular problem in reconciling these two affiliations. The strong rhetoric documented by Dominy is instructive with regard to the depth of feelings involved. Her analysis vividly illustrates the fact that ethnic, or cultural, identities are part of a larger set of social categories, and that the potentials for alliance and disengagement are considerable.

It is important to remember that all of these issues of categorization are being raised within a broader context of macrostructural constraints and increasing sociocultural complexity. It is to these issues that we now turn.

Macrostructural Aspects of Identity

To summarize my discussion to this point, it appears that before European intrusion, Oceanic identities were rooted in relational networks based on genealogical ties and locality. In time, Pacific peoples were incorporated, to a greater or lesser degree, into an economic and political macrosystem dominated by an alien (Western) culture. The critical comparative question, then, is what this conjunction of cultures (Oceanic with West, Oceanic with Oceanic) has to tell us about the dynamics of identity—how it shapes, and is shaped by, the social order.

Western administrators imposed ethnic categories as they organized their colonial worlds. They used ethnicity as a means of political subjugation and promulgated the notion that personal worth depends on the ethnic group to which one is assigned. Decolonialization left a substantial residue of these conceptions in emergent political formations,[9] and the Western cultural paradigm still dictates the nature of the political game in Oceania. To a considerable extent, but in new and rather interesting ways, ethnic consciousness remains part of the conceptual and attitudinal equipment used to play it.

As identity issues are drawn into political arenas by indigenous leaders they become subject to all the forms of dialogue and action that constitute political gamesmanship. Campaigning with an eye toward ethnic categories, for example, has become a way to generate political constituencies, and local politicians often assume the prerogative not only to redefine groups for political purposes, but to provide alternative bases for assessing the social value of membership in them. An important consequence is that a handful of leaders—a small elite—has come to have an inordinate amount of influence over how ethnicity is defined in public arenas.

The politicization of cultural identity raises some important questions about social constructions of personal worth. Many precontact Oceanic societies were egalitarian in structure,[10] with prestige based upon fulfilling obligations within networks of kinsmen and community mates. When drawn into more complex, hierarchical sociopolitical systems, people from such societies confront new criteria for evaluating an individual's social standing. An example is provided by the Micronesians from Sapwuahfik Atoll, who distinguish themselves on behavioral grounds from Pohnpeians, whom they describe on occasion as self-enhancing political entrepreneurs. Sapwuahfik people on Pohnpei have the option of playing the Pohnpei game and gaining status in the broader community, or remaining committed to the central bases of Sapwuahfik identity, which is rooted in an egalitarian ethic (Poyer, chapter 6). What this signifies, on a more general plane, is a shift in the bases for determining prestige. Social worth in the political world of contemporary Oceania is embedded in a context of competing populations. To be successful in this larger arena, Sapwuahfik people are required to act in ways contrary to the very way they define their identity. Currently their sense of self-worth is sufficiently strongly rooted in traditional values to sustain them, but one wonders what the consequences of long-term socioeconomic competition will be.

At the heart of the issue is how the bases for cultural identity relate to peoples' attempts to control their own destinies. Indigenous social movements, such as Marching Rule and other millenarian sects, must be seen against this backdrop. They represent, as Linnekin (chapter 7) points out, attempts by colonially subjugated peoples to regain some measure of control over their lives. Colonial history is rife with less dramatic instances, including a wide variety of economic ventures and the dogged maintenance of indigenous medical practices (Howard 1979). The thrust toward self-determination remains strong in the postcolonial Pacific, as the essays in this volume attest (see, for example, Pomponio's analysis of Mandok attempts to defend their way of life by buying a trading vessel and by resisting relocation of a school, chapter 3). Cultural identity is an important part of this thrust, as Pacific peoples explore the most effective ways of balancing political potency in larger arenas against greater control of home communities. By affiliating with other groups, small, potentially distinctive communities are able to enhance their political clout, but they correspondingly must give up a measure of control over their own sovereignty. It is this dilemma that, at least in part, provides a framework for expression of "nested" identities. Cultural identity in Oceania thus has a generative quality, as people search for appropriate alliances and tolerable levels of inclusion.

The fact that much of the discourse concerning cultural identity takes place within political arenas raises questions about its relevance for social reconstruction and social transformation. Can political discourse and action effectively generate commitment to cultural identities, particularly newly formed ones? To what extent do political definitions of cultural identity carry over into other areas of social life? What are the organizational effects of redefining "tradition" for political purposes? Obviously Oceanic societies are not the first to face these dilemmas. They are part and parcel of nation building everywhere, especially where indigenous social, linguistic, religious, and cultural divisions are pronounced.

One of the central issues confronting leaders of emergent nations is how to symbolize unity within contexts of increasing complexity. In contemporary Oceania sociocultural differentiation is taking place along a number of dimensions at once, as individuals move into new occupational roles, receive differential education, spend time abroad, obtain wealth in varying degrees, and so on. Once-isolated Pacific Islanders are being exposed to a multiplicity of world views, ranging from the highly particularistic and provincial to cosmopolitan universalism. As the parameters of cultural experience are altered from relatively closed, redundant modes to a relatively open, diversified mode, the symbolization of identity has become increasingly problematic. A plentitude of possible identities is matched by a multiplicity of ways for symbolizing each particular identity, with the choice of symbols having profound consequences for breadth of inclusion and degree of commitment. Some symbols—particularly those closely associated with a particular person or place—can be divisive, while others are unifying. The case of Maori *tangihanga* 'mourning ceremonies' described by Sinclair (chapter 10) is an excellent example of the latter. It is a powerful symbol for a variety of reasons, including its association with the ancestors and its strong emotional loading. Because they are situationally confined, tangi provide a focused context for affirming Maoriness in which participants do not have to deal with the wider array of potentially divisive symbols.

While the concept of "tradition" is a rallying cry for contemporary leaders, there also seems to be a move toward contemporaneous, social symbolizations of identity. An instance is the case of the Mewun of Vanuatu. In her analysis Larcom makes the important point that for the Mewun "authenticity" (of identity) was previously entwined with the land on which they lived—their sociomythic place—but that this is changing as a result of the establishment of village courts and a preoccupation with *kastom*, "which is rapidly being redefined by the national government as a concept that explains essential differences between Vanuatu and the West, or between indigenous linguistic groups" (Larcom, p. 175).

Another major trend involves trimming the range of salient diacritics by emphasizing a limited number of key symbols to which large segments of a population can relate. The selection of slit-gongs, pigs' teeth, and decorative leaves in Vanuatu is an example, but much of the talk about kastom in Melanesia can also be seen as a pruning process. In various Melanesian societies specific "traditional" customs and practices, some of which were previously confined to domestic spheres, are being selected and given salience in the public arena (Larcom, chapter 8; Linnekin, chapter 7).

Perhaps the most pervasive symbolism employed throughout Oceania, as in most of the rest of the postcolonial Third World—the symbolism by which indigenous peoples are able both to define themselves and to forge links with each other—is white colonial society itself. For many Oceanic intellectuals, white society, with its emphases on individualism, material consumerism, and racialism, provides an oppositional category that allows clearest self-definition (see Dominy, chapter 11, for a detailed example). By contrasting Oceanic values of relatedness to Western (white) individualism and racialism these observers have anticipated (and informed) the major thesis of this volume.

Conclusion

The chapters presented in this book encourage us to take a fresh view of ethnicity and the role that cultural identity plays in social life. While group categorization is probably everywhere more flexible than has been portrayed in the scholarly literature, in Oceania it is process rather than structure that commands our attention. There we have an opportunity to examine ethnicity in the making. Events implicating issues of ethnicity and cultural identity are occurring with increasing regularity, and we are challenged to explore the interplay between cultural paradigms and historical events, to examine how cultural propositions concerning sameness and difference affect events and are modified by them. Much work remains to be done. To set the stage for meaningful comparisons, we will need a much more extensive array of richly textured descriptions than is now available. But ultimately it is through comparisons—with cultures outside as well as within the region—that our deepest insights are likely to emerge.

The prospects for comparison raise some interesting questions regarding meaningful boundaries at various levels. In addition to imposing ethnic categories on Pacific Islanders, Europeans imposed the categories of Micronesia, Melanesia, and Polynesia on the region. The rationales of race, language, and custom were used, along with geography, to distinguish these "culture" areas. Until recently anthropologists accepted this division, and indeed may have further entrenched it. Thus the terms *Micronesian, Melanesian,* and *Polynesian* have considerable potential for being converted into significant ethnic designations (Linnekin, p. 167), although as yet, it seems, they are only occasionally used that way. One wonders, as alliances are forged between the newly formed nations within Oceania, whether this level of contrast will become institutionalized, or whether new, crosscutting, distinctions will emerge. It would be ironic if the indigenous peoples of Oceania were to adopt these classic divisions as ethnic categories just as anthropologists have come to question their validity.

I would like to conclude by pointing out some profound value issues embedded in questions of ethnicity and cultural identity that must be faced both by the people of Oceania and by anthropologists. The boundaries and borders that distinguish populations one from another are indeed, as Linnekin (chapter 7) persuasively argues, cultural constructions, but they also hold the potential for channeling very powerful emotions. That group identities are subject to hate-filled manipulation has been made all too clear in places like Northern Ireland and the Middle East. When people come to hate one another on the basis of ethnic categories, when they punctuate their interactions with frequent violence, they institutionalize social schisms that are demeaning and maladaptive for everyone involved.

Although much of Oceania has mercifully been spared the more destructive aspects of institutionalized ethnic antagonisms, residues of colonial structuring are clearly evident and portend difficult times ahead. In Australia, Hawaii, and New Zealand, descendants of the original inhabitants have clearly become an underclass, with all of the economic, social, and health disadvantages thereby entailed. One can well understand the bitterness, the anger experienced by these people. One can empathize with their attempts to redefine cultural identities in the interest of political efficacy. The extent to which class antagonisms will develop along ethnic lines in newly emergent Pacific nations remains to be seen, but the potential is definitely present, as recent events in Fiji and Vanuatu clearly demonstrate.

But we should not forget that cultural differences provide a source of diversity that humankind can ill afford to abandon. With the pressures that exist toward homogenizing the world into one version or another of Western society, we are in danger of losing cultures that contain critical elements needed for adaptations to change we do not yet anticipate (Yinger 1985, 173). Oceania, by providing models of cultural diversity based on flexible group formations with porous boundaries, on mutable criteria for inclusion, presents us with a vision of what a pluralistic world might look like, free from the institutionalized schisms that have structured so much of European history. Whether that vision will be realized, even in Oceania, ought to concern us all.

NOTES

1. In a recent review of ethnicity, Yinger (1985, 159) reports that "there is now widespread if not universal agreement among scholars that 'racial differences derive social significance from cultural diversity' " (citing Kuper in Kuper and Smith 1971, 13). That such a statement is necessary in a contemporary review is itself remarkable, and an indicator of the persistence of racialism in Western thought, even among scholars.

2. That sociopolitical considerations are fundamental, and underlie conceptual distinctions based on race, is suggested by the fact that Europeans have often conferred "honorary white status" on selected groups or individuals where it has been expedient to do so (as in South Africa where Japanese have been designated as honorary whites; see also Tonkinson, chapter 9).

3. It is interesting to note that the evolutionists did not rank *cultures* as we now understand the term, but rather populations among whom race, language, and culture were assumed to cohere. Despite their essentially liberal perspective, they were, on the whole, unable to disentangle one from the other (Harris 1968, 137–141).

4. This is an extension of what Pettigrew (1979) calls "the ultimate attribution error," by which negatively valued acts of outgroups are seen as caused by their immutable characteristics, while their positively valued acts are explained by transitory, situational forces (cited in Yinger 1985, 164).

5. Since I am more familiar with the Polynesian materials I may have skewed things somewhat in their direction, although the inspiration for my analysis has come from all the chapters in this book.

6. This assumption poses a serious problem for indigenous leaders who are attempting to use a common notion of tradition to define pan-community identity in modern political settings. As Tonkinson points out (chapter 9), they tend not to define the terms of identity and avoid specifying its components. One

tack is to focus on shared experiences since European contact, but that, too, has its problems since different groups have been differently affected.

7. These conditions are not exclusive to Oceania, of course (see Yancey, Eriksen, and Juliani 1979 for a more general assessment of emergent ethnicity), but they are especially salient there.

8. A "prototypical them" can be thought of as a categorical opposite that is least subject to contextual variation within a broad cultural frame (e.g., as black Africans are for white South Africans).

9. Fiji, where political parties are institutionalized along ethnic lines, provides an outstanding example.

10. I do not mean to imply that they adhered to an egalitarian ideology in the modern sense. In fact, many Oceanic societies were hierarchical in orientation but remained egalitarian in practice because of practical constraints, such as a small population.

REFERENCES

Aboriginal Newsletter
  1983   NADOC: 1938–1983. *Aboriginal Newsletter,* no. 126(A) (June/July): 1, 5.
Alkire, William H.
  1965   *Lamotrek Atoll and Inter-Island Socioeconomic Ties.* Illinois Studies in Anthropology, no. 5. Urbana: University of Illinois Press.
  1970   Systems of Measurement on Woleai Atoll, Caroline Islands. *Anthropos* 65:1–73.
  1978   *Coral Islanders.* Arlington Heights, Ill.: Harlan-Davidson.
Allace, L.
  1976   Siassi Trade. *Oral History* 4 (10): 2–22.
Anderson, Christopher
  1985   On the Notion of Aboriginality: A Discussion by Christopher Anderson, Ian Keen, Tim Rowse, J. R. von Sturmer, Kenneth Maddock, Colin Tatz, Stephen Thiele. *Mankind* 15:41–55.
Archer, Dane, and Mary Archer
  1970   Race, Identity and the Maori People. *Journal of the Polynesian Society* 79:201–218.
Ardener, Edwin
  1972   Belief and the Problem of Women. In *The Interpretation of Ritual,* edited by J. Fontaine, pp. 135–158. London: Tavistock Publications.
Aronson, Dan R.
  1976   Ethnicity as a Cultural System: An Introductory Essay. In *Ethnicity in the Americas,* edited by F. Henry, pp. 9–19. The Hague: Mouton.
Austin, W. G., and S. Worchel, eds.
  1979   *The Psychology of Intergroup Relations.* Monterey, Calif.: Brooks/Cole.
Awatere, Donna
  1980   Korero-Tia Wahine Ma! *Broadsheet* 84 (November).
  1981   Rugby, Racism and Riot Gear: New Zealand in the Winter of 1981. *Broadsheet* 94 (November).
  1984   *Maori Sovereignty.* Auckland: Broadsheet Publications.
Babayan, Chad, Ben Finney, Bernard Kilonsky, and Nainoa Thompson
  1987   Voyage to Aotearoa. *Journal of the Polynesian Society* 96:161–200.
Banton, Michael
  1987   *Racial Theories.* Cambridge: Cambridge University Press.

Barrère, Dorothy, Mary Kawena Pukui, and Marion Kelly
   1980   *Hula: Historical Perspectives.* Pacific Anthropological Records, no.
          30. Honolulu: Bernice P. Bishop Museum.
Barth, Fredrik
   1956   Ecologic Relationships of Ethnic Groups in Swat, North Pakistan.
          American Anthropologist 58:1079–1089.
   1971   Tribes and Intertribal Relations in the Fly Headwaters. *Oceania*
          41:171–191.
Barth, Fredrik, ed.
   1969   *Ethnic Groups and Boundaries: The Social Organization of Culture
          Difference.* Boston: Little, Brown and Co.
Barwick, Diane
   1964   The Self-Conscious People of Melbourne. In *Aborigines Now*, edited
          by M. Reay, pp. 20–31. Sydney: Angus and Robertson.
Bascom, William R.
   1950   Ponape: The Tradition of Retaliation. *Far Eastern Quarterly* 10:56–
          62.
   1965   *Ponape: A Political Economy in Transition.* University of California
          Anthropological Records, vol. 22. Berkeley: University of California
          Press.
Bateson, Gregory
   1972   *Steps to an Ecology of Mind.* New York: Ballantine Books.
Battaglia, S.
   1984   Living through Death: Survival and Identity in Urban Papua New
          Guinea. Unpublished ms. (in author's files).
Beaglehole, Ernest, and Pearl Beaglehole
   1945   Contemporary Maori Death Customs. *Journal of the Polynesian Soci-
          ety* 54:91–116.
Beckett, Jeremy
   1964   Aborigines, Alcohol, and Assimilation. In *Aborigines Now*, edited by
          M. Reay, pp. 32–47. Sydney: Angus and Robertson.
Bedford, Richard
   1973   A Transition in Circular Mobility. In *The Pacific in Transition*, edited
          by H. Brookfield, pp. 187–227. New York: St. Martin's Press.
Belshaw, Cyril S.
   1954   *Changing Melanesia: Social Economics of Culture Contact.* Mel-
          bourne: Oxford University Press.
Bentley, G. Carter
   1987   Ethnicity and Practice. *Comparative Studies in Society and History*
          29 (1): 24–55.
Bernart, Luelen
   1977   *The Book of Luelen.* Edited and translated by J. Fischer, S. Riesen-
          berg, and M. Whiting. Honolulu: University Press of Hawaii.
Berndt, Ronald M.
   1977   Aboriginal Identity: Reality or Mirage? In *Aborigines and Change:
          Australia in the 1970s*, edited by R. Berndt, pp. 1–12. Atlantic High-
          lands, N.J.: Humanities Press.

Berndt, Ronald M., and Catherine H. Berndt
  1985   *The World of the First Australians: Aboriginal Traditional Life, Past and Present.* Adelaide, Australia: Rigby.
Berreman, Gerald
  1975   Bazaar Behavior: Social Identity and Social Interaction in Urban India. In *Ethnic Identity: Cultural Continuities and Change,* edited by G. De Vos and L. Romanucci-Ross, pp. 71–105. Palo Alto, Calif.: Mayfield Publishing Co.
Best, Elsdon
  1924   *Maori Religion and Mythology.* Dominion Museum Bulletin, no. 10. Wellington: Dominion Museum.
  1926   Notes on Customs, Rituals and Beliefs Pertaining to Sickness, Death and Burial. *Journal of the Polynesian Society* 35:6–30.
Blainey, Geoffrey
  1984   *All for Australia.* North Ryde, Australia: Methuen Haynes.
Blank, Arapeha
  1980   The Role and Status of Maori Women. In *Women in New Zealand Society,* edited by P. Bunckle and B. Hughes, pp. 34–51. Auckland: George Allen and Unwin.
Bleakley, J. W.
  1929   The Aboriginals and Half-Castes of Central Australia and North Australia: Report by the Chief Protector of Aborigines, Queensland. Commonwealth Parliamentary Paper, no. 21.
Bloch, Maurice
  1982   Death, Women and Power. In *Death and the Regeneration of Life,* edited by M. Bloch and J. Parry, pp. 211–230. Cambridge: Cambridge University Press.
Bloch, Maurice, and Jonathon Parry, eds.
  1982   *Death and the Regeneration of Life.* Cambridge: Cambridge University Press.
Blong, R.
  1982   *The Time of Darkness.* Seattle: University of Washington Press.
Blu, Karen
  1980   *The Lumbee Problem: The Making of an American Indian People.* Cambridge: Cambridge University Press.
Bonnemaison, Joel
  1985   The Tree and the Canoe: Roots and Mobility in Vanuatu Societies. *Pacific Viewpoint* 26 (1): 30–62.
Bourgois, Philippe
  1988   Conjugated Oppression: Class and Ethnicity among Guaymi and Kuna Banana Workers. *American Ethnologist* 15:328–348.
Bowman, Pierre
  1985   Royal and Regal. *Sunday Honolulu Star-Bulletin and Advertiser,* 23 June: C-1, 16.
Brady, Ivan, ed.
  1976   *Transactions in Kinship: Adoption and Fosterage in Oceania.* Honolulu: University Press of Hawaii.

Braroe, Niels
  1975   *Indian and White.* Stanford: Stanford University Press.
Brookfield, H. C., and Doreen Hart
  1971   *Melanesia: Geographical Interpretations of an Island World.* London: Methuen.
Broome, Richard
  1982   *Aboriginal Australians.* The Australian Experience, no. 4. Sydney: George Allen and Unwin.
Burridge, Kenelm O. L.
  1978   Introduction: Missionary Occasions. In *Mission, Church and Sect in Oceania,* edited by J. Boutelier, D. Hughes, and S. Tiffany, pp. 1–30. Ann Arbor: University of Michigan Press.
Burris, Jerry
  1982   A Close Look at the "Hawaiian Renaissance." *Pacific Islands Monthly* 53 (1): 31–32.
Burrows, Edwin, and Melford E. Spiro
  1953   An Atoll Culture: Ethnography of Ifaluk in the Central Carolines. *Behavior Science Monographs* (CIMA Reports, nos. 16 and 18). New Haven: HRAF Press.
Butterworth, G. W.
  1973   Highpoint and Hiatus. In *Polynesian and Pakeha in New Zealand Education,* edited by D. Bray and C. Hill, pp. 7–17. Auckland: Heineman.
Carrier, James G.
  1979   School and Community on Ponam. *In* The Community School, edited by D. Lancy. *Papua New Guinea Journal of Education* Special Issue 15:66–77.
  1981a   Education as Investment: Education, Economy and Society in Ponam. *Papua New Guinea Journal of Education* 17:17–35.
  1981b   Labour Migration and Labour Export on Ponam Island. *Oceania* 51:237–255.
Carroll, Vern
  1970a   Adoption on Nukuoro. In *Adoption in Eastern Oceania,* edited by V. Carroll, pp. 121–157. Honolulu: University Press of Hawaii.
  1975   The Demography of Communities. In *Pacific Atoll Populations,* edited by V. Carroll, pp. 3–19. Honolulu: University Press of Hawaii.
  1977   Communities and Non-Communities: The Nukuoro on Ponape. In *Exiles and Migrants in Oceania,* edited by M. Lieber, pp. 67–79. Honolulu: University Press of Hawaii.
Carroll, Vern, ed.
  1970b   *Adoption in Eastern Oceania.* Honolulu: University Press of Hawaii.
Castile, George Pierre, and Gilbert Kushner, eds.
  1981   *Persistent Peoples: Cultural Enclaves in Perspective.* Tucson: University of Arizona Press.
Caughey, John L.
  1977   *Faanakkar: Cultural Values in a Micronesian Society.* University of Pennsylvania Publications in Anthropology, no. 2. Philadelphia: Department of Anthropology, University of Pennsylvania.

Chapman, Murray
  1970 Population Movement in Tribal Society: The Case of Duidui and Pichahila, British Solomon Islands. Ph.D. diss., Geography Department, University of Washington.
  1975 Mobility in a Non-Literate Society. In *People on the Move*, edited by L. Kosinski and R. Prothero, pp. 129–145. London: Methuen.
  1985 Mobility and Identity in the Island Pacific. *Pacific Viewpoint* Special Issue 26 (1).
Chapman, Murray, and R. Mansell Prothero, eds.
  1985 *Circulation in Population Movement: Substance and Concepts from the Melanesian Case.* London: Routledge and Kegan Paul.
Chase, Athol
  1981 Empty Vessels and Loud Noises: Views About Aboriginality Today. *Social Alternatives* 2 (2): 23–27.
Chodorow, Nancy
  1978 *The Reproduction of Mothering.* Berkeley: University of California Press.
Clifford, James
  1988 *The Predicament of Culture: Twentieth-Century Ethnography, Literature, and Art.* Cambridge: Harvard University Press.
Cohen, Abner
  1969 *Custom and Politics in Urban Africa: A Study of Hausa Migrants in Yoruba Towns.* Berkeley: University of California Press.
  1974a Introduction: The Lesson of Ethnicity. In *Urban Ethnicity*, edited by A. Cohen, pp. ix–xxiv. London: Tavistock Publications.
  1974b *Two Dimensional Man: An Essay on the Anthropology of Power and Symbolism in Complex Society.* Berkeley: University of California Press.
Cohen, Ronald
  1978 Ethnicity: Problem and Focus in Anthropology. *Annual Review of Anthropology* 7:379–403.
Cohn, Bernard S.
  1980 History and Anthropology: The State of Play. *Comparative Studies in Society and History* 22:198–221.
Colbung, Ken
  1979 On Being Aboriginal: A Personal Statement. In *Aborigines of the West: Their Past and Present*, edited by R. Berndt and C. Berndt, pp. 100–105. Nedlands: University of Western Australia Press.
Cole, Keith
  1979 *The Aborigines of Arnhem Land.* Adelaide: Rigby.
Collins, J.
  1985 Do We Want Blainey's Australia? *Australian Quarterly* 57 (1–2): 47–56.
Comaroff, Jean
  1985 *Body of Power, Spirit of Resistance.* Chicago: University of Chicago Press.
Coombs, H. C., M. Brandl, and W. Snowdon
  1983 *A Certain Heritage.* Canberra: Centre for Resource and Environmental Studies, Australian National University.

Crowley, Frank
   1980   *Colonial Australia 1875–1900.* A Documentary History of Australia,
           vol. 3. Melbourne: Thomas Nelson Australia.
Crowley, Frank, ed.
   1974   *A New History of Australia.* Melbourne: William Heinemann.
Dallmayr, Fred R.
   1981   *Twilight of Subjectivity: Contributions to a Post-Individualist Theory
           of Politics.* Amherst: University of Massachusetts Press.
Damm, H., and E. Sarfert
   1935   Inseln um Truk. In *Ergebnisse der Südsee Expedition 1908–1910.* II.
           B. 6, subvolume 2, edited by G. Thilenius. Hamburg: Friederichsen,
           de Gruyter & Co.
Danforth, Loring M.
   1982   *The Death Rituals of Rural Greece.* Princeton: Princeton University
           Press.
Dansey, Harry
   1977   A View of Death. In *Te Ao Hurihuri,* edited by M. King, pp. 129–
           142. Wellington: Hicks Smith/Methuen New Zealand.
Deacon, A. B.
   1934   *Malekula: A Vanishing People in the New Hebrides.* London:
           G. Routledge and Sons.
Dean, Eddie, and Stan Ritova
   1988   *Rabuka: No Other Way.* Sydney, Australia: Doubleday.
Dening, Greg
   1980   *Islands and Beaches: Discourse on a Silent Land—Marquesas, 1776–
           1880.* Honolulu: University Press of Hawaii.
Deshen, Schlomo, and Moshe Shokeid
   1974   *The Predicament of Homecoming: Cultural and Social Life of North
           African Immigrants in Israel.* Ithaca: Cornell University Press.
De Vos, George
   1975   Ethnic Pluralism: Conflict and Accommodation. In *Ethnic Identity:
           Cultural Continuities and Change,* edited by G. De Vos and L. Ro-
           manucci-Ross, pp. 5–41. Palo Alto, Calif.: Mayfield Publishing Co.
De Vos, George, and Lola Romanucci-Ross
   1975   Ethnicity: Vessel of Meaning and Emblem of Contrast. In *Ethnic
           Identity: Cultural Continuities and Change,* edited by G. De Vos and
           L. Romanucci-Ross, pp. 363–390. Palo Alto, Calif.: Mayfield Pub-
           lishing Co.
   1982   Introduction 1982. In *Ethnic Identity: Cultural Continuities and
           Change.* Rev. ed., edited by G. De Vos and L. Romanucci-Ross, pp.
           ix–xvii. Chicago: University of Chicago Press.
Dominy, Michele D.
   1983   Gender Conceptions and Political Strategies in New Zealand Wom-
           en's Networks. Ph.D. diss., Anthropology Department, Cornell Uni-
           versity.
   1985   Gender Complementarity, Aging and Reproduction Among New
           Zealand Pakeha Women. In *Aging and Its Transformations: Moving*

Toward Death in Pacific Society, edited by Dorothy Counts and David Counts, pp. 49–65. Lanham, Md.: University Press of America.

1986 Lesbian-Feminist Gender Conceptions: Separatism in Christchurch, New Zealand. *Signs: Journal of Women in Culture and Society* 11 (2): 25–40.

Douglas, Mary
1970 *Natural Symbols.* New York: Pantheon Press.

Drummond, Lee
1980 The Cultural Continuum: A Theory of Intersystems. *Man,* n.s. 15:352–374.
1981 Ethnicity, "Ethnicity," and Culture Theory. *Man,* n.s. 16:693–696.

Dunstall, G.
1981 The Social Pattern. In *The Oxford History of New Zealand,* edited by W. Oliver, pp. 396–430. Wellington: Oxford University Press.

Durkheim, Emile
[1912] *The Elementary Forms of the Religious Life.* New York: Free Press.
1965

Eades, Diana
1981 "That's Our Way of Talking": Aborigines in Southwest Queensland. *Social Alternatives* 2 (2): 11–14.

Eckermann, A.-K.
1977 Group Organization and Identity within an Urban Aboriginal Community. In *Aborigines and Change: Australia in the 1970s,* edited by R. Berndt, pp. 288–319. Canberra: Australian Institute of Aboriginal Studies.

Edwards, Coral
1982 Is the Ward Clean? In *All that Dirt: Aborigines 1938, An Australia 1938 Monograph,* edited by B. Gammage and A. Markus, pp. 4–8. Canberra: History Project, Australian National University.

Eisendstadt, S. N.
1973 Post-Traditional Societies and the Continuity and Reconstruction of Tradition. *Daedalus* 102 (Winter): 1–28.

Elbert, Samuel H.
1972 *Puluwat Dictionary.* Pacific Linguistics, ser. C., no. 24. Canberra: Linguistic Circle of Canberra.

Emerick, Richard
1960 Homesteading on Ponape: A Study and Analysis of a Resettlement Program of the United States Trust Territory Government of Micronesia. Ph.D. diss., Anthropology Department, University of Pennsylvania.

Emory, Kenneth P.
1965 *Kapingamarangi: Social and Religious Life of a Polynesian Atoll.* Bernice P. Bishop Museum Bulletin no. 228. Honolulu: The Museum.

English, A.
1985 *Land Rights and Birthrights (The Great Australian Hoax).* Bullsbrook, Western Australia: Veritas Publishing Co.

Enloe, Cynthia H.
   1973   *Ethnic Conflict and Political Development.* Boston: Little, Brown
          and Co.
Errington, Fredrick
   1974   *Karavar: Masks and Power in a Melanesian Ritual.* Ithaca, N.Y.:
          Cornell University Press.
Evans, Raymond
   1975   "The Nigger Shall Disappear . . .": Aborigines and Europeans in
          Colonial Queensland. In *Exclusion, Exploitation and Extermination:
          Race Relations in Colonial Queensland,* edited by R. Evans,
          K. Saunders, and K. Cronin, pp. 25–145. Sydney: Australia and
          New Zealand Book Co.
Evans, Raymond, Kay Saunders, and Kathryn Cronin, eds.
   1975   *Exclusion, Exploitation and Extermination: Race Relations in Colo-
          nial Queensland.* Sydney: Australia and New Zealand Book Co.
Evans, Rebecca
   1982   Rebecca Evans on Her Life. *Broadsheet* 103 (October).
Fajans, Jane
   1986   The Person in Social Context. In *Person, Self, and Experience:
          Exploring Pacific Ethnopsychologies,* edited by G. White and
          J. Kirkpatrick, pp. 367–397. Berkeley: University of California Press.
Falgout, Suzanne
   1984   Persons and Knowledge on Ponape. Ph.D. diss., Anthropology De-
          partment, University of Oregon.
Farr, Jan
   1978   Bastion Point. *Broadsheet* 62 (January).
Feinberg, Richard
   1981   What Is Polynesian Kinship All About? *Ethnology* 20:115–131.
Fernandez, James
   1972   Fang Representations under Acculturation. In *Africa and the West,*
          edited by P. Curtin, pp. 3–48. Madison: University of Wisconsin
          Press.
Finney, Ben R.
   1973   *Polynesian Peasants and Proletarians.* Cambridge: Schenkman.
   1979   *Hōkūle'a: The Way to Tahiti.* New York: Dodd, Mead.
Finney, Ben, Bernard Kilonsky, Steven Somsen, and Edward D. Stroup
   1986   Reviving a Vanishing Art. *Journal of the Polynesian Society* 95:41–
          90.
Fischer, John L.
   1957   *The Eastern Carolines.* New Haven, Ct.: Pacific Science Board.
   1974   The Role of the Traditional Chiefs on Ponape in the American Period.
          In *Political Development in Micronesia,* edited by D. Hughes and
          S. Lingenfelter, pp. 166–177. Columbus: Ohio State University Press.
Fishman, Joshua A.
   1983   Language and Ethnicity in Bilingual Education. In *Culture, Ethnic-
          ity, and Identity,* edited by W. McCready, pp. 127–137. New York:
          Academic Press.

Fitzgerald, Thomas K.
  1974   Maori Acculturation: Evolution of Choice in a Post-Colonial Situa-
          tion. *Oceania* 44:209–215.
  1977   *Education and Identity*. Wellington: New Zealand Council for Edu-
          cational Research.
Fortune, Reo
  [1932] *Sorcerers of Dobu*. New York: E. P. Dutton and Co.
  1963
Foster, Brian L.
  1974   Ethnicity and Commerce. *American Ethnologist* 1:437–448.
  1977   Mon Commerce and the Dynamics of Ethnic Relations. *Southeast
          Asian Journal of Social Science* 5 (1–2): 111–122.
Foster, George
  1965   Peasant Society and the Image of Limited Good. *American Anthro-
          pologist* 67:293–315.
Franklin, Margaret Ann
  1976   *Black and White Australians: An Inter-racial History 1788–1975*.
          South Yarra, Victoria: Heinemann Educational (Australia).
Freedman, Michael P.
  1967   The Social and Political Organization of the Siassi Islands. Ph.D.
          diss., Anthropology Department, University of Michigan.
Galaty, John
  1982   Being Maasai: Being "People of Cattle": Ethnic Shifters in East
          Africa. *American Ethnologist* 9:1–20.
Gale, F., and J. Wundersich
  1982   *Adelaide Aborigines: A Case Study of Urban Life 1966–1981*. Can-
          berra: Development Studies Centre, Australian National University.
Gallimore, Ronald, and Alan Howard, eds.
  1968   *Studies in a Hawaiian Community: Na Makamaka o Nanakuli*.
          Pacific Anthropological Records, no. 1. Honolulu: Bernice P. Bishop
          Museum.
Garvin, Paul, and Saul S. Riesenberg
  1952   Respect Behavior on Ponape: An Ethnolinguistic Study. *American
          Anthropologist* 54:210–220.
Geertz, Clifford
  1966   Religion as a Cultural System. In *Anthropological Approaches to the
          Study of Religion*, edited by M. Banton, pp. 1–46. London: Tavistock
          Publications.
  1973   *The Interpretation of Cultures*. New York: Basic Books.
Gell, A.
  1975   *Metamorphosis of the Cassowaries: Umeda Society, Language, and
          Ritual*. London: The Athlone Press.
Gewertz, Deborah
  1983   *Sepik River Societies: A Historical Ethnography of the Chambri and
          Their Neighbors*. New Haven: Yale University Press.
Gilbert, Kevin J.
  1973   *Because a White Man'll Never Do It*. Sydney: Angus and Robertson.

1977   *Living Black: Blacks Talk to Kevin Gilbert.* Melbourne: Allen Lane, Penguin.

1981   The Aboriginal Question. *Social Alternatives* 2 (2): 34–35.

Gilligan, Carol

1982   *In a Different Voice: Psychological Theory and Women's Development.* Cambridge: Harvard University Press.

Ginzburg, Benjamin

1933   Lamarck, Chevalier de. Encyclopedia of the Social Sciences, vol. 9, pp. 21–22.

Gladwin, Thomas, and Seymour B. Sarason

1953   *Truk: Man in Paradise.* New York: Wenner-Gren Foundation for Anthropological Research.

Glazer, Nathan, and Daniel P. Moynihan

1975   *Ethnicity: Theory and Experience.* Cambridge: MIT Press.

Goldman, Irving

1970   *Ancient Polynesian Society.* Chicago: University of Chicago Press.

Golomb, Louis

1978   *Brokers of Morality: Thai Ethnic Adaptation in a Rural Malaysian Setting.* Honolulu: University Press of Hawaii.

1985   *An Anthropology of Curing in Multiethnic Thailand.* Illinois Studies in Anthropology, no. 15. Urbana: University of Illinois Press.

Goodale, Jane C.

1971   *Tiwi Wives: A Study of the Women of Melville Island, North Australia.* Seattle: University of Washington Press.

1985   Pigs Teeth and Skull Cycles: Both Sides of the Face of Humanity. *American Ethnologist* 12:228–244.

Goodenough, Ward, and Hiroshi Sugita

1980   *Trukese-English Dictionary.* Memoirs of the American Philosophical Society, vol. 141. Philadelphia: American Philosophical Society.

Gould, Stephen Jay

1979   Shades of Lamarck. *Natural History* 88 (8): 22–28.

Green, Vera M.

1981   Blacks in the United States: The Creation of an Enduring People? In *Persistent Peoples: Cultural Enclaves in Perspective,* edited by G. Castile and G. Kushner, pp. 69–77. Tucson: University of Arizona Press.

Group for the Advancement of Psychiatry

1987   *Us and Them: The Psychology of Ethnonationalism.* New York: Brunner/Mazel.

Guiart, Jean

1963   *The Arts of the South Pacific.* New York: Golden Press.

Gumbert, Marc

1984   *Neither Justice nor Reason: A Legal and Anthropological Analysis of Aboriginal Land Rights.* St. Lucia: University of Queensland Press.

Habermas, Jurgen

1975   *Legitimation Crisis.* Translated by Thomas McCarthy. Boston: Beacon Press.

Halkyard, Hilda
   1982   Hilda Halkyard, an Interview with Donna Awatere. *Broadsheet* 101
          (July/August).
Hallowell, A. I.
   1963   American Indians, White and Black: The Phenomenon of Trans-
          culturation. *Current Anthropology* 4:519–531.
Hambruch, Paul, and Anneliese Eilers
   1936   Ponape: Gesellschaft und Geistige Kultur, Wirtschaft, und Stoffliche
          Kulture. In *Ergebnisse der Südsee Expedition 1908–1910.* Edited by
          G. Thilenius. Hamburg: Friederichsen, de Gruyter & Co.
Handler, Richard
   1984   On Sociocultural Discontinuity: Nationalism and Cultural Objectifi-
          cation in Quebec. *Current Anthropology* 25:55–71.
   1985a On Dialogue and Destructive Analysis: Problems in Narrating Na-
          tionalism and Ethnicity. *Journal of Anthropological Research* 41 (2):
          171–182.
   1985b On Having a Culture: Nationalism and the Preservation of Quebec's
          Patrimoine. In *History of Anthropology,* vol. 3, *Objects and Others,*
          edited by G. Stocking, pp. 192–217. Madison: University of Wiscon-
          sin Press.
Handler, Richard, and Jocelyn Linnekin
   1984   Tradition, Genuine or Spurious. *Journal of American Folklore*
          97:273–290.
Harawira, Titewhai
   1982   Wahine Ma Korerotia. Interviews edited by Donna Awatere. *Broad-
          sheet* 101 (July/August).
Harding, Thomas G.
   1967   *Voyagers of the Vitiaz Strait: A Study of a New Guinea Trade System.*
          Seattle: University of Washington Press.
   1970   Trading in Northeast New Guinea. In *Cultures of the Pacific,*
          edited by T. Harding and B. Wallace, pp. 94–111. New York: Free
          Press.
Harris, Marvin
   1964   *Patterns of Race in the Americas.* New York: Walker and Co.
   1968   *The Rise of Anthropological Theory: A History of Theories of Cul-
          ture.* New York: Crowell.
   1970   Referential Ambiguity in the Calculus of Brazilian Racial Identity.
          Southwestern Journal of Anthropology 26:1–14.
Hasluck, Paul
   [1942] *Black Australians: A Survey of Native Policy in Western Australia,*
   1970   *1829–1897.* Carlton, Victoria: Melbourne University Press.
Hawke, Sharon
   1983   Mira Szaszy. *Broadsheet* 112 (September).
Hechter, Michael
   1986   Theories of Ethnic Relations. In *The Primordial Challenge: Ethnicity
          in the Contemporary World,* edited by J. Stack, Jr., pp. 13–24. New
          York: Greenwood Press.

Herdt, Gilbert
  1981   *Guardians of the Flutes: Idioms of Masculinity.* New York: McGraw-Hill.
Hertz, Robert
  1960   A Contribution to the Study of the Collective Representation of Death. In *Death and the Right Hand,* edited by R. Needham, pp. 27–86. Glencoe, Ill.: Free Press.
Heuer, Berys N.
  1969   Maori Women in Traditional Family and Tribal Life. *Journal of the Polynesian Society* 78:448–494.
Hezel, Francis X.
  1978   The Education Explosion in Truk. *Micronesian Reporter* 26 (4): 24–33.
Hiatt, L. R.
  1965   *Kinship and Conflict: A Study of an Aboriginal Community in Northern Arnhem Land.* Canberra: Australian National University Press.
Hicks, George L.
  1977a Introduction: Problems in the Study of Ethnicity. In *Ethnic Encounters: Identities and Contexts,* edited by G. Hicks and P. Leis, pp. 1–20. North Scituate, Mass.: Duxbury Press.
  1977b Separate But Similar: Adaptation by Two American Indian Groups. In *Ethnic Encounters: Identities and Contexts,* edited by G. Hicks and P. Leis, pp. 63–83. North Scituate, Mass.: Duxbury Press.
Hobsbawm, Eric
  1983   Introduction: Inventing Traditions. In *The Invention of Tradition,* edited by E. Hobsbawm and T. Ranger, pp. 1–14. Cambridge: Cambridge University Press.
Hobsbawm, Eric, and Terence Ranger, eds.
  1983   *The Invention of Tradition.* Cambridge: Cambridge University Press.
Hoetink, H.
  1967   *The Two Variants in Caribbean Race Relations: A Contribution to the Sociology of Segmented Societies.* Translated by E. Hooykas. London: Oxford University Press.
Hohepa, Pat
  1970   *A Maori Community in Northland.* Auckland: A. H. and A. W. Reed.
Honour, Hugh
  1975   *The New Golden Land: European Images of America from the Discoveries to the Present Time.* New York: Pantheon Books.
Hooley, B.
  1971   Austronesian Languages of the Morobe District, Papua New Guinea. *Oceanic Linguistics* 10 (2): 79–151.
  1976   Austronesian Languages: Morobe Province. In *New Guinea Area Languages and Language Study,* edited by S. Wurm, pp. 335–348. Pacific Linguistics, ser. C, 39 (2).

Hooley, B., and K. McElhanon
  1970 Languages of the Morobe District, New Guinea. In *Pacific Linguistic Studies in Honour of Arthur Capell*, edited by S. Wurm and D. Laycock, pp. 1065–1094. Canberra: Australian National University, ser. C, no. 13.
Howard, Alan
  1963 Conservatism and Non-Traditional Leadership in Rotuma. *Journal of the Polynesian Society* 72:65–77.
  1979 The Power to Heal in Colonial Rotuma. *Journal of the Polynesian Society* 88:243–275.
  1985 Ethnopsychology and the Prospects for a Cultural Psychology. In *Person, Self and Experience: Exploring Pacific Ethnopsychologies*, edited by G. White and J. Kirkpatrick, pp. 401–420. Berkeley: University of California Press.
Howard, Alan, and Irwin Howard
  1977 Rotumans in Fiji: The Genesis of an Ethnic Group. In *Exiles and Migrants in Oceania*, edited by M. Lieber, pp. 161–194. Honolulu: University Press of Hawaii.
Hughes, Daniel
  1972 Integration of the Role of Territorial Congressman into Ponapean Society. *Oceania* 43:140–152.
  1982 Continuity of Indigenous Social Structure and Stratification. *Oceania* 53:5–18.
Huntington, Richard, and Peter Metcalfe, eds.
  1979 *Celebrations of Death. The Anthropology of Mortuary Ritual.* Cambridge: Cambridge University Press.
Husband, Charles
  1982 Introduction: "Race"—The Continuity of a Concept. In *"Race" in Britain: Continuity and Change*, edited by C. Husband, pp. 11–26. London: Hutchinson.
Hymes, Dell
  1975 Folklore's Nature and the Sun's Myth. *Journal of American Folklore* 88:345–369.
Institute of Pacific Studies
  1980 *Vanuatu.* Suva, Fiji: University of the South Pacific.
Isaacs, Harold
  1975 *Idols of the Tribe: Group Identity and Political Change.* New York: Harper and Row.
Isoaimo, A.
  1980 Circular to All Headmasters and Teachers: Grade 6 Class Achievements 1979. Morobe Province Department of Education. Mimeo.
Jackson, Hana
  1982 Wahine Ma Korerotia. Interviews edited by Donna Awatere. *Broadsheet* 101 (July/August).
Jackson, Michael
  1968 Some Structural Considerations of Maori Myth. *Journal of the Polynesian Society* 77:147–162.

Jacobs, Patricia
  1986   Science and Veiled Assumptions: Miscegenation in W. A. 1930–1937. *Australian Aboriginal Studies* 2:15–23.
Jacobson-Widding, A.
  1983   *Identity: Personal and Sociocultural.* Atlantic Highlands, N.J.: Humanities Press.
Jayawardena, Chandra
  1980   Culture and Ethnicity in Guyana and Fiji. *Man*, n.s. 15:430–450.
Jones, Delmos, and Jacquetta Hill-Burnett
  1982   The Political Context of Ethnogenesis: An Australian Example. In *Aboriginal Power in Australia*, edited by M. Howard, pp. 215–246. St. Lucia: University of Queensland Press.
Jordan, D. F.
  1985   Census Categories—Enumeration of Aboriginal People, or Construction of Identity? *Australian Aboriginal Studies* 1:28–36.
Jorgensen, Joseph
  1972   *The Sun Dance Religion.* Chicago: University of Chicago Press.
Kahn, Miriam
  1986   *Always Hungry, Never Greedy: Food and the Expression of Gender in a Melanesian Society.* New York: Cambridge University Press.
Kanahele, George S.
  1982   *Current Facts and Figures about Hawaii.* Honolulu: Project WAIAHA.
Kane, Herb Kawainui
  1976   A Canoe Helps Hawaii Recapture Her Past. *National Geographic* 149:468–489.
Keen, Ian
  1988   *Being Black: Aboriginal Cultures in "Settled" Australia.* Canberra: Australian Institute of Aboriginal Studies.
Keesing, Roger M.
  1968   Chiefs in a Chiefless Society: The Ideology of Modern Kwaio Politics. *Oceania* 38:276–280.
  1978   Politico-Religious Movements and Anticolonialism on Malaita: Maasina Rule in Historical Perspective. *Oceania* 48:241–261.
  1982a *Kwaio Religion.* New York: Columbia University Press.
  1982b Kastom in Melanesia: An Overview. *Mankind* 13:297–301.
  1982c Kastom and Anticolonialism on Malaita: "Culture" as Political Symbol. *Mankind* 13:357–373.
Keesing, Roger M., and Robert Tonkinson, eds.
  1982   Reinventing Traditional Culture: The Politics of Kastom in Island Melanesia. *Mankind* Special Issue 13 (4).
Kernot, B. J.
  1981   Race Relations and the Growth of Community in New Zealand—A Response. In *Christians in Public Planning*, edited by C. Nichol and J. Veitch, pp. 135–152. Wellington: Religious Studies Department.
Keyes, Charles F., ed.
  1981   *Ethnic Change.* Seattle: University of Washington Press.

King, Michael
 1981 Between Two Worlds. In *The Oxford History of New Zealand*, edited by W. Oliver, pp. 279–301. Wellington: Oxford University Press.
 1983 *Whina: A Biography of Whina Cooper.* Auckland: Hodder and Stoughton.
Kiste, Robert
 1974 *The Bikinians: A Study in Forced Migration.* Menlo Park, Calif.: Cummings Press.
Krämer, Augustin
 1935 Inseln um Truk. In *Ergebnisse der Südsee Expedition 1908–1910.* II. B. 6, subvolume 1. Edited by G. Thilenius. Hamburg: Friederichsen, de Gruyter & Co.
Kuper, Leo, and M. G. Smith, eds.
 1971 *Pluralism in Africa.* Berkeley: University of California Press.
Kushner, Gilbert
 1970 The Anthropology of Complex Societies. *Biennial Review of Anthropology* 6:80–131. Stanford: Stanford University Press.
Labby, David
 1976 *The Demystification of Yap.* Chicago: University of Chicago Press.
Lal, Brij
 1986 *Politics in Fiji: Studies in Contemporary History.* Laie, Hawaii: Institute for Polynesian Studies.
 1987 Letter. *Pacific Islands Monthly* 58 (10): 7.
 n.d. *Power and Prejudice: The Making of the Fiji Crisis.* Auckland: New Zealand Institute for International Affairs. In press.
Landsman, Gail H.
 1985 Ganienkeh: Symbol and Politics in an Indian/White Conflict. *American Anthropologist* 87:826–839.
 1987 Indian Activism and the Press: Coverage of the Conflict at Ganienkeh. *Anthropological Quarterly* 60 (3): 101–113.
Langton, Marcia
 1981 Urbanizing Aborigines: The Social Scientists' Great Deception. *Social Alternatives* 2 (2): 16–22.
Larcom, Joan
 1980 Place and the Politics of Marriage: The Mewun of Malekula, New Hebrides. Ph.D. diss., Anthropology Department, Stanford University.
 1982 The Invention of Convention. *Mankind* 13:330–337.
 1983 Following Deacon: The Problem of Ethnographic Reanalysis, 1926–76. In *History of Anthropology*, vol. 1., edited by G. Stocking, Jr., pp. 175–195. Madison: University of Wisconsin Press.
Larson, Eric H.
 1977 Tikopia in the Russell Islands. In *Exiles and Migrants in Oceania*, edited by M. Lieber, pp. 242–268. Honolulu: University Press of Hawaii.
Lawrence, Peter
 1964 *Road Belong Cargo.* Manchester: Manchester University Press.

Layard, John
  1928   Degree-taking Rites in South West Bay, Malekula. *Journal of the
          Royal Anthropological Institute* 7:139–223.
Leenhardt, Maurice
  [1947] *Do Kamo: Person and Myth in the Melanesian World.* Chi-
  1979   cago: University of Chicago Press.
Lehmann, A. J.
  1983   *The Decline of White-Race Survival Intelligence.* Perth, Western
          Australia: Access Press.
Lessa, William A.
  1950   Ulithi and the Outer Native World. *American Anthropologist* 52:27–
          52.
  1956   Myth and Blackmail in the Western Carolines. *Journal of the Polyne-
          sian Society* 65:66–74.
  1966   *Ulithi: A Micronesian Design for Living.* New York: Holt, Rinehart,
          and Winston.
LeVine, Robert A.
  1966   *Dreams and Deeds: Achievement Motivation in Nigeria.* Chicago:
          University of Chicago Press.
LeVine, Robert A., and Donald T. Campbell
  1972   *Ethnocentrism: Theories of Conflict, Ethnic Attitudes, and Group
          Behavior.* New York: John Wiley and Sons.
Lieber, Michael D.
  1968   *Porakiet: A Kapingamarangi Colony on Ponape.* Eugene: University
          of Oregon, Department of Anthropology.
  1970   Adoption on Kapingamarangi. In *Adoption in Eastern Oceania,*
          edited by V. Carroll, pp. 158–205. Honolulu: University Press of
          Hawaii.
  1974   Land Tenure on Kapingamarangi. In *Land Tenure in Oceania,* edited
          by H. Lundsgaarde, pp. 70–99. Honolulu: University Press of
          Hawaii.
  1977a   The Processes of Change in Two Kapingamarangi Communities. In
          Exiles and Migrants in Oceania, edited by M. Lieber, pp. 35–67.
          Honolulu: University Press of Hawaii.
  1984   Strange Feast: Negotiating Identities on Ponape. *Journal of the Poly-
          nesian Society* 93:141–189.
Lieber, Michael D., ed.
  1977b   *Exiles and Migrants in Oceania.* Honolulu: University Press of
          Hawaii.
Lindstrom, Lamont
  1982   Leftamap Kastom: The Political History of Tradition on Tanna
          (Vanuatu). *Mankind* 13:316–329.
Lini, Walter
  1982   Lini Pleads for Understanding of "Melanesian Renaissance." *Pacific
          Islands Monthly* 53 (4): 25–28.
Linnekin, Jocelyn
  1983   Defining Tradition: Variations on the Hawaiian Identity. *American
          Ethnologist* 10:241–252.

1985 *Children of the Land: Exchange and Status in a Hawaiian Community.* New Brunswick, N.J.: Rutgers University Press.

Lippmann, Lorna
1973 *Words or Blows: Racial Attitudes in Australia.* Harmondsworth: Penguin Books.
1981 *Generations of Resistance: The Aboriginal Struggle for Justice.* Melbourne: Longman Chesire.

Littlewood, R. A.
1972 *Physical Anthropology of the Eastern Highlands.* Anthropological Studies in the Eastern Highlands of New Guinea, vol. 2. Seattle: University of Washington Press.

MacCannell, Dean
1984 Reconstructed Ethnicity: Tourism and Cultural Identity in Third World Communities. *Annals of Tourism Research* 11:375–391.

McDonald, Geoff
1982 *Red Over Black: Behind the Aboriginal Land Rights.* Bullsbrook, Western Australia: Veritas.

McGregor-Alegado, Davianna
1980 Hawaiians: Organizing in the 1970s. *Amerasia* 7 (2): 29–55.

McKaughan, Howard, ed.
1973 *The Languages of the Eastern Family of the East New Guinea Highlands Stock.* Anthropological Studies in the Eastern Highlands of New Guinea, vol. 1. Seattle: University of Washington Press.

McKellar, Hazel
1981 Aborigines in Rural Queensland: Land and Identity Not "Ethnicity." *Social Alternatives* 2 (2): 61–63.

McKnight, Robert
1977 Commas in Microcosm: The Movement of Southwest Islanders to Palau, Micronesia. In *Exiles and Migrants in Oceania,* edited by M. Lieber, pp. 10–33. Honolulu: University Press of Hawaii.

McTagget, Sue
1984 Te Herenga Waka: The Place of Protocol. *New Zealand Listener,* November.

Maddock, Kenneth
1974 *The Australian Aborigines: A Portrait of Their Society.* Ringwood, Victoria: Penguin Books.
1983 *Your Land is Our Land.* Ringwood, Victoria: Penguin Books.

Manning, Frank
1973 *Black Clubs in Bermuda: Ethnography of a Play World.* Ithaca, N.Y.: Cornell University Press.

Manuel, George
1974 *The Fourth World: An Indian Reality.* Ontario: Collier-Macmillan.

Marcus, George E., and Michael M. J. Fischer
1986 *Anthropology as Cultural Critique: An Experimental Moment in the Human Sciences.* Chicago: University of Chicago Press.

Markus, Andrew
1982 After the Outward Appearance: Scientists, Administrators and Politicians. In *All that Dirt: Aborigines 1938, An Australia 1938 Mono-*

    graph, edited by B. Gammage and A. Markus, pp. 83–106. Canberra: History Project, Australian National University.

Marshall, Mac
    1975   Changing Patterns of Marriage and Migration on Namoluk Atoll. In *Pacific Atoll Populations,* edited by V. Carroll, pp. 160–211. Honolulu: University Press of Hawaii.

Mason, Leonard
    1947   Economic Organization of the Marshall Islands. Economic Survey of Micronesia. U.S. Commercial Company Report, no. 9. (Available in microfilm from the Library of Congress.)

Massola, Aldo
    1975   *Corranderrk: A History of the Aboriginal Station.* Kilmore, Victoria: Lowden.

Matthews, Janet
    1977   *The Two Worlds of Jimmie Barker: The Life of an Australian Aboriginal 1900–1972.* Canberra: Australian Institute of Aboriginal Studies.

Mead, Margaret
    1967   Homogeneity and Hypertrophy: A Polynesian-Based Hypothesis. In *Polynesian Culture History: Essays in Honor of Kenneth P. Emory,* edited by G. Highland, R. W. Force, A. Howard, M. Kelly, and Y. H. Sinoto, pp. 121–140. Bernice P. Bishop Museum. Special Publication no. 56. Honolulu: The Museum.
    1977   End Linkage: A Tool for Cross-Cultural Analysis. In *About Bateson,* edited by J. Brockman, pp. 171–234. New York: E. P. Dutton.

Mead, Sidney M.
    1976   The Production of Native Art and Craft Objects in Contemporary New Zealand Society. In *Ethnic and Tourist Arts—Cultural Expressions from the Fourth World,* edited by N. Graburn, pp. 285–298. Berkeley: University of California Press.

Meggitt, Mervyn J.
    1962   *Desert People: A Study of the Walbiri Aborigines of Central Australia.* Sydney: Angus and Robertson.

Meintel, Dierdre
    1984   *Race, Culture and Portuguese Colonialism in Cabo Verde.* Syracuse: Maxwell School of Citizenship and Public Affairs, Syracuse University.

Merlan, Francesca
    1981   Land, Language and Social Identity in Aboriginal Australia. *Mankind* 13:133–148.

Metge, Joan
    1976   *The Maoris of New Zealand.* Rev. ed. London: Routledge and Kegan Paul.

Miller, James
    1985   *Koori: A Will to Win.* London: Angus and Robertson.

Mitchell, J. Clyde
    1969   Structural Plurality, Urbanization and Labour Circulation in Southern Rhodesia. In *Migration,* edited by J. Jackson, pp. 156–180. Cambridge: Cambridge University Press.

Moerman, Michael
1965 Ethnic Identification in a Complex Civilization: Who Are the Lue? *American Anthropologist* 67:1215–1230.
1968 Being Lue: Uses and Abuses of Ethnic Identification. In *Essays on the Problem of Tribe*, edited by J. Helm, pp. 153–169. Seattle: University of Washington Press.

Molisa, Grace N., Nikenike Vurobarabu, and Howard VanTrease
1982 Vanuatu: Overcoming Pandemonium. In *Politics and Melanesia*, edited by R. Crocombe and A. Ali, pp. 84–115. Suva, Fiji: Institute of Pacific Studies, University of the South Pacific.

Morgan, Sally
1987 *My Place*. Fremantle, Australia: Fremantle Art Centre Press.

Morris, H. F., and J. S. Read
1972 *Indirect Rules and the Search for Justice: Essays in East African Legal History*. Oxford: Clarendon Press.

Mortensen, Annette
1983 Theory: Maori Sovereignty and Matriarchy. *Broadsheet* 111 (July/August).

Muga, David
1984 Academic Sub-Cultural Theory and the Problematic of Ethnicity: A Tentative Critique. *Journal of Ethnic Studies* 12:1–52.

Myers, Fred R.
1987 *Pintupi Country, Pintupi Self*. Washington, D.C.: Smithsonian Institution Press.

Nagata, Judith
1974 What is a Malay? Situational Selection of Ethnic Identity in a Plural Society. *American Ethnologist* 1:331–350.
1981 In Defense of Ethnic Boundaries: The Changing Myths and Charters of Malay Identities. In *Ethnic Change*, edited by C. Keyes, pp. 88–116. Seattle: University of Washington Press.

Nason, James
1975 The Strength of the Land: Community Perception of Population on Etal Atoll. In *Pacific Atoll Populations*, edited by V. Carroll, pp. 117–159. Honolulu: University Press of Hawaii.

National Aboriginal Conference (NAC)
1980 World Council of Indigenous Peoples. *NAC Newsletter* (November): 9, 25.

Neville, A. O.
1947 *Australia's Coloured Minority: Its Place in the Community*. Sydney: Currawong Publishing Co.

Newfong, John
1972 The Aboriginal Embassy—Its Purposes and Aims. *Identity* 1 (5): 4–6.

Ngwele, S. B.
1981 Customary Law: Should It Have a Role to Play in the Legal System of Vanuatu? In *Navara: Voice of Vanuatu Students*. Port Moresby, Papua New Guinea: University of Papua New Guinea.

Noonan, Ros, and Judith Aitken
1981 Ros Noonan and Judith Aitken. *Broadsheet* 94 (November).

Norton, R.
1983   Ethnicity, "Ethnicity" and Culture Theory. *Man*, n.s. 18:190–191.
O'Brien, Jay
1986   Toward a Reconstitution of Ethnicity: Capitalist Expansion and Cultural Dynamics in Sudan. *American Anthropologist* 88:898–907.
O'Donoghue, Lois
1985   Proposal for an Aboriginal and Islander Consultative Organisation: Discussion Paper. Canberra: Government Printer.
Oliver, Douglas
1975   *The Pacific Islands*. Rev. ed. Honolulu: University Press of Hawaii.
1989   *Oceania: The Native Cultures of Australia and the Pacific Islands*. 2 vols. Honolulu: University of Hawaii Press.
Oppenheim, Roger S.
1973   *Maori Death Customs*. Wellington: A. H. and A. W. Reed.
Orange, Claudia
1987   *The Treaty of Waitangi*. Wellington: Allen and Unwin.
Ortner, Sherry
1973   On Key Symbols. *American Anthropologist* 75:1338–1346.
Owens, J. M. R.
1968   Christianity and the Maoris to 1840. *The New Zealand Journal of History* 2:18–40.
Palmer, K., and C. McKenna
1978   *Somewhere Between Black and White: The Story of an Aboriginal Australian*. Melbourne: Macmillan.
Panoff, Michael
1968   The Notion of Double Self Among the Maenge. *Journal of the Polynesian Society* 46:275–295.
Papali'i, Mona
1983   May 24: Can 20000 Women Be Wrong? *Broadsheet* 111 (July/August).
Parkin, D. J.
1966   Urban Voluntary Associations as Institutions of Adaptation. *Man*, n.s. 1:90–95.
Parr, C. J.
1963   Maori Literacy, 1843–1867. *Journal of the Polynesian Society* 72:211–234.
Parsonson, Ann
1981   The Pursuit of Mana. In *The Oxford History of New Zealand*, edited by W. Oliver, pp. 140–168. Wellington: Oxford University Press.
Pataki-Schweizer, K. J.
1980   *A New Guinea Landscape: Community, Space, and Time in the Eastern Highlands*. Anthropological Studies in the Eastern Highlands of New Guinea, vol. 4. Seattle: University of Washington Press.
Patrol Reports
        National Archives, Port Moresby, Papua New Guinea.
Perkins, Neville
1974   The Central Australian Aboriginal Congress: An Expression of Pan-Aboriginalism and Self-Determination. *Identity* 2 (1): 27–32.

Petersen, Glenn
  1977 Ponapean Agriculture and Economy. Ph.D. diss., Anthropology Department, Columbia University.
  1979 External Politics, Internal Economics and Ponapean Social Formation. *American Ethnologist* 6:25–40.
  1982a *One Man Cannot Rule a Thousand: Fission in a Ponapean Chiefdom.* Ann Arbor: University of Michigan Press.
  1982b Ponapean Matriliny: Production, Exchange, and the Ties That Bind. *American Ethnologist* 9:129–144.
  1984 The Ponapean Culture of Resistance. *Radical History Review* 28–30:347–366.
Peterson, Nicolas, and Marcia Langton
  1983 *Aborigines, Land and Land Rights.* Canberra: Australian Institute of Aboriginal Studies.
Pettigrew, Thomas
  1979 The Ultimate Attribution Error: Extending Allport's Cognitive Analysis of Prejudice. *Personality and Social Psychology Bulletin* 5:461–476.
Phillips, W. J.
  1954 European Influence on Tapu and Tangi. *Journal of the Polynesian Society* 63:175–198.
Pitt, David C.
  1970 *Tradition and Economic Progress in Samoa.* Oxford: Clarendon Press.
Ploeg, A.
  1984 Development Administration in an Isolated Sub-District. *Administration for Development* 22:1–17.
Pomponio, A.
  1983 Namor's Odyssey: Education and Development on Mandok Island, Papua New Guinea. Ph.D. diss., Anthropology Department, Bryn Mawr College.
Pomponio, A., and D. F. Lancy
  1986 A Pen or a Bushknife? School, Work, and "Personal Investment" in Papua New Guinea. *Anthropology and Education Quarterly* 17 (1): 40–61.
Poyer, Lin
  1983 The Ngatik Massacre: History and Identity on a Micronesian Atoll. Ph.D. diss., Anthropology Department, University of Michigan.
  1988a Maintaining "Otherness": Sapwuahfik Cultural Identity. *American Ethnologist* 15:472–485.
  1988b History, Identity, and Christian Evangelism: The Sapwuahfik Massacre. *Ethnohistory* 35:209–233.
Protect Kaho'olawe 'Ohana
  1981 Aloha 'Aina (newsletter). Winter. Kaunakakai, Molokai, Hawaii.
Prothero, R. Mansell, and Murray Chapmen, eds.
  1985 *Circulation in Third World Countries.* London: Routledge and Kegan Paul.
Rabinow, Paul
  1977 *Reflections on Fieldwork in Morocco.* Berkeley: University of California Press.

Ranger, Terence
    1983   The Invention of Tradition in Colonial Africa. In *The Invention of Tradition*, edited by E. Hobsbawm and T. Ranger, pp. 211–262. Cambridge: Cambridge University Press.

Rangihau, John
    1975   Being Maori. In *Te Ao Hurihuri: The World Moves On*, edited by M. King, pp. 221–233. Wellington: Hicks Smith/Methuen New Zealand.

Read, Peter
    1982   A Double Headed Coin: Protection and Assimilation in Yass 1900–1960. In *All that Dirt: Aborigines 1938, An Australia 1938 Monograph*, edited by W. Gammage and A. Markus, pp. 9–28. Canberra: History Project, Australian National University.
    1984   *Down There with Me on the Cowra Mission*, edited by P. Read. Sydney: Pergamon Press.

Reece, R. H. W.
    1974   *Aborigines and Colonists: Aborigines and Colonial Society in New South Wales in the 1830s and 1840s.* Sydney: Sydney University Press.

Reminick, Ronald A.
    1983   *Theory of Ethnicity: An Anthropologist's Perspective.* Lanham, Md.: University Press of America.

Reusch, Jurgen, and Gregory Bateson
    1951   *Communication: The Social Matrix of Psychiatry.* New York: W. W. Norton.

Reynolds, Henry
    1972   *Aborigines and Settlers: The Australian Experience 1788–1939.* Stanmore, New South Wales: Cassell Australia.
    1987   *Frontier: Aborigines, Settlers and Land.* Sydney: Allen and Unwin.

Riesenberg, Saul
    1948   Magic and Medicine on Ponape. *Southwestern Journal of Anthropology* 4:406–429.
    1968   *The Native Polity of Ponape.* Smithsonian Contributions to Anthropology, vol. 10. Washington, D.C.: Smithsonian Institution.

Ritchie, James
    1973   Recognition. In *Polynesian and Pakeha in New Zealand Education*, edited by D. Bray and C. Hill, pp. 68–74. Auckland: Heinemann.

Ritter, Philip L.
    1980   Kosraen Circulation, Out-Marriage, and Migration. *Anthropological Forum* 4 (3–4): 352–374.

Robbins, Sterling
    1982   *Auyana: Those Who Held onto Home.* Anthropological Studies in the Eastern Highlands of New Guinea, vol. 6. Seattle: University of Washington Press.

Rogers, Susan C.
    1975   Female Forms of Power and the Myth of Male Dominance: A Model of Female/Male Interaction in Peasant Society. *American Ethnologist* 2:727–756.

Rothschild, Joseph
   1981   *Ethnopolitics: A Conceptual Framework*. New York: Columbia University Press.
Rothwell, Nicholas
   1987   Rabuka's Republic. *Pacific Islands Monthly* 58 (11): 10–13.
Rowley, C. D.
   1972a   *The Destruction of Aboriginal Society*. Harmondsworth: Penguin Books.
   1972b   *Outcasts in White Australia*. Harmondsworth: Penguin Books.
Rowse, Tim
   1985   On the Notion of Aboriginality: A Discussion by Christopher Anderson, Ian Keen, Tim Rowse, J. R. von Sturmer, Kenneth Maddock, Colin Tatz, Stephen Thiele. *Mankind* 15:41–55.
Sack, P.
   1972   Dukduk and Law Enforcement. *Oceania* 43:96–103.
Sahlins, Marshall
   1963   Poor Man, Rich Man, Big-man, Chief: Comparative Types in Melanesia and Polynesia. *Comparative Studies in Society and History* 5 (3): 285–303.
   1965   On the Sociology of Primitive Exchange. In *The Relevance of Models in Social Anthropology*, edited by M. Banton, pp. 139–236. London: Tavistock Publications.
   1981   *Historical Metaphors and Mythical Realities: Structure in the Early History of the Sandwich Islands Kingdom*. Ann Arbor: University of Michigan Press.
   1985   *Islands of History*. Chicago: University of Chicago Press.
Salamone, Frank A.
   1985   Colonialism and the Emergence of Fulani Identity. *Journal of Asian and African Studies* 20:193–202.
Salmond, Anne
   1975   *Hui: A Study of Maori Ceremonial Gatherings*. Wellington: A. H. and A. W. Reed.
   1978   Te Ao Tawhito: A Semantic Approach to the Traditional Maori Cosmos. *Journal of the Polynesian Society* 87:5–28.
Sansom, Basil
   1982   The Aboriginal Commonality. In *Aboriginal Sites, Rights and Resource Development*, edited by R. Berndt, pp. 117–138. Perth: University of Western Australia Press.
Saussure, Ferdinand de
   1959   *Course in General Linguistics*. New York: McGraw-Hill.
Schieffelin, Edward
   1976   *The Sorrow of the Lonely and the Burning of the Dancers*. New York: St. Martin's Press.
Schiller, Nina Glick
   1977   Ethnic Groups Are Made, Not Born: The Haitian Immigrant and American Politics. In *Ethnic Encounters: Identities and Contexts*, edited by G. Hicks and P. Leis, pp. 23–35. North Scituate, Mass.: Duxbury Press.

Schmitt, Robert C.
  1968   *Demographic Statistics of Hawaii: 1778–1965.* Honolulu: University of Hawaii Press.
Schneider, David M.
  1968   *American Kinship: A Cultural Account.* Englewood Cliffs, N.J.: Prentice-Hall.
  1984   *A Critique of the Study of Kinship.* Ann Arbor: University of Michigan Press.
Schutz, Alfred
  1962   *Collected Papers,* vol. 1: *The Problem of Social Reality.* Edited by M. Natanson. The Hague: M. Nijhoff.
Schwalbenberg, Henry M.
  1984   The Plebiscite on the Future Political Status of the Federated States of Micronesia: Factionalism, Separatism, and Sovereignty. *Journal of Pacific History* 19 (3): 172–184.
Schwartz, Theodore
  1963   Systems of Areal Integration: Some Considerations Based on the Admiralty Islands of Northern Melanesia. *Anthropological Forum* 1:56–97.
  1982   Cultural Totemism: Ethnic Identity Primitive and Modern. In *Ethnic Identity: Cultural Continuities and Change.* Rev. ed., edited by G. De Vos and L. Romanucci-Ross, pp. 106–131. Chicago: University of Chicago Press.
Schwimmer, Erik
  1966   *The World of the Maori.* Wellington: A. H. and A. W. Reed.
  1972   Symbolic Competition. *Anthropologia* 14:117–155.
  1977   What Did the Eruption Mean? In *Exiles and Migrants in Oceania,* edited by M. Lieber, pp. 296–341. Honolulu: University Press of Hawaii.
Shils, Edward
  1957   Primordial, Personal, Sacred and Civil Ties. *British Journal of Sociology* 8 (2): 130–145.
  1981   *Tradition.* Chicago: University of Chicago Press.
Shore, Bradd
  1982   *Sala'ilua: A Samoan Mystery.* New York: Columbia University Press.
Silverman, Martin G.
  1969   Maximize Your Options: A Study in Symbols, Values, and Social Structure. In *Forms of Symbolic Action,* edited by R. Spencer, pp. 97–115. Seattle: University of Washington Press.
  1971   *Disconcerting Issue: Meaning and Struggle in a Resettled Pacific Community.* Chicago: University of Chicago Press.
  1977a Introduction: Locating Relocation in Oceania. In *Exiles and Migrants in Oceania,* edited by M. Lieber, pp. 1–9. Honolulu: University Press of Hawaii.
  1977b Making Sense: A Study of a Banaban Meeting. In *Exiles and Migrants in Oceania,* edited by M. Lieber, pp. 121–160. Honolulu: University Press of Hawaii.

Sinclair, Karen P.
  1983   A Comment on Professor F. Allan Hanson's Essay on Dynamic Forms
         in the Maori Concepts of Reality. *Ultimate Reality and Meaning*
         6:321–332.
  1984   Maori Women at Midlife. In *In Her Prime: A New View of Middle-
         aged Women*, edited by J. Brown and V. Kerns, pp. 117–134. South
         Hadley, Mass.: J. S. Bergen, Publishers.
  1985   'Koro' and 'Kuia': Aging and Gender Among the Maori of New
         Zealand. In *Aging and its Transformations: Moving Toward Death in
         Pacific Society*, edited by Dorothy Counts and David Counts, pp. 27–
         46. Lanham, Md.: University Press of America.
  n.d.   The Journey to Waitangi: A Maori Pilgrimage. In *Sacred Journeys*,
         edited by A. Morinis. (in prep.).
Sinclair, Keith
  1969   *A History of New Zealand*. Harmondsworth: Penguin Books.
Smith, Anthony D.
  1981   *The Ethnic Revival*. Cambridge: Cambridge University Press.
Smith, L. R.
  1980   *The Aboriginal Population of Australia*. Canberra: Australian
         National University Press.
Sorrenson, M. P. K.
  1981   Maori and Pakeha. In *The Oxford History of New Zealand*, edited by
         W. Oliver, pp. 168–197. Wellington: Oxford University Press.
Stack, John F., Jr., ed.
  1981   *Ethnic Identities in a Transnational World*. Westport, Ct.: Green-
         wood Press.
  1986   *The Primordial Challenge: Ethnicity in the Contemporary World*.
         New York: Greenwood Press.
Stanner, W. E. H.
  1979   *White Man Got No Dreaming: Essays 1938–1973*. Canberra: Austra-
         lian National University Press.
State of Hawaii
  1974   *The State of Hawaii Data Book*. Honolulu: Department of Planning
         and Economic Development.
Stevens, Frank, ed.
  1971– *Racism: The Australian Experience*. 3 vols. Sydney: Australia
  1972   New Zealand Book Co.
Stirling, Amiria Manutahi, and Anne Salmond
  1976   *Amiria: The Life Story of a Maori Woman*. Wellington: A. H. and
         A. W. Reed.
Stone, Linda
  1977   East Indian Adaptations on St. Vincent. In *Ethnic Encounters: Iden-
         tities and Contexts*, edited by G. Hicks and P. Leis, pp. 37–47. North
         Scituate, Mass.: Duxbury Press.
Stone, Sharman
  1974   *Aborigines in White Australia*. South Yarra, Victoria: Heinemann
         Educational (Australia).

Strauss, Anselm L.
  1977   *Mirrors and Masks: The Search for Identity.* London: Martin Robin-
         son.
Sutton, Peter, and Arthur Palmer
  1981   *Daly River (Malak Malak) Land Claim.* Darwin: Northern Land
         Council.
Tajfel, H., ed.
  1982   *Social Identity and Intergroup Relations.* Cambridge: Cambridge
         University Press.
Tatz, Colin
  1979   *Race Politics in Australia: Aborigines, Politics and Law.* Armidale,
         Australia: University of New England Publishing Unit.
  1982   *Aborigines and Uranium, and Other Essays.* Richmond, Victoria:
         Heinemann Educational (Australia).
Tauroa, Hiwi, and Pat Tauroa
  1987   *Te Marae: A Guide to Customs and Protocol.* Auckland: Reed
         Methuen.
Thiele, S. J.
  1984   Anti-Intellectualism and the "Aboriginal Problem": Colin Tatz and
         the "Self-Determination" Approach. *Mankind* 14:165–178.
Thomas, Mary Durand
  1978   Transmitting Culture to Children on Namonuito Atoll, Caroline
         Islands. Ph.D. diss., Anthropology Department, University of Hawaii.
Tindale, Norman B.
  1941   Survey of the Half-Caste Problem in South Australia. *Proceedings of
         the Royal Geographical Society of Australia, South Australia Branch*
         42 (1): 66–161.
Tindale, Norman B., and B. George
  1979   *The Australian Aborigines.* Melbourne: Curry O'Neil.
Tonkinson, Robert
  1974   *The Jigalong Mob: Aboriginal Victors of the Desert Crusade.* Menlo
         Park, Calif.: Cummings.
  1977   The Exploitation of Ambiguity: A New Hebrides Case. In *Exiles and
         Migrants in Oceania,* edited by M. Lieber, pp. 269–295. Honolulu:
         University Press of Hawaii.
  1978   *The Mardudjara Aborigines: Living the Dream in Australia's Desert.*
         New York: Holt, Rinehart, and Winston.
  1982a National Identity and the Problem of Kastom in Vanuatu. *Mankind*
         13:306–315.
  1982b Kastom in Melanesia: Introduction. *Mankind* 13:302–305.
  1984   Semen versus Spirit-Child in a Western Desert Culture. In *Religion in
         Aboriginal Australia: An Anthology,* edited by M. Charlesworth, H.
         Morphy, D. Bell, and K. Maddock, pp. 107–123. Brisbane: Univer-
         sity of Queensland Press.
Trigger, D.
  1988   Racial Ideologies in Australia's Gulf Country. Paper delivered at the
         Fifth International Conference on Hunting and Gathering Peoples,
         Darwin, Australia.

Trosper, Ronald L.
  1981 American Indian Nationalism and Frontier Expansion. In *Ethnic Change*, edited by C. Keyes, pp. 247–270. Seattle: University of Washington Press.
Tucker, Margaret
  1983 *If Everyone Cared*. Melbourne: Grosvenor.
Tupouniua, Sione, Ron Crocombe, and Clare Slatter, eds.
  1980 *The Pacific Way*. Suva, Fiji: South Pacific Social Sciences Association.
Turner, Victor
  1967 *The Forest of Symbols*. Ithaca, N.Y.: Cornell University Press.
Tuzin, Donald
  1972 Yam Symbolism in the Sepik: An Interpretive Account. *Southwestern Journal of Anthropology* 28:230–254.
Tylor, Edward B.
  [1871] *Primitive Culture*. London: John Murray.
  1920
Uchendu, Victor C.
  1975 The Dilemma of Ethnicity and Polity Primacy in Black Africa. In *Ethnic Identity: Cultural Continuities and Change*, edited by G. De Vos and L. Romanucci-Ross, pp. 265–275. Palo Alto, Calif.: Mayfield Publishing Co.
United States Department of State
  1980 Annual Report to the United Nations on the Administration of the Trust Territory of the Pacific Islands.
United States Navy
  1944 *Civil Affairs Handbook: East Caroline Islands*. Washington, D.C.: Navy Department.
Valentine, C. A.
  1963 Men of Anger, Men of Shame: Lakalai Ethnopsychology and Its Implications for Social Psychological Theory. *Ethnology* 2:441–477.
van den Berghe, Pierre L.
  1981 *The Ethnic Phenomenon*. New York: Elsevier.
Vincent, Alex
  1973 Two Brothers. In *The Languages of the Eastern Family of the East New Guinea Highlands Stock*. Anthropological Studies in the Eastern Highlands of New Guinea, vol. 1, edited by H. McKaughan, pp. 638–651. Seattle: University of Washington Press.
Vincent, Joan
  1974 The Structuring of Ethnicity. *Human Organization* 33:375–379.
von Sturmer, J. R.
  1973 Changing Aboriginal Identity in Cape York. In *Aboriginal Identity in Contemporary Australia*, edited by D. Tugby, pp. 16–26. Milton, Australia: Jacaranda Press.
Wagner, Roy
  1981 *The Invention of Culture*. Chicago: University of Chicago Press.
Walker, Ranginui
  1973 Biculturalism and Education. In *Polynesian and Pakeha in New*

    Zealand Education, edited by D. Bray and C. Hill, pp. 110–122. Auckland: Heinemann.

1975   Marae: A Place to Stand. In *Te Ao Hurihuri: The World Moves On,* edited by M. King, pp. 21–34. Wellington: Hicks Smith/Methuen New Zealand.

Wallerstein, Immanuel

1973   The Two Modes of Ethnic Consciousness: Soviet Central Asia in Transition? In *The Nationality Question in Soviet Central Asia,* edited by E. Allworth, pp. 168–175. New York: Praeger.

1974   *The Modern World-System.* New York: Academic Press.

Walsh, A. C.

1973a   *More and More Maoris.* Wellington: Whitcombe and Tombs.

1973b   Developments Since the Hunn Report and Their Bearing on Education. In *Polynesian and Pakeha in New Zealand Education,* edited by D. Bray and C. Hill, pp. 18–28. Auckland: Heinemann.

Ward, Alan

1974   *A Show of Justice: Racial "Amalgamation" in 19th Century New Zealand.* Canberra: Australian National University Press.

Ward, Roger

1977   Curing on Ponape: A Medical Ethnography. Ph.D. diss., Anthropology Department, Tulane University.

Warner, W. Lloyd

[1937]   *A Black Civilization.* New York: Harper.

1958

1959   *The Living and the Dead: A Study of the Symbolic Life of Americans.* New Haven: Yale University Press.

Watson, James B.

1963   A Micro-Evolution Study in New Guinea. *Journal of the Polynesian Society* 72 (3): 188–192.

1983   *Tairora Culture: Contingency and Pragmatism.* Anthropological Studies in the Eastern Highlands of New Guinea, vol. 5. Seattle: University of Washington Press.

Watson, James B., and Virginia D. Watson

1972   *Batainabura of New Guinea.* 3 vols. New Haven, Ct.: HRAF Press.

Watson, Virginia Drew, and J. David Cole

1977   *Prehistory of the Eastern Highlands of New Guinea.* Anthropological Studies in the Eastern Highlands of New Guinea, vol. 3. Seattle: University of Washington Press.

Weaver, Sally M.

1983   Australian Aboriginal Policy: Aboriginal Pressure Groups or Government Advisory Bodies? *Oceania* 54 (1–2) 1–22, 85–108.

White, Geoffrey M., and John Kirkpatrick, eds.

1985   *Person, Self, and Experience: Exploring Pacific Ethnopsychologies.* Berkeley: University of California Press.

Williams, John

1969   *Politics of the New Zealand Maori: Protest and Cooperation 1891–1909.* Seattle: University of Washington Press.

Williams, Nancy M.
  1986   *Black Earth: The Yolngu and Their Land—A System of Land Tenure.*
          Stanford: Stanford University Press.
Williams, Raymond
  1977   *Marxism and Literature.* Oxford: Oxford University Press.
Willmot, Eric
  1982   Higher Order Identity in Polygeneric Societies. Barry Scott Memorial
          Lecture, Macquarie University, Sydney, April.
Wolf, Eric
  1982   *Europe and the People Without History.* Berkeley: University of Cali-
          fornia Press.
Woolmington, Jean
  1973   *Aborigines in Colonial Society.* North Melbourne: Cassell Australia.
Worsley, Peter
  1959   Cargo Cults. *Scientific American* 200 (5): 160–167.
  1964   *The Third World.* Chicago: University of Chicago Press.
  1968   *The Trumpet Shall Sound.* 2d ed. New York: Schocken Books.
Wright, Harrison
  1959   *New Zealand 1769–1840: Early Years of Western Contact.* Cam-
          bridge: Harvard University Press.
Yancey, J. M., E. P. Eriksen, and R. N. Juliani
  1979   Emergent Ethnicity: A Review and Reformulation. *American Socio-
          logical Review* 41:391–402.
Yinger, J. Milton
  1985   Ethnicity. In *Annual Review of Sociology* 11:151–180.
Zelenietz, Martin, and Jill Grant
  1981   Kilenge Narogo: Ceremonies, Resources and Prestige in a West New
          Britain Society. *Oceania* 51:98–117.

CONTRIBUTORS

Michèle D. Dominy is professor of anthropology at Bard College and review editor for the *Journal of History of Sexuality*. She received her A.B. from Bryn Mawr in 1975 and her Ph.D. from Cornell University in 1983. She conducted field research in Christchurch, New Zealand, with urban women's networks in 1979 and 1980. Since 1986 she has been working with New Zealand South Island high-country sheep station families, where she has been examining cultural identity and place attachment. She has published on this work in *American Ethnologist*, *Cultural Anthropology*, *Anthropology Today*, *Anthropological Forum*, and *Landscape Review*. In 1995 she was research scholar in residence at the University of Canberra while conducting research in the Australian Alps.

Juliana Flinn is a professor of anthropology at the University of Arkansas at Little Rock. She received her A.B. in anthropology from Barnard College in 1972 and her Ph.D. from Stanford University in 1982. Through a postdoctoral traineeship from the National Institute of Mental Health, she received her M.P.H. from Columbia University in 1984. Her fieldwork in Micronesia includes two years (1974–1976) as a Peace Corps volunteer on Namonuito Atoll, fieldwork on Pulap Atoll and among Pulap migrants in 1980–1981 and the summers of 1986 and 1989, and research among Carolinians of Saipan during the summers of 1992 and 1993.

Alan Howard has been a professor of anthropology at the University of Hawai'i since 1970. He earned all of his academic degrees from Stanford University (Ph.D. 1962). He has conducted research on Rotuma (Republic of Fiji), among Hawaiian-Americans, and with Samoan migrants. He is currently engaged in a study with his wife, Jan Rensel, of Rotuman migrants abroad. His major publications include *Learning to be Rotuman* (1970), *Ain't No Big Thing: Coping Strategies in a Hawaiian-American Community* (1974), and *Hef Ran Ta (The Morning Star): A Biography of Wilson Inia* (1994). He is also co-editor of *Devel-*

opments in Polynesian Ethnology (1989) with Robert Borofsky, and
Spirits in Culture, History, and Mind (1996) with Jeannette Mageo.

Joan Larcom received her Ph.D. from Stanford University and an
M.B.A. from Simmons Graduate School of Management. She has taught
at the University of Californa (Santa Cruz) and Mount Holyoke College.
Since her original research in Vanuatu in 1972–1974, she has returned
to the islands three times to continue her research on political change
and economic development. She is now a human resources development officer with the regional USAID office in West Africa.

Michael D. Lieber is a professor of anthropology at the University of
Illinois at Chicago. He received his B.A. in history from Trinity College
in 1960 and his Ph.D. in anthropology from the University of Pittsburgh
in 1968. He conducted field research on Pohnpei and Kapingamarangi
in 1965, 1966, 1977, 1978–1980, and again during the summers of 1980
and 1982. He completed a lexicon of the Kapingamarangi language in
1971. He has taught at the University of Nevada, the University of
Washington, the Community College of Micronesia on Pohnpei, and at
Bryn Mawr College. Lieber has also conducted fieldwork with Western
Shoshone, with urban Black Americans, and in community power structures in small communities in western Pennsylvania.

Jocelyn Linnekin is a professor of anthropology at the University of
Hawai'i. She received her Ph.D. from the University of Michigan in
1980. Fieldwork in a rural Hawaiian community in 1974–1975 served as
the basis for her book *Children of the Land: Exchange and Status in a
Hawaiian Community* (1985). Her second solo-authored book, *Sacred
Queens and Women of Consequence: Rank, Gender, and Colonialism in
the Hawaiian Islands*, was published in 1990. She has made several trips
to Western Samoa and has conducted ethnohistorical research on
Samoa in New Zealand and Australia. This work has resulted in a number of articles and book chapters on the Samoan contact encounter. She
is currently developing a project on cross-cultural constructions of
democracy.

Alice Pomponio is a professor of anthropology at St. Lawrence University. She received her Ph.D. in anthropology from Bryn Mawr College in
1983. Her original work in the Siassi Islands focused on education and
economic development. She returned to pursue a follow-up study in
1986–1987. In 1988–1989 she was an Andrew Mellon Postdoctoral Fellow at the University of Pittsburgh. She is the author of *Seagulls Don't Fly
into the Bush: Cultural Identity and Development in Melanesia* (1992).

Lin Poyer is an associate professor of anthropology at the University of Cincinnati. She received her Ph.D. from the University of Michigan in 1983. She conducted field research with the people of Sapwuahfik, in the Federated States of Micronesia, in 1979–1980. Her research concerns cultural identity, ethnohistory, and symbolic anthropology. Her book *The Ngatik Massacre* was published in 1993.

Karen P. Sinclair received her Ph.D. from Brown University. She is currently a professor of anthropology at Eastern Michigan University. She has written articles on Maori tradition and innovation and is a major contributor to *The Cross-cultural Study of Women* (Feminist Press, 1986). Since her initial fieldwork in the early 1970s, she has continued to conduct research in New Zealand with the support of such agencies as the National Endowment for the Humanities.

Myrna Ewart Tonkinson received her Ph.D. in anthropology from the University of Oregon in 1976. She conducted fieldwork with Aborigines at Jigalong, an Aboriginal community in Western Australia, focusing on health, traditional medicine, and social change. She has also conducted research at Alice Springs on the life histories of elderly women of mixed Aboriginal-white ancestry. She is a member of the Australian Institute of Aboriginal Studies and is currently teaching in the Department of General Practice (Faculty of Medicine) at the University of Western Australia.

James B. Watson is a professor emeritus of anthropology at the University of Washington. He conducted field research in New Guinea in 1953–1955, 1959, 1963–1964, and 1967. He has also carried out fieldwork in Brazil and the western U.S. He was principal investigator for the New Guinea Micro-Evolution Project, begun in 1959, and has published extensively on New Guinea ethnology and wider anthropological topics.

INDEX

Aboriginality, 192, 195–201, 208, 215

Aboriginal Land Rights Act, 214

Aborigines, Australian, 12, 16n.4, 159; British categorization of, 201–202, 204–207; colonial subjugation of, 202–204; diversity of, 191–195; emergent identity of, 195–198, 215; laws restricting, 209–212, 214; passing as white, 212–213; and political movements, 196–199, 267; white antagonism toward, 208. *See also* Aboriginality

Acculturation, 19, 25, 117–119, 124

Adoption, 7, 54, 80–82, 100n.2, 115, 130, 138, 141, 161, 265–266

Alcohol, 212, 223, 230, 236nn.17, 18

Alliance, 20, 114, 144. *See also* Exchange; Marriage

American Indians. *See* Native Americans

Ancestors, teachings of, 34, 56, 251

Ancestry: identity defined by, 2, 4, 8–9, 74–80, 132, 100n.2, 149, 154–157, 169–170, 192, 194, 200, 265; status varying with, 61

Aotearoa, 251, 254, 255. *See also* New Zealand

Arrows, 23, 25

Ascription, group, 7–9, 12, 127, 134–135, 153, 155–157, 170. *See also* Categorization; Identity; Lamarckian identity

Assimilation, 206, 213–214, 254

Atavism, 195, 206, 265. *See also* Biology; Race

Atolls, 5, 74, 93, 103–106, 127–128

Australia, 9, 12, 149; colonial history of, 202–203; race relations in, 204–208, 214, 259. *See also* Aborigines, Australian

Authenticity, 186, 188, 276

'Ava. *See* Kava

Awatere, Donna, 239, 250–251, 253, 255, 256n.9

Bananas, 24, 128

Barth, Fredrik, 1–3, 6, 10, 11, 15n.1, 46, 133, 136, 164

Bastion Point, 239, 246–248, 250, 256n.7

Behavior: as diacritic, 192, 194; inherited, in racial theories, 206–207. *See also* Biology; Performance; Stereotypes

Belau, 130, 168

Beliefs: differences in, as diacritic, 22–25, 29, 192; traditional, asserted, 227. *See also* Religion; *Tangihanga*

Betel nut, 110

Biculturalism, 223, 238, 254

Big-men, 51, 163, 178–179, 183, 184. *See also* Entrepreneurs

Bingo, 86

Biographies, 72, 76, 79, 91

Biology: behavior explained by, 72–74, 206–207, 264; ethnicity determined by, 2, 4, 6–8, 11–12, 18–19, 38, 53, 103, 146, 152–153, 157, 172, 194, 263, 267; in racial ideologies, 192, 199, 203–208, 265. *See also* Blood; Mendelian identity; Race

Bishop Estate, Bernice P., 157

"Black," as label, 207–208, 244, 248–249, 255, 267. *See also* Race

Black Women's Movement, 239, 247. *See also* Awatere, Donna

Bleakley, J. W., 205–206

Blood: in ethnic ideologies, 2; Pacific metaphors of, 9, 37, 43, 53, 54, 61, 153; Western metaphors of, 192, 204–206, 209, 211, 218n.11. *See also* Mendelian identity

Boats, commercial, 61–63, 66–67

Bone, as metaphor of identity, 9, 37

Boundaries, group, 6–7, 10–11, 15n.1, 18, 74, 93, 99, 264; administrative, 14; permeable, in Oceania, 266, 271, 278;